DEVELOPING LEADERSHIP

All royalties from the book are going to two charities:

Prospect Burma is dedicated to providing educational scholarships for Burmese nationals. This is funded by the Nobel peace Prize awarded to Aung San Suu Kyi, who observes: 'If people are educated they can check the government abuse of power, if people remain uneducated the government can rule and oppress as it wishes.'

www.prospectburma.org/about-prospect-burma.html

MODEM is a UK ecumenical Christian network, which encourages authentic dialogue between exponents of leadership, organization, spirituality and ministry to aid the development of better disciples, community, society and world.

www.modem-uk.org/About.html

SAGE was founded in 1965 by Sara Miller McCune to support the dissemination of usable knowledge by publishing innovative and high-quality research and teaching content. Today, we publish more than 750 journals, including those of more than 300 learned societies, more than 800 new books per year, and a growing range of library products including archives, data, case studies, reports, conference highlights, and video. SAGE remains majority-owned by our founder, and after Sara's lifetime will become owned by a charitable trust that secures our continued independence.

Los Angeles | London | Washington DC | New Delhi | Singapore | Boston

Edited by

Christopher Mabey & Wolfgang Mayrhofer

DEVELOPING LEADERSHIP

¿ Questions Business Schools Don't Ask ?

Los Angeles | London | New Delhi
Singapore | Washington DC | Boston

Los Angeles | London | New Delhi
Singapore | Washington DC | Boston

SAGE Publications Ltd
1 Oliver's Yard
55 City Road
London EC1Y 1SP

SAGE Publications Inc.
2455 Teller Road
Thousand Oaks, California 91320

SAGE Publications India Pvt Ltd
B 1/I 1 Mohan Cooperative Industrial Area
Mathura Road
New Delhi 110 044

SAGE Publications Asia-Pacific Pte Ltd
3 Church Street
#10-04 Samsung Hub
Singapore 049483

Editor: Kirsty Smy
Editorial assistant: Molly Farrell
Production editor: Sarah Cooke
Copyeditor: Gemma Marren
Proofreader: Audrey Scriven
Indexer: Silvia Benvenuto
Marketing manager: Catherine Slinn
Cover design: Francis Kenney
Typeset by: C&M Digitals (P) Ltd, Chennai, India
Printed in India at Replika Press Pvt Ltd

© Christopher Mabey and Wolfgang Mayrhofer 2015

First published 2015

Chapter 1 © Christopher Mabey and Wolfgang Mayrhofer 2015
Chapter 2 © Tim Harle 2015
Chapter 3 © Aidan Ward and Wolfgang Mayrhofer 2015
Chapter 4 © Ricky Yuk-Kwan Ng 2015
Chapter 5 © Yuliya Shymko 2015
Commentary: Jerry Biberman
Chapter 6 © Molly Scott Cato 2015
Chapter 7 © Ken Parry and Audun Fiskerud 2015
Chapter 8 © David Beech 2015
Chapter 9 © Andrew Henley 2015
Chapter 10 © Leah Tomkins 2015
Commentary: J.-C. Spender
Chapter 11 © Karen Blakeley 2015
Chapter 12 © Mervyn Conroy 2015
Chapter 13 © Hugo Gaggiotti and Peter Simpson 2015
Chapter 14 © Pare Keiha and Edwina Pio 2015
Commentary: Laurence Freeman
Chapter 15 © Rickard Grassman 2015
Chapter 16 © Doirean Wilson 2015
Chapter 17 © Phil Jackman 2015
Chapter 18 © Pamsy Hui, Warren Chiu, John Coombes, and Elvy Pang 2015
Chapter 19 © Mary Hartog and Leah Tomkins 2015
Chapter 20 © Daniel Doherty 2015
Commentary: David W. Miller
Chapter 21 © Chris Mabey and Wolfgang Mayrhofer

Library of Congress Control Number: 2014953797

British Library Cataloguing in Publication data

A catalogue record for this book is available from the British Library

ISBN 978-1-44629-610-3
ISBN 978-1-44629-611-0 (pbk)

MIX
Paper from
responsible sources
FSC
www.fsc.org   FSC® C016779

At SAGE we take sustainability seriously. Most of our products are printed in the UK using FSC papers and boards. When we print overseas we ensure sustainable papers are used as measured by the Egmont grading system. We undertake an annual audit to monitor our sustainability.

CONTENTS

LIST OF FIGURES AND TABLES

FIGURES

TABLES

ABOUT THE CONTRIBUTORS

David Beech is an organizational psychologist and registered as a practitioner psychologist by the UK Health and Care Professions Council. Since 1989 he has designed and delivered leadership development initiatives in postgraduate and executive education across private, public and not-for-profit enterprises, including projects in China, Europe and the USA, and projects to develop executive director and community leadership capabilities. David is passionate about action centred learning in leadership and organization development that supports individuals and groups with high performance working and continuous improvement and change for the good life in today's tough and turbulent global markets. Currently he is a lecturer in people management at Salford Business School.

Dr Jerry Biberman is Professor Emeritus of Management at the University of Scranton (retiring from full-time teaching in 2012). For 12 years he served as chair of the Management/Marketing Department at the University of Scranton. He obtained his MS, MA and PhD from Temple University. His current interests are in the areas of holistic coaching and consulting and transformative education. Jerry has co-edited several books and has published many articles in the areas of work and spirituality and on organizational behaviour teaching. Jerry currently lives with his wife Linda in Las Vegas, Nevada.

Karen Blakeley's research interests focus on responsible leadership development. She has worked with leading global organizations in the delivery and assessment of their responsible leadership development programmes and has designed and delivered responsible leadership courses for undergraduate and post-graduate students at the University of Winchester Business School. She has published articles on responsible leadership, a book on leadership blind spots and is particularly interested in the role of spirituality as a means for personal transformation and character development. Prior to joining the business school, Karen was a leadership development consultant working with companies all over the world. She currently heads up the Doctorate of Business Administration at Winchester and is researching the role of values, learning and spirituality in responsible leadership development.

Dr Warren Chiu's expertise is in the field of leadership and creativity. He has published in various international journals and provided consultancy services to public and private organizations relating to leadership development and human resource management. He is currently the co-director of the Center for Leadership and Innovation. He paints as a hobby.

Mervyn Conroy is a senior fellow at the Health Services Management Centre, University of Birmingham. He is co-director of the MSc Leadership for Health Services Improvement modules, Leadership in Context and Applied Leadership Learning at Birmingham University. He has worked in NHS mental health services as a clinician, manager and researcher. His research, teaching and consultancy over the last decade have focused on change, leadership ethics, the sustainability of health service reform and connected health and social care communities.

Dr John Coombes is a teaching fellow of the Department of Management and Marketing at the Hong Kong Polytechnic University. He teaches systems concepts in environmental management for business, management and organization, corporate social responsibility and systems dynamics. He researches information systems, learning strategies and technology, idea generation and social media, multimedia information systems and systems support for stakeholder thinking.

Daniel Doherty enjoyed 30 years of providing organization and business strategy to a number of global multinational players before returning to business school life ten years ago. Daniel is senior lecturer at Middlesex University Business School, London, where he teaches across the syllabus but more recently has been focusing on teaching and research into coaching and organization learning. His research passion is for narrative approaches to learning.

Audun Fiskerud has been teaching at the Bond University Business School for eight years, following the completion of four Master's degrees at Bond University (MBA, Master of Finance, Master of Communication and Master of Accounting). Audun has for the last three years worked on the Business Spirituality Research Project, a collaboration between Bond University and the Sunland Group.

Laurence Freeman (OSB) is a Benedictine monk and the spiritual guide and director of the World Community for Christian Meditation, a contemporary, contemplative community. He is also the director of Meditatio, the outreach programme of the same community, which engages with the secular world on the themes of education, mental health, business, addiction and recovery, and medicine. He travels widely as an international speaker and retreat leader, and is the author of many articles and books including, *The Selfless Self* (2009), *Jesus: The Teacher Within* (2010) and *First Sight: The Experience of Faith* (2011).

Dr Hugo Gaggiotti is principal lecturer in Organization Studies and director of the Bristol MBA at the University of the West of England, Bristol. He studies contemporary ethnic groups by shadowing and by connecting with them during long periods of time. Among the groups he is studying are international MBA students, Italian and Brazilian nomadic engineers and British university administrators, project managers and their teams. Cultural descriptions figure in his writings about power, ethics, post-colonialism, the construction of symbolic spaces, organizational careers, work routines and work rites, like meetings and academic ceremonies. His recent publications examine the exclusion of theorizing in business schools.

Dr Rickard Grassman is a research fellow at the Department of Engineering Sciences in Uppsala University. His primary research explores social media technologies and their interrelation with innovation and social movements. However, what perhaps more clearly comes to light in this volume is his interest in cultural aspects of knowledge work, which among other sectors has led him to explore our financial world and its influence on identity and the economy. His range of work, including his PhD, testifies to a consistently critical sensitivity that accentuates what is often overshadowed in the mainstream.

Tim Harle works at the overlap of business and faith. He is programme leader for Sarum College's MA in Christian Approaches to Leadership and a visiting research fellow at Bristol Business School. He has worked in a range of companies in the service sector, and undertook advanced management studies at INSEAD. Tim's publications cover both business and faith perspectives for practitioner and academic audiences. His research interests include post-Newtonian approaches to leadership, and leadership in schools (www.timharle.net).

Dr Mary Hartog is the director of Organization and Leadership Practice for Middlesex University Business School, London. This is an externally facing post working with organizations to help them achieve their strategic goals in leadership and organization development. Mary is an academic with a practitioner background in human resource development and change. She specialises in action learning and reflective practice helping leaders navigate the complexities of organizational life, including the political and emotional. She obtained her PhD from the University of Bath in 2004 from the Centre for Action Research in Professional Practice. Mary was awarded a National Teaching Fellowship in 2006 for excellence in teaching and learning and she achieved recognition as a Principal Teaching Fellow of the Higher Education Academy in 2014.

Andrew Henley is Professor of Entrepreneurship and director of the Institute of Management, Law and Information Science at Aberystwyth University, having previously been the head of the School of Business and Economics at Swansea University. Between 2009 and 2012 he was director of the LEAD

Wales programme for Welsh entrepreneurs. He has written and published extensively on ethics, leadership, entrepreneurial motives and characteristics, and on regional economic development issues. He has served in a range of policy advisory and consultancy roles in the public and private sectors.

Dr Pamsy Hui received her PhD in organization science from the University of Texas at Austin and is a senior teaching fellow of management at the Hong Kong Polytechnic University. Her research focuses on management education, and the management of stakeholder reactions towards information communicated in the marketplace. Prior to joining Hong Kong Polytechnic University, she taught at the University of Texas at Austin (USA), Nanyang Technological University (Singapore), and Chinese University of Hong Kong. Her research has appeared in *Decision Sciences* and *Journal of Social Issues*, as well as *The Oxford Handbook of Inter-Organizational Relationships* (2008).

Phil Jackman is the UK director of the Agape Workplace Initiative, with 37 years of experience in mentoring and leadership development, and a relational network which now extends to 200 countries. As a seasoned communicator and spiritual entrepreneur he is committed to the rehumanization of the workplace. The originator of the course 'Habits of the Heart', Phil has built a team of 20 facilitators and mentors over the last six years, teaching and coaching leaders in health, education, business and church.

Pare Keiha (QSO, MSC, PhD, MBA, MComLaw, FRSA, MInstD, MRSNZ) is the Pro Vice Chancellor for Māori Advancement, the Pro Vice Chancellor for Learning and Teaching, and Dean of Te Ara Poutama, the Faculty of Māori and Indigenous Development at the Auckland University of Technology, New Zealand. He has an extensive background in the governance of public and private companies in New Zealand. He was honoured by the Queen in 2008 when he was made a Companion of the Queen's Service Order (QSO) for his services to business, education and Māori.

Chris Mabey is a chartered psychologist and Professor in Leadership at Middlesex University Business School. Chris has held a career-long interest in leadership development as a counsellor for a charity, as a practitioner with British Telecom and Rank Xerox, and as a consultant. More recently he has researched, taught and written on this topic with four different business schools. He co-authored *Management and Leadership Development* (2008).

Wolfgang Mayrhofer is Full Professor and head of the Interdisciplinary Institute of Management and Organisational Behaviour, WU Vienna, Austria. He has previously held full-time positions at the University of Paderborn, Germany, and at Dresden University of Technology, Germany. He conducts research in comparative international human resource management and leadership, work careers, and systems theory and management, and has received national and international rewards for outstanding research and service to the academic community. Wolfgang Mayrhofer authored, co-authored and co-edited 28 books, more than 110 book chapters and 70 peer-reviewed articles. He is a member of the editorial or advisory board of several international journals and research centres.

David W. Miller serves as director of the Princeton University Faith and Work Initiative. His research, teaching, and writing focus on the intersection of faith and work. He teaches business ethics drawing on the resources of the Abrahamic traditions. He is the author of *God at Work: The History and Promise of the Faith at Work Movement* (2007). David brings an unusual bilingual perspective to his scholarship. Before studying for his PhD, he spent sixteen years in business, including eight years with IBM, and eight years in London as a senior executive in international finance. David also serves as an advisor to CEOs and executives on ethics, values, leadership and faith at work.

Ricky Yuk-Kwan Ng is a senior education development officer in the Centre for Learning and Teaching, Vocational Training Council, Hong Kong. His research interests are in the workspace personalization in organizations, using photo-ethnography in organizational studies and critique in art and design education.

Dr Elvy Pang obtained a doctorate in business administration. Her research and teaching focuses are in the areas of leadership, team effectiveness, generic competencies, and technology-assisted learning. Prior to joining academia, she was an entrepreneur and a business practitioner in a diverse range of areas in Hong Kong and mainland China, including executive development and HR consultancy. Elvy has qualifications for the Big-Five, FIRO-B, MBTI, DISC and NLP.

Ken Parry is Professor of Leadership Studies at Deakin University. He was founding director of the Centre for the Study of Leadership in Wellington, New Zealand. He has written or edited eight books, mainly on the topic of leadership, with several published by Sage. Ken was founding editor of the *Journal of Management and Organization*, the research journal of the Australian and New Zealand Academy of Management. He has addressed the Senior Executive Service of the Australian Public Service at the National Press Club. He is widely used as a speaker at professional conferences and industry events.

Edwina Pio is the first Professor of Diversity in Aotearoa/New Zealand. In addition to her role at the business school at AUT University, she is a visiting professor at Boston College in the USA, is on the board of the Australia New Zealand Academy of Management and is an associate director of the New Zealand India Research Institute. Her principal area of research interest is diversity in business and education, and through her interdisciplinary scholarship, research, publications and international presentations, she seeks to change the parameters of the debate, particularly focusing on marginality, ethnicity, gender and religion/spirituality. Professor Pio has published widely in internationally ranked journals and is the author of several books.

Molly Scott Cato is an MEP for the South West of England and sits in parliament's Green Group. She was formerly Professor of Green Economics at Roehampton University. Molly is an expert on economics and finance and has published a number of books and papers, including most recently *The Bioregional Economy: Land, Liberty and the Pursuit of Happiness* (2012), which develops ideas for a new model of stable and sustainable economic life. She has also written widely on themes concerned with mutualism, social enterprise, policy responses to climate change, banking and finance, and local economies. Molly is the Green Party's national speaker on finance and a member of its political committee.

Yuliya Shymko is Assistant Professor of Strategy at the Vlerick Business School (Belgium) and a visiting professor of Sociology at IE University (Spain). She has a helpful mix of academic and managerial backgrounds. Trained as an economist with a specialization in international relations, she has also dedicated her time to research the socio-political and economic reality of post-Soviet republics in affiliation with the University of Alberta (Canada). Her current academic interests include the application of feminist theories to business ethics, cross-sector collaboration in creative industries, and the emergence of hybrid organizations to address the problems of sustainable development and social deterioration.

Peter Simpson is Associate Professor in Organization Studies at Bristol Business School. Throughout his career he has held a range of leadership roles and consulted to senior managers on strategic change. He studies leadership through the theoretical lenses of complexity, spirituality and psychodynamics and has published widely in this field. His latest book is *Attention, Cooperation, Purpose: An Approach to Working in Groups Using Insights from Wilfred Bion* (2014, with Robert French). Current projects include the ESRC Seminar Series 'Ethical Leadership: The Contribution of Philosophy and Spirituality', and the BA/Leverhulme funded 'Group Decision-making in Times of Crisis: Promoting Peace Dialogue Processes after the Arab Spring'.

J.-C. Spender retired in 2003 as Dean of the School of Business and Technology at FIT/SUNY in Manhattan. He was previously on the faculty at UCLA, Rutgers, York (Toronto), and City (now Cass). Prior to an academic career he worked for Rolls-Royce and Associates on nuclear power, IBM (in the City), and Slater-Walker. His most recent books include *Business Strategy: Managing Uncertainty, Opportunity, and Enterprise* (2014) and *Strategic Conversations: Creating and Directing the Entrepreneurial Workforce* (2014, with Bruce Strong).

Leah Tomkins is senior lecturer at Middlesex University London. Her research concerns different facets of the lived experience of work and organization, drawing principally on phenomenological philosophy. Previously a management consultant with Accenture and KPMG, then Director of Change for the UK Civil Service, she is interested in exploring the things that are relatively silent in organizational conversations, such as feelings, bodies and existential meanings. Her projects seek to expose the implicit functionalism of 'organizational strategy' and 'change management', not to undermine calls for organizational effectiveness, but rather, to consider alternative ways of thinking about what we mean by 'effective'.

Aidan Ward is an organizational systems consultant who looks at how structures drive behaviours. He works across public, private and third sectors. His current work is in how pension fund investment ends up destroying value, and in alternative economic models for local community development.

Doirean Wilson is a fellow of the CIPD, a Fellow of the European SPES Institute, and an HRM senior lecturer (Practice) at Middlesex University Business School, London. Her previous roles include consultant, journalist and projects manager. She teaches various business and HRM topics and her research interests and publications are in the area of leadership, gender disparity and cross-cultural team working. Doirean recently drew on her study to launch a high profile practitioner diversity conference at Middlesex.

PRAISE FOR *DEVELOPING LEADERSHIP*

'A rare thing, this book gives more than the label promises. The title is about "questions", yet each chapter gives us answers to *why* important issues are not addressed in business schools – and what to do about it. This is a manifesto for reform, and the next big question is what will you, reader, do about it?'

Jonathan Gosling, Professor of Leadership,
University of Exeter

'Reading this book makes you think about leadership and, most of all, educating potential leaders! The book builds on an astonishing multiplicity of theoretical, philosophical and spiritual traditions, providing the reader with a critical understanding of leadership processes – including moral responsibilities and accountabilities.'

Jörg Sydow, Professor of Management,
Freie Universität Berlin

'Exploring the intrinsic link between spirituality, ethics and business, is a critical step in ensuring the unified vision of individuals, institutions of society and the community, to achieve a harmonious and sustainable future. It is incumbent upon us all to become the *"agents of change".'*

Soheil Abedian, Chairman of Sunland Group,
Australia

'This is a very timely publication. Business school education needs a critical examination from people who inhabit that world and know what they're talking about. The presence and prominence of teleological, spiritual and ethical perspectives are especially welcome.'

Richard Higginson, Director of Faith in Business, Ridley Hall,
University of Cambridge

'The authors have undertaken a courageous exploration of the ills that never seem to go away in the capitalist model. Courageous because the authors examine their own roles in perpetuating those ills. It is an important book which I hope the leaders of business schools and leaders of business will read.'

Vincent Neate, Head of Sustainability,
KPMG

'This collection of readings is an excellent antidote to what can be seen as the ignominy of our age – the relentless and unremitting proliferation of corporate scandals culminating but not ceasing with the 2008 global financial crisis. More specifically, it focuses on one of the travesties of the modern university – the incapacity of business schools to challenge the myopic economic instrumental values of business. By raising problems and possible solutions to questions that business schools rarely ask, it facilitates a debate that could help to challenge the inadvertent complicity of higher education to sustain and reproduce an unenlightened individualistic self-seeking managerial cadre. It provides an illuminating insight into current business school and business practices and their failures to provide a more enlightened ethical leadership that would benefit both students and practitioners of business as well as society more generally.'

David Knights, Professor of Organisation Studies,
Lancaster University Management School and
Open University Business School

'This book is a badly needed, but underestimated – and perhaps unwanted? – wake-up call for main stream business schools, which are providing smooth, normative, maple syrup flavoured managerialist answers to important, current and future leadership challenges. The book will help academics, students and practitioners to get out of the inner paradigmatic prison, where answers are provided, before the questions are raised, where socially desirable rhetoric shade for critical questioning, and where "what's in it for me?" repress important societal, ethical considerations.'

Henrik Holt Larsen, Professor of Human Resource Management,
Institute for Organisation, Copenhagen Business School

'We live in interesting times. Wealth and power are concentrated in the hands of a very small elite, while the dispossessed are complicit because they have made money their god. We are racing towards cataclysmic collapse, as infinite growth is not possible when we live on a finite planet. Within this aberration Business Schools have become the servants of corporate power. Thinking is seen as dangerous because it threatens power, and ethics is equally subversive within materialistic consumerism. Without challenging the idea of business, this book asserts that universities at least ought to be asking questions. However, speaking truth to power is not easy when universities themselves have become just another corporate business. This book is vast and complex in its scholarship, with something for everyone. Enjoy and be challenged.'

Tony Watkins, Fellow of the New Zealand Institute of Architects,
Chartered Member of the Royal Institute of British Architects

'Finally! For too long the role of business education, and the MBA as its global flagship, has remained shockingly unquestioned in today's crisis of enterprise and economics. This book has to be highly commended for its collaborative, cross-cultural courage, reviewing and renewing not only the underlying assumptions of business and business education, but also for tapping deeply into an impressive variety of philosophical, ethical, cultural and spiritual resources of humanity as vital ingredients for a much needed transformation of an entire discipline and practice. *Developing Leadership*'s main merit is to be a well-composed, deeply substantiated and profoundly challenging "door opener" to a crucial debate – to be held across borders, cultures, disciplines and institutions. It is an example and urgent invitation for co-engagement between management educators, business students and practitioners alike. Congratulations!'

Alexander Schieffer, Co-Author of *Transformation
Management: Towards the Integral Enterprise*

THE PARROT'S TRAINING

'Once upon a time there was a bird. It was ignorant. It sang all right, but never recited scriptures. It hopped pretty frequently, but lacked manners. Said the Raja to himself: "Ignorance is costly in the long run. For fools consume as much food as their betters, and yet give nothing in return." He called his nephews to his presence and told them that the bird must have a sound schooling. The pundits were summoned, and at once went to the root of the matter. They decided that the ignorance of birds was due to their natural habit of living in poor nests. Therefore, according to the pundits, the first thing necessary for this bird's education was a suitable cage.'[1]

Rabindranath Tagore

Is it too far-fetched to liken business schools to the bejewelled cage in Tagore's exotic fable? As he goes on: 'crowds come to see it from all parts of the world. "Culture, captured and caged!" exclaimed some, in a rapture of ecstasy and burst into tears.' But while a succession of pundits, goldsmiths and numerous nephews benefit from elaboration of the cage, the bird inside is neglected and finally breathes its last. Guarded by the kotwal and the sepoys and the sowars, the bird is brought to the Raja and in a poignant ending: 'he poked its body with his finger. Only its inner stuffing of book-leaves rustled.'

---

[1]Excerpted from: V. Bhatia (ed.) 1994. Rabindranath Tagore: Pioneer in Education. New Delhi: Sahitya Chayan.

FOREWORD

This book is music to my ears ... When I first saw the draft, the first line of Etta James' iconic blues ballad, 'At last, my love has come along ...' kept repeating in my head. I have long thought that there is a desperate need to be critically reflexive about the paradigm of leadership and management promoted by business schools. However, because business discourse is so pervasive, this felt a lonely place to be. I'm really glad that this book has come along!

According to some scholars, business has become such a dominant force in the West that Western Society is now characterized as being a 'business culture'. More recently, the colonization of market language has spread to education, medicine, religion, politics, art, sports and leisure sector has even permeated into family life, and into our constructions of love, affection and personal identity. In this sense, commerce and culture have become inextricably combined. Noted anthropologist, Stephen Gudeman, refers to this as the 'long term shift from community to market' that 'is often justified as modernization, progress, and the triumph of rationality'.

In organizations, this trend is manifested by the wide-spread adoption the Masters of Business Administration (MBA) approach. During my twenty-five years as a Human Resource professional, twenty-one of which have been in the Christian NGO sector, I have frequently wrestled with the incongruity of having to subscribe to a transactional model of organizing based on market principles. It strikes me as ironic that faith-based organizations are attempting to foster life-giving communities, and deal with issues of inequality, poverty, politics and power, using the managerialist practices of a capitalist/business discourse that, arguably, created the inequality in the first place.

I delight in the fact that this book is a collection of narratives aimed at picking the lock of this twenty-first century psychic prison. It feels emancipatory. They do this by:

- inviting readers to be critically reflexive about managerial practice;
- identifying taken-for-granted assumptions of business discourse;
- challenging what we now take as 'normal' ways of perceiving, conceiving and acting in organizations; and
- imaging and exploring extraordinary alternatives.

For me, this is a long overdue and must read book.

Patrick Goh
Head of Global Human Resources
Tearfund

1 WHAT KIND OF LEADER ARE YOU BECOMING?

Chris Mabey and
Wolfgang Mayrhofer

INTRODUCTION

Business schools teach a mix of subjects, from strategy, international business and operations management to marketing, accounting and HRM, drawing upon a wide range of disciplines including economics, political science, psychology and sociology. Implicit in this offering is the intention to develop leadership capability in whatever sphere of activity students graduate into. Increasingly, leadership studies, in one guise or another, feature ever more explicitly in the curriculum of undergraduate and Master's level programmes. We might anticipate therefore a growing degree of competence, integrity and wisdom among alumni as, year by year, they take up influential roles in business, government, public services and the third sector. In actual fact, the evidence is far from encouraging (Collinson, 2012; Kellerman, 2012; Khurana, 2007; Mintzberg, 2004). As each month passes, it seems that new scandals emerge concerning financial impropriety, reckless risk-taking, dubious morality bordering on illegal behaviour and self-serving arrogance among public figures,[1] most of whom are well educated and hitherto trusted to act responsibly on behalf of those constituencies they serve. At a more personal level, the demands on leaders continue to intensify: having to achieve more with less, dealing with multi-stakeholder accountability, subject to heightened scrutiny and surveillance and working with technologies that blur work/non-work boundaries and confound the work–life balance, to name just a few.

---

[1]Collinson (2012) refers to a prevalence of 'prozac leadership' in a study of 200 organizations, which is fuelled by wishful thinking, naivety, hubris or more deliberately manipulative motives. Designed to promote happiness, this style of leadership actually discourages critical reflection and ill equips companies to deal with setbacks.

For those concerned about such matters, a series of disconcerting questions arise:

- Given that business schools are typically enmeshed in capitalist regimes, to what extent do they throw light on the material conditions which give rise to the financial crises and leadership failures of our age? How well equipped are they to examine the instruments, the processes, the environment within which dubious business practices flourish?
- To what extent are business schools guilty of inventing language, models and metrics to give the appearance of order and sufficiency, when the employees and organizations they research and study are invariably complex, mystifying and defy rational representation?
- By relying upon conventional teaching methods where the faculty pose as experts and students are there to listen, learn and produce assignments according to prescriptive criteria, are not business schools, by controlling the learning process in this way, creating learner dependency and passivity? By failing to explore the emotions and micro-politics generated by this system of management teaching and learning, are not business schools simply reproducing the operation of power relations that typically prevail in work organizations and thus failing to help individuals to prepare for and negotiate this contested terrain?
- In times of national austerity, how can business schools, which continue to grow and accumulate material resources, justify their societal leadership development role? Apart from a token nod towards corporate social responsibility and business ethics, to what extent are students encouraged to explore the competing moralities, the community implications and the ecological consequences of various business strategies? To what extent does debate take place about the philosophical and spiritual roots of wisdom as against the often arid pursuit of commodified knowledge?
- Given the increasing global reach of business schools is it tenable to continue to promote a Western mono-cultural worldview in terms of secular assumptions, conceptual content, case material and style of teaching? How respectful, relevant and empowering is this for students and staff of different ethnicities, traditions and faiths?

The relationship between universities and their offspring business schools has been played out over the last half century with a degree of predictability. Starting as experimental children in an untested marketplace, they then grew rapidly to become troublesome adolescents seeking their institutional identity and autonomy before finally being welcomed by their university parents as bankable adults, progressing – if progress this is – from out-of-line calves to assembly-line cash-cows. But along the way, have business schools lost something of their original ambition and promise to make better leaders for society?

Of course these are sweeping criticisms clothed in the form of questions and we are not the first to make them. There are many examples of business and management schools which have bucked the trend, radically re-thought their *raison d'être* and experimented with fresh approaches.[2] We have no wish to simply continue the chorus of criticism that has rumbled on from Mintzberg's early and influential debunking of conventional MBAs in 2004. The intention of this book is to add a neglected perspective to the diagnosis of the problem, and aided by that understanding, to go on to offer some antidotes. Our contention is that three issues substantially contribute to the difficulties faced by business schools: inadequate theorizing about leadership; a failure of nerve concerning the centrality of moral values to sound leadership; and impoverished curriculum design when it comes to the teaching of and learning about leadership. In short, the typically unasked, and therefore ill-considered, question is: what kind of leader are you becoming? Or to personalize it further and challenge one's own comfort zones, what kind of leader am I becoming?

Before we visit these issues we need to diagnose the problem a little further. We turn to this issue next.

A CASE OF COLLUSION

It appears that business schools find themselves at the centre of a collusive cycle. To differing degrees, each stakeholder group, whether this is students, faculty members, research funders, journal review boards, accreditation bodies, employers or the universities to which they are attached, are aware of this collusion, but find themselves unwilling or unable to break the cycle. Figure 1.1 shows the participants in this cycle.

The difficulty with collusion is that it represents an unspoken agreement, the impact is difficult to determine and it is often only discovered after significant damage has occurred. Despite unease, each party benefits sufficiently not to blow the whistle. Let us look at each stakeholder constituency a little more closely.[3]

Students

Although it would be unfair to make generalizations about any of the stakeholders in Figure 1.1, it may be assumed that behind the students' desire to develop their skills and to acquire knowledge, the underlying mindset of most students is instrumental: they want to gain a qualification that will enhance

---

[2]For some examples see Ghoshal (2005), Mitroff (2004) and Harle, this volume, although Neubaum et al. (2009) have disputed the link between business education and the negative moral philosophies of students.

[3]This list of stakeholders is not exhaustive. The government is a key player in some countries as in the German language area, where most business schools are largely (80–95 per cent) state financed. Many business schools in the USA are supported by private donors. It might be argued that another stakeholder contributing to this collusion is the popular media.

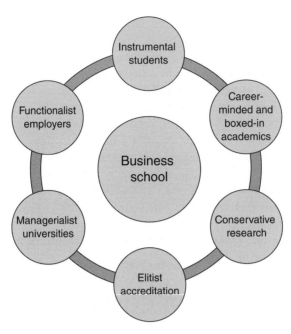

Figure 1.1 Business schools: caged in a collusive cycle

their career prospects. This explains why the ranking and reputation of universities are so closely scrutinized by would-be students. There is evidence that few students are satisfied with a didactic pedagogy delivered by ivory tower, subject-matter experts. Rather, a staff development style of tuition is preferred, lighter on theory and heavier on relevance to the workplace and preferably taught by those with a strong business/practitioner background. This may be more digestible and feel more 'alive' but can be at the expense of academic rigour and the provocation to reflect and deepen self-awareness. Contrasting with both of these is a 'critical approach' which uses the work and non-work experiences of students – such as their experiences of authority and being managed, of being consumers of different products and services, or their enjoyment of privileges compared to other groups in society – to problematize rather than simply validate management theories and assumptions. However, based on a case study of an MBA programme at a UK business school, Currie and Knights (2003) note that this critical reflection on conventional managerial practice may be resisted by students for a number of reasons. Many students, especially those from South East Asian countries, reinforced in some cases by being female, are culturally conditioned not to challenge teachers or engage in classroom dialogue.[4] For them a critical approach confronts the privileges of

---

[4]David Beech – one of our contributors – notes that this assertion may in fact reflect a Western view, even one influenced by Foucault, which risks overly privileging the Greek orientation to the primacy of the individual actor. Creative (individualistic) competition (Greece) under the rule of law (Rome) is at the heart of the Western

belonging to an MBA cadre and undermines a model of managerial behaviour deemed necessary to learn in order to obtain employment in a Western global company. Even for students more inclined to debate in a classroom setting critical pedagogy, which counters the reduction of topics like leadership to morally neutral techniques and encourages engagement with emotions and the anxieties they evoke, may prove too uncomfortable. In such an environment it becomes too easy for students and faculty to collude: 'Students do the minimum necessary to satisfy the examiners by regurgitating, without personal conviction, the knowledge acquired from their management teachers, while, at the same time, teaching becomes a legitimate cover for management teachers to pursue their research interests' (Currie and Knights, 2003: 43).

Academics

Teaching staff in business schools may sense dissatisfaction with the quality of teaching and the learning environment more generally in their institutions, yet perceive themselves unable or ill equipped to remedy the situation. Why is this? First, as noted above, is the straightforward matter of career progression: research output is expected, possibly mandated, and hence rewarded and prioritized; teaching comes second and even though student feedback is increasingly under scrutiny, the line of least resistance is to keep students happy rather than to stretch them. There is an irony here. While business school tutors may regard themselves as separate from the wider neo-liberal project which characterizes modern capitalist economies, able to stand back, commentate and interpret from the outside, they themselves are part of the 'constructivist project [that] does not presume the ontological givenness of a thoroughgoing economic rationality for all domains of society but rather takes as its task the development, dissemination and instrumentalization of such a rationality' (Brown, 2006: 40–1). It could be argued that university faculty are prime producers of this rationality, not least because it serves to consolidate and develop their (and we might add 'our') careers.

Second, to take a conventional, 'disciplinary' approach, i.e. delivering a body of knowledge about management as a subject matter expert, in a compartmentalized fashion and unconnected to other modules in the chosen course, is what most students expect; adopting a more critical and challenging subject matter and pedagogy is likely to lead to student discomfort and resistance as well as teacher anxiety due to a loss of power in controlling the class (Reynolds, 1999).

---

tradition; while in recent centuries Yahweh's principles for humanity (Judaism) have been progressively neglected. However the Judaic tradition tends to prioritize individuals too. The Chinese tradition of yinyang prioritizes duties and obligations to others and to self in the context of changing circumstances. The deontology (duties and obligations) of yinyang are to know the other, know the self, know nature (and human technologies), and know the situation configured by others, selves and the material world and to act appropriately. There are potential links here to Aristotle's approach to finding an appropriate balance – 'golden mean' – across competing requirements.

Third, even when business school tutors do attempt to venture into more critical territory, encouraging their students to reflect on the often unexamined mental models that inform their managerial actions, they *can* find themselves institutionally isolated. For example, there is pressure to increase income results in larger class sizes, making more intensive, experiential work more difficult, and a limit on resources where, for example, break-out rooms are not available and extra tutors/coaches not fundable; meanwhile peers may remain sceptical and/or unsupportive and accreditation regimes are unyielding since, for example and as we shall see in a moment, professional bodies like the Association of Masters in Business Association (AMBA) and the Chartered Institute of Personnel and Development (CIPD) tend to promote a traditional, functionally focused curriculum.

Research

Surely business school research, which by definition concerns the testing of assumptions and venturing into uncharted intellectual territory, is one area which breaks free from the collusion we are discussing? Due to the way research is conceived and funded, and its findings are disseminated, this is often far from the case. A strategic issue for organizations and governments alike concerns the dissemination of knowledge gained from university research in a way which benefits the wider economy and society as a whole. Studies on knowledge management and diffusion seek to tackle the problem of stickiness, causal ambiguity, and issues like trust, with an emphasis upon choosing appropriate governance systems in order to positively impact organizational performance or competitive advantage. The problem is that the more codified, and therefore transferable, knowledge is, the less likely it is to be valuable for the receiving parties. As the literature on communities/networks of practice demonstrates (Orlikowski, 2002; Ormrod et al., 2007; Swan and Scarborough, 2005), much of what is considered precious knowledge, tacit or otherwise, remains embedded within social structures and the unique relationships and informal routines of a given network.

In an effort to secure value for money in R&D environments, government sponsors and public/private funding agencies place increasing emphasis on deliverables and highly specified outcomes. This is true of private sector organizations as well as inter/national publicly funded research (The Bellagio Statement, 2011). All of this rests on a flawed premise. It is assumed that new knowledge, once identified, can be readily commodified and commercialized. Ironically, though well intentioned, this can actually subvert innovation and constrain the research process so that it leads to non-surprising, pre-determined outputs, and at worst, the arrival at faddish, best-practice solutions (Newell et al., 2001). By definition, the outcomes of research are unknowable at the outset; fresh insights arising from the research process are emergent and socially constructed – in other words, their meaning and significance are highly depended on the context, complex relationships and differing motives of all those involved such as the research group, respondents and case organizations, sponsors and disseminators. This is especially true of social science-informed research, which crosses disciplinary boundaries and involves multinational research teams.

Work on the triple helix collaboration between university, industry and government also shows the innovative knowledge gain to be emergent, not easily controlled and multi-level (organizational, regional and national) (Etzkowitz and Leydesdorff, 2000). In the common pursuit of realizing value-creating innovation, each party is subject to complex dynamics like shifts in market forces, political power, institutional control and IT regimes. To some extent each can take on the role of the other. The challenge for business schools is evident, both for the kind of research conducted (in terms of research questions, methods and analysis) and the means for disseminating the fruits of their research enquiry (internally to peers and externally to funding bodies, policy-makers, government and the media). Such empirically derived insights have the potential to enhance the way organizations perform and benefit society more generally, but a common lament of governments and research sponsors is that this impact fails to materialize. Part of the problem here is that the causal connection between business research and business results is notoriously difficult to demonstrate. But there are other lines of enquiry that business school research can and should be pursuing. For example, given that truly mould-breaking knowledge is typically tacit and embedded, this calls for interpretive analysis which pays close attention to the cultural and symbolic expressions of knowledge, to the narratives and stories that are told and how they are deployed to evoke meaning. On this reading, the who, what and how of knowledge exchange (Fletcher, 2004) are re-cast as a distributed and interdependent set of practices which are enacted by all. And given that the current orthodoxy in a given organization tends to resist more radical findings which threaten to disrupt the status quo, this calls for critical research which is capable of surfacing unheard voices rather than reproducing the ideologies and power relations of the dominant elite. We return to this in the section 'More Adequate Theorizing'.

University

Criticism is not confined to the business school, but expands to the university as a whole. Part of the critique focuses on the fundamental mission of universities as reflected in the subjects taught. It has been argued, for example, that studying the humanities is vital for the cultivation of aesthetic rather than political judgement: 'The works of Shakespeare contain important knowledge. But it is not scientific knowledge, nor could it ever be built into a theory. It is knowledge of the human heart. Shakespeare doesn't teach us what to believe: he shows us how to feel – case by case, person by person, mood by mood'.[5]

The other part of the critique is more institutional. The preoccupation with quantifiable targets, league tables and auditable data leads some to describe the modern university as paranoid-schizoid: 'in face of the on-going struggle for excellence, growth and survival and the attempt to gain greater market share ... [there is] ... no space for the experience of guilt, the desire for love, mourning or reparation' (Sievers, 2006: 15, cited in Craig et al., 2014). Writing as a Professor of English, Docherty (2011) laments the fact that the university, in common with much of public life in general, has become preoccupied with the need to present itself to the world through the twin pillars of Transparency and Information as the means of securing that university's prevailing social or governmental status and dogma. While apparently laudable, transparency is too easily traded for truth (or the scholarly search for it) and raw, comodifiable information has too easily supplanted curiosity-driven demands for critical knowledge. He goes on to contrast the 'official' university, its formal face contained in excellence rankings, mission statements and an attractive web presence, to the clandestine university where most academics do their daily work. And the gap between the two is widening: 'Senior managers are condemned to live in the official realm, conjuring facts and figures that have absolutely no bearing on, or even interest for, the academics who keep the university alive. The clandestine academic exists in the interstices of officialdom, and has to remain in the shade because the university is in grave danger of being betrayed' (Docherty, 2011). In a boldly written case study, which recounts the unfolding of change management led by the assertive dean of a European business school, Parker (2014) broadly concurs with this verdict. Perhaps most surprising – given their professional autonomy, investment in critical traditions and membership of trade unions – was the inability or unwillingness of academics at this school to resist the inexorable march of a managerialist agenda.

The current audit culture which is present in a number of countries, particularly with middle-class universities trying to enhance their status, is questionable on several fronts. At worst, it can lead to excessive bureaucracy, short-term measures to produce quick wins and punitive performance management. The problem with this trend is that it undermines collegiality and blunts the aspiration of most academics, namely to tackle societal issues of enduring significance. Among faculty, who invariably signed up for the opportunity to autonomously pursue research interests and share that passion with students,[6] a wider university culture

---

[5]Source URL: http://spectator.org/articles/41571/farewell-judgement by Roger Scruton (accessed 1 July 2014).

[6]A study of 347 faculty staff in 38 business schools from 12 countries found 'academic freedom' to be the most important factor in attracting and retaining talent (Verhaegen, 2005).

which erodes trust and discourages risk will ultimately lead to passivity and cynicism. As an antidote to this pessimistic picture and turning back to the business school as a key contributor to the intellectual and social vitality of the university, Ferlie et al. (2010) advocate a public interest school of management. This would be characterized by three core principles: first, a recovery of the professional standards of responsible management – this would be reflected in a socialization process which inculcates norms of conduct, a curriculum that includes ethical and philosophical considerations of the role of business in society and a pedagogy that encourages reflective, personal development. Second, the cultivation of a broad knowledge base founded on social science-informed research and active partnering with other social science departments like law, international relations, anthropology. And third, active engagement with a variety of public, private and governmental constituencies to make an impact beyond the academy, while avoiding the danger of corporate capture. This reformed model of a public interest school of management would offer a modernized version of the original vision of early American schools such as Wharton (Khurana, 2007) with the 'three pillars of profession building, integration in a research intensive university and a (social) science base' (Ferlie, 2010: S69).

Accreditation and rankings

It has become commonplace for governing agencies to introduce audits, league tables, ranking systems and formal assessment processes on most arenas of public life; one might argue this is a reasonable bureaucratic response to an area which feels out of control and where trust has been breached. Business schools have not escaped. Motivated by the desire to have objective measures of high-class outputs from journals, scholars and academic institutions, a host of metrics have grown up. International accreditation systems include EQUIS, assessing institutions as a whole with an underlying implicit normative model of structures and processes of 'good' academic institutions (www.efmd.org/accreditation-main/equis); the Association to Advance Collegiate Schools of Business (AACSB), with its emphasis on teaching and its link to the goal of the academic institutions (www.aacsb.edu); or AMBA, with its focus on individual MBA, DBA and MBM programmes (www.mbaworld.com). For ranking universities within and across countries, different methods and databases are used. They include, among others, the *Financial Times* top 40 journals in economics and business (*FT*40), the University of Dallas list of the top 24 business journals (UTD), the Research Assessment Exercise (Research Evaluation Framework in the UK), Performance Based Research Funding (New Zealand), the field-specific journal ranking of the Association of Business Schools (ABS) in the UK, and the ISI Social Science Citation Index. Calling for a radical re-think of the way university scholarship is assessed and rewarded, Adler and Harzing (2009) identify a number of flaws in academic ranking systems. They question the emphasis on journal papers which often are read by few and relatively un-influential compared to books and open access publishing, the bias towards

English as the *lingua franca*, the skew towards a very limited number of 'elite' journals, the arbitrary nature of the decision criteria used to construct journal ranking, and the confusion between productivity (number of publications) and impact (citation counts). They conclude that '[i]t is not just that ranking systems are inconsistent, volatile and in many ways inherently unfair; it is that the motivation systems they engender – including encouraging blatant individual self-interest and a consequent lack of loyalty to any particular university or broader societal mission – undermine the very essence of good scholarship' (Adler and Harzing, 2009: 84).

Bowing to similar public pressure to distinguish the best, good and not-so-good business schools, accreditation bodies tend to base their quality kite-marks on blunt measures of worth, including publications in A-listed journals.[7] The FT, for example, publishes its ranking of top 100 global MBAs each year, a highly influential register for prospective students and employers alike. This is derived from several factors, such as the extent to which alumni fulfilled their stated goals for doing an MBA, which three schools alumni would recruit from, their change in level of seniority and size of employer, their success in finding a job within three months of graduation, their salary enhancement and a perception of their MBA's value for money. While not disputing the importance of such measures (although they can be criticized in their own right), one wonders whether the very instrumentality of such indices might drive out other dimensions of good scholarship. As we saw earlier, most students when asked what they seek from their business school will invariably answer: a career-enhancing qualification. Yet this may well be followed by other responses including: the opportunity to engage with ground-breaking research, exposure to a learning environment that stretches, challenges and provokes via innovative pedagogy, the chance to sharpen their cultural sensitivity by working with an international student body and the opportunity to develop their self-awareness, capability and vision as future leaders. Ask employers the same question and they may refer to the desire for graduates to bring original thinking to their work, to pursue fresh and innovative business ideas and get them speedily to market, to be prepared to question outmoded orthodoxies in order to improve professional practice; more enlightened employers may also wish for graduates capable and courageous enough to run ethical businesses, with an eye for high safety, low rejects, mutual respect, for ecologically sustainable and socially responsible strategies. Where, we might ask, do such qualities, individual and corporate, feature in the league tables and assessment criteria, and – indeed – are such metrics at all pertinent to these wider and deeper examples of scholarship?

---

[7]At the time of writing, 59 schools worldwide claim 'triple accreditation'. Those not on the list include Harvard, Stanford, Wharton, McGill and IIM Calcutta, hardly also-rans in the global picture. And inevitably a further question arises: *Quis custodiet ipsos custodes* [Who will guard the guardians themselves]? As Grugulis (2007: 54–70) points out, accreditation schemes are often self-generating industries.

Some commentators have criticized this audit culture as attempting 'to construct a vocabulary of knowledge that legitimizes managerial power at the expense of more traditional and collegial visions of the university. Indeed, managerial power elites have a vested interest in legitimizing the deployment of audit-based performance management systems in universities, thereby rendering such systems immune to falsification' (Craig et al., 2014: 2). This may appear to be too jaundiced; surely one legitimate role of business schools is to engage students in a way which contributes to a profitable and sustainable business base in society. The problem arises with the attempt to impose a New Public Management philosophy upon university faculties with the intent of increasing efficiency, monitoring output and driving up institutional reputation because this runs a real risk of creating the opposite.

Employers

For all the other benefits they might name, such as a desire to develop their high potential staff, to tap into latest ideas, to be seen to take scholarship seriously and so on, an over-riding calculation for those employers sponsoring or releasing their staff to participate in business school programmes is that the financial and opportunity costs associated with study will reap dividends in terms of their contribution to corporate performance. This is based upon a beguiling premise that well-conceived and well-designed training and development will enhance leadership capability which, in turn, will lead to a cadre of gifted visionaries who can collectively restore the fortunes of the organizations they lead.[8] But of course, corporates might be equally wary of business school tuition being *too* good, since this would potentially serve to release critically minded graduates into their ranks who might probe dubious practices and upset comfortable orthodoxies. Given that employers will tend to focus on 'business-ready' skills when recruiting, business schools are likely to have 'balancing the status quo' as their presiding motivation.[9] Despite its undoubted contribution, the shortcomings of such a functionalist approach to management and leadership development have been well-rehearsed. These include a bias towards unitarist instrumentalism, reflected not least in the language used (see Box 1.1); a tendency to privilege the managerial concerns of private companies and large scale administrative organizations and neglect SMEs, third sector and alternative forms of organization like co-operatives; a persistent preoccupation with

---

[8]And governments harbour the hope that this, in time, will trickle through to enhance national competitiveness (Russon and Reinelt, 2004).

[9]In a national UK survey of employers (CMI, 2014), the top attributes most sought after in new managers were: communication skills (67 per cent), problem-solving and critical analysis (48 per cent), team-building skills (47 per cent), motivating others (46 per cent) and project management skills (17 per cent). Only 16 per cent mentioned 'the ability to reflect and self-awareness'.

enhancing the qualities of the individual as against more contextualized, distributed or team-based development approaches (Day et al., 2006; Gronn, 2002; Iles and Preece, 2006); a tendency to assume the notion of *leader* to be a self-evident entity; and, following on from this, the likelihood that management and leadership remain un-interrogated activities, needing only to be improved upon or *developed*.

BOX 1.1   CHOOSING OUR CURRENCY

A small but telling example of the performance paradigm concerns the language we choose. In the very act of coining such a terms as 'human resource 'and 'social capital' and proclaiming that 'people are our greatest asset' and 'if you can't measure it, you can't manage it', some scholars and practitioners appear not to consider how the appropriation of such language from the arena of accounting into the broader realm of leadership development might contribute to a certain (contestable) construction of the world and the individuals within it.

So then, there are many factors which conspire against business schools fulfilling their original mission to be capitalism's conscience, to ask questions other institutions are afraid to ask, to use their privileged societal position to promote multi-disciplinary dialogue, and to use their finely-honed educational skills to provoke deeper self- and other-awareness.[10] The stakeholder constituencies we have listed in the collusive cycle are, to differing degrees, aware of the collusion. What is clear, however, is that none appear to be prepared to break ranks and confront this stultifying inertia: instrumentally oriented students meet career-minded academics who are driven by elitist accreditation and managerialist universities to produce conservative research and traditional teaching, which are consumed by functionalist organizations and so the self-serving cycle continues.

By way of prefacing what is to come in this book, we now turn to three potential ways of breaking the deadlock. Although each appears to be the province of just one of the collusive parties, namely business school academics, we propose that once initiated by academics, these avenues have the capacity to create a far-reaching re-appraisal of how business schools and universities conduct themselves.

MORE ADEQUATE THEORIZING

It may seem odd and somewhat esoteric to suggest that one way of breaking the collusive cycle outlined above is to revisit the underlying theories promoted by business schools. Yet surely questions such as 'What constitutes knowledge?', 'What sources of evidence are trustworthy?' and 'How can the fruits of research

---

[10]Several chapters in this volume pick up this theme in more detail.

improve our understanding of organizations?' are fundamental to the *raison d'être* and influence of business schools. When it comes to guiding social and organizational enquiry, two axes with different sets of assumptions have been put forward: those concerning social order and those concerning epistemology (Burrell and Morgan, 1979). They can help differentiate the syllabus and underpinning research of all business school courses according to the stance each takes towards these. To start with the *social order* axis, some set out with the premise of underlying consensus and therefore both seek order and treat order production as the dominant feature of business and organizations, thus 'through the highlighting of ordering principles, such existing orders are perpetuated' (Alvesson and Deetz, 2000: 26). In contrast, scholarly work located towards the dissensus extreme of this axis considers conflict, tension, inequality and struggle to be natural ingredients of the social world. As such, any semblance of order is to be treated with suspicion and as an indication that the full variety of human interests is in some way being suppressed. The *epistemological* axis concerns the nature of knowledge and how it is ascertained, ranging from fixed or *a priori* at one extreme to emergent at the other. A fixed ontology seeks to answer the question 'What is the focus of our study?' and implies either/or thinking which prompts the enquirer or researcher to look for theoretically driven classifications and taxonomies. It is assumed that with the appropriate research tools and validated methods, definitive answers, solutions and evidence-based truths can be determined. At the emergent extreme, the intention is to highlight the unfolding nature of individual and collective behaviour rather than treating this as objective, analysable and ultimately measurable. Because the object of study is continuously shaping and being shaped by situated practice, theorizing is associated with emergence and cyclical causality. Rather than pursuing replicable truths, meanings are socially constructed and multiple.

From these two axes four distinct research perspectives or, more precisely, *discourses* can be derived which might be termed functionalist, interpretive, dialogic and critical. A discourse can be thought of as a connected set of statements, concepts, terms and expressions which constitutes a way of talking and writing about a particular issue. Discourses are not intended to be theoretically watertight boxes (like paradigms) and their permeability allows us to be more imaginative about the way they might flow into each other. It is important to note that the discourses with which we engage are not inconsequential details of speech but have the capacity to either broaden or restrict our thoughts, actions, beliefs and behaviours. So if we consider that a primary goal of business schools is to deepen our understanding of leadership and its development, we arrive at quite different conceptualizations of this task (Figure 1.2).

Functionalist discourse (a priori/consensus) emphasizes consensus and a fixed view of knowledge; although the term may not be familiar to the majority of students, this discourse is the one that they and business schools will identify with most readily, because it concerns the means-end calculation of how to

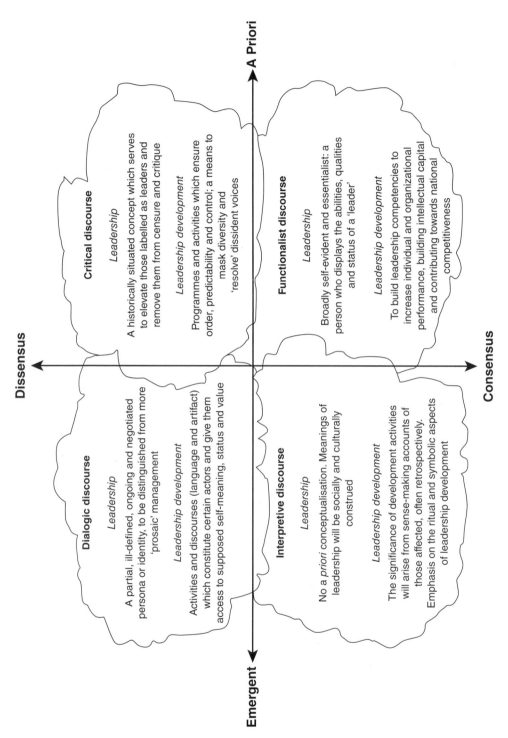

Dissensus

Critical discourse

Leadership

A historically situated concept which serves to elevate those labelled as leaders and remove them from censure and critique

Leadership development

Programmes and activities which ensure order, predictability and control; a means to mask diversity and 'resolve' dissident voices

A Priori

Functionalist discourse

Leadership

Broadly self-evident and essentialist: a person who displays the abilities, qualities and status of a 'leader'

Leadership development

To build leadership competencies to increase individual and organizational performance, building intellectual capital and contributing towards national competitiveness

Consensus

Dialogic discourse

Leadership

A partial, ill-defined, ongoing and negotiated persona or identity, to be distinguished from more 'prosaic' management

Leadership development

Activities and discourses (language and artifact) which constitute certain actors and give them access to supposed self-meaning, status and value

Interpretive discourse

Leadership

No a *priori* conceptualisation. Meanings of leadership will be socially and culturally construed

Leadership development

The significance of development activities will arise from sense-making accounts of those affected, often retrospectively. Emphasis on the ritual and symbolic aspects of leadership development

Emergent

Figure 1.2 Four ways in which business schools might view leaders and their development (adapted from Mabey, 2013: 361)

maximize efficiency and success for the project or organization concerned. This will be reflected in the strategic priorities of business school management as well as in the tools, models and metrics enshrined in their teaching (cases, texts, assessment strategies and the like). All of this is premised on the questionable assumption that the interests of the employer and the employee are mutual (Fournier and Grey, 2000).

Interpretive discourse (emergent/consensus) does not regard knowledge as an objective commodity and strategic capability as an individual asset, both being typical for a functionalist view. Rather, it sees such things more as a fluid consequence, naturally arising from, contributing to and being shaped by social practices. This view emphasizes relationships and contextual setting. So business school management and pedagogy would encourage the exploration of subjectivity and plurality, while remaining largely consensus-oriented. The focus will be as much on the experience of collective learning as on the actual topics taught, more on the cultural significance of joining an educated elite as on grades and merits awarded, as much on access to privileged networks as tapping the expertise of tutors. The serried lines of class photographs that adorn business school corridors and the desks of alumni give some symbolic indication of this.

Dialogic discourse (dissensus/emergent) has a strong post-modern flavour, so the single and static notion of 'leadership' is open to question; rather, within this ontology, there is only 'leading' – with leadership identity being accomplished, negotiated and regulated through everyday practices. So the paraphernalia of business schools such as accreditation systems, league tables, general theories, key texts, marketing USPs and so on would be regarded suspiciously as attempts to produce or privilege dominant interests. It takes a courageous business school to entertain this kind of challenge and 'deconstruction'. Yet it could be argued that the very notion of dialogue, inherent in dialogic discourse, is precisely where business schools can make their contribution. An example might be drawing students' attention to aspects of their managerial activities and the language they use that they would otherwise not notice and giving credence to the precise, bodily feelings aroused by such encounters (see Tomkins in this volume).

Finally, *critical discourse* (dissensus/a priori) tends to represent the world in terms of analytically distinct divisions like: truth and falsity, oppressors and oppressed, agency and structure, individual and collective; like dialogic discourse, it takes a dissensus stance maintaining that our means of accessing social truths will always be historically and politically mediated via, among other things, competing ideologies. Of course business schools can be, and often are, part of a managerialist ideology which would seek to protect its interests, but this does not have to be the case. Encouraging self-reflexivity has the potential to be emancipating for students, as well as its staff; for example, by discussing and exposing 'false consciousness' where individuals unthinkingly acquiesce to social dynamics or ideologies that do not serve their own 'true' or 'real' interests.

Why is this consideration of discourse so important? Because these four different discourses[11] lead to contrasting conceptions of who leaders are and how organizations, like business schools themselves, are best led; this in turn has profound implications for the way leadership research questions are framed, how subjects are 'taught' in undergraduate and Master's programmes and how such learning might be used to inform practice – bearing in mind that discourses are by definition permeable and fluid, not water-tight boxes. It is our contention that there are three risks facing business schools and their primary agenda of developing effective leadership, all of which sell students short. The first is simply to ignore or gloss over the underlying discourses (with all their taken-for-granted assumptions) of different works that are studied and models that are examined. In a recent analysis of the dominant discourses in refereed journal articles dealing with leadership development, only a fraction were found to adopt non-functionalist approaches (see Table 1.1) and these were almost exclusively European. It is perhaps unsurprising that business schools are sometimes branded as too conformist in what and how they teach.

Table 1.1 Review of leadership development literature (2000–11) by discourse, journal location and first author location

Dominant discourse		Journal location			First author location		
	TOTAL	USA	Europe	Other	USA	Europe	Other
Functionalist	188	64	117	7	110	35	43
Interpretive	24	4	20	–	4	17	3
Dialogic	7	–	7	–	1	5	1
Critical	9	–	9	–	–	9	–

Source: Mabey (2013)

The second is that the management and faculty of business schools remain wedded to their favoured discourse(s) and fail to engage with the work of other discourses, especially those which start from quite different assumptions about consensus and dissensus, subjectivity and objectivity, emergent and a priori knowledge and what constitutes a leadership 'problem' in the first place (Lewis and Keleman, 2002). Surely, the creative and theoretical challenge of business schools is to present and critique a *variety* of discourses concerning the nature, purpose, morality and contribution of organizations in society and to draw upon cross-disciplinary approaches to do so. Each discourse brings its own fascinating and distinctive lens through which to view the leadership of MNCs, charities, SMEs, third-sector enterprises, R&D networks and the like, and each set of actors in that process

---

[11]This is just one way of differentiating discourses. See, for example, Western (2008) for a fascinating chronological account of leadership discourses over the last century, concluding with eco-leader discourse.

(see Figure 1.1) will be drawn towards the discourse(s) that would appear appropriate for them at any one point in time. When different interest groups operate within a single discourse in an unquestioning manner, collusion can naturally follow.

The third is to fight shy of identifying and labelling our own ontological preference and values standpoint. Inevitably, we are all embedded within, and subject to, competing sets of discursive assumptions.[12] However, part of the business school's role is to encourage students to become more critically reflexive and attuned to different 'readings' of what it means to be an effective change agent, a successful entrepreneur or business leader and, hence, how different modules/sub-disciplines might be best employed to develop these types of leadership. To do this, it surely behoves the tutor to do the same and pin his or her philosophical colours to the mast. Personally, with regard to ontological preference, we have most sympathy with *critical realism*, which comes closest to that of interpretive discourse. This construes leadership as a contextually based process of social influence and, as such, it is not possible to arrive at universal, replicable leadership theories. However, this critical realist stance parts company with more extreme interpretivists who propound multiple realities, by maintaining that there is a single reality but that it is perceived and interpreted differently. In other words, the social world is real in the sense that it generates affect and exists independent of its identification. So when discussing the design and impact of leadership development activities (see Box 1.2), we might refer to common practice and even similar language but at the same time recognize that the impact and influence of this 'intervention' will vary according to other influences within a particular organizational context.[13]

BOX 1.2   CAN COMPETENCY BE CONTROLLED?

A UK-headquartered multinational launched a tailored personal development programme catalysed by a sophisticated capability framework. The context was constituted, on the one hand, by structures: namely the nexus of leadership ideology within the company, the quasi-religious meanings invested in documents launching the programme and the relationships prescribed by accompanying learning workshops, assessment and appraisal processes. On the other hand, interviews revealed that these meanings, practices and relationships were sustained by the agents themselves as they participated in the programme: in some cases they aligned themselves with the organization's ideology and in other cases directly, though implicitly, they were opposed to it.

---

[12]As one of our contributors comments: 'I say I am a multi-epistemic creature. When I board a plane I am a positivist; when I counsel my children I am interpretivist; when I make sense of my political world I am a critical realist; when I make sense of art and religion I am a postmodernist'. The issue is less about boxing our behaviour and more to do with self-awareness about the assumptions, language and technologies we inhabit.

[13]For more on this standpoint, see Fleetwood (2004) and Kempster and Parry (2011).

This leads us on to a second way of confronting the collusive cycle in Figure 1.1 to which we turn now.

RECOVERY OF MORAL AUTHORITY

In the previous section we made a case for business schools – both management and faculty – to be clearer in their articulation of discourse and associated philosophical stance.[14] To this we would now add the need for business schools to give greater attention to ethical and spiritual dimensions of leadership. This inescapably practical and personal question is concerned more with what kind of a person each of us might become and the leadership that this then evokes, rather than the rules that we ought to obey or the skills we should acquire. Policy-makers time and again turn to deontological or utilitarian rule compliance in the face of crisis – even when similar regulatory frameworks have failed (e.g. Turner Review, 2009). This is evident in the recent past where the effectiveness of the UK regulatory response to the 2008 banking crisis is, as yet, unknown and potentially 'inadequate' (Davies, 2012: 206); and recent crises in the UK Health Services (e.g. Francis Inquiry Report, 2010) have led to a focus on ethical practice, the quality of leadership and a return to the National Health Service's founding principles of care and compassion. It is timely for business schools to debate this reliance on regulatory responses to ethical challenges by becoming more self-conscious about their values.

Business schools have been criticized for many years for their pedagogies, curricula and culture and following the events of 2007/8 at the onset of the global crisis, that criticism became more concentrated. Most significantly for this volume is the criticism levelled by Ghoshal (2005) and others that by propagating ideologically inspired amoral theories, often under the rubric of leadership, business schools have removed any sense of moral responsibility from their students. In response, calls are being heard for a more critical approach to leadership studies (Alvesson and Spicer, 2012) and for the involvement of 'more than engineers and accountants. We must also harness the ideas of artists, philosophers, designers, ecologists, anthropologists, and theologians' (Hamel, 2012: 254). Fresh approaches are emerging, such as those that embrace aesthetics, eco-leadership, embodiment and spirituality.[15]

It is not that business ethics has been absent from business school curricula, it is more that the treatment of the subject invariably falls short in its scope. Even if a mandatory course (which is rare), the syllabus tends to draw upon a

---

[14]Something we have encouraged contributors to do in this volume.

[15]See, for example, Mabey et al. (forthcoming); Western (2008); Melina et al. (2013); special issues in the *Journal of Management Development* (2010–12); *Organization* (2012); *Journal of Management Inquiry* (2005) and edited collections like *Religion and Organization Theory* edited by Paul Tracey, Nelson Phillips and Michael Lounsbury (2015).

very limited philosophical base, typically propounds a universal ethics of business, focuses upon specific issues like bribery or human rights rather than surfacing the ethical threads in everyday thought and action, and frequently fails to step outside the capitalist ideology and political economy of business (Bolden et al., 2011). More fundamental still is the question of how ethical is the management – not just the teaching – of business schools? Students and the organizations they represent are left asking: how can we develop our leaders to be successful at delivery without compromising their human values?

To be fair, some help is at hand. Those researching and writing in the area of leadership have expressed a growing interest in the philosophical and spiritual dimensions of ethical leadership. Three levels of analysis can be discerned:

- First, at an organizational practice level, this can be seen in the growth of such workplace initiatives as mindfulness and meditation (Vogus and Sutcliffe, 2012; Williams and Penman, 2011). Many organizations across the world now promote meditation as a means for promoting health and improved performance, including Google which developed a meditation training programme, *Search Inside Yourself*, that has evolved into a Leadership Institute. The place of meditation in business has become a focus of attention in the last decade and academics have scrutinized the influence of meditation on, for example, stress management and performance ethics.
- Second, at a theoretical level, there is a range of approaches informed by a rainbow of disciplines from economics to theology, from Greek philosophy to organizational behaviour (OB) theory, which seek to recover the spiritual roots of effective leadership. Of particular prominence is spiritual leadership theory (SLT) which has emerged over the last decade as an approach – some suggest a paradigm – that brings together individual spirituality and the creation of an innovative, motivated learning organization (e.g. Fry, 2008), with an impact on the 'triple bottom line'. Some commentators, however, claim that it introduces impoverished definitions of spirituality and proceeds to operationalize them in empiricist terms to produce proxy measures of spiritual leadership and corporate spirituality (Case and Gosling, 2010; Nehemya et al., 2009). SLT, its critics maintain, renders organizational spirituality in theologically denuded, disenchanted and strictly performative terms.
- At a third level are the belief systems which support practical and theoretical exploration. The number of authors drawing upon faith-based approaches to leadership, whether they be Māori (Holmes, 2007), American Indian (Warner and Grint, 2006), existentialist (Lawler, 2005), Taoist (Prince, 2005), Confucian (Tan and Khoo, 2002), or Judeo-Christian (Pattison, 1997) is testimony to a perceived moral vacuum in leadership studies.

We recognize the need to tread carefully as this is a path in contested territory. As mentioned above, there is a tendency within some literature to employ spirituality in instrumental terms, which can evolve into another form of utilitarian rule compliance – something that is readily associated with religious institutions. One way to tackle this is an initial focus upon *askesis*, self-transformative exercises that can be found in all forms of spirituality, religious and secular. Indeed mindfulness and meditation linked directly to an ethic of practice may provide a place of commonality between competing belief systems, as well as a point of connection between spirituality and philosophy. For example, Foucault saw his practice of philosophy as *askesis* (McGushin, 2007). His code of ethics attempts to connect an understanding and critique of power with a personal project of self (Crane et al., 2008). With similar attention given to the formation of our own subjectivity it may be possible to engage with an ethics of practice through paying attention to theories of moral imagination, virtue ethics and values-based management. Some propose that we critically engage with the notion of ethics as a practical concept, 'used to denote the possibilities of individual agency ... rather than following a religiously-based norm, or acting in accordance with some Kantian transcendental imperative' (Styhre, 2001: 799).

With regard to spiritual values, we need to take a small detour. Individualistic conceptions of leadership have met with great scepticism in Europe over recent years (see again the small but distinct difference in Table 1.1). *Pars pro toto*, heroic leadership theories have come under fire because of putting too little emphasis on the context and accepting, as intended or unintended consequences, manipulation by seniors (sometimes resisted, as Box 1.2 shows) and normative followers. This scepticism has good reasons, among them the importance of adapting leadership thinking and practice to a changing landscape of organizations and the increasing importance of relational, community and network elements. Yet, we argue that – in our view well-founded – the critique of *charisma* and getting rid of unjustified heroism must not purge *character*[16] from the discussion.

Leaders do not operate under full autonomy and, for a long time, followers were only partially included in the picture. But is not the assertion that the power of leaders arises exclusively from the actions of followers rather than being the cause of such action, going too far? Surely power, influence, resistance, cynicism, envy and dependency are just some of the emotions that flow among constituent players in a given context and it is more realistic to see the leader–follower relationship as one of interdependence, a dynamic tension between like and dislike of the leadership, between varying degrees of dependency and denigration (Western, 2008). Leaders continue to wield influence, but this resides less in their ability to objectively diagnose a given situation and propose a way forward – as propagated by contingency theorists – and more in the way they co-construct a persuasive account of the context which then legitimates a given form of authority (whether coercive, calculative or ideological) (Grint, 2005). Leadership, then, requires mutual respect, trust and commitment. Such a view cautions us against

---

[16]The study of leader character, focusing on *who* one is rather than *what* one does, is a topic of growing importance among management researchers. See, for example: Cameron (2011), Crossan et al. (2013), Dufresne and Offstein (2012), Hannah and Avolio (2011).

essentialist views of leadership where some individuals 'possess' leadership. Rather, it underscores the importance of individuals and their relationships, encompassing all members of an organization. In a similar vein, competency frameworks including the essentials for effective leadership (Box 1.2) can be misleading. Instead of being seen as a reflection of complex interactions between different types of actors, e.g. leaders, peers, subordinations and actors in the various segments of context, these frameworks are often interpreted as showing objective properties of individual actors. As such, they do not pay enough tribute to the moral, spiritual and emotional dimensions of leadership, which are not readily captured by behavioural dimensions.

The missing moral dimension is crucial then for leadership education in business schools. While we partly support the critique aiming at competency frameworks and their individualistic stance, this reference to moral character points towards the importance of moral power and personal integrity for strategic change. Underlying this is, among others, the commitment to a higher purpose (Quinn and Sonnenshein, 2008).

We now come to the third area for challenging the collusive cycle in which business schools are so easily enmeshed, and this concerns the influential arena of the classroom.

RE-APPRAISAL OF PEDAGOGY

As noted earlier, there would appear to be two extremes when it comes to business school teaching. On the one hand is the disciplinary approach where the syllabus has a strong theory content, is taught in a didactic manner by subject matter 'experts', who remain in control of the classroom experience, aided and abetted by prescriptive learning objectives, traditional pedagogy and an assessment strategy which emphasises memory and regurgitation. On the other hand is what Currie and Knights (2003) refer to as the staff development approach, 'where teachers simply become highly skilled, professional communicators of materials that are at least partially derived from "real-life" cases and are therefore seen as relevant to practising managers' (2003: 40–1). They go on to advocate a 'critical' approach which combines the best of both, namely academic rigour and participative teaching methods. This has several advantages. Crucially, it encourages students to learn *about* management as well *for* management and opens up a number of rich learning opportunities: to test some of the assumptions that are often taken for granted in the disciplinary and staff development approaches; to challenge gendered and Western ethnocentric models which marginalize non-Anglo-American and female voices; to give credence to the ethical and moral dimensions of managing, acknowledging the multiple roles and responsibilities of students, e.g. to their family, their community, their spiritual and political allegiance, to the wider planet, and not least to their own health and wellbeing; and to explore the highly politicized nature of everyday workplace activities and the often unexamined models that inform managerial actions, recognizing that, as practising managers, MBA students are already drawing upon complex theoretical ideas in an intuitive way in their day-to-day lives.

Why is it that this approach is often discussed but less often pursued? Part of the reason is the interlocking of stakeholders referred to in the collusive cycle, which collectively creates institutional, political and social pressure to leave things as they are. Another part of it lies with the anxieties of teaching and administrative staff provoked by more ambiguous and unsettling learning activities, by the discomfort of disrupting classroom expectations and by the challenge of working with 'here-and-now' dynamics and emotions in the classroom. As one business tutor, who has tried it, notes: 'In the same way that anxiety underpins students' avoidance of learning, anxiety also underpins political avoidance strategies in management practice' (Vince, 2010: S36). Perhaps a further, less discussed, reason is that the critical approach potentially ventures into ethical and spiritual territory and for many, particularly in the Cartesian, post-Enlightenment West, this is still taboo. Yet, moral authority should not be confused with moral certitude. Being clear where one stands morally, ethically and spiritually does not imply dogmatism, nor does it necessarily lead to the desire to impose one's values or position of faith/non-faith on others. Of course in fundamentalist circles, be they religious, political or ideological, it can, but it doesn't necessarily have to. The number of authors drawing upon faith-based approaches to leadership is testimony to a perceived moral vacuum in leadership studies. And given that faith is essentially a matter of personal decision and ongoing moral choices, rather than something received vicariously or even co-created, this re-situates the individual as a central figure in leadership development, and therefore centre-stage on the business school stage. We might also note that the model of servant leadership sees *leadership of self* as a prerequisite to leading others. It has been noted that deep learning and sustained change are often driven by desperation, crisis or aspiration and the real territory of change is *in here* with the consequences being *out there*, deeply private yet inherently collective (Senge, 2002). A servant leader is committed and invites, rather than demands, commitment from others; crucially there is room for choice; this allows one to be committed and still live in the domain of doubt, which fosters humility and tolerance[17] (Box 1.3).

BOX 1.3   LEADING WHO AND FOR WHAT PURPOSE?

Henri Nouwen, a Catholic theologian-priest with 20 years' success as an academic at Notre Dame, Yale and Harvard, changed vocation to work at L'Arche, a community for mentally disabled people. After a short time at the centre he noted that '[i]t seemed as though I was starting my life all over again. Relationships, connections, reputations could no longer be counted on', leading him to conclude

---

[17]Box 1.3 recounts the reflections of Henri Nouwen (1978: 12–13; 1989: 16–17).

that 'the leader of the future is called to be completely irrelevant and to stand in this world with nothing to offer but his or her own vulnerable self'.

Elsewhere in a reference to radical pedagogy well ahead of its time, Nouwen notes that: 'A redemptive teaching relationship is bilateral … The teacher has to learn from his [sic] student. Teachers and students are fellowmen [sic] who together are searching for what is true, meaningful and valid and who give each other the chance to play each other's roles'.

The risk of re-instating the individual leader as a prime mover in the curriculum and pedagogy of business schools is that we slide back into charismatic territory with all its attendant ambushes. However, once character and charisma have been de-coupled we can begin to explore more fully what individuals in all their relational and ethical richness bring to the leader–follower dynamic. Given that leadership is intrinsically going on a journey together, surely the moral purpose of that journey is an essential and fascinating dimension of what business schools offer their students. As two commentators on the field have stated: 'We really must look past the charisma and into the motives of the leader. We must look past leader behaviours and into the heart of the leader. We really need to have an insight into leadership for a higher purpose' (Jackson and Parry, 2008: 98).

CONCLUSION

We began by posing some questions of business schools and their apparent incapacity to answer, or even address, these. This was attributed to a cycle of collusion which thwarts the rich societal contribution business schools should be making and three potential avenues were outlined for breaking this mould. This book is intended to explore and clarify the contours of this contested and complex terrain more fully. Although it is authored by, and tends to reflect the interests of, just one of the stakeholder groups in Figure 1.1, i.e. academics, albeit from a wide variety of disciplines, it seeks to rise above the immediate parochial concerns of its constituency to engage with the broader issues we have raised.

In Part I we discern more carefully where business schools have lost their way (Harle), become incapable of addressing certain questions (Ward and Mayrhofer), lost touch with the world of work (Ng), indeed with the very 'humanness' of organizations (Shymko); and each contribution starts to delineate a route back.

Part II confronts some of the sacred shibboleths of business schools, questioning whether all businesses have to grow (Scott Cato), whether leadership can ever be values-free (Parry and Fiskerud), whether market capitalism (Beech) and modern economics (Henley) are morally suspect and what we lose ethically by treating ourselves and others as disembodied and de-politicized subjects (Tomkins).

Having already hinted at antidotes along the way, the remainder of the book goes on to offer a more full-bodied, but by no means exhaustive, riposte to the ills we have described.

Part III proposes that business schools can regain their ethical high-ground by drawing upon a number traditions and faith positions: spirituality (Blakeley), MacIntyre's virtue (Conroy), classical Greek philosophy (Gaggiotti and Simpson) and the Māori notion of *wairua* (Keiha and Pio).

In the Part IV we consider not just what and why we teach in business schools, but how. Drawing upon their first-hand experience in the MBA classroom, we encounter: the genre-crossing and century-hopping relevance of Balzac to the demise of Lehmann Brothers (Grassman), how a cross-cultural fist-fight in the classroom led to learning about respect (Wilson) and the contemporary resonance of ancient Hebrew wisdom (Jackman); this is followed by three raw pedagogic challenges: teaching cosmopolitan values to mainland China students (Hui, Chiu, Coombes and Pang), modelling an ethic of care in the face of public sector redundancies (Hartog and Tomkins) and creating critical legitimacy for students to revise their view of a favourite management 'blockbuster' (Doherty). Recognizing that all this is more of a conversation than precise prognosis, we have enlisted rapporteurs, each well qualified to engage with the issues raised in respective sections (Biberman, Spender, Freeman, and Miller). We are grateful to them for their provocation and hope that some of you as readers will continue the dialogue at www.ethicalleadership.org.uk

In sum, by divining more fundamentally the nature and resilience of business school collusion, we are proposing that these result as much from a collective failure of moral authority – in the best sense – as they do from the parochial protection of partisan interests. Following on from this assessment, the book offers a range of philosophical, ethical and spiritual approaches which are potentially capable of unlocking the institutional, socio-political, cultural and pedagogic chains that beset business schools caught in a collusive cycle. In so doing, we hope to have moved the argument on.

REFERENCES

Adler, N. and Harzing, A.-W. (2009) 'When knowledge wins: transcending the sense and nonsense of academic rankings', *Academy of Management Learning and Education*, 8 (1): 72–95

Alvesson, M. and Deetz, S. (2000) *Doing Critical Management Research*. London: Sage.

Alvesson, M. and Spicer, A. (2012) 'Critical leadership studies: the case for critical performativity', *Human Relations*, 65: 367–90.

Bellagio Statement (2011) 'EU/US Roadmap to Measuring the Results of Investments in Science'. Report following the EU/US Science of Science Policy, Rockefeller Foundation Bellagio Centre Workshop, June 27–30.

Bolden, R. and Gosling, J. (2006) 'Leadership competencies: time to change the tune?', *Leadership*, 2 (2): 147–63.

Bolden, R., Hawkins, B., Gosling, J. and Taylor, S. (2011) *Exploring Leadership: Individual, Organizational and Societal Perspectives*. Oxford: Oxford University Press.

Brown, W. (2006) *Edgework: Critical Essays on Knowledge and Politics*. Princeton, NJ: Princeton University Press.

Burrell, G. and Morgan, G. (1979) *Sociological Paradigms and Organizational Analysis*. London: Heinemann.

Cameron, K. (2011) 'Responsible leadership as virtuous leadership', *Journal of Business Ethics*, 98: 25–35.

Case, P. and Gosling, J. (2010) 'The spiritual organization: critical reflections on the instrumentality of workplace spirituality', *Journal of Management, Spirituality and Religion*, 7 (4): 257–82.

CMI (Chartered Management Institute) (2014) '21st century leaders'. Retrieved from: www.managers.org.uk/21CLeaders (accessed 14 November 2014).

Collinson, D. (2012) 'Prozac leadership and the limits of positive thinking', *Leadership*, 8 (2): 87–107.

Craig, R., Amernic, J. and Tourish, D. (2014) 'Perverse audit culture and accountability of the modern public university', *Financial Accountability and Management*, 30 (1): 2–24

Crane, A., Knights, D. and Starkey, K. (2008) 'The conditions of our freedom: Foucault, organization, and ethics', *Business Ethics Quarterly*, 18 (3): 299–320.

Crossan, M., Mazutis, D., Seijts, G. and Gandz, J. (2013) 'Developing leadership character in business programs', *Academy of Management Learning and Education*, 12: 285–305.

Currie, G. and Knights, D. (2003) 'Reflecting on a critical pedagogy in MBA education', *Management Learning*, 34 (1): 27–49.

Davies, H. (2012) 'Regulatory responses to the financial crisis: an interim assessment', *International Journal of Disclosure and Governance*, 9 (3): 206–16. doi:10.1057/jdg.2012.5.

Day, D., Gronn, P. and Salas, E. (2006) 'Leadership in team-based organizations: on a threshold of a new era', *The Leadership Quarterly*, 17: 211–16.

Docherty, T. (2011) 'The unseen academy', *Times Higher Education*, 10 November.

Douglas, T. (1983) *Groups: Understanding People Gathered Together*. London: Tavistock.

Dufresne, R.L. and Offstein, E.H. (2012) 'Holistic and intentional student character development process: learning from West Point', *Academy of Management Learning and Education*, 11: 570–90.

Etzkowitz, H. and Leydesdorff, L. (2000) 'The dynamics of innovation: from national systems and "mode 2" to a triple helix of university – industry – government relations', *Research Policy*, 29: 109–23.

Ferlie, E., McGivern, G. and Moraes, A. (2010) 'Developing a public interest school of management', *British Journal of Management*, 21: S60–S70.

Fleetwood, S. (2004) 'The ontology of organisation and management studies', in S. Fleetwood and S. Ackroyd (eds), *Realism in Action in Management and Organisation Studies*. London: Routledge, pp. 27–53.

Fletcher, J.K. (2004) 'The paradox of post-heroic leadership: an essay on gender, power and transformative change', *Leadership Quarterly*, 14: 647–61.

Fournier, V. and Grey, C. (2000) 'At the critical moment: conditions and prospects for critical management studies', *Human Relations*, 53 (1): 7–32.

Francis, Robert, QC (2010) *Robert Francis Inquiry Report into Mid-Staffordshire NHS Foundation Trust*. London: House of Commons.

Fry, L.W. (2008) 'Spiritual leadership: state-of-the-art and future directions for theory research, and practice', in J. Biberman and L. Tishman, L. (eds), *Spirituality in Business: Theory, Practice, and Future Directions*. New York: Palgrave, pp. 106–24.

Ghoshal, S. (2005) 'Bad management theories are destroying good management practices', *Academy of Management Learning and Education*, 4 (1): 75–91.

Grint, K. (2005) *Leadership: Limits and Possibilities*. Basingstoke: Palgrave.

Gronn, P. (2002) 'Distributed leadership as a unit of analysis', *The Leadership Quarterly*, 13: 423–51.

Grugulis, I. (2007) *Skills, Training and Human Resource Development: A Critical Text*. Basingstoke: Palgrave.

Hamel, G. (2012) *What Matters Now*. San Francisco, CA: Jossey-Bass.

Hannah, S. and Avolio, B. (2011) 'The locus of leader character', *The Leadership Quarterly*, 22: 979–83.

Holmes, J. (2007) 'Humour and construction of Maori leadership at work', *Leadership*, 3 (1): 5–27.

Iles, P. and Preece, D. (2006) 'Developing leaders or developing leadership?', *Leadership*, 2 (3): 317–40.

Jackson, B. and Parry, K. (2008) *A Very Short, Fairly Interesting and Reasonably Cheap Book About Studying Leadership*. London: Sage.

Kellerman, B. (2012) *The End of Leadership*. New York: HarperBusiness.

Kempster, S. and Parry, K. (2011) 'Grounded theory and leadership research: a critical realist perspective', *Leadership Quarterly*, 22 (1): 106–20,

Khurana, R. (2007) *From Higher Aims to Hired Hands: The Social Transformation of American Business Schools and the Unfulfilled Promise of Management as a Profession*. Princeton, NJ: Princeton University Press.

Lawler, J. (2005) 'The essence of leadership? Existentialism and leadership', *Leadership*, 1 (2): 215–33.

Lewis, M. and Keleman, M. (2002) 'Multiparadigm enquiry: exploring organizational pluralism and paradox', *Human Relations*, 55 (2): 251–75.

Mabey, C. (2013) 'Leadership development in organizations: multiple discourses and diverse practice', *International Journal of Management Reviews*, 15 (4): 359–469.

Mabey, C., Parry, K. and Egri, C. (forthcoming) 'Ethical leadership: philosophical and spiritual approaches', *Academy of Management Learning and Education*.

McGushin, E.F. (2007) *Foucault's Askesis: An Introduction to the Philosophical Life*. Evanston, IL: Northwestern University Press.

Melina, L., Burgess, G.J., Falkman, L. and Marturano, A. (eds) (2013) *The Embodiment of Leadership*. San Francisco, CA: Jossey-Bass.

Mintzberg, H. (2004) *Managers Not MBAs: A Hard Look at the Soft Practice of Managing and Management Development*. Harlow: FT Prentice Hall.

Mitroff, I. (2004) 'An open letter to the deans and faculties of American business schools', *Journal of Business Ethics*, 54: 185–9.

Nehemya, I., Goldstein-Gidoni, O. and Zaidman, N. (2009) 'From temples to organizations: the introduction and packaging of spirituality', *Organization*, 16 (4): 597–621.

Neubaum, D., Pagel, M., Drexler, J., McKee-Ryan, F. and Larson, E. (2009) 'Business education and its relationship to student personal moral philosophies and attitudes towards profits: an empirical response to critics', *Academy of Management Learning and Education*, 8: 9–24.

Newell, S., Swan, J. and Kautz, K. (2001) 'The role of funding bodies in the creation and diffusion of management fads and fashions', *Organization*, 8 (1): 97–120.

Nouwen, H. (1978) *Creative Ministry*. Garden City, NY: Doubleday.

Nouwen, H. (1989) *In the Name of Jesus: Reflections on Christian Leadership*. London: Darton, Longman and Todd.

Orlikowski, W. (2002) 'Knowing in practice: enacting a collective capability in distributed organizing', *Organization Science*, 13: 249–73.

Ormrod, S., Ferlie, E., Warren, F. and Norton, K. (2007) 'The appropriation of new organizational forms within networks of practice: Founder and founder-related ideological power', *Human Relations*, 60: 745–67.

Parker, M. (2014) 'University, Ltd: changing a business school, *Organization*, 21 (2): 281–92.

Pattison, S. (1997) *The Faith of the Managers*. London: Cassell.

Prince, L. (2005) 'Eating the menu rather than the dinner: Tao and leadership', *Leadership*, 1 (1): 105–26.

Quinn, R. and Sonnenshein, S. (2008) 'Four general strategies for changing human systems', in T. Cummings (ed.), *Handbook of Organization Development*, London: Sage, pp. 69–78.

Reynolds, M. (1999) 'Grasping the nettle: possibilities and pitfalls of a critical management pedagogy', *British Journal of Management*, 10 (2): 171–84.

Russon, C. and Reinelt, C. (2004) 'The results of an evaluation scan of 55 leadership development programs', *Journal of Leadership and Organizational Studies*, 10 (3): 104–7.

Senge, P. (2002) 'Afterword', in R. Greenleaf, *Servant Leadership* (25th anniversary edn). New Jersey: Paulist Press.

Sievers, B. (2006) 'The psychotic organization: a socio-analytic perspective', *Ephemera: Theory and Politics in Organizations*, 6 (2): 104–20.

Styhre, A. (2001) 'Kaizen, ethics, and care of the operations: management after empowerment', *Journal of Management Studies*, 38 (6): 795–810.

Swan, J. and Scarborough, H. (2005) 'The politics of networked innovation', *Human Relations*, 58: 913–43.

Tan, K. and Khoo, H. (2002) 'The relevance of Confucianism to national quality awards in South East Asia', *International Journal of Cross-Cultural Management*, 2 (1): 65–82.

Verhaegen, P. (2005) 'Academic talent: Quo Vadis? Recruitment and retention of faculty in European Business Schools', *Journal of Management Development*, 24 (9): 807–18.

Vince, R. (2010) 'Anxiety, politics and critical management education', *British Journal of Management*, 21: S26–29.

Vogus, T.J. and Sutcliffe, K.M. (2012) 'Organizational mindfulness and mindful organizing: a reconciliation and path forward', *Academy of Management Learning and Education*, 11 (4): 722–35.

Warner, L. and Grint, K. (2006) 'American Indian ways of leading and knowing, *Leadership*, 2 (2): 225–44.

Western, S. (2008) *Leadership: A Critical Text*. London: Sage.

Williams, M. and Penman, M. (2011) *Mindfulness: A Practical Guide to Finding Peace in a Frantic World*. London: Piatkus.

PART I

HOW DO BUSINESS SCHOOLS PREPARE STUDENTS FOR LEADERSHIP?

2 QUESTIONING BUSINESS SCHOOLS

Tim Harle

INTRODUCTION

As the global financial crisis unfolded in 2008, researchers from a Carnegie Foundation study were doing fieldwork on business education at US institutions. The authors of the subsequent report, noting how professions such as medicine and engineering focus on understanding failure as a way to improve practice, expected to see urgent attention being paid 'within business programs to probing such a frightening, large-scale catastrophe, one that threatened to destroy the global economic system itself' (Colby et al., 2011: 11). The reality was very different: 'Instead, in many of the sites we visited, the crisis was characterized as a kind of natural event … previous understandings of the workings of the business world were so strong that, even in the face of massive problems, neither business faculty nor students cracked open these understandings to reveal the need for alternative points of view and new approaches' (Colby et al., 2011: 11). At best, this reveals a gulf in understanding, at worst, a state of denial.

Tourish and Hargie (2012) observe a similar lack of appreciation of responsibility in their study of British bankers' response to the post-2008 crisis. Where did business schools lose their way, how did such a disconnect between theory and practice, between cause and effect, between personal and corporate responsibility, arise? In this chapter, I address that question first by summarizing contributions to the debate about business schools in recent years. Much of this is highly critical but there are also seeds of hope. In the second section I explore these more hopeful avenues, under the thematic headings of leadership, paradigms and complexity. This leads to a final section where I suggest ways in which business schools can promote responsible reconnections and begin to re-discover their social and economic contribution to society.

BUSINESS SCHOOLS: HAVE THEY LOST THEIR WAY?

The observed disconnects are not a new challenge for educators. Citing the corrupt culture behind the collapse of Enron and Arthur Andersen, Ian Mitroff wrote an open letter to US business school deans and faculty expressing his outrage at how business educators (with whom he identified himself) allowed the situation to develop. Among his criticisms was that business schools promulgated 'a narrow, outdated, and repudiated notion of ethics', which leads to 'a learned sense of helplessness and hopelessness among faculties, students and workers regarding control of their lives and careers' (Mitroff, 2004: 185). Pfeffer and Fong (2002) questioned the self-satisfaction of business schools and joined other critics in focusing on the impact of the MBA on students and society. Following the events of 2008, criticism of business schools became more concentrated. Much of this soul-searching comes from within business schools themselves (see Box 2.1). Such is the perceived state of emergency, that O'Doherty and Jones (2005: 2) shed the usual protocols of polite academic discourse by likening the business school to 'a cancerous machine spewing out sick and irrelevant detritus'. In the face of such attacks, there is evidence of robust responses, particularly from beyond the North American and Western European context (Durand and Dameron, 2008; Morsing and Rovira, 2011).

BOX 2.1 *FROM HIGHER AIMS TO HIRED HANDS*

This is the title of a 2007 book by Rakesh Khurana, Leadership Development Professor at Harvard Business School, in which he provides a scorching historic critique of US business education. He summarizes his thesis as follows:

> … by aiming to legitimate themselves, in the second half of the twentieth century, in terms of the era's successively dominant discourses – first of science and rationality, and then of the superiority of markets to all other forms of social organization, including management itself – university-based business schools in America have contributed to their own delegitimation. In so doing, they have not only undermined their own competitive position vis-a-vis other providers of management education but also virtually abandoned any idea of social purpose, once part of the price of admission to the revered institution of the American university. (Khurana and Penrice, 2011: 9)

Criticism of business schools is not confined to the USA and Europe, as an Indian business school professor discovered when he met a 'business icon'. Asha Bhandarker was taken aback to receive this response when proudly telling his fellow citizen of his role: 'Do business schools really groom leaders? My experience with scores of MBAs from the top Indian schools tells me that business schools

---

tend to produce job-hoppers, careerists, and climbers. Their life ambition seems to be reaching high positions rather than make contributions to nation building. It's a pity because, these are some of the brightest minds this country produces' (Bhandarker, 2008: xix).

Underlying the polemic are some important debates. First there is the gap between theory and practice, a theme that continues to surface (Alvesson and Sandberg, 2013; Pfeffer, 2007). In a widely cited posthumous article, Sumantra Ghoshal (2005) challenged the impact of managerial theory on practice and pedagogy. Second, there is the trend towards instrumentality at the expense of more socially, ethically and ecologically oriented goals. This is expressed in the persistent focus on publications in highly ranked journals, too readily subverted by a managerialist agenda which further removes academics from the ecosystem inhabited by their students, and also by an obsession with reputation rankings, which Thomas et al. (2013: 153) state has set back the value mission of business schools. Third, we now have schemes, such as the Thinkers 50, which are widely regarded as the 'Oscars of management thinking'.[1] Social media traffic following publication of the 2013 list suggests that business schools are more than happy to draw attention to their 'thinkers'. While this is potentially laudable, there is a tendency to elevate some authors and speakers to the overused status of guru. As Thomas et al. (2013: 119–20) remark, some of these individuals are now 'almost industries in themselves'. Finally there is a debate about the harnessing of new technologies for business school education. Onzoño (2011) is one author who draws attention to the impact of new technologies, although it is too early to offer considered comment on the rush to MOOCs (massive open online courses). Starkey and Tempest (2009) emphasize the need for business schools not simply to focus on organization technology, but to raise fundamental questions about knowledge and society.

Amann et al., with Shiban Khan (2011: 447–69) highlight three interdependent tasks facing business schools wishing to embrace a humanistic approach. Two, covering research and teaching, are familiar, but the third may come as a surprise – administration. The authors draw attention to the role of business school leaders and the importance of such initiatives as PRME[2] (see Blakeley, this volume), EFMD[3] and GRLI.[4] The need for business schools to have sustainable business models in a globalized world poses an increasing challenge to administrators and deans (Thomas and Peters, 2012).

A growing number of authors address the challenges, and offer some ways forward (see Box 2.2). For example, Dameron and Durand (2011) provide a

---

[1]www.thinkers50.com/about/ (accessed 26 March 2014).

[2]Principles for Responsible Management Education, www.unprme.org.

[3]European Foundation for Management Development, www.efmd.org.

[4]Globally Responsible Leadership Initiative, www.grli.org.

distinctive European voice, while an edited collection by Canals (2012) advances European interaction with dominant North American discourses. One group that has taken up the challenge of responding to these criticisms is CEMS, originally the Community of European Management Schools, but now describing itself as the Global Alliance in Business Education.[5] Morsing and Rovira (2011: xix) write how 'Asian, Latin American and European geo-political and socio-economic contexts provide other points of departure for business schools than their Anglo-Saxon counterparts'. Rather than comparing Anglo-Saxon and non-Anglo-Saxon models, the CEMS collection aims to provide a global voice.

Reporting on research[6] from the Aspen Institute Center for Business Education, Samuelson (2011: 158) notes how, 'The financial crisis has opened the door for fresh, scholarly enquiry about the very purpose of business and sparked debate about how key frameworks are communicated to students, especially in finance and economic classrooms' (see Box 2.2). But, as Ford et al. (2010) point out, critical scholars need to consider their own role, calling for a 'reflexive journey' that may involve uncomfortable questions. Their questions, based on examples from their own experience, include whether their critical approach is understood by students as a judgemental stance, and whether such students interpret nuanced critical questioning as simply another 'truth'.

BOX 2.2   QUESTIONS BEING ASKED BY BUSINESS SCHOOLS

Aspen Institute, Colorado:

- What is the purpose, in business and societal terms, of a business activity or investment?
- What is the social context of such a decision? Who needs to be consulted to secure a decision that stands the test of time? What are the impacts on quality of life for the community?
- How are performance and profitability assessed? Over what period? What is, and isn't, being counted?

Source: Samuelson (2011: 155–6)

ESADE, Spain:

We need to develop an identity in business schools, in relation to ethics and social responsibility, which transcends the curriculum. 'There is a need for self-examination and answering fundamental questions such as: What is our purpose? What type of people and professionals do we aim to educate?

---

[5] www.cems.org.

[6] See www.beyondgreypinstripes.org.

What kind of business leader is necessary for the welfare of society? What practices must we implement to responsibly manage our own school? What new roles and responsibilities should our school adopt to serve society's future needs?'

Source: Losada et al. (2011: 163)

In the next section, I draw upon current debates to briefly explore how business schools might respond to the sustained critique of the last decade. Three hopeful directions present themselves: a better understanding of leadership, questioning unspoken paradigms and embracing complexity. Space allows only a light sketch of the salient issues, but subsequent chapters in this volume will develop these ideas in more depth.

BUSINESS SCHOOLS: FINDING A WAY BACK

Developing a better understanding of leadership

Tourish (2013: 199) summarises the situation well: 'leadership, as traditionally envisaged, is a key part of the problems we now face, rather than the solution'. In a critique of transformational leadership, he urges business schools to revisit how they approach the teaching of leadership (2013: 7). Writing from within the industry she describes, Barbara Kellerman's list of criticisms is stark:

> … the leadership industry is self-satisfied, self-perpetuating and poorly policed; that leadership programs tend to proliferate without objective assessment; that leadership as an area of intellectual inquiry remains thin; and that little original thought has been given to what leader learning in the second decade of the twenty-first century should look like. (Kellerman, 2012: 169)

In recent years it has become fashionable to repudiate individualistic conceptions of leadership, especially on the European side of the Atlantic. There are good reasons to explain the fascination with collective, and the relegation of individual, expressions of leadership. The nature of organizations and boundaries of identity are changing, prompting a re-assessment of the way leadership is exercised in relational, community and networked enterprises. Leadership of *place*, as against positional leadership, emphasizes more fluid relational processes and the primacy of collaboration between individuals, institutions, firms and other community level groups. And conventional, 'heroic' leadership theories have been critically dismantled because they are said to neglect context, to reproduce normative followers and to facilitate manipulation by seniors. There are undoubted flaws in an individualized approach to, and teaching of, leadership, but in our haste to discredit *charisma* and banish it to the outmoded shores of heroism, are we not in danger of also ditching *character*?

Certainly a given leader does not operate with infinite autonomy and the leadership literature has, until recently, neglected the importance of those being led. Leadership requires individuals to give and receive respect, build trust in face to face encounters and generate mutual commitment. This rightly deflects us from a preoccupation with leadership competence being invested in certain individuals, but nevertheless reminds us that a multitude of everyday 'leadership acts' by a combination of actors, from the cleaner to the CEO, make up collective organizational capability. The individual actor cannot be written out of the leadership play.[7] Another way in which individualistic notions of leadership have become discredited is the way organizations have devised competency frameworks in an effort to capture the essential qualities, traits and behaviours necessary for effective leadership. The problem here is that of seeing competency as an objective property of the individual rather than a fluid consequence of the interpretive interaction between a leader, colleagues and their organizational and cultural context. This disembodied approach also under-emphasizes the moral and relational dimensions of leadership and the need for an emotional engagement with others (Bolden and Gosling, 2006).

I find this reference to the missing moral dimension of particular interest. A business school module dealing with leadership surely cannot dodge such issues. In the headlong rush to denounce competency frameworks with their focus on individualized skills and behaviours (for all sorts of legitimate theoretical and pragmatic reasons), it would be easy to overlook this reference to moral character which is undeniably individual at core. Some authors go so far as to say that personal integrity and moral power, derived from reduced defensiveness, the examination of personal hypocrisy and commitment to a higher purpose, constitute the essential mainspring of leading effective strategic change (Quinn and Sonenshein, 2008).

> It is odd, to say the least, that the education which we have devised for the best of our managers has so little in it about personality theory, what makes people what they are; or about learning theory, how people grow and develop and change; or political theory, how people seek power, resist power and organize themselves; or moral philosophy, how they decide between right and wrong. (Charles Handy, 1996, quoted in Thomas et al., 2013: 255)

There have been attempts to introduce a more ethical basis to leadership development into business school curricula, such areas as a greater emphasis on business ethics, corporate social responsibility (CSR) and social entrepreneurship. But, as Box 2.3 suggests, there is still a long way to go. At the risk of oversimplification, business schools should spend more time asking 'why?' rather than 'what?' and 'how?', a theme taken up by many chapters in this book.

Referring to the Association to Advance Collegiate Schools of Business globalization report (AACSB International, 2011), the taskforce's chair calls for

---

[7]As Douglas observes: 'there is no such thing as a leaderless group, only groups with differing degrees of leadership residing in the actions of one person or several' (1983: 43, cited in Western, 2008: 47).

business schools to take the opportunity to focus on 'the *whole individual*' (Bruner et al., 2012: 5). One person who has done much to promote more thoughtful engagement, combining questions of spirituality with practical CSR, is Philippe de Woot; a biennial award is now made in his honour.[8]

BOX 2.3   CALLS FOR ETHICAL LEADERSHIP

… We must encourage more human (and humane) values in management, especially forgiveness and health at work. Leadership training, which may well be the centerpiece of a reshaped business education, should aim at developing a style of management that promotes these values. (Eric Corneul, EFMD, in Hardy and Everett, 2013: x)

Business schools could become 'important agents of cultural change if they were willing to transform and rise up to the level of challenges facing us. But their assurance, if not their arrogance, makes one doubt their will fundamentally to question themselves … The *raison d'être* of most of these schools is to equip their students to run the existing system in an ever more effective way without asking questions about its aims, its faults or the dangers it poses. In this way, the majority of professors are the thurifers of an ideology, the clergy and the celebrants of a unidimensional way of thinking. They claim to train citizens and yet they more often train mere robots of a system without a clear *raison d'être*. They constitute a major obstacle to the establishment of a culture of sustainable development. This is also true for most universities or schools of Christian tradition. (Philippe de Woot, Emeritus Professor, Catholic University of Louvain, 2013: 44–5)

Hamel (2012: 10) summarizes the challenge facing business schools succinctly: 'The worst economic downturn since the 1930s wasn't a banking crisis, a credit crisis, or a mortgage crisis – it was a moral crisis'. Reflecting a view that what got us into the current situation will not get us out of it, he offers the widest compass of all, calling for management development to involve 'more than engineers and accountants. We must also harness the ideas of artists, philosophers, designers, ecologists, anthropologists, and theologians' (Hamel, 2012: 254).

Questioning unspoken paradigms

A second theme which poses a fundamental challenge concerns the paradigms, often unspoken, underlying business school curricula and understandings of leadership.

For some time the reliance by MBA programmes upon liberal capitalist models, especially the primacy of shareholder value, has been criticized (Datar et al., 2010).

---

[8]www.solvay.edu/philippe-de-woot-award (accessed 31 March 2014).

Durand and Dameron (2008: 17) observe that business schools 'are struggling with the overhang of two centuries of commitment to rationality as the appropriate methodology for investigating social and economic questions'. This takes us back to where we started, viewing the global financial crisis as a natural disaster. Thomas Bieger of St Gallen notes a key criticism of business schools: 'Their basic concepts, models and theories [are] based mainly on a mechanistic and economic view of human nature. In search of a Newton-like paradigm, closed, axiomatic models are favored' (2011: 105). Locke and Spender (2011) also challenge Newtonian paradigms. They conclude their broad-ranging critique, including historical and religious dimensions, thus:

> The choice is not between socialism and unregulated US neoliberal market capitalism, but between the latter and an internationally regulated form of dynamic capitalism in which firms are more efficient because of participative management, and the markets function better because of a more equitable distribution of wealth in society. Unless a combination of domestic and international political pressures brings the necessary reforms to managerialism and business schools in the US, they will not be part of the solution to current woes but a continued cause of dislocation in American society and in the world economy. (2011: 192)

The influence of agency theory in recent decades is an example of the combined impact of underlying paradigms of liberal capitalism and mechanistic models, affecting both markets and the behaviour of organizations and individuals. Colby et al. (2011: 45) report that, 'although few deans or faculty endorsed this "shareholder primacy" [agency] view, it appeared to be strongly entrenched in key parts of the curriculum'. Tourish et al. (2010) provide a sustained critique of agency theory in the context of business education, while Muff et al. (2013: 179) lament that initiatives such as CEMS (see above) 'remain for the most part marginal, leaving core subjects in finance and economics untouched'.

A further paradigm rarely addressed by business schools is the fact that individuals are not isolated, self-serving workers but active members of communities. Referring to Adam Smith's foundational text on the importance of self-interest, Strand (2011: 214) comments how, 'Friedman ... and others have failed to focus on the significant detail that Smith's baker, butcher and brewer lived within communities that they served and directly interacted with their stakeholders on a daily basis'. Bolden and Kirk (2012) describe a relational approach to leadership which involves an engagement with the ethical values of the community in which leadership is enacted. They suggest that leadership development 'could be conceived as ... a potential antidote to overly heroic or instrumental accounts of leadership but one that may also require sacrifice: the possible subordination of self-interest to that of the community' (2012: 49). A good example of this contrary understanding is Keith Grint's (2005: 105) observation of inverse learning in the military and families: 'while leaders think they are teaching followers to follow, in fact it is the followers who do most of the teaching and the leaders who do most of the learning'. The community dimension of leadership is developed further by Parry (this volume).

All this implies that conventional teaching paradigms in business schools require re-appraisal. Standing in the tradition of Paolo Freire, Brookfield and Holst (2011) call for deep engagement with political structures that can help create a more just world. Their 'holy trinity' of contemporary adult learning could be mapped with interest onto business school programmes: transformative adult learning; critical reflection; self-directed learning (2011: 32–41). Fotaki and Prasad (2014) also draw on Freire's work, including his emphasis on 'conscientization' in their challenge to business school academics to be more critically engaged with issues of social justice and values. Toubiana (2014) also calls on faculty to raise their awareness on questions of social justice: noting the hegemonic forces at play in a typical MBA programme, she is pessimistic about whether such change will occur without disruptive change. However, initiatives we have considered above, together with later chapters in this volume addressing questions of justice, humanity, ethics and community, indicate that there may be at least some grounds for realistic optimism.

Embracing complexity

The third underlying theme is one that derives from radical new insights from complexity theory. The world of education has a vital contribution to make in exposing hidden assumptions and introducing new perspectives (Mason, 2008). As research in a range of scientific fields came together in what is now termed complexity theory, it is no surprise that philosophers and theologians considered the implications (Kauffman, 2008). Faced with the longstanding observation that entropy and disorder are properties of organisms and organizations alike, the concepts of emergence and self-organization require radically new understandings for both the scientist and philosopher. Tsoukas and Chia (2002) examine such questions as the continuing nature of change, the significance of microscopic actions and the emergence of organization. There has been a growing interest in complexity theory to help understand economics and the geopolitical system (Beinhocker, 2006; Stacey, 2010). Such fundamentally different perspectives challenge received notions of control, rationality and efficiency: they are thus highly relevant to business school curricula and pedagogies. The first scholarly handbook in this field (Allen et al., 2011) includes contributions on limits to knowledge (Allen and Boulton, 2011) and organizational learning (Mitleton-Kelly and Ramalingam, 2011). The former highlight the importance of learning to live with uncertainty; they recognize the importance of modelling and counsel against the wholesale replacing of classical scientific approaches with tools derived from complexity science. The latter explore similarities and differences between complexity thinking and existing approaches, including social constructionism and systems thinking. For business schools, this raises questions both for the curriculum and the interplay between pedagogical approaches and learning styles.

However, as Cilliers (2002: 83) cautions, we cannot use the uncertainties of complexity theory to excuse ourselves from addressing moral dilemmas: 'What we need, therefore, are ways of dealing with that which we cannot calculate, of coping with our ignorance. There is a name for this. It is called "ethics", and no amount of complexity theory will allow us to escape it'. Complexity perspectives are also important in new understandings of leadership; though, as Uhl-Bien and Marion (2009) point out, there may need to be a mix of complexity and traditional approaches: they explore how the interaction between a complexity-based approach to leadership and a Weberian bureaucracy can generate emergent outcomes, such as learning and innovation. Van Velsor (2008) approaches leadership development from a complexity perspective, emphasizing the need to cultivate an organization's capacity for promoting emergent collective leadership practices. Mowles (2011) describes his work as a consultant who teaches complexity in a university. He cites a provocative insight about alternatives to performance management, based on the concept of improvisation. Here is a challenge to the functionalist managerialist agenda, with performance on an implied stage proving hard both to control and to measure (2011: 217–18).

The literature for academics and practitioners continues to grow, but are fundamental shifts in mindset happening? Educational institutions, including business schools, are well placed to transmit radically new ways of thinking about self, others, organizations and the world by exposing faculty to such new paradigms as complexity thinking. New insights into such questions as notions of control and links between cause and effect mean that the potential impact, and practical usefulness, of complexity thinking are widespread. From corporate strategy to project management, from government regulation to management development programmes, there are challenges for both organizations and individual leaders. These should surely be given more prominence in business schools.

SO WHERE NOW FOR BUSINESS SCHOOLS?

The period since the financial crisis of 2008 has been one of questioning, even soul searching. But does this simply reflect a readjustment of the market, or is something more fundamental happening? A definitive answer is not yet possible, but we can at least identify some areas for action, several of which are explored in this volume.

Business schools are responsible to a vast array of stakeholders, not all of whom are immediately apparent. They are responsible to their students. And these students are responsible to the communities which they represent, including past and future generations. They are responsible to one another. They are responsible to themselves. And they are responsible to this fragile planet. Teaching such responsibility should form an integral part of business school curricula. And such teaching should not be left to business ethicists or regulatory experts: such attitudes should form an integral part of twenty-first century leaders (see Box 2.4). Four themes, all of which are taken up by subsequent chapters in this volume, appear to have particular salience to this challenge:

- The growth in *sustainability* education is an area to watch. But we need to ensure that the focus is not simply on the 'green' agenda and physical renewables – what of the sustainability of our organizations and our very selves? Questions of community and spirituality are surely relevant here: in addressing this question, Elvira and Davila (2012) emphasize the importance of a humanistic approach to leadership.
- Another area to address is that of *connectedness*. This may involve silo-breaking curricula where links between subjects and functional specialisms are highlighted. And it may be embodied in a more holistic understanding of our humanity, expressing our responsibility to self, others and planet. The next phase of management education may be characterized less by the proliferation of providers than by the development of connections between them (AACSB International, 2011: 23).
- Business schools need to see beyond hegemonic North American worldviews. We have seen glimpses of a post-Newtonian understanding, informed by complexity sciences. And we have heard echoes of non-Western perspectives where the community embraces the individual. Business schools are crying out for *wisdom*, wisdom that will not be found in the plethora of rankings, or accreditation schemes, still less the academic chase to irrelevance in journal publication.
- One area where these themes weave together to provide new patterns is in understandings of *leadership*. Responsibility – both individual and collective – and connectedness are integral to sustainable leadership. Business schools would do well to reflect this in their governance and curricula and, in their pedagogy, to emphasize another key feature of leadership, which provides a good stepping-off point for the rest of this volume: the lifelong nature of learning.

BOX 2.4 PROGRAMMES GOING BEYOND A NARROW BUSINESS VIEW

Business schools operate in highly competitive markets. It is not always easy to discern whether they are setting trends, or responding to demands from prospective students or wider society. Taking a sample of UK courses, we can see a number of recent developments:

Sustainability

Ashridge Masters in Sustainability and Responsibility www.ashridge.org.uk/Website/Content.nsf/wDEG/MSc+in+Sustainability+and+Responsibility?open document

Cambridge Masters in Sustainability Leadership www.cpsl.cam.ac.uk/Graduate-Study/Masters-in-Sustainability-Leadership.aspx

(Continued)

(Continued)

Cranfield MSc in Management and Corporate Sustainability www.som.cran field.ac.uk/som/p19936/Programmes-and-Executive-Development/MSc/Corporate-Sustainability

Exeter One Planet MBA Programme http://business-school.exeter.ac.uk/mba atexeter/oneplanetmba/oneplanetmbaprogramme/

Social entrepreneurship

Essex MSc in Social Entrepreneurship www.essex.ac.uk/coursefinder/course_details.aspx?course=MSC+N10512

Goldsmith MA in Social Entrepreneurship www.gold.ac.uk/pg/ma-social-entre preneurship/

We are even beginning to see the appearance of rankings for such programmes, though attempts such as Net Impact's local chapter rankings are US-focused:

www.socialenterprisebuzz.com/2013/03/06/which-social-entrepreneurship-program-should-you-choose/

Non-profits

Cass MSc in NGO Management www.cass.city.ac.uk/courses/masters/charity-courses/ngo-management

Lancaster MA in Hospice Leadership www.lancaster.ac.uk/lums/business/executive-education/open-executive/ma-hospice-leadership/

All websites accessed 31 March 2014.

FURTHER READING

For long-standing criticisms of business schools, see Mintzberg (2004) and Bennis and O'Toole (2005).

For post-crisis reviews of business schools and management learning, see Currie et al. (2010) and Edwards et al. (2013).

For hopeful responses from the business school community, see Morsing and Rovira (2011) and Muff et al. (2013).

For leadership and complexity theory, see Goldstein et al. (2010) and McGonagill and Doerffer (2011).

REFERENCES

AACSB International (2011) *Globalization of Management Education: Changing International Structures, Adaptive Strategies, and the Impact on Institutions.* Bingley: Emerald.

Allen, P. and Boulton, J. (2011) 'Complexity and limits to knowledge: the importance of uncertainty', in Allen et al. (eds), *The Sage Handbook of Complexity and Management*, pp. 164–81.

Allen, P., Maguire, S. and McKelvey, B. (eds) (2011) *The Sage Handbook of Complexity and Management*. London: Sage.

Alvesson, M. and Sandberg, J. (2013) 'Has Management Studies lost its way? Ideas for more imaginative and innovative research', *Journal of Management Studies*, 50 (1): 128–52.

Amann, W., Pirson, M., Dierksmeier, C., von Kimakowitz, E. and Spitzeck, H. (eds) (2011) *Business Schools Under Fire: Humanistic Management Education as the Way Forward*. Basingstoke: Palgrave.

Beinhocker, E.D. (2006) *The Origin of Wealth: Evolution, Complexity, and the Radical Remaking of Economics*. Boston, MA: Harvard Business School Press.

Bennis, W. and O'Toole, J. (2005) 'How business schools lost their way', *Harvard Business Review*, 83 (4): 96–104.

Bhandarker, A. (2008) *Shaping Business Leaders: What B-Schools Don't Do*. New Delhi: Sage.

Bieger, T. (2011) 'Business schools – from career training centers towards enablers of CSR: a new vision for teaching at business schools', in Morsing and Rovira (eds), *Business Schools and Their Contribution to Society*, pp. 104–13.

Bolden, R. and Gosling, J. (2006) 'Leadership competencies: time to change the tune?', *Leadership*, 2 (2): 147–63.

Bolden, R. and Kirk, P. (2012) 'Leadership development as a catalyst for social change: lessons from a pan-African programme', in S. Turnbull, P. Case, G. Edwards, D. Schedlitzki and P. Simpson (eds), *Worldly Leadership: Alternative Wisdoms for a Complex World*. Basingstoke: Palgrave, pp. 32–51.

Brookfield, S.D. and Holst, J.D. (2011) *Radicalizing Learning: Adult Education for a Just World*. San Francisco, CA: Jossey-Bass.

Bruner, R.F., Conroy, R.M. and Snell, S.A. (2012) 'The development of general management capabilities in a global world', in Canals (ed.), *Leadership Development in a Global World: The Role of Companies and Business Schools* pp. 3–28.

Canals, J. (ed.) (2012) *Leadership Development in a Global World: The Role of Companies and Business Schools*. Basingstoke: Palgrave.

Cilliers, P. (2002) 'Why we cannot know complex things completely', *Emergence*, 4 (1/2): 77–84.

Colby, A., Ehrlich, T., Sulllivan, W.M. and Dolle, J.R. (2011) *Rethinking Undergraduate Business Education*. San Francisco, CA: Jossey-Bass.

Currie, G., Knights, D. and Starkey, K. (2010) 'Introduction: a post-crisis critical reflection on business schools', *British Journal of Management*, 21: S1–S5.

Dameron, S. and Durand, T. (eds) (2011) *Redesigning Management Education and Research: Proposals from European Scholars*. Cheltenham: Edward Elgar.

Datar, S.M., Garvin, D.A. and Cullen, P.G. (2010) *Rethinking the MBA: Business Education at a Crossroads*. Boston, MA: Harvard Business School Press.

de Woot, P. (2013) *Spirituality and Business: A Christian Viewpoint*. Leeds: GSE Research.

Douglas, T. (1983) *Groups: Understanding People Gathered Together*. London: Tavistock.

Durand, T. and Dameron, S. (2008) *The Future of Business Schools: Scenarios and Strategies for 2020*. Basingstoke: Palgrave.

Edwards, G., Elliott, C., Iszatt-White, M. and Schedlitzki, D. (2013) 'Critical and alternative approaches to leadership learning and development', *Management Learning*, 44 (1): 3–10.

Elvira, M.M. and Davila, A. (2012) 'Globalization and sustainable leadership', in Canals (ed.), pp. 163–87.

Ford, J., Harding, N. and Learmonth, M. (2010) 'Who is it that would make business schools more critical? Critical reflections on Critical Management Studies', *British Journal of Management*, 21: S71–S81.

Fotaki, M. and Prasad, A. (2014) 'Social justice interrupted? Values, pedagogy, and purpose of business school academics', *Management Learning*, 45 (1): 103–6.

Ghoshal, S. (2005) 'Bad management theories are destroying good management practices', *Academy of Management Learning and Education*, 4 (1): 75–91.

Goldstein, J., Hazy, J.H. and Lichtenstein, B.B. (2010) *Complexity and the Nexus of Leadership: Leveraging Nonlinear Science to Create Ecologies of Innovation*. New York, NY: Palgrave.

Grint, K. (2005) *Leadership: Limits and Possibilities*. Basingstoke: Palgrave.

Hamel, G. (2012) *What Matters Now*. San Francisco, CA: Jossey-Bass.

Hardy, G.M. and Everett, D.L. (eds) (2013) *Shaping the Future of Business Education: Relevance, Rigor, and Life Preparation*. Basingstoke: Palgrave.

Kauffman, S.A. (2008) *Reinventing the Sacred: A New View of Science, Reason, and Religion*. New York: Basic Books.

Kellerman, B. (2012) *The End of Leadership*. New York: HarperBusiness.

Khurana, R. (2007) *From Higher Aims to Hired Hands: The Social Transformation of American Business Schools and the Unfulfilled Promise of Management as a Profession*. Princeton, NJ: Princeton University Press.

Khurana, R. and Penrice, D. (2011) 'Business education: the American trajectory', in Morsing and Rovira (eds), pp. 3–15.

Locke, R.R. and Spender, J.-C. (2011) *Confronting Managerialism: How the Business Elite and Their Schools Threw Our Lives Out of Balance*. London: Zed Books.

Losada, C., Martell, J. and Lozano, J.M. (2011) 'Responsible business education: not a question of curriculum but a raison d'être for business schools', in Morsing and Rovira (eds), *Business Schools and Their Contribution to Society,* pp. 163–74.

Mason, M. (ed.) (2008) *Complexity Theory and the Philosophy of Education*. Chichester: Wiley-Blackwell.

McGonagill, G. and Doerffer, T. (2011) *Leadership and Web 2.0: The Leadership Implications of the Evolving Web*. Gütersloh: Bertelsmann.

Mintzberg, H. (2004) *Managers Not MBAs: A Hard Look at the Soft Practice of Managing and Management Development*. Harlow: FT Prentice Hall.

Mitleton-Kelly, E. and Ramalingam, B. (2011) 'Organisational learning and complexity science: exploring the joint potential', in Allen et al. (eds), *The Sage Handbook of Complexity and Management*, pp. 349–65.

Mitroff, I.I. (2004) 'An open letter to the deans and the faculties of American business schools', *Journal of Business Ethics*, 54 (2): 185–9.

Morsing, M. and Rovira, A.S. (eds) (2011) *Business Schools and Their Contribution to Society*. London: Sage.

Mowles, C. (2011) *Rethinking Management: Radical Insights from the Complexity Sciences*. Farnham: Gower.

Muff, K., Dyllick, T., Drewell, M., North, J., Shrivastava, P. and Haertie, J. (eds) (2013) *Management Education for the World: A Vision for Business Schools Serving People and Planet*. Cheltenham: Edward Elgar.

O'Doherty, D. and Jones, C. (2005) 'Inducement', in C. Jones and D. O'Doherty (eds), *Manifestos for the Business School of Tomorrow*. Turku: Dvalin, pp. 1–9.

Onzoño, S.I. (2011) *The Learning Curve: How Business Schools are Re-Inventing Education*. Basingstoke: Palgrave.

Pfeffer, J. (2007) 'A modest proposal: how we might change the process and product of managerial research', *Academy of Management Journal*, 50 (6): 1334–45.

Pfeffer, J. and Fong, C. (2002) 'The end of business schools? Less success than meets the eye', *Academy of Management Learning and Education*, 1 (1): 78–95.

Quinn, R.E. and Sonenshein, S. (2008) 'Four general strategies for affecting change in human systems', in T. Cummings (ed.), *Handbook of Organization Development*. Thousand Oaks: Sage, pp. 69–78.

Samuelson, J. (2011) 'The new rigor: beyond the right answer', in Morsing and Rovira (eds), pp. 149–60.

Stacey, R.D. (2010) *Complexity and Organizational Reality: Uncertainty and the Need to Rethink Management after the Collapse of Investment Capitalism* (2nd edn). Abingdon: Routledge.

Starkey, K. and Tempest, S. (2009) 'The winter of our discontent: the design challenge for business schools', *Academy of Management Learning and Education*, 8 (4): 576–86.

Strand, R. (2011) 'A plea to business schools: tear down your walls', in Morsing and Rovira (eds), pp. 213–22.

Thomas, H., Lorange, P. and Sheth, J. (2013) *The Business School in the Twenty-First Century: Emergent Challenges and New Business Models*. Cambridge: Cambridge University Press.

Thomas, H. and Peters, K. (2012) 'A sustainable model for business schools', *Journal of Management Development*, 31 (4): 377–85.

Toubiana, M. (2014) 'Business pedagogy for social justice? An exploratory investigation of business faculty perspectives of social justice in business education', *Management Learning*, 45 (1): 81–102.

Tourish, D. (2013) *The Dark Side of Transformational Leadership: A Critical Perspective*. Hove: Routledge.

Tourish, D., Craig, R. and Amernic, J. (2010) 'Transformational leadership education and agency perspectives in business school pedagogy: a marriage of inconvenience?', *British Journal of Management*, 21: S40–S59.

Tourish, D. and Hargie, O. (2012) 'Metaphors of failure and the failure of metaphors: a critical study of bankers' explanations for the banking crisis', *Organization Studies*, 33 (8): 1045–69.

Tsoukas, H. and Chia, R. (2002) 'On organizational becoming: rethinking organizational change', *Organization Science*, 13 (5): 567–82.

Uhl-Bien, M. and Marion, R. (2009) 'Complexity leadership in bureaucratic forms of organizing: a meso model', *Leadership Quarterly*, 20 (4): 631–50.

Van Velsor, E. (2008) 'A complexity perspective on leadership development', in M. Uhl-Bien and R. Marion (eds), *Complexity Leadership, Part 1: Conceptual Foundations*. Charlotte, NC: Information Age Publishing, pp. 333–46.

Western, S. (2008) *Leadership: A Critical Text*. London: Sage.

3 QUESTIONS BUSINESS SCHOOLS ARE UNABLE TO ASK

Aidan Ward and
Wolfgang Mayrhofer

INTRODUCTION

What questions are business schools unable to ask? Although this is a sweeping question, in practice business schools are quite homogeneous, both in terms of how they are structured internally and in terms of how they are coupled to their social and political environments. In this chapter, we propose that the combination of these two factors – the way business schools organize themselves and their relationship with the external environment – lead to systemic blind spots and seriously compromise their capability to operate the way they were originally intended. Drawing upon systems theory, in particular a cybernetic perspective about the structure of teaching and learning systems, and a self-referential systems perspective, we conclude that there are systemic reasons beyond the intentions of individual actors such as deans, professors or students, why business schools cannot see what they are supposed to see. In short it is not simply a case of which questions business schools do not ask, but which questions business schools cannot ask.

Our key example is from one of the first business schools in the UK. Stafford Beer, the famous cybernetician, was highly influential in the initial design of Manchester Business School. The UK government's concern at the time was to increase the competitiveness of British businesses and Beer's design focused on equipping students to help solve business problems that stood in the way of innovation and efficiency. Indeed the vast majority of the distinguished alumni from Manchester Business School (MBS) took a degree called Management Science, not an MBA. Their education had a cybernetic underpinning design that with hindsight was more effective than the current designs but which has been allowed to languish. We discuss this case further below, but it is pertinent to note that the Association of Business Schools in the UK recently conducted a government sponsored study of all 130 British business schools, suppliers of business education in a global context. One conclusion was that, compared to MBS 50 years ago, in many ways the business schools of today are less able to fulfil their fundamental goal.

We will develop our argument in three steps. After briefly giving an overview of systems theory and its development, we will first look at internal structural issues, using a cybernetic angle to uncover some of the mechanisms at work which lead to problematic outcomes in terms of the economic system and the society as a whole. Second, we will focus on the link between business schools and their environment, using social systems theory and in particular a self-referential view of organizations to identify blind spots as the result of specific coupling decisions made by society as well as the specific business school. Finally, we will conclude with reflections on the relationship between the individual and the business school.

SYSTEMS THEORIES

Systems theory is the theoretical underpinning of this chapter. We will outline in more detail the two perspectives used for our argument – cybernetics and self-referential closure – in the following sections. They constitute major discourses within a broader set of approaches. There is no unified systems theory, although some kind of consensus seems to exist that systems are units differentiated from the environment and consist of at least two interrelated and distinguishable elements. Box 3.1 gives a short overview about these major discourses in systems theory (for more details see Mayrhofer, 2004).

BOX 3.1   SYSTEMS THEORIES: CYBERNETICS AND SELF-REFERENTIAL SYSTEMS

Cybernetic descriptions of systems view the information and decision-making *structures* to show how they lead to the observed *behaviour*. Of particular interest are the ways in which an organization maintains its viability in its environment and behaviours that are preserved when the environment changes. In general organizations are not aware of their own cybernetic structure and their conceptualization of how they make decisions can differ markedly from the cybernetic evidence. Often cybernetic descriptions use a nested model where larger systems are made of smaller systems with the same set of cybernetic concerns at each scale.

Self-referential descriptions of systems emphasize that the set of conversations, actions and decisions that are taken within the system refer to its internal

(Continued)

(Continued)

world and not, directly, to its environment. The environment only enters into these internal processes via a set of interpretations of meaning that are themselves dependent on that same set of internal conversations, actions and decisions. The response of an organization to external events and change is understood to be a function of how they are seen and understood.

Both these *system views* are important in gaining critical distance from the management self-description of particular business schools and of business schools in general. The self-reflective ability to see what management is and is not dealing with in an organization ought to be a major aspect of business education. Sadly that ability is often entirely missing ...

The reason for choosing a systemic angle for our analysis is the conviction that the focus on the dynamic interplay between various elements within social systems, in this case business schools, and between the social system and its broader environment, helps us to better understand the emergence of blind spots and their systemic rather than individual roots. Instead of regarding the consistency of the business school approach to be evidence of its effectiveness, we regard it as a structural inability to address the key issues in business education. We will now turn to our first step, looking inside business schools and how they react to their environment from a cybernetic point of view.

CYBERNETICS AND IMPLIED PURPOSE

Cybernetics (Wiener, 1948) assigns an important role to the environment. It provides influencing forces that contribute to the steering of systems. The primary mechanism is the cybernetic feedback loop is illustrated by a thermostat. Through positive and negative feedback mechanisms, a system changes its states. It is important to note that the system does not directly react to environmental influences. The system itself translates inputs from the environment into its own language, creating its own informational image about the environment. The dominating differentiation is between system and environment. Systems constitute themselves by differentiation from the environment with which they are tightly or loosely coupled. Vague environmental complexity is transformed in selective systems complexity. Order emerges from selectivity.

The metaphor in cybernetics is the steersman, the Odysseus figure straining all his senses and guile to maintain a course. In personal conversation Beer was fond of poking fun by analysing what the implied purpose of a system was, what the steersman was in practice steering towards, given the way it maintained certain invariants in the face of change. He would state polemically that the Purpose Of a System Is What It Does – POSIWID.

From a system design perspective this approach implies a control loop that detects (measures) whether the desired course is being maintained and takes corrective action if it is not. For this discussion of business schools and real businesses in the domestic economy, the detection must be of some desired change in the performance of businesses, at least: some impact either from direct work on business problems by the business school or work by alumni who really know how to solve problems. The Association of Business Schools report mentioned above concludes that in general this registering of impact is absent, although there are local and domain-specific examples where it is attempted. Indeed the commissioning of the report itself is a tacit admission that these measures are lacking.

The available corrective action to the course being steered is within the business schools themselves, to adjust what is taught, how it is taught and how it is applied in such a way that the impact is enhanced. It is our thesis that this latter aspect of governance is in practice unacceptable to business schools as they are currently embodied. They can neither see this problem (the self-reference argument) nor act on it, because the structures they use do not contain this loop and cannot support it when it is introduced, as in the London Business School experiment, MLab (see Box 3.2).

This situation, of not addressing the situation for which the institution was set up, is serious enough, but these are schools of management. What they purport to teach is how to manage businesses better. They supply organizations of all types with people who will be in responsible management positions; however, as in the case of the cobbler's children going without shoes, they often do not see their own management failings. Least of all do they recognize their own inability to pursue purpose, thus undermining the education they provide.

Just as business schools can be seen not to have the cybernetics structures they require to pursue questions of national and international business innovation and efficiency, they *do* possess cybernetic structures that pursue other goals. Any organization reacts with its own interpretation of certain things in its environment. We might ask which aspects of the environment do business schools pay attention to and how do they make internal decisions based on this interpretation? From inside the management system of a business school it appears that there are certain aspects of the external world that drive decisions: perhaps the number and calibre of applicants, perhaps the perceived status of the school and its ranking in league tables, perhaps the ability to attract star staff. Any management system pays attention to a very narrow selection of variables in its environment. The important question is whether the cybernetic structure, the connectedness of decision-making, allows the organization to pursue its stated purposes, or whether in practice it blinds the organization to what it needs to know. Is the management system actually paying attention to the right things to allow it to navigate an appropriate course, to equip its students for future leadership roles? There is evidence to suggest that business school staff themselves are dubious about the efficacy of the education their schools offer. Many chapters in this book are the result of respective authors' frustrations in trying to maintain a focus on educational need.

Stafford Beer's (1979) estimate was that, at most, half of what a student would need to know to solve a real business problem would or could be found in syllabus material. The rest had to be developed *in situ*. Beer's view was that the joint investigation and discovery of problems in real organizations between staff and students was the real teaching situation. Yet, despite the international reputation of this 'Manchester Method' there is little understanding of what it consists of or how to deliver it among staff at Manchester Business School today. This illustrates the systemic blindness of a business school as an institution. Something of great significance and value can be in full view without people being able to see it (see Box 3.2).

Whether it is designed into the structure of a business school or not, there is a cybernetic structure that controls what, over time, is paid attention to and what is not. Beer proposed that management of the school should be based on a design that promoted a certain sort of information about purpose in pursuing changes to business practice. That design was effective in promoting a form of education where the quality of the syllabus and the teaching were always being critiqued against their effectiveness on real-world, real-time problem-solving. Since that time, other cybernetic structures have prevailed that create knowledge silos and where effectiveness is only judged by academic peer processes. Since a cybernetic understanding is not in general taught or available, the systemic blindness that these structures produce is itself hidden. To be blunt, this is about whether students can see whether what they are being taught works in practice.

To summarize, due to the way they internally organize, business schools have become largely incapable of fulfilling their original purpose of benefiting society. This becomes clear when we consider the radical model of Beer, which contains three salient differences to the way business schools typically function today:

1. The absence of modules based on academic disciplines – finance, marketing and so on. Instead all courses were trans-disciplinary.
2. Learning-based approaches rather than teaching-based. An emphasis on students learning through addressing actual business problems on projects with real businesses – action research or problem-based learning rather than lectures.
3. The close integration of academic research with student learning. Students are an integral part of the research context, contributing their work and insights to original work on real world problems.

A SELF-REFERENTIAL VIEW: THE IMPORTANCE OF COUPLING

An ABS report from 2013 claims in its title that business schools are there in part to 'drive innovation and growth in the domestic economy' (Thorpe and Rawlinson, 2013). Our argument from the theory of self-referential systems is that such a purpose falls within one of the many blind spots of business schools as institutions. Questions about contribution to the economy are among the questions business schools are unable to ask.

Self-referential closure of systems (Maturana, 1992; Maturana and Varela, 1987) originally focused on biological aspects. However, these ideas have also been applied to social systems. The dominant differentiation within self-referential closure approaches is the distinction between self- and other-referent views. Systems constitute themselves through observation of difference and through relating themselves to those differences. Order emerges through processing noise from turbulent environments, i.e. 'order from noise'.

More specifically, social systems theory as coined by Luhmann (1995) and its application and specification for organization theory (e.g. Seidl, 2005), sees organizations as autopoietically closed and consisting of communications or – in the case of formalized organizations – decisions. In short, actions are under the all-pervasive pressure of expectations. At the basal level they are not open to their environment, but they are constantly self-referencing (autopoietically closed): they reproduce the elements they consist of out of the elements they consist of. Social systems are non-trivial machines that constantly alter their internal states and relationships (von Foerster, 1985).

It is evident that pure self-reference, i.e. looking only within the system, is not enough. Beyond the internal horizon, social systems have to relate to the external world such as finance and labour markets, global competitors, new legal regulations and so on. These relationships are formed and influenced by the internal structure of rules, the internal mode(s) of operation and the guiding differences used in the organization. Such guiding differences are the main yardsticks or touchstones that organizations use to make sense of their internal and external environment and guide their action. For instance they may have a dominant logic such as market or social responsibility, a focus on specific financial benchmarks which underlies all action, or a certain ideology which pre-formats all views. Overall, we can define the relationship between social systems and their environments in a dual way. Systems are 'without' their environment in their basal structure, their self-organizing processes and their operative closure. At the same time, they are dependent on the environment since this is what systemically enriches and interpunctuates their internal operations (Willke, 1987).

Social systems such as organizations are structurally coupled to their environment through psychic systems, namely 'individuals', who sensitize them to specific sections of the organization's environment. Thus marketing people notice new trends in how to sell an MBA to the broader public; quality assurance managers alert the business schools to the necessary requirements for the accreditation process; course managers scan for the latest pedagogic fads and fashion to be added to curricula. At the same time, structural coupling allows social systems to *disregard* many parts of the environment. Given the enormous number of possibilities, social systems are impressed only by very few 'instances' and sharply selective towards the environment as well as towards their own possibilities of 'reaction' (Luhmann, 1988). It is indifference, not action, which follows on from most environmental incidents.

Against this backdrop, we argue that due to the dependence of business schools on specific sub-systems of society such as economy, politics or science, they have to focus on some questions and, hardly surprising, ignore others. To be sure, business schools, like all other organizations, can and usually are coupled with several societal sub-systems at the same time. In particular education, science and economics constitute the primary societal sub-systems on which business schools depend. These sub-systems provide both the necessary resources and expectations. Examples of the former include research grants, reputational rankings or funding opportunities; examples of the latter include the provision of well-educated graduates, solutions for important business problems or answers to questions relevant for society as a whole.

Through their specific programmes and strategic positioning, business schools make choices about the kind of coupling they want to develop. Some business schools put the emphasis primarily on education and economics, with science taking a less important role in their activities; other schools favour the scientific sub-system and have comparatively less regard for education. Other configurations also exist, of course. No matter what these decisions look like, once they are made, certain issues have to be relegated and become non-issues out of structural necessity. When leaning towards economics, business schools can hardly raise the issue of whether managers are needed at all or whether they are capable of preparing students for their life in business. Likewise, if they are strongly coupled to science as a societal sub-system, it does not make very much sense for them to question basic scientific progress or take a solipsistic epistemological stance by assuming that most likely no reality exists 'out there'. If they elevate education, it is hard to see business schools declaring that they are not interested in their graduates' later careers or the quality of their pedagogy relative to other institutions. Note that this does not mean that there are no individual actors within business schools who go down such routes, take such stances, or do teach along these lines. Of course, there are. As *collective* actors (Coleman, 1990), however, this is not an option for business schools. Imagine a dean of study welcoming new undergraduate students with a fiery speech outlining that a Bachelor's or Master's in business administration is to no avail; think of an academic director of PhD programmes announcing on the web-page of the business school that research in business schools is not real science, but only everyday wisdom cloaked as scientific output; picture the head of the business school's executive training unit questioning the role of business schools published statement of purpose. Hard to do? Yes, rightly so. But statements like these are clearly within reach for other collective actors such as think tanks, political parties or lobbying institutions because they are linked to and dependent on different types of societal sub-systems. Political parties do not depend on science and its quest for truth, lobbying institutions rely on the worldview of their clients such as employers' associations, and think tanks might rely on a single source of material income such as a big donor having a certain agenda with regard to education and the role of business schools in society. All of this allows such institutions to question issues which are 'taboo', i.e. in their structural blind spot, something which business schools, due to their specific dependencies, cannot do.

Business schools contribute to society in a number of ways. Beyond the manifest and obvious level, they also support the various societal sub-systems through more latent, not immediately visible, contributions. A few examples may suffice. Entry requirements in terms of previous experience, subjects taken or test results provide legitimacy for a number of arrangements in earlier phases of the educational chain such as schools, test institutes or preparatory courses. Companies not only expect well-educated graduates, but also well-socialized ones. Thus, a great degree of conformity, disciplining and procrastination is part of the hidden agenda that business schools, usually without an explicit decision, have – and have to have – if they want to prepare their graduates for a capitalist, hierarchical economy and a market system.

This again underlines our point: due to the systemic set-up of business schools in the broader environment and their link to a specified set of societal sub-systems, they not only fail to address certain questions, they are also structurally myopic – which prevents these issues coming to the fore. Structural coupling produces blindness and a cybernetic structure produces an inability to ask, or address, key questions.

THE INDIVIDUAL AND THE CONTEXT

We have presented two analyses of the business school as a social system, using two different sets of theory. The default understanding of what business schools produce, however, is couched in terms of an individual student. This student chooses his or her school and course, pays his or her fees and leaves as product, with a set of credentials and a set of skills and knowledge that make the overall proposition worthwhile in their own eyes.

The dichotomy between the social system view and the individualized view raises questions about the learning model. Taking the questions that business schools are unable to ask first, we note that many MBA students are mature students coming with questions already formed about the nature of business and the role of education. It is not simply a matter of business schools not having the capability to address important questions, it is also a matter of being unable to frame a meaningful response to student inquiry.

Secondly the question of learning context is central to the cybernetic view. The meta-learning implications of basing learning around the classroom and small projects, compared to anchoring it in real-world problems that may not have a solution, are clearly vast. The notion that management effectiveness is about high-powered individuals armed with a raft of management theory could not be more misleading.

What is actually required as the core of management education is an understanding of management as having a limited but key role in a (business) social system. To solve a business or organizational problem is to shift how the situation is seen by the organization at the same time as providing an alternative set of connections. The solution to organizational problems in general implies that the organization and the individuals within it must think differently. Although there needs to be some different underpinning theory for such a change, this core is a thoroughly practical and grounded understanding, as much about tacit knowledge as about the syllabus.

The question that is furthest from business schools' agenda is also the question that must concern every student that passes through their institutions. In the popular imagination this question concerns 'management's right to manage'. What is the real justification for giving managers positional authority? Everyone has a story about a new graduate, still wet behind the ears, being made to look idiotic by the experienced staff they are supposed to be managing.

Business schools are structurally coupled, and individuals too are structurally coupled into their context. It necessarily follows that a manager in a situation that requires a business transformation cannot remain the same individual after the transformation as they were before. This crucial insight is at the heart of many management failures yet it is rarely discussed or understood. This is also at the heart of our argument here. Do managers, and students of management, understand that their own identity is caught up in the ways they understand organization and management action in organizations?

This exposure to personal risk and change is precisely what will be learnt experientially and possibly existentially in a learning situation that is cybernetically structured the way that Beer advised. It would be desirable indeed if students who did not want to engage with this level of personal risk and change did not become managers. The core question that business schools are unable to ask is whether students have what it takes to become a manager: not whether they can pass the exams, carry out assignments and do the projects, not whether their attendance and their fee paying are up to scratch, but whether they are prepared to engage with issues that will change them as people.

CONCLUSION

Business schools are not general purpose educational machines, able to turn their attention to whatever appears important or meets the demand from students. On the contrary, business schools come to make structural choices, often without understanding the implications, and those choices then constrain the nature of the education they can provide and the questions they can ask.

If we ask the POSIWID question: if we look at the implied purpose of business schools, given observations of their behaviour, then both outside observers and concerned staff tend to point to the financial bottom line. Business schools want to protect the perceived value of the credentials they sell, and are risk averse in experimenting with their pedagogical model.

Some of the questions that cannot be asked given current structures are surprising. The questions raised in the Association of Business Schools report about the contribution to innovation in the economy, for instance, are clearly not on the agenda and have to be the subject of a government sponsored report. Equally there have been many questions raised in the popular press about the implied ethics of MBA graduates and their involvement in major business scandals.

It is the governance of business schools that ought to be concerned with both the nature of the social systems that each business school is coupled to and the cybernetic structures that control the nature of the education experience. In a chicken and egg fashion, however, it is not clear where people with governance responsibility would have to be educated to ensure these systems work in practice. As ever, real education is a precondition to supplying real education to the next generation.

FURTHER READING

For a classic text discussing the importance of cybernetic thinking in management, see Beer (1959).

For a book that conceptualizes organizations by building on insights into the human nervous system and the theory of viable systems, see Beer (1981).

For an edited collection of various major texts looking at the development and facets of self-organization as a major theoretical angle in various disciplines, see Krohn et al. (1990).

For a basic text about how we acquire knowledge and understanding and the underlying processes, see Maturana and Varela (1987).

For an edited volume about the importance and application of social systems theory for understanding and managing organizations, see Seidl and Becker (2005).

REFERENCES

Beer, S. (1959) *Cybernetics and Management*. New York: Wiley.

Beer, S. (1979) *The Heart of Enterprise*. Chichester: Wiley.

Beer, S. (1981) *Brain of the Firm* (2nd edn). Chichester: Wiley.

Coleman, J.S. (1990) *Foundations of Social Theory*. Cambridge, MA: Harvard University Press.

Krohn, W., Küppers, G. and Nowotny, H. (eds) (1990) *Self-organization: Portrait of a Scientific Revolution*. Dordrecht: Kluwer.

Luhmann, N. (1988) 'Organisation', in W. Küpper and G. Ortmann (eds), *Mikropolitik*. Opladen: Westdeutscher Verlag, pp. 165–86.

Luhmann, N. (1995) *Social Systems*. Stanford: Stanford University Press.

Maturana, H. (1992) 'The origin of the theory of autopoietic systems', in H.R. Fischer (ed.), *Autopoiesis* (2nd edn). Heidelberg: Auer, pp. 121–3.

Maturana, H.R. and Varela, F.J. (1987) *The Tree of Knowledge: The Biological Roots of Human Understanding*. Boston, MA: Shambhala.

Mayrhofer, W. (2004) 'Social systems theory as theoretical framework for human resource management – benediction or curse?', *Management Revue*, 15 (2): 178–91.

Seidl, D. (2005) 'The basic concepts of Luhmann's theory of social systems', in D. Seidl and K.H. Becker (eds), *Niklas Luhmann and Organization Studies*. Malmö: Liber and Copenhagen Business School Press, pp. 21–53.

Seidl, D. and Becker, K.H. (eds) (2005) *Niklas Luhmann and Organization Studies*. Malmö: Liber and Copenhagen Business School Press.

Thorpe, R. and Rawlinson, R. (2013) *The Role of UK Business Schools in Driving Innovation and Growth in the Domestic Economy*. London: Association of Business Schools.

von Foerster, H. (1985) *Sicht und Einsicht: Versuche zu einer operativen Erkenntnistheorie*. Braunschweig: Vieweg.

Wiener, N. (1948) *Cybernetics, or Control and Communication in the Animal and the Machine*. New York: MIT Press.

Willke, H. (1987) 'Strategien der Intervention in autonome Systeme', in D. Baecker, J. Markowitz, R. Stichweh, H. Tyrell and H. Willke (eds), *Theorie als Passion*. Frankfurt: Suhrkamp, pp. 333–61.

4 PREPARING MANAGERS FOR 'EXILE' AT WORK? THE HONG KONG EXPERIENCE

Ricky Yuk-Kwan Ng

INTRODUCTION

The primary aim of this chapter is to see how employee 'identity' is regulated in contemporary workplaces. I want to explore the concept of 'exile' in an Asian context and investigate how work has the capacity to 'detach' an employee from where he/she belongs so as to create a simultaneous sense of being ever-present at work and yet with an absence of meaning. Although there is a ready recognition of this state, the ill-balance of work/personal life and the loss of self and identity in the workplace are topics rarely addressed in business schools. My intention is to shed light on the human side of organizations: hopefully this will point the way for business schools to devise more academic debates and effective strategies in order to prepare students to cope with the identity struggles and estrangement in workplaces during their 'exile' at work.

THE SENSE OF BEING ALIENATED, STRIPPED AND IMPRISONED

Work environments in private and commercial business sectors are generally described in critical studies and accounts of personal experience as places of hegemony, authority and compulsion, shaping the employees into the organization's culture and homogeneous behavioural patterns. Once in the workplace, employees are deemed to be selling their personal time in exchange for wages and status. Unsurprisingly, people often speak of their work experience as one which is regulated and controlled by others and many studies describe work life as mundane and exhausting. In view of Taylor's scientific management system, the deprivation of individual characteristics aims to emphasize unity, efficiency and productivity in workplaces (Taylor, 1911). Work imposes a discipline on the worker by their mere presence in the workspace. Time is regulated, attendance monitored, behaviour governed by rules of conduct and of social interaction as implied by McGregor's Theory X (McGregor, 1960). Language is specific to the workspace, and workspaces themselves have their own traditions and cultures (Roy, 1959); a lot of time is spent on organizational learning, whose purpose is the 'remodelling of cognitive, emotional and behavioural patterns' (Gherardi and Strati, 1988: 161) and thus shaping employees into a specific organizational role and identity. It is a process of identity being constructed rather than being fixed (Sveningsson and Alvesson, 2003). Following the same vein, it is noted that the capitalist system monopolizes not only the worker's labour time but also their self-identity (Newitz, 2006 as cited in Bell, 2008: 76). Uniforms and strictly applied codes of practice are other attempts to generate the 'totalitarian state-of-mind' in some organizations, like factories, banks and theme parks. Employees are expected to stick to their roles once they put on their uniforms. For example, Disney's staff demonstrate the concept of 'emotional labour' since they are expected to immerse themselves in their own roles once they step out from back stage to face visitors. Speaking specifically about total institutions, it has been argued that 'the level of conformity engendered within total institutions is achieved by removing the things and relationships that sustain an individual's sense of self in a process of "stripping", exposing them instead to physical and psychological subjugation and humiliation' (Bell, 2008: 81). Therefore, the 'totalitarian state-of-mind' can be considered as both a physical state of the environment and a psychological state-of-mind.

THE CONTEMPORARY WORKPLACE

Addressing both physical and psychological 'authoritarianism', Höpfl claims that the site of performance as seen in religious rituals is nevertheless regulated by an anterior authority; metaphorically, organizations are hierophantic spaces and their sites of performance are regulated by the absent author-creator from afar in order to turn the individual 'I' into the collective 'We'. These 'converts' or 'believers' actively demonstrate their commitment to the values and customs of their new land (Höpfl, 2007: 15). Work in the industrial era was considered a 9-to-5 responsibility, especially for those who worked in factories. Factory workers worked extensively on assembly lines and because of the nature of the work environment, personal workspaces and individual work stations did not exist. Instead, lockers were provided in changing rooms and personal belongings were temporarily stored and retrieved after work. In these workplaces, the boundary between home and work was clearly defined. The employees were expected to achieve productivity by following the rules and regulations at work. Self, identity and homeliness were automatically eliminated in these workplaces, where working in the factory signified entry onto the stage of a particular type of work or work role and being 'detached' to create an absence of self. By contrast, the situation is more subtle in contemporary workplaces. Instead, employees are being 'attached' to create an ever-presence of self. Work environments in contemporary organizations are located away from industrial factories with 'rigid hierarchies, procedures, products and boundaries, in favour of constant and continuous reinvention, redefinition and mobility' (Gabriel, 2005: 13). There is a major difference between the contemporary workplaces and industrial factories. In modern offices, whereas the character of work might have some superficial similarities to factory work in being notionally time-bound, in practice the psychological boundary around the role extends well into non-work life, sometimes to the extent that there is little left in terms of a vestigial self to protect against the intrusion of work into all areas of life (Costea et al., 2005; Land and Taylor, 2010). It is this extension of the work role and the 'colonization of the self' which has come to characterize the nature of contemporary work. The experience of alienation is concealed by the appropriation of all areas of life as work and by a false consciousness of work as 'homely'. There is always a fine line between office and home in contemporary workplaces, because the less rigid boundaries and work mobility generate the inseparability of work and personal life. The feeling of 'being connected' and 'being attached' best describes the overlapping of work life and personal life. Such work is made flexible and possible using technologies and micro-electronic equipment. Once connected by any means of communication, the boundaries between work life and personal life have become blurred. The habit of checking short messages and emails related to work at home or on vacation is familiar to managers, financial analysts and sale agents, not to mention working late at night and working at home on holidays. It is this extension of the work role and the colonization of the self which here come to characterize the nature of contemporary work (see Box 4.1).

BOX 4.1   GOOGLE'S HOME AWAY FROM HOME

The cross-over of office and home can be seen in the design of Google's offices, where the employee can bring in his/her kids and pets to work. There is no doubt that Google's practice to a certain degree relieves the feeling of alienation by making the workplaces more comfortable, enabling the employee to retain their self and identity and generating a sense of belonging by making his/her workspace feel like home. A second glance at the practices reveals that the homeliness in turn merges work life and personal life, by making the concepts of office and home even more inseparable. It is not surprising to hear people mentioning that the office is their second home and Google's office seems to act as a surrogate home and thus to create the sense of 'home away from home' or re-forming the

(Continued)

'lost community'. People who are too attached to work gradually lose their place of belonging and eventually fall into a dilemma of not being able to differentiate between the real and the unreal. The trouble is that it provides a supreme example of the complete colonization of the workplace. All life is work or presumably home under such a regime. So, whereas Google's offices seem to act as a 'home away from home' and while it must be accepted that this approach might carry much appeal for the employee, it must also be acknowledged that it carries a further loss of autonomy.

A cynical interpretation would be that such practices are a strategy for the further colonization of even the small areas of resistance open to the individual. The pretence that work can be a substitute for the lost homeland is a travesty which implicitly contravenes the notion of a straightforward psychological contract of work. It is the American dream at corporate level with a melting pot mentality to support it. However, the goals are corporate and the individual merely instrumental to their achievement.

EXILED TO WORK

What is meant by the concept of 'exile from home' in relation to the workplace? The idea seeks to capture the sense of being imprisoned, stripped of one's liberty, and of a melancholia that might be experienced in the workplace. In other words, it is possible to conceive of the workspace in terms of an absence of meaning (Sievers, 1986), melancholia and estrangement. Significantly the experience of exile not only exists in factory work but also in post-industrial white-collar work. Literally and metaphorically, the employee is being exiled from his/her homeland, and the nostalgic dislocation from geographical origins is seen as an analogy for the workplace (Braziel and Mannur, 2003). According to the work of Höpfl, going to work might be viewed as a temporary condition of exile from home, where work performance requires that the personal is either suspended in the service of the role or else is drawn upon to support its interpretation; in this sense, the day-to-day experiences of work draw on the estrangement and accommodations of exile. Milosz uses the Genesis story, the Exclusion from the Garden of Eden, in his essay to describe the psychological feelings of exile: 'The nostalgic thinking about a return to the once happy existence [that] is intensified by their awareness of prohibition' (Milosz, 1997: 4). Milosz describes exile as a stage of alienation and loss of harmony with the surrounding space. The diasporic experience creates anxiety about the unfamiliar and nostalgia. Exile thus carries this dual notion of exclusion from the *locus amoenus* (the delightful place) into a place of estrangement and, at the same time, an implicit notion of prohibition or punishment which places the responsibility for the condition of exile on the exiles themselves. Given that, the extent to which work functions as a state of exile or evokes a sense of nostalgia is extremely problematic. In other words, the post-modern employee is exiled from his/her 'homeland' into the world of work, where he/she becomes a stranger, with all the negotiations of entry and accommodation that this demands. This prompts feelings of 'being faraway, yet so close' and being simultaneously 'detached' and 'attached' during exile at work. In the rest of this chapter, I will explore these issues in an Asian context and discuss how business schools can address this 'loss'.

FROM THE WORLD'S FACTORY TO THE LAST FRONTIER

With an attempt to look into the migrants' work life in *Factory Girls: Voices from the Heart of Modern China*, Chang's ethnographic study unveils the contemporary work life and conditions of factory assembly lines in Dongguan, an industrial city in China's Pearl River Delta (Chang, 2008). This mass migrant workforce movement from rural villages to cities is a remarkable phenomenon that transforms the way we perceive work in a contemporary Chinese context. Literally, the migrant workers are being detached and exiled from their homelands. As a belated industrial revolution in the post-modern era, the work conditions of factories are unsatisfactory according to Western standards, and to a certain extent this has been intensified into a kind of non-humanistic situation. Repressive management regimes are being used, overtime pay is never mentioned and as the manager of one factory announced, 'this is your task and if you have to stay up three days and nights, you do it' (Chang, 2008: 114). It is undeniable that the notorious 'sweat shop' prevails in contemporary China. The painstaking 14 hours per day assembly line factory work best describes the deprivation of individuality and the stripping of 'self' and 'identity'. Life in a post-modern factory is significantly different from that in the modern age. With the overly thoughtful arrangement of daily living necessities in the factory town, work therefore further penetrates into workers' private lives (see Box 4.2).

BOX 4.2 FACTORY GIRLS: VOICES FROM THE HEART OF MODERN CHINA

The factory described in Chang's (2008) book is large enough to house its own dormitories, restaurants, hospital and fire department, as well as entertainment facilities such as a movie-theatre and karaoke bars. With the kindness designed to eliminate the feeling of alienation by furnishing the workplace as a surrogate home, factory work in China colonizes every single moment of the individual's life

(Continued)

(Continued)

and provides a false consciousness of a temporary homeland that soothes the melancholic and nostalgic feelings resulting from the dislocation of geographical origins during the exile to work. At the end of the book, Chunming, one of the main characters, expresses her view that 'I am the same as you', and this notion indicates the prevalence of a 'totalitarian state-of-mind' at work by transforming the individual 'I' into the collective 'We': namely the 'Converts' and the 'Believers'. This phenomenon is neither new nor isolated: the colonization of work and life widely exists in a majority of the factories across mainland China.

Such an account is not confined to factory work but also occurs in many occupations and roles. Recent news discloses that guidance on dress codes and personal belongings brought to work is announced to clerical staff and teachers by China's government officials. The suggestions are rather imperative: ladies are expected to put on light make-up while eyebrows should be nicely clipped to a given standard. Although no uniforms are required in offices and classrooms, it is suggested that the outfit should be limited to three colours. It is also recommended that they should not take off their jackets or clothes in front of guests and students even on a hot summer day. There are also some interesting suggestions given to gentlemen: their socks need to be long enough so that no flesh and hair on their legs will be shown when they sit down. In addition, any loose buttons should be repaired to avoid the look and the feel of a pathetic 'bachelor'. The officials further advise that personal belongings such as family photographs, trinkets, knick-knacks, mementos and souvenirs are distractions that will reduce work efficiency and should not be brought to work (Next Media, 2011). While following such advice is claimed to be voluntary, it reveals the officials' strong intention to remodel the cognitive and behavioural patterns of white-collar staff. In China's contemporary offices, rather than the alienation of individuality, very often the estrangement experience is from a 'given identity' to create a psychological absence of self. Similar to factory work, once taking up a given role in the office, the 'I' automatically turns into a collective 'We'. It is a result of traditional Chinese politics and culture that absolute obedience is expected in workplaces. It is, however, well reported that not all workers are happy to be shaped by organizations. Such socialization does not occur without provoking resistance, for example, in one OEM manufacturer several workers jumped off the roof due to the unfair treatment and anxieties raised from pressure of work. For similar reasons, it is also reported that riots recently took place in one of the Japanese car manufacturing plants. Although these are some extreme cases, it is clear that psychological factors significantly influence the dilemma raised by the balance of work and individuality.

Certainly, work culture is bounded by ideologies and traditions, and to better understand the issue in a broader ethnic Chinese context, it is instructive to take another look at the issue in Hong Kong: a city within a stone's throw of

Shenzhen, China (Ng and Höpfl, 2014). Being the last frontier of China, Hong Kong has the advantage of being a global city with a mixed East and West culture. It is assumed that organizations in Hong Kong may have adopted Western management practices and that work conditions are relatively accommodating and managers more caring about employees' feelings. So what is the experience of employees at work in Hong Kong and does this reveal similarities or differences between working in mainland China and Hong Kong?

Apparently, the negotiation of the home/work boundaries is shaped by specific organizational cultures and norms (see Box 4.3).

BOX 4.3   FORGING WORK IDENTITIES IN HONG KONG

A study of Hong Kong employees reveals many examples of their being exiled from their homeland, emotional detachment and being stripped of their freedom in the workplace. The earliest they can be home for dinner on a work day is seven o'clock but on a busy day it will be much later. There is an underlying practice that one should not leave earlier than the supervisor or boss; sometimes the boss brings in food for dinner in the office to show the employees that he/she is busy and claims, 'I am the same as you'. High competition, and long working hours with a low salary seem to be acceptable norms in some types of office work. Employees are crowned with attractive work titles, for example, the title of manager instead of supervisor and officer instead of clerk. It is this 'given identity' that regulates and deprives the 'self' and 'identity' at work. Once employees are given a specific title, they are responsible for the absence and the ever-presence of self. Most, though not all, employees reported going to work as, in effect, a temporary exile from home; one is supposed to leave one's personal life (or 'home') behind.

These are typical examples of work penetrating into personal life. Because of the job nature and the location of factories, a number of employees in Hong Kong have to make frequent business trips across the border to China, and very often they have to stay over for days, literally being 'cast away' from families and friends. A student who came to my evening classes told me that he had to go back to the office after class in order to finish his remaining work tasks. Interestingly, another student said that he had a membership at the nearby gym in order that he can take a hot shower before spending the night in his office. These examples reflect people's feelings of being exiled from their homeland, experiencing the dullness and the negative 'being faraway, yet so close' feelings because of the length of time spent at work, feeling the distance and cold and emotional detachment of being grounded in the workplace. Yet these limitations at work are more than physical, they are also psychological. Yes, there is geographic dislocation, but also the intrusion of work demands into one's personal life that generates the sense of confinement. The issues which emerge are more deeply related to the 'psychological contract of work' constituting a demand for an ever-presence of self, so that there is no longer a clear contractual boundary between 'work' and 'non-work'. This clearly suits the organization's purpose and strategic direction since, in a way, it diminishes the concept of estrangement and accommodates any sense of exile within a common goal under one roof. So, clearly in Chinese workplaces and with the Chinese work culture, employees hold a fundamental belief that they are supposed to sacrifice their personal attributes at work for the homogeneity of office etiquette. This emerging theme matches Leung's assertion that Chinese culture is characterized as collectivistic, following group norms to generate harmony and prosperity (Leung, 2010). In sum, the earlier mentioned cases in China's factories and this research into Hong Kong's organizations point to an imbalance of work/life resulting from organizations' excessive stress on input and output, effectiveness and efficiency. This kind of work culture, the imbalance of work/personal life and the loss of self and identity at work, are inconvenient truths for businesses and business schools alike.

CAN BUSINESS SCHOOLS ADDRESS THE LOSS OF THE HUMAN SIDE IN ORGANIZATIONS?

Typically, business and management programmes in Hong Kong place a strong emphasis on functional knowledge and technical skills. Personally, I recall learning concepts designed to increase production and generate income, for example: scientific management, total quality management, project management, effectiveness and efficiency, input and output, human resources management's theory X and Y. On the other hand, topics on the caring and soft side of management were hardly mentioned in textbooks. A recent review of the undergraduate and graduate programmes offered by Hong Kong's various universities shows that the majority of undergraduate programmes being offered are in accountancy, economics and finance, information systems, management sciences, human resources management and marketing, with the exception of one postgraduate programme in organizational behaviour: the MSc in Human Resource Management (HRM) and Organizational Behaviour (OB) programme offered by the Department of Management, Lingnan University, since September 2010 (Education Bureau, Hong Kong, 2014). In the hope of altering the prevailing learning concepts in Hong Kong's business and management curricula, I propose three ways forward for a paradigm shift. Firstly, following Pink's (2006) suggestion, the business sector needs a whole new mindset: it would be more meaningful that business schools not only produce Master of Business and Administration (MBA) graduates but also graduates with the added-on attributes of Master of Fine Arts (MFA) to enhance students' social awareness, sensitivity and creativity. In view of that, business schools' curricula need to build a range of mindset changing subjects and soft management skills, such as role expectations, identity regulations and work psychology to generate organizational discourses from a broader social and cultural perspective. This would include topics such as philanthropy and community enterprise, ethics, equality and social responsibilities, job satisfaction and commitment, human connection, wellbeing and positive psychology, staff capability building and development, along with the use of good practices from the caring organizations as case studies in textbooks. These would equip would-be managers to build preferred work environments and caring organizations.

Secondly, as managers become aware that human resources are the most valuable assets in contemporary organizations, there is a need to soften the sharp edges of the 'totalitarian state-of-mind' to generate desirable work conditions for staff commitment and satisfaction. I contend that there is an urgent need to discuss controversial topics concerning the totalitarian state-of-mind, alienation and deprivation of individuality. This will help generate discourses and theories which will enable students to challenge deep rooted 'totalizing tendencies' at work. Realizing the repressive management culture in most South East Asian organizations, it is necessary to look into the soft side of management and to reconsider the correlation between productivity and employees' job satisfaction. With reference to the practices of most OEM companies in China, I would like to further propose establishing caring groups in organizations to accommodate employees, which creates a more meaningful and pleasant life at work.

Thirdly, conventional business and management teaching relies heavily on the study of well-established theories and cases. The famous 'if you were the manager, what would you do?' textbook exercise may not truly reflect the complexity of the specific cases, and as we have seen, problems in real life are fuzzy, elusive and exile-inducing. Further attempts should be made to focus on engaging students in internships or workplace attachments to enable them to see what actually happens in factories or offices for a better understanding of management theories and managers in action. This will build on programmes that prolong engagement in the workplace as a partial fulfilment of the study, where students will spend perhaps a year on the job to enhance their first-hand experiences for a better development of their final projects or dissertations before they come back to school to finish their final year. Finally, I would suggest the use of ethnography (Chang, 2008) and narrative story-telling (Ibarra and Barbulescu, 2010) as ways to immerse students in the field, so as to 'enter the "back regions" of organizations' (Sveningsson and Alvesson, 2003: 1170) in order to obtain an insider's view to observe behaviours and patterns and to draw insights and reflections from behind-the-scenes organizational activities.

To conclude, I believe that a close link and mutual influence between academics and industries would be beneficial for knowledge advancement; therefore, collaborations, dialogues and idea exchanges between academics and practitioners are equally important to facilitate the development of management curricula with a humanistic perspective. I am hoping that this short chapter will shed light on the human side of organizations and point the way for business schools to better prepare students to cope with real-life work situations.

REFERENCES

Bell, E. (2008) *Reading Management and Organization in Film*. New York: Palgrave, Macmillan.

Braziel, J. Evans and Mannur, A. (eds) (2003) *Theorizing Diaspora*. Oxford: Blackwell.

Chang, T. Lesile (2008) *Factory Girls: Voices from the Heart of Modern China*. New York: Spiegel and Grau.

Costea, B., Crump, N. and Holm, J. (2005) 'Dionysus at work? The ethos of play and the ethos of management', *Culture and Organization*, 11 (2): 139–51.

Education Bureau, Hong Kong (2014) 'Local higher education'. Retrieved from: www.edb.gov.hk/en/edu-system/postsecondary/local-higher-edu/index.html (accessed 1 December 2011).

Gabriel, Y. (2005) 'Glass cage and class palaces: images of organization in image-conscious times', *Organization*, 12 (1): 9–27.

Gherardi, S. and Strati, A. (1988) 'The temporal dimension in organisational studies', *Organisational Studies*, 9 (2): 149–64.

Höpfl, H. (2000) 'On being moved', *Studies in Cultures, Organisations and Societies* [now *Culture and Organisation*], 6 (1): 15–22.

Höpfl, H. (2007) 'Master and convert: women and other strangers', *Journal of Critical Organizational Inquiry*, 6 (4): 116–131.

Ibarra, H. and Barbulescu, R. (2010) 'Identity as narrative: prevalence, effectiveness, and consequences of narrative identity work in macro work role transitions', *Academy of Management Review*, 35 (1): 135–54.

Land, C. and Taylor, S. (2010) 'Surf's up: life, balance and brand in a new age capitalist organization', *Sociology*, 44 (3): 395–413.

Leung, K. (2010) *Beliefs in Chinese Culture: The Oxford Handbook of Chinese Psychology*. Hong Kong: Oxford University Press.

McGregor, D. (1960) *The Human Side of Enterprise*. New York: McGraw-Hill.

Milosz, C. (1997) 'On exile'. Introductory essay in J. Koudelka (ed.), *Exiles* (2nd edn). London: Thames and Hudson.

Next Media (2011) Retrieved from: http://hk.apple.nextmedia.com/international/art/20111201/15850810 (accessed 1 December 2011).

Ng, R. Yuk-Kwan, and Höpfl, H. (2014) 'The aesthetic diaspora: a photographic study of objects in the workspace', *International Journal of Work Organisation and Emotion*, 6 (1): 92–129.

Pink, H.D. (2006) *A Whole New Mind: Why Right-Brainers Will Rule the Future*. New York: Penguin.

Roy, D.F. (1959) 'Banana time: job satisfaction and informal interaction', *Human Organization*, 18: 158–68.

Sievers, B. (1986) 'Beyond the surrogate of motivation', *Organisational Studies*, 7 (4): 335–51.

Sveningsson, S. and Alvesson, M. (2003) 'Managing managerial identities: organizational fragmentation, discourse and identity struggle', *Human Relations*, 56 (10): 1163–93.

Taylor, F.W. (1911) *Principles of Scientific Management*. New York: Harper.

5 THE FORGOTTEN HUMANNESS OF ORGANIZATIONS

Yuliya Shymko

His answers were quite often like that. When she spoke of beauty, he spoke of the fatty tissue supporting the epidermis. When she mentioned love, he responded with the statistical curve that indicates the automatic rise and fall in the annual birthrate. When she spoke of the great figures in art, he traced the chain of borrowings that links these figures to one another. (Robert Musil, *The Man Without Qualities*, 1965)

CULTIVATING ATTITUDES IN THE AGE OF DISENCHANTMENT

'The disenchantment of the world', the narrative decrying 'specialists without spirit' and 'sensualists without heart', was the diagnosis that the sociologist Max Weber gave to new technocratic bureaucracies in the early twentieth century. Canadian philosopher Charles Taylor took over and extended it to economic rationality in modern secular societies. *Disenchantment* was also the way Austrian writer Robert Musil portrayed Vienna after the First World War. The concerns of Musil about the values of truth and opinion, and how society organizes ideas and plants them into the minds of individuals, are as important today as they were one hundred years ago. Just like the inhabitants of the slowly decaying Austro-Hungarian Empire, Western societies have been living in the atmosphere of disenchantment with the grand meta-narratives of the past and in the desperate search of new meaningful existential orienteers.

The dismantling of popular ideologies accompanied by the crash of normative certitudes, once provided by the state and church, has made universities inadvertently assume the role of primary cultivators of attitudes and mores. They perform this mission by creating, structuring, popularizing and disseminating knowledge or, in other words, by organizing ideas and turning them into individual beliefs and convictions. Forming an increasingly important part of the educational landscape across the world, business schools also embark on this mission – they cultivate attitudes in their students, either intentionally or subliminally. Later these attitudes become manifest in the choices and practices of management professionals and bear all sorts of social consequences. Thus taking a closer look at the values of truth and opinion that shape modern business school education strikes me as a very valuable exercise.

Disenchantment with the humanistically inspired collective utopias of liberation has made many social scientists turn towards a politically dispassionate and aloof 'scientific' explanation of the human condition. This shift has coincided with, and been partly driven by, rapid technological changes in the economic organization of production and consumption. The growing complexity of organizational processes and the increasing allure of natural science discourse in explaining the essence and the purpose of human systems have resulted in the birth and proliferation of ostensibly mechanistic and functionalist management theories. This predicament has been noted and reflected upon by management writers. For example, Peter Drucker emphasizes that '*an organization is a human, a social, and indeed a moral phenomenon*' (Clutterbuck and Crainer, 1991: 107, emphasis added), and Tom Peters has famously remarked that in the business school where he went, '*the only facts that many of us considered "real data" were the ones we could put numbers on*' (Peters and Waterman, 2004: 30, emphasis added). Consequently, the apparent ambivalence of business education towards morals and the general indifference of technocratic management theories towards the actual pains and joys of daily organizational life have brought many of us to a state of analytical passivity. It is this state of normative hibernation that Musil astutely attacks when he refers to Ulrich, a 32-year old mathematician and one of the novel's main protagonist, as being 'without qualities'. So where does the disenchantment with the political ideals, the draining of humanness from our understanding of organizations and the loss of empathetic reflection from our professional mission leave us as business school professionals? The aim of this chapter is to study this question by offering some critical reflections on knowledge creating and teaching approaches that dominate the institutional culture of many business schools. As an example, I take a closer look at the popular topic of 'organizational change' and its current presentation in management courses and illuminate new pedagogic avenues that may help bring humanistic tradition back to the core of management science and practice.

The reason I choose to explore the theme of change is its ubiquitous presence in the rhetoric of political, social and economic policy-makers. The talk of globalization is inseparable from the talk of change and challenges that accompany the new reality of interdependence and the increasing pace of interorganizational competitiveness. Hardly any business school curriculum falls short on the courses that place 'change management' in the centre of their educational value proposition. Many students aspire to work in 'agile and change promoting organizations' like Google or Apple or to join the ranks of powerful consulting companies like McKinsey or BCG. In the school where I work at least 30 per cent of all graduates end up in some kind of consulting company. They are also taught and encouraged to think of themselves as 'the agents of change' in times when rule-breaking is extolled and 'rebellious' CEOs are widely celebrated as the new role models. This excessiveness of enthusiasm and attention with regard to the topic of change makes me wonder if there is anything missing in its current educational representation.

THE UNCHANGING DISCOURSES OF CHANGE

The stories of organizational change are at the very basis of the educational edifice of business schools. Change capabilities are at the centre of managerial practices, the devotion to change is the epitome of effective leadership, the pursuit of change is the ethos of organizational existence. For example, one of the most popular products on the Harvard Business Publishing site for Educators (http://hbsp.harvard.edu) is a change management simulation 'Power and Influence'. The preface and the introductory paragraph of Beer and Nohria's *Breaking the Code of Change* state:

> We live in a world in which the nature of organizations and the practice of management are being profoundly changed. Most people accept that we are living through a period of great business turmoil. And most managers and organizations have accepted Tom Peter's dictum that they must 'change or die'. The demands of an ever competitive and changing environment are increasing the need for knowledge about how to lead and manage organizational change rapidly, efficiently, and effectively. (Beer and Nohria, 2000: 1)

Speed, efficiency and effectiveness are put at the centre of superior management capabilities in promoting and implementing change in organizations. One cannot help but notice that in this Superman style of acting, very little space is left for thoughtfulness, hesitation and empathy. Richard Sennett argues that such callous attitudes toward change management are a direct result of the shift from managerial to shareholder power in the age of corporate capitalism (Sennett, 2006). Companies experience enormous pressure to look beautiful in the eyes of 'impatient capital' and pursue change (even when unnecessary) to demonstrate signs of internal flexibility and dynamism (Sennett, 2006: 56). Consequently, unlike historians or political theorists, management educators tend to see change in bright colours as long as the numbers look good. The reassuring rhetoric that many business school professors employ to talk about organizational change establishes a strong semantic linkage to words like 'evolution', 'progress', 'transformation'. This celebration of perpetual transition from 'good to great' in case studies (see Doherty, this volume), textbooks and bestselling teaching materials creates a strong bias in students towards 'creative destruction' and forms an attitude that is almost entirely oblivious to the vicissitudes and hardships of any change project that involves humans (see Box 5.1).

I believe that such a technocratic and ethically sterile appraisal of organizational change is the direct outcome of scientific and pedagogical approaches that have taken over business education in the last decades.

THE SCIENTIFIC AND PEDAGOGICAL TRIVIALIZATION OF CHANGE

Popular strategic frameworks, deeply rooted in the epistemic tradition of economics, tend to explain changes and shifts in organizational practices and management techniques as a rational response to the challenges of efficiency, legitimacy and technology. Though the definition of 'efficiency' may vary depending on the paradigmatic proclivities of management scholars, the description of the mechanics of change remains invariably functional and rationality centred. Organizations wilfully change reacting to external pressures, legitimacy requirements, resource contingencies, competitive dynamics, a rise in transaction costs, etc. In the field of strategy, tightly connected to the industry of professional consulting, change theorists tend to peddle nomothetic rationalizations and directive prescriptions. Essentially, organizational players are conceived as rational actors who strive to adapt to and succeed in the battlefield of market competitiveness. Case studies, business games and simulation methods that accompany theoretical elaborations to provide students with 'real-life experiences' generally serve to demonstrate the universal usefulness of a framework or a theory rather than unveiling its limitations. Arguably, case studies are just factually circumscribed narratives of problems and solutions that nourish one specific type of sense-making and discourage all other ways of seeing. To narrow down and simplify the reality of organizational life further, some business schools promote the use of simulations and business games as a prominent and technologically advanced teaching technique (e.g. 'Power and Influence' simulation mentioned earlier). Thus the further cultivation of attitudes takes place in 'a phantom world which may mimic real life *with abstract actors* that impersonate humans and cast them in conceptual conditions that emulate actual circumstances' (Gross, 2009: 364, emphasis added). But how does one simulate the human consequences of change that Sennett describes in his compassionate story of the BBC restructuring, or the Boston Bakers (see Box 5.2)?

BOX 5.2   GREEK BAKERS IN BOSTON

In another absorbing book, *The Corrosion of Character* (1999), Richard Sennett provides more heart-wrecking examples of the personal consequences of work in the age of perpetual corporate re-engineering. He describes the dilution of professional dignity and self-regard among Greek bakers in Boston who used to treat and cherish their professional skills as the fundamental part of their ethnic and social identity. A giant food conglomerate that bought the business undertook a radical modernization of the processes following the management hype of the day – flexible specialization facilitated by the use of sophisticated reconfigurable machines. The change may have achieved its intended results – more efficient production of bread – but it also brought the consequences on which typical case study narratives usually remain silent. Sennett places these in the daylight of his readers' imagination:

> The bakers now no longer know how to bake bread. Automated bread is no marvel of technological perfection; the machines frequently tell the wrong story about the loaves rising within. The workers can fool with the screen to correct somewhat for these defects; what they can't do is fix the machines, or more important, actually bake bread by manual control when the machines all too often go down. Program-dependent laborers, they can have no hands-on knowledge. The work is no longer legible to them, in the sense of understanding what they are doing. In place of alienation, their sense of daily life in the bakery is marked by indifference. Here are the people whose work identities are weak. (1999: 68)

To enhance the credibility of their strategic change theories, management scholars actively borrow vocabulary from various disciplines in natural sciences such as evolutionary biology and physics. This enables them to produce a scientific discourse that rationalizes and objectifies the behaviour of individuals and collectivities as goal oriented and driven, uniformly predictable, and void of any idiosyncratic and intricate deviations. Not surprisingly, students end up construing the experience of organizational change as a re-engineering process organizational elements are denoted and made sense of in the language of abstract and 'professionally' sounding terms such as assets, business units, capabilities, optimal relocation, efficient recapitalization, etc. Inevitably, their understanding of change and how it should be practised in organizations gets infused with highly functionalist and mechanistic accounts of organizational life.

DEBUNKING CHANGE THEORIES

Humanistically minded scholars in management research seek to take a more ethically sensitive stand on explaining the phenomenon of organizational change. Notwithstanding the complexity and the notion that the space of human action looks messier and less rational than some of us tend to believe, these approaches bring more realism and insightfulness to our understanding of organizations and the individuals who constitute them. They engender what Hannah Arendt calls 'thinking without a banister' (in Strong, 2012: 1). Finding things out without deterministic theoretical assumptions (e.g. people are self-interested, tireless utility calculators who would follow a command if properly incentivized) is what may help business school teachers in seeking to offer a more holistic and humane understanding of organizational change.

A prominent approach that business schools may adopt in teaching change management is the multifaceted examination of management practices to carry out the processes of organizational reordering, reshaping and identity construction. Here I offer an example of such an approach. By discussing an article on plant restructuring at Caterpillar Inc., I demonstrate how adding a few alternative interpretations of the phenomenon can intellectually enrich students' analytical and normative comprehension of the case at hand. This overview is a simple demonstration of the importance of multiple narratives and counterfactual assessments in classroom discussions and deliberations.

BOX 5.3   CATERPILLAR INC.

Caterpillar Inc. is the world's leading manufacturer of construction and mining equipment, diesel and natural gas engines, industrial gas turbines and diesel-electric locomotives. With more than US$70 billion in assets, Caterpillar was ranked number 1 in its industry and number 44 overall in the 2009 Fortune 500. Caterpillar's historical manufacturing home is in Peoria, Illinois, which is also the location of its world headquarters and core research and development activities. Due to the radical restructuring of business operations which began in the 1990s, there are now 20,000 fewer union jobs in the Peoria, Illinois area, while employment outside the US has increased. Whereas in traditional case studies Caterpillar's modernization is used as an example of a successful and operationally impeccable 'change story', more critically minded scholars offer a radically different assessment of the necessity and the dynamics of change that Caterpillar sought to implement.

Finding things out

Miller and O'Leary (1994) present the lengthy and problematic modernization of the Caterpillar plant Decatur between 1985 and 1994 as a story of intertemporal wrestling with competing rationalizations, discourses and reconciliations in the flux of successes and failures. In the first lines of the explanatory note to their article Miller and O'Leary claim their freedom from methodological concerns in building their analysis of the 'most extensive corporate wide programs of factory modernization' (Miller and O'Leary, 1994: 15). They contend that managers were keen on providing continuous but incoherent diagnostics of the plant's economic viability and the search for subsequent remedies was contingent on what managers conceived as 'a problem'. Consequently, they primarily see the modernization efforts of Caterpillar as a transformation of identity and meaning that required a shared and consensual understanding of common challenges (e.g. global competition) and the responses to them (creating an ethos of innovativeness). They seek to demonstrate that this transformation took place through the introduction of new accounting techniques and sense-making heuristics that twisted workers' self-assessment and augmented the construction of *economic citizenship* as a vital regulatory and governance mechanism. Conveying their story by centring it on management discourses and narratives, they insist that Marxist binary oppositions and fixed identities such as manager–worker, capital–labour, are too restrictive and deterministic to provide a satisfactory explanation 'for the processes by which the multiple components of a factory modernization program are assembled together at a particular point in time, *and possibly reassembled and refocused subsequently*' (Miller and O'Leary, 1994: 16, emphasis added). Moreover, they deem as anachronistic the idea of patterned labour bargaining and resistance in the context of a modern multidivisional organizational structure. Instead, they emphasize the provisional and shifting nature of alliances that may emerge between management and non-management employees due to some shared identity and perceived congruence of interests. In short, they offer an intriguing and unconventional storytelling of organizational change.

However, a problem emerges when one tries to understand the individual phenomenon of factory modernization within the broader context of socio-political and economic forces. Where do the boundaries of alternative explanations lie in this exercise of relativism? How contestable is this representation of what really happened at Caterpillar? Can we claim that the Caterpillar modernization was a unique experience? Or are there any common symptoms that reflect the institutional struggles of post-industrial free market economies? Would the same conclusions be drawn had Miller and O'Leary decided to pay closer attention to what workers had to say about their own experiences?

Many mirrors for the same face

Such persistent questioning constitutes an important role for business schools in exposing multiple aspects of organizational reality and inviting competing interpretations of the case in hand. To exemplify how this might be achieved I briefly examine the commentary of three sets of authors, each bringing their own distinctive 'take' on the Caterpillar story.

Ezzamel et al. (2004) concur with two fundamental insights in Miller and O'Leary's study. First, they embrace the concern to shift the terms of reference of the debate on accounting change from the purely economic such as transaction costs theory to the realm of the political, where the processes of deliberation and interpretative struggles mesh with the reality of managing and organizing. Second, they share the basic premise of Foucauldian analysis that the de-legitimation of certain practices (e.g. specific accounting techniques) is inseparable from the strategies used to promote the authority and value of commending alternatives. However, they offer a substantive enrichment to the story by indicating that the politics of production, and the subtleties of power and coercion in an ordained setting, are a crucial omission from Miller and O'Leary's interpretation of change at Caterpillar. Specifically, they point out that the notion of resistance is completely overlooked in the presented account of reality and 'the voice of labor is conspicuous by its absence as its cooperation is tacitly implied' (Ezzamel et al., 2004: 299). By integrating some theoretical insights from labour process theory and identity literature these researchers restore the importance of agency in workers' resilience to the new logics of efficiency and organizational practices imposed by the management.

Arnold (1998) is another writer who offers a fresh layer to the narrative of Caterpillar's transformation and demonstrates that the class struggle is not a matter of discursive constructions or anachronistic categorizations. For her, the same phenomenon (a plant modernization) when explained through the prism of historical materialism can be understood to exemplify the inherent ideological contradictions of modern capitalism. She dismantles the concept of 'economic citizenship' that implies an individualized notion of identity, ignores the historical embeddedness of individuals and trivializes their sense of solidarity. Drawing extensively from the interviews with workers in Caterpillar's Decatur plant, many of them representing the local trade union, she vividly demonstrates the presence of the class consciousness and solidarity that underlie the history of industrial conflict at Caterpillar. According to her interpretation, the story of Decatur restructuring is one of class struggle and the experience of collective resistance to what is perceived as 'capitalist exploitation'.

Finally, Froud et al. (1998) add yet another layer to the multiplicity of different narratives on Caterpillar. They focus on the empirical assessment of management discourses that Miller and O'Leary use to make sense of Caterpillar's transformation. Their approach involves the use of numbers from the company's accounts and official sources to reveal the gap between intention and outcome. By putting management discourses in the context of industry and sector dynamics of the period they offer what Miller and O'Leary do not – the actual validation of managerial claims. Their contextual analysis reveals that Caterpillar's management was fighting imaginary problems and failed to understand the impact of exogenous factors, such as exchange rates, as major determinants of Japanese competitive advantage. They show how the managers were trapped in their own sense-making and cognitive rigidities: they were offering and rationalizing solutions to non-existent challenges, thus failing to deliver and ending up creating ever more fantasies about the state of reality. Their story of Decatur restructuring unveils the dual identity of Caterpillar management: self-serving power prompting professionals to be selective about their facts and justifications, on the one hand, and on the other they can be seen as honest manufacturers undone by external turbulences combined ironically with the results of their own making.

CONCLUSION

So, what educational value can business schools derive from exposing students to multiple interpretations in this case, organizational change at Caterpillar? I see at least three important aspects here.

The first aspect is the *intellectual abandonment of habitual and manager-centric approaches* to a problem formulation typically encountered in case studies on organizational change management. Understanding the cognitive and professional biases in managerial behaviour and sense-making enables students to loosen some of their taken-for-granted assumptions about why certain organizational forms and practices all of a sudden have to be changed or replaced.

The second aspect is *building awareness of the problems of power and domination* in any organizational setting. Any serious discussion of organizational change cannot ignore the questions of group interests, political manipulation and the nature of individual resistance to a project of change.

Finally, the third aspect consists of the *development of the moral imagination* of students as in their attempts to understand the essence of change they can no longer adhere to the normatively neutral and comfortable heuristics of technocratic analysis.

The obsession with 'scientism' in management research and the hyperbolized professional pragmatism of teaching in business schools makes us forget that we study people made up of flesh and blood, individuals with dreams, frustrations, hopes, aspirations, fears and vanities. Amidst the complexity of socio-economic and political transformation that the world is experiencing on a global scale, one cannot help but notice that many business schools have been growing surprisingly economical in their ideas and ethos. All too often we rely on simple mechanistic notions of behaviour to explain complex social phenomena adopting even simpler quantifications and schemes of infinite human desires and grievances. Our management theories 'normalize' bad behaviour, invade public thinking with dehumanizing concepts such as 'human resources' or 'human capital', and one of our now rarely questioned exercises in mainstream theoretical deliberation is what John K. Galbraith once called '*the search for a superior justification for selfishness*' (cited in Cornwell, 2002, emphasis added).

Yet we take very little responsibility for the consequences of our work, for the recommendations we give to managers, for the beliefs we encourage and cultivate, and most importantly – for the disastrous policies based on these beliefs and recommendations. We claim to be amoral, value neutral, objective, rigorous and detached. Humanistic accounts of individual struggles inside organizations bring us back to our sensibilities. Their generous and sympathetic portrayals of people and their circumstances in the context of organizational life make us realize that there is nothing 'objective' in our epistemic claims for truth. The most urgent change needed in the current business education is the return of actual human beings into our discourses of management practices and organizational missions. One of the ways to bring personal experiences of people affected by organizational change to the empathetic attention of students is to stop treating ethical issues of management as a separate course under the generic title of 'CSR' and to instil every syllabus of core management subjects with polemical potential. This potential can be derived from combining classical cases and texts with artistic representations of human experiences in organizational reality. For example, I accompany my seminar on competitive dynamics and game theory with the movie *Glengarry Glenn Ross* and excerpts from the BBC documentary *The Century of the Self*. At least 40 per cent of my current syllabus on globalization consists of award winning documentaries and films that sympathetically depict human struggles in the globalizing world.

Finally, I argue that the best thing business schools can do to substantiate their vocal awareness of institutional responsibility towards society is to open their classroom space to contesting multidisciplinary views on the philosophy of management. Rigor and the relevance of a management education can greatly benefit from encouraging and cultivating ideological polyphony among teachers and students. Polyphony is a crucial attribute of any creative process, equally indispensable for promoting a humanistic vision and intellectual diversity across management education. The 2008 economic crisis has sadly demonstrated that the spread of voices that claim expertise and the authority of knowledge is to a large extent the product of power and institutional entrenchment rather than a result of open-minded intellectual polemics driven by the awareness of an important social mission. As management education grows its intellectual presence in public decision-making, we must make sure that its normative sensitivities are up to the task.

FURTHER READING

For the criticism of modern knowledge models, see Lyotard (1984).
For the cognitive re-shaping of learning experiences, see Bauman (2009).
For an ethnographic look at moral education in business schools, see Anteby (2013).
For a witty and thoughtful analysis of popularized management mantras, see Wooldridge (2011).

REFERENCES

Anteby, M. (2013) *Manufacturing Morals*. Chicago: University of Chicago Press.

Arnold, P.J. (1998) 'The limits of postmodernism in accounting history: the Decatur experience', *Accounting, Organizations and Society*, 23 (7): 665–84.

Bauman, Z. (2009) *Does Ethics Have a Chance in the World of Consumers?* Cambridge, MA: Harvard University Press.

Beer, M. and Nohria, N. (2000) *Breaking the Code of Change*. Cambridge, MA: Harvard Business School Press.

Clutterbuck, D. and Crainer, S. (1991) *Makers of Management*. London: Papermac.

Cornwell, R. (2002) 'Stop the madness', interview (6 July). *Toronto Globe and Mail*. Retrieved from: http://wist.info/galbraith-john-kenneth/7463/ (accessed 15 December 2014).

Ezzamel, M., Willmott, H. and Worthington, F. (2004) 'Accounting and management-labour relations: the politics of production in the "factory with a problem"', *Accounting, Organizations and Society*, 29 (3/4): 269–302.

Froud, J., Williams, K., Haslam, C. and Johal, S. (1998) 'Caterpillar: two stories and an argument', *Accounting, Organizations and Society*, 23 (7): 685–708.

Gross, N. (2009) 'The pragmatist theory of social mechanisms', *American Sociological Review*, 74 (3): 358–79.

Lyotard, J.F. (1984) *The Postmodern Condition: A Report on Knowledge*. Minneapolis, MN: University of Minnesota Press.

Miller, P. and O'Leary, T. (1994) 'Accounting, "economic citizenship" and spatial reordering of manufacture', *Accounting Organizations and Society*, 19 (10: 15–43.

Musil, R. (1965) *The Man Without Qualities*. New York: Perigee Books.

Peters, T. and Waterman, R.H. (2004) *In Search of Excellence: Lessons from America's Best-Run Companies*. London: Profile Books.

Sennett, R. (1999) *The Corrosion of Character: Personal Consequences of Work in the New Capitalism*. New York: W.W. Norton and Company.

Sennett, R. (2006) *The Culture of the New Capitalism*. New Haven, CT: Yale University Press.

Strong, T.B. (2012) *Politics without Vision: Thinking without a Banister in the Twentieth Century*. London: University of Chicago Press.

Wooldridge, A. (2011) *The Masters of Management*. New York: HarperCollins Publishers.

PART I

RAPPORTEUR

Jerry Biberman

Every ten years or so an ethical crisis or incidence occurs which results in businesses and corporations at least paying lip service to their interest in ethics and social responsibility, and which prompts a call for business schools to pay more attention to teaching their students business ethics or social responsibility. Past incidents in the United States have included several cases involving car manufacturers (e.g. the Ford Pinto and more recently General Motors), the BP oil spill, the bank mortgage crisis that resulted in a massive recession, and the way in which workers are mistreated in manufacturing plants in third world countries. Businesses have responded to these incidents by creating pages on their websites devoted to social responsibility and producing television advertisements touting their interest in ethics and social responsibility. Business schools respond by creating single courses in business ethics and by saying in their curricula descriptions that they are committed to teaching the importance of business ethics, and accrediting agencies such as AACSB respond by calling for more attention to be paid to ethics and social responsibility in business school courses. And yet, despite all these calls throughout the years for changes in the way business schools teach business ethics and social responsibility, people and corporations continue to act unethically, and corporations and their leaders continue to act in their own best interests to maximize profits with little regard for the welfare of their workers or for the greater social and global environment.

Calls for changes in the way managers and leaders are taught and the way that managers and leaders should behave are nothing new. Almost 30 years ago (Biberman and Hynson, 1986) I argued that organizational behaviour and leadership theories go in a cyclical nature from calls for managers and leaders to be more streamlined and task oriented (as Theory X managers have been described) to calls for leaders to be more humanistic and people oriented (e.g. Theory Y). In more recent years, writers have started writing about spirituality at work and spiritual leadership as a way to get leaders and managers to become more concerned with the souls or spirits of the people who work in corporations. So why has there been no real change in the way most managers and leaders behave towards their workers and towards the environment in organizations, or in the way they deal with ethical dilemmas?

One possible explanation is that business schools are responsible, because of both the way in which they structure their curricula and the way they teach the subjects of business ethics, organization behaviour, and social responsibility. These subjects are often taught as separate stand-alone courses, without being tied in to the overall business school curriculum. Students are thus given the impression that while their professors may say one thing in these courses, in the 'real world' (as represented by their finance, accounting and other courses) the only thing that really matters is maximizing profits. As one of my students said to me, he will tell any teacher what she or he wants to hear to get a good grade in the particular course, but he knows that in the real world increasing profits is all that matters. Students may also get the same impressions from the way in which their courses are taught.

The four chapters in Part I help to explain how this situation came about and is still occurring in most business schools. They each describe the failure of today's business schools to deal with the disenchantment – or loss of soul – of modern businesses.

Using the two systems theory perspectives of cybernetics and self-referential closure, Ward and Mayrhofer argue that the systemic setup of business schools produces an inability on their part to ask and address the key questions involved in determining whether students are changed as people by business schools so that they can become better managers – as opposed to just being able to pass exams and carry out assignments.

Shymko describes the 'disenchantment' of business schools, and their 'technocratic and ethically sterile appraisal of organizational change', as being the result of business schools being obsessed with scientism and valuing speed, efficiency and effectiveness, and their using case studies and business games and simulations that consider managers to simply be rational actors, while paying little or no attention to such humanistic values as thoughtfulness, hesitation and empathy. To combat this, Shymko suggests that business schools consider abandoning manager-centric approaches to problem-solving, greater awareness of organizational power and domination, and the development of the 'moral imagination' of students.

Harle addresses the question of how business schools lost their way, leading to a 'disconnect between theory and practice, between cause and effect, between personal and corporate responsibility'. He attributes these trends to the emphasis on science and rationality and the superiority of markets, and to business schools wanting to legitimate themselves. Harle states that:

> The *raison d'être* of most of these schools is to equip their students to run the existing system in an ever more effective way without asking questions about its aims, its faults or the dangers it poses. In this way, the majority of professors are the thurifers of an ideology, the clergy and the celebrants of a unidimensional way of thinking. They claim to train citizens and yet they more often train mere robots of a system without a clear *raison d'être*. They constitute a major obstacle to the establishment of a culture of sustainable development. This is also true for most universities or schools of Christian tradition.

Finally, Ng's chapter describes the effect of corporations on employee 'identity', where 'work has the capacity to "detach" an employee from where he/she belongs so as to create a simultaneous sense of being ever-present at work and yet with an absence of meaning'.

All four of the chapters prescribe ways in which business schools' curricula should be changed to add more soft management skills, and prescribe different ways in which the subject areas should be taught. These include more use of internships and service learning experiences, and less reliance on case analyses and lectures.

I agree with the authors' assessment of the current state of business school education, and I also agree with their prescriptions for change. It seems to me that the areas of business ethics and social responsibility need to be incorporated throughout the curriculum into every business course, and not only as separate standalone courses. Even more significant, in my opinion, is the importance of changing the way in which business courses are taught, so that the whole student is taught – not just their intellect and case problem-solving skills. Students should also be exposed to experiences that have the potential to reach their emotions and to stimulate their compassion. In my experience, techniques such as using films and music can be helpful. Even more potentially helpful, in my opinion, is the use of spiritual methodologies such as meditation, which can help students to calm their thinking and to access their 'higher selves'. This is the main reason that I became involved with the spirituality at work movement. The history of the spirituality at work movement to date demonstrates the challenges to researchers and particularly teachers who want to really provide learning situations for students to become more ethical and socially aware leaders, and mirrors in many ways the problems in business schools that the chapter authors describe.

It has been almost 20 years since the publication of several books that can be viewed as beginning interest in the area of spirituality of business. These include *The Reinvention of Work: A New Vision of Livelihood for Our Time* (Fox, 1995); *Leading with Soul: An Uncommon Journey of Spirit* (Bolman and Deal, 1995); and *A Spiritual Audit of Corporate America: A Hard Look at Spirituality, Religion, and Values in the Workplace* (Mitroff and Denton,1999).

Around the time that these books were appearing, interest in spirituality at work began to surface in such academic bodies as the International Academy of Business Disciplines (IABD, where a track on spirituality at work was created) and the Academy of Management (AOM, where the interest group on Management, Spirituality and Religion or MSR was created; Biberman, 2003). Research in the area of management and spirituality led to several articles on the subject appearing in academic journals and the publication of the *Journal of Management, Spirituality and Religion*, as well as several edited texts containing theoretical and empirical articles on the subject (e.g. Biberman and Tischler, 2008; Biberman and Whitty, 2007).

As one of the early writers in this area (as well as being the founder of the IABD track and first chair of the AOM MSR division), I remember a feeling of excitement at the creation of a new research area, and thinking that this new research area might have some impact on changing the way organizations do business and the way in which business schools teach management and business. Looking back at the 'field' almost 20 years later, I am forced to question whether this interest in spirituality has so far had any impact at all on either management research, the teaching of management in business schools, or management practice – beyond preaching to the choir for those of us who were involved in doing the writing and research on the subject. My reasons for saying this are as follows:

1. I have so far not seen any major or bestselling management or organization behaviour textbook have a chapter or section on spirituality.
2. Very few courses in organization behaviour or management have sections in their courses or syllabi devoted to the area of management and spirituality.
3. Whereas early writing and research on the subject contained an interesting mix of theoretical speculation on the subject, various kinds of innovative qualitative research, and empirical research, most of the more recent research has tended to be empirical research, with an emphasis on how spirituality somehow leads to the improvement of either worker productivity or a company's financial 'bottom line'. I believe that this shift in research methodology has been largely the result of three factors – doctoral students and untenured faculty fearing that research on spirituality would hurt their chances of getting their degrees and gaining tenure; universities and their accrediting agencies demanding that faculty publish in top tier research journals that prefer mainstream quantitative research to innovative qualitative research; and the desire by members of the relevant group within academic society to gain legitimacy and division status within the society.

So where do we go from here? While, as I stated earlier, I agree with all of the points and prescriptions of the authors of the four chapters, I believe that the only real possible change in the teaching of leader behaviour will come from individual faculty having the courage to teach these subjects using those techniques that have the greatest potential to change the souls of their students.

In teaching their courses, professors can make greater use of possible soul-stirring techniques such as music, films, poetry and especially such spiritual techniques as meditation. Examples of how these techniques could be used include:

1. Having a period of time at the beginning and/or end of each class for meditation. Students could then be asked to reflect on and write about their meditation experience.
2. Showing either portions of films or entire films that illustrate major course themes – particularly those films or clips of films that affect a person emotionally. *Joe vs. the Volcano* has a number of spiritual themes. Other possible films that can be used include *Glenn Gary Glenn Ross* and *Office Space*. There are several books that describe how films and film excerpts can be used in teaching business classes.
3. Assigning course writing assignments and projects that have a heavy emphasis on student self-reflection. For example, students could be asked to reflect on their experiences after completing 'service learning' projects; or students could be asked to describe or give examples of how certain specific course theories apply to their own behaviour.
4. Using more experiential exercises in class – particularly those that involve self-reflection and analysis during and after the exercise.

Even more important, professors and their institutions need to 'walk the talk' and show through their actions that they actually practise what they preach. By this I mean that professors should ensure that in taking on consulting practices, and especially in describing their consulting experiences to their students, their consulting behaviour conforms to the ethical and leadership practices that they are teaching. Similarly, business schools should only engage with or participate in projects with those businesses and organizations that they consider to be ethical, and should ensure that their practices or involvement with these organizations conform to the ethical standards they espouse. In addition, business schools should pay as much attention to evaluating and rewarding good teaching as they do to evaluating and rewarding publication.

Moreover, professors and their business schools should be encouraged to do more pro bono and non-profit work with non-profit and socially conscious institutions, and students should be encouraged to do more service learning experiences with these institutions. For example, one business school in its capstone course has its students engage in consulting projects with non-profit agencies in their community.

Students and future leaders are more influenced by what they actually observe in their teachers and mentors than by what their teachers and mentors profess to believe or do.

REFERENCES

Biberman, G. and Hynson, L.M., Jr. (1986) 'A combined perspective on corporate culture', in John C. Glidewell (ed.), *Corporate Cultures: Research Implications for Human Resources Development*. Alexandria, VA: American Society for Training and Development, pp. 87–93.

Biberman, J. (2003) 'How workplace spirituality becomes mainstreamed in a scholarly organization', in Robert A. Giacolone and Carole L. Jurkiewicz (eds), *Handbook of Workplace Spirituality and Organizational Performance*. Armonck, NY: M.E. Sharpe, pp. 421–8.

Biberman, J., and Tischler, L. (eds) (2008) *Spirituality in Business: Theory, Practice, and Future Directions*. New York: Palgrave MacMillan.

Biberman, J. and Whitty, M.D. (eds) (2007) *At Work: Spirituality Matters*. Scranton, PA: University of Scranton Press.

Bolman, L.G. and Deal, T.E. (1995) *Leading with Soul: An Uncommon Journey of Spirit*. San Francisco, CA: Jossey-Bass.

Fox, M. (1995) *The Reinvention of Work: A New Vision of Livelihood for Our Time*. San Francisco, CA: Harper.

Mitroff, I. and Denton, E.A. (1999) *A Spiritual Audit of Corporate America: A Hard Look at Spirituality, Religion, and Values in the Workplace*. San Francisco, CA: Jossey-Bass.

PART II

HOW ROBUST ARE THE THEORETICAL AND MORAL ASSUMPTIONS OF BUSINESS SCHOOLS?

6 IS ECONOMIC GROWTH A FORCE FOR GOOD?

Molly Scott Cato

One of the features of the globalized capitalist economy, that inherently challenges our path to a just and sustainable future, is the hegemonic nature of economic growth. Growth is an idea and an unquestioned objective for enterprises of all sorts and in all sectors. The focus on economic growth has led to lengthy supply chains, which waste energy and produces unnecessary carbon emissions. Growth has also facilitated the creation of complex group structures for business corporations, obscuring methods of audit and reducing accountability and transparency. In an era when scientific evidence indicates clearly the importance of setting 'prosperity without growth' (Jackson, 2009) as a social and economic objective, I argue that business schools need to question the growth paradigm at the level of the enterprise and the economy as a whole. The rush towards growth is driven at a micro-level by the idea of 'economies of scale', which operates as a mantra within neoclassical economics. This is theoretically problematic since it runs counter to the idealized market model of the same economic theory, which assumes a multiplicity of small companies in competition with each other, and free access for new players to enter markets. While in strategy courses we teach how companies in the real world find ways to consolidate their market power, in economics classes the same students are learning about a market model that idealizes competitive markets. For green economists the idea of 'appropriate scale' as popularized by Schumacher, and developed by his teacher Leopold Kohr, is both more constructive and more sustainable than idealizing growth. This chapter explores alternative forms of business that might better encapsulate the design imperative of appropriate scale, particularly the worker-managed firm.

THE ORIGIN OF THE GROWTH IMPERATIVE

The idea of growth is now so inherent in our understanding of how economies function that it is difficult to imagine an economy that is in balance with its environment or a firm that has successfully reached its optimal level of functioning. This is precisely why it is difficult for business schools to question whether growth is necessarily advantageous in terms of a society or enterprise. In this section I examine how this idea came to dominate our understanding of economic life at the micro- and macro- levels.[1]

Micro-growth and the theory of the firm

The rush towards growth is driven theoretically by the idea of 'economies of scale', which operates as a mantra within neoclassical economics (Mankiw, 2012: 272).[2] This is theoretically problematic since it runs counter to the idealized market model of the same economic theory (Mankiw, 2012: 66), which assumes a multiplicity of small companies in competition with each other, and free access for new players to enter markets. Interestingly, many of those who have developed and who teach the field of study labelled 'strategy' are themselves economists, so they need to undergo a mental compartmentalization in teaching the theory of competition in one class and then moving on to teach students how to develop strategies to subvert this competition. While in strategy courses they teach how companies in the real world find ways to consolidate their market power, in economics classes the same students are learning about a market model that makes such consolidation impossible in theory and which does not exist in reality.

The commonsense view of economies of scale is simple and immediately appealing: in any process of manufacture certain costs are unavoidable (designated 'fixed costs'), such as the cost of renting a factory or arranging to advertise the availability of your products. Other costs (designated 'variable costs') result from purchasing inputs to the production process and are proportional to the amount produced. It is obvious that, while variable costs relate directly to the level of output, fixed costs diminish as production is increased. Hence it is more efficient to produce at a larger scale, since the proportional impact of fixed costs declines. Leaving aside the idea of diseconomies of scale, to which we will return in the third section below, the issue of exploiting scale economies is, accordingly to neoclassical economic theory, to be theoretically limited by the operation of market competition. A company exploiting economies of scale will make large profits which will attract other entrepreneurs to enter the same sector of production, thus ensuring a

---

[1]The Green House think tank is engaged in a Post Growth Project, more details of which can be found at www.greenhousethinktank.org/page.php?pageid=postgrowth (accessed 8 January 2015).

[2]Mainstream textbooks are fairly standard in terms of the theory they include; I have used Mankiw here because it is probably the most widespread text used in teaching in US universities and because Mankiw has also worked as a government advisor in the USA.

limit on the size of expansion and a time-limit on the ability of what are called 'super-normal profits'.

Since the ability to earn such excessive profits is a characteristic feature of contemporary capitalism we need to question why the theory no longer applies. The answer taught in strategy courses is that capitalist firms have an incentive to use the means at their disposal to limit market competition. They have a number of ways to do this: controlling their design and technological advantages through the use of intellectual property laws; making strategic alliances with potential competitors; diversifying horizontally (taking over competitors) or vertically (extending along their supply chain) to exercise greater control within their market. Most importantly of all, the ability of new small producers to enter the market and ensure that there is competition to drive prices down and keep profits within a reasonable limit is seriously restricted by the sheer size and power of existing companies. In fact the real reason for corporations to expand is to enable themselves to exercise this power both economically and politically, rather than merely to exploit the economies of scale in terms of input costs. So, in summary, economic growth is about market power rather than productive efficiency.

Macro-growth and the war-fighting economy

The importance of growth to any economic policy-maker or politician is clear from the fact that the key indicator of the success of a national economy is considered to be the percentage increase in GDP or gross domestic product: an indication of the increase in the measure of economic activity. Regardless of what the economic activity achieves or fails to achieve, expansion is always judged to be good and contraction is always judged to be bad. This is a perverse and narrow way to measure a national economy, especially because it focuses solely on quantity, ignoring quality entirely. To illustrate this, the pioneering ecological economist Herman Daly famously if somewhat facetiously gave the example of a country deciding to cut down its entire national forest and to use the timber to manufacture gambling chips: in a conventional GDP approach to success this would be an economic advance.

The most swingeing and trenchant attack on both GDP and the growth obsession was Marilyn Waring's (1988) book *If Women Counted*. As a feminist she was deeply critical of the way that a narrow economic measure failed to value women's caring and reproductive labour, but she was also appalled by the origin of GDP in the war years as the means to maximize the destructive capacity of a war economy. She discovered that the system that was later established as a global standard by the UN in the post-war world was actually based largely on the UK system of maximizing the output of war material during the Second World War. What had been necessary during a national emergency had now come to dominate the world, with destructive social and environmental consequences.

PROBLEMS WITH THE GROWTH IMPERATIVE

Both within the individual enterprise and at the level of national economies, the central motivation is now to expand, to such an extent that a period of stability or shrinkage is labelled as 'negative growth', as though growth were the normal state of affairs, and 'growth' has become the hegemonic idea within economic theory. A range of authors including Douthwaite (1992), Cato (2009), Jackson (2009) and Dietz and O'Neill (2013) has provided critical accounts of the social and environmental impacts of this growth obsession, questioning the substitution of quantity for quality as the key economic goal and sharing US environmentalist Edward Abbey's critical comment that 'Growth for the sake of growth is the ideology of the cancer cell'. In this section I briefly reprise some of the arguments problematizing growth, first at the level of the enterprise and then at the level of the economy as a whole.

Within the enterprise (micro)

Although it is Schumacher who is known for the adage 'small is beautiful', he was greatly influenced in his thought by the Austrian economist Leopold Kohr, whose (1957) masterpiece *The Breakdown of Nations* established a critique of globalization before it had even been named and argued that there are natural boundaries to human communities. Kohr critiqued the inefficiency of the excessive scale of modern society, whose origin he found in the over-production of two types of goods the need for which increases as society expands in scale: power commodities and density commodities. The first include such things as 'tanks, bombs or the increase in government services required to administer increased power'; the second are 'rendered necessary as a result of population increases, such as traffic lights, first-aid equipment, tube services, or replacement goods for losses which would never have occurred in less harassed smaller societies' (Kohr, 1957: 146). Kohr's critique is focused on social systems but a similar critique could be made of the multinational corporation, which now spends vast amounts of energy and time co-ordinating the individual enterprises of which it is comprised. Although a capitalist, growth-based economy revels in the additional demand that power and density commodities create, from an ecological point of view sustainability tends more towards ecological efficiency.

The increasing size and consequent power of global corporations have also generated problems of political control, since many multinational corporations are now larger than many of the world's national economies and their structure of operation, basing their production in countries with low environmental and employment standards, and their headquarters for taxation purposes in countries with the lowest tax rates, enables them to avoid the social responsibilities that any enterprise should carry, while maximizing the financial returns to shareholders. The example of transfer-pricing, where companies sell commodities from one part of their business to another to achieve an artificial internal market that minimises their tax liabilities, is the foremost example of this behaviour that is facilitated by the size and global reach of companies, of which Starbucks is the most egregious example. The ability of large companies to manipulate markets rather than be subject to their laws (as in the example of the LIBOR price-fixing scandal) and to suborn the activities of the accountants who should be auditing their practices as a result of the massive accounts they are contracted for (as in the case of the Enron-Anderson scandal) is an example of the undermining of corporate standards as scale expands and both accountability and responsibility are consequently diminished.

Within an economy (macro)

Nationally and globally our economies are growing out of control. This process is heedless of the environmental impact of infinite growth within a limited planet which, as the heterodox economist Kenneth Boulding quipped, could only seem rational to a madman or an economist. Since most economic activity requires the use of raw materials and almost everything that contributes to growth measured as GDP requires the use of energy, most frequently carbon-emitting fossil-fuel energy, the environmental consequences of the growth obsession are devastating. In his 1992 critique, Douthwaite also makes clear that the social consequences are also destructive, citing such examples as an increase in crime that results from increased material wealth and a reduction in the quality of relationships that follows on from the longer working hours of 'more successful' economies. Finally, since GDP is a measure of total output, the economic growth that is bought at such a heavy social and environmental price could all accrue to one person, because our central economic measure does not include any consideration of distribution.

We can gain a practical insight into the inefficiency of this bloated economic system by considering the system of international trade. Historically, trade was conducted in rare commodities or goods that were exchanged between countries where they were not available: the Vikings brought furs and amber and exchanged them for glass and silks. Such trade was a marginal activity, with the products of daily subsistence being produced domestically and varying from region to region depending on the climate. Today, trade is an opportunity to exploit the profits of arbitrage (the price differential between two markets), the ability to manipulate currencies, and to take advantage of economies whose labour force are too powerless to negotiate themselves decent wages. It is a system that has created vastly extended supply chains, in which the components for final products may cross the world several times before reaching a market, and where the same goods pass each other either at sea or on over-crowded domestic road networks. The scale of this trade is profitable but hugely costly in terms of carbon emissions that generate no additional human welfare (see Box 6.1).

BOX 6.1   ADVERTISING, GROWTH AND OVER-CONSUMPTION

The advertising industry is a good example of the built-in tendency towards growth and greater consumption being conceived as a productive part of our economy. At the end of the Second World War, it made sense to encourage greater consumption, since the origin of the war was partly the result of the economic instability and unemployment of the 1930s. This led to the deliberate creating of death-dated goods that would expire once they had passed their warranty date as well as the creation of short-term fashions to encourage the need for replacing goods and clothing before they had worn out. The modern advertising industry sells objects apparently to satisfy a certain need when really they satisfy a deeper and perhaps even subliminal desire. Beautiful women draped over fast cars persuade young men that they will acquire sexual allure as well as a set of wheels. In this way our desires and needs are themselves distorted, ultimately leading us towards lives of dissatisfaction and longing. The role of Edward Bernays, Freud's nephew, was seen as central to this broader use of psychological insights, which he first described in his uncritical book on propaganda. As a green economist I would challenge the role of the advertising industry in creating dissatisfaction to drive greater production for profit. In the growth paradigm because its services can be sold it contributes to GDP, but from a sustainability perspective it reduces human wellbeing and drives the over-use of resources – and hence is largely destructive.

IS SMALL STILL BEAUTIFUL?

In this section I turn to the issue of how the question of scale might be included in a business school curriculum. Following the suggestion made in the film *The Corporation* and other academic work along similar lines, it is crucial to make students aware of the particular restrictions of the corporate firm's legal identity, although I do not have time to cover this here (for further information see Byrne, 2010). As demonstrated in the first section above, raising questions about the power that results from the excessive size of some corporations is possible within economic theory itself. However, it can also arise from a moral, ethical or spiritual position which takes a radical view of the equality or even the inherent divinity of each human person. An example can be found in the religious organization the Society of Friends or Quakers, who have a unique business model, which seeks ethical and even divine inspiration before a decision is reached.[3] The process of globalization and the dominating position of certain (largely US-based) corporations negate this equality and so are inherently unethical. Similarly, the control of the world's resources by a small number of corporations, and the quest to exert greater control as those resources become scarce

---

[3]Forbes website discusses the Quaker business model at www.forbes.com/2009/10/09/quaker-business-meetings-leadership-society-friends.html (accessed 14 January 2015).

(see Dobbs et al., 2011), stand counter to the view of human beings as having an equal right to access the resources they need to ensure a decent life. It is in this context that I am proposing a return to appropriate scale as part of the business school curriculum.

The appropriately scaled enterprise

One response to the problem of excessive scale, and the excessive power it enables global corporations to exercise, is to use the anti-trust legislation that exists in all jurisdictions to ensure that markets are open to new entrants and not unduly concentrated. In an era of multinational corporations this control must also of necessity be exercised at a global level. While this is a task for politicians it is important that students of business understand the abuse of power that global consolidation constitutes.

Can we suggest a form of business that does not have the same incentive to grow? I believe that the self-managed firm or worker co-operative might be such a form. In a worker co-operative power is shared, so each individual employee or manager does not gain from an increase in the size of the firm. Since the governance form requires democratic engagement, increasing size can be argued to work against the central motivation of the firm. In addition, because profits are shared according to effort rather than ownership share, there is little advantage to owners in increasing turnover beyond a certain size (Johanisova et al., 2013). The size of the enterprise is naturally limited by the ability of those employed there rather than the desire of the owners to accumulate value (Box 6.2).

BOX 6.2 CO-OPERATIVES: WHY SIZE MATTERS

Co-operatives are limited by the size of their membership, since once the enterprise expands beyond the size at which all members can be present in the same meeting the mutual principle becomes watered down. Although some of the most successful co-operatives are very large, this can lead to a degeneration of their co-operative values, as we have seen recently in the case of the UK's Co-operative Bank. The need to elect representatives reduces engagement and ends direct accountability. It can also lead to complex, nested management structures which reduce transparency and accountability. For this reason co-operatives are more likely to expand by networking and by creating spin-offs than by expanding into ever-larger businesses. This tension was faced in the past by the Mondragon Group, which split co-operatives in two when the membership grew above 500 in order to maintain personal relationships and the ability to make democratic decisions. However, more recently the Group has operated more like a conventional corporate, with offshore subsidiaries, partly as a result of pressure from capitalist competitors. For similar reasons the UK retail co-operatives went through a period of consolidation, where local links and democratic accountability were undermined.

The threats of the globalized economy

In 1973 E.F. 'Fritz' Schumacher published the book that provided the mantra for the environmental movement: *Small Is Beautiful*. He based his critique of the post-war obsession with scale on his observation of the operation of the UK National Coal Board, when he worked there as an economist. He was concerned about the wasteful use of energy inherent in larger and more complex social and economic systems, but he also argued for the importance of human scale for personal and spiritual reasons, identifying the 'dangers to the integrity of the individual when he feels as nothing more than a small cog in a vast machine and when the human relationships of his daily working life become increasingly dehumanized' (Schumacher, 1973: 242). He believed that beyond a certain scale the human spirit could not flourish and argued for a human-scale economy and for technology appropriate for community use that did not alienate the people who produced or consumed it.

Rather than analysing the historical development and existing operation of systems such as the EU single market or the NAFTA free-trade area, students should be encouraged to critique such vast and dominating structures. They should be free to consider how these organizations are impacting on the ability of countries in the majority world to achieve an acceptable material lifestyle.

PEDAGOGY FOR A HUMAN-SCALE ECONOMY

Given the wider context, what can business schools do to address the question of whether growth is necessarily good at the firm or economy level? The economy operates on a number of taken-for-granted assumptions and is supported in this by the narrow way that economics is taught in our universities. Business schools have a role in supporting a critical examination of the wider business context. At a micro- and macro-level faculty can question some of these assumptions and support students to change the status quo. This section explores a particular pedagogy of teaching 'pluralist economics' which might help business schools to begin to engage with the problem.

Pluralist economics

As previously stated, 'growth' is the hegemonic idea within the capitalist economy and the neoclassical economic theory that supports and reinforces it. Hence the most important first step in questioning growth is to adopt a pluralist approach to the teaching of economics within business schools. Pluralist economics is based on a critical approach to pedagogy, in contrast to the neoclassical approach which is taught as a self-contained system of ideas, more akin to a catechism than an intellectual discipline. Unlike most other disciplines outside theology, economics as a system of education is monist not pluralist;

orthodoxy is encouraged while heterodoxy is discouraged (Negru, 2009). The consequence of this was that when the 2008 financial crisis hit there was only one tool in the toolbox and that tool, a globalized market economy based on the corporation, has failed to fix the economy.

A pluralist approach to teaching economics requires us to demonstrate respect for alternative views and to have a practical approach to the problems that the discipline seeks to solve. The conflict between opposing theories is likely to be most effective in generating solutions rather than clinging to received wisdom and unchanging views of reality. To quote the editor of the *International Journal of Pluralism and Economics Education*, 'pluralism instills empathy, dialogue, humility, and understanding. Monism [its opposite], by filtering out different views, prevents one from knowing which view is better in certain situations. Monism is antithetical to pluralism and antithetical to education' (Reardon, 2009: 267).

Pluralist economics focuses on the key questions of economics – the production and allocation of resources and goods – but within the context of a commitment to social justice and sustainability. In the forthcoming text *Introducing Economics* (Reardon et al., 2014) insights from a range of theory and set contemporary discussions are placed within a historical context. The impact of the growth imperative on sustainability and its blindness to questions of equity will inevitably be covered since it is only the narrow view of neoclassical economics that we need not concern ourselves with resource scarcity.

In introducing a pluralist approach to economics education we need to begin when students first encounter the subject, whether in school or university. Most importantly, we need to begin with the questions, rather than with offering a precooked theoretical system, which is the way most economics courses are structured. In my own university I have recently introduced such a course, beginning with the central question facing any economic actor: how do I achieve a livelihood? This question makes no presumption about how resources are allocated or whether I choose to make my living directly using resources or through seeking a job. It thus seeks to be culturally as well as historically neutral. In discussing production, the course offers a range of alternative structures within which production might take place, from the family firm, to the co-operative and the corporation.

It is at the macro, or international, level that most existing economics courses fall so far short of the ideal. In spite of the gross inequalities of wealth demonstrated by the global economy, it is often the case that issues of allocation and equity are left to the final few chapters of a book, which the course frequently does not reach at all. The issue of sustainability and a wise use of resources is also often left for second- or third-year courses, which many business students do not take. By contrast, the pluralist course at my university teaches all macroeconomics topics through the prism of equity and sustainability. It also includes examples from a range of societies rather than the exclusive focus on 'developed' Western societies that typifies most courses. Finally, it includes a range of theoretical approaches, from the work of Brazilian economist Celso Furtado to the insights of Polish economist Michal Kalecki.

The role of 'critical' faculty

It is important for teachers to be explicit about the inconsistency between the theory of perfect competition as taught in economics and the techniques of market control taught in strategy. For example, teaching staff could introduce the model of perfect competition and then compare it with the actual behaviour of companies, and with the dominant theories of strategy. Students could discover how market power is really exercised, and see how reality challenges the strictures of economic theory. Students should be invited to critique the reality of market domination, and to explore some of the ethical questions this raises. For example, many students will be committed to finding jobs with global corporations or to be consumers of their brands, and so this is challenging for them.

The challenge of teaching economics from the real world that we live in is that this can present students with immediate ethical dilemmas. I teach in London, the heart of the global finance industry, and many of my students are aspiring to work in the city of London. Explaining to them how the global financial institutions guarantee that many in the world will be left in poverty naturally causes them some concern. However, the advantage of the globalized education system of the twenty-first century is that other students have experience of societies where many people still earn a living directly from the land. So students are able to bring their diverging and stimulating experience to questions about sources of livelihood.

CONCLUSION

The teaching of economics is a key barrier to the development of progressive and sustainable economic systems in our modern world. Central to the misleading nature of conventional economic theory is the idealization of growth. As pedagogues it is essential that we raise the question of whether growth is the unalloyed benefit that economic theory suggests. Challenging the centrality and hegemony of growth is the first step towards developing a participatory and inclusive economics curriculum.

REFERENCES

Byrne, T.P. (2010) 'False profits: reviving the corporation's public purpose', *UCLA Law Review*, Discourse 25, 57: 25–49.

Cato, M.S. (2009) *Green Economics: An Introduction to Theory, Policy and Practice*. London: Earthscan.

Dietz, R. and O'Neill, D. (2013) *Enough is Enough*. London: Earthscan.

Dobbs, R., Smit, S., Remes, J., Manyika, J., Roxburgh, C. and Restrepo, A. (2011) *Mapping the Economic Power of Cities*. Washington, DC: McKinsey Global Institute, McKinsey and Co.

Douthwaite, R. (1992) *The Growth Illusion*. Totnes: Green Books.

Jackson, T. (2009) *Prosperity without Growth: Economics for a Finite Planet*. London: Earthscan.

Johanisova, N., Crabtree, T. and Frankova, E. (2013) 'Social enterprises and non-market capitals: a path to de-growth?', *Journal of Cleaner Production*, 38: 7–16.

Kohr, L. (1957) *The Breakdown of Nations*. London: Routledge and Kegan Paul.

Mankiw, N.G. (2012) *Principles of Economics* (6th edn). Mason, OH: Cengage.

Negru, I. (2009) 'Reflections on pluralism in economics', *International Journal of Pluralism and Economics Education*, 1 (1/2): 7–21.

Reardon, J. (2009) *The Handbook of Pluralist Economics Education*. London: Routledge.

Reardon, J., Madi, A.M. and Cato, M.S. (2014) *Introducing Economics*. London: Pluto.

Schumacher, E.F. (1973) *Small Is Beautiful*. London: Blond and Briggs.

Waring, M. (1988) *If Women Counted: A New Feminist Economics*. New York: Harper and Row.

7 CAN LEADERSHIP BE VALUE-FREE?

Ken Parry and Audun Fiskerud

HOW DID WE LEAVE MORALITY AND ETHICS OUT OF THE STUDY OF LEADERSHIP?

Well, we think the quick answer to that question is that we introduced into the curriculum greed, anger, pride, envy and gluttony. Unfortunately, morality and ethics never were in the curriculum of business schools, let alone of leadership courses. These two topics have been given lip-service over the years and still are treated as a platitude or an add-on to business programmes. Indeed, the morality of leadership is a very contestable discourse. Our colleagues Bernie Bass and Paul Steidlmeier differentiated between pseudo-transformational and authentic transformational leadership. More recently, Fred Walumbwa and others have differentiated authentic from in-authentic leadership. Quite recently, there is still an empirical investigation into destructive leadership, the implication being that even though it is destructive, it is still leadership. The immediacy with which Adolf Hitler emerges in classroom discussions about leadership illustrates the contestability of morality within notions of leadership. To be fair, he is used as an extreme example in order to make a point, yet many people still see him as a benchmark for leadership. As most scholars do, we consider morality to be the sum of the rights and wrongs of action within a particular social setting; and ethics to be the art and science of thinking about morality.

A less confrontational and more amoral advocate of this message was Milton Friedman (1970), one of the most prominent exponents of free-market, neo-liberal economics. He proposed that a corporation's social responsibility is to increase its profits, working within legal and social norms, but generally left to pursue its own self-interest as much as it likes. Within this narrative, morality and ethics are seen as the responsibility of government. Friedman was not writing about leadership. Rather, he was writing about people who run companies; people who have become known as 'leaders'. This traditional view of the role of corporations has permeated management theory and practice for decades, and such a narrative for business is still a reality in the minds of many managers today. This traditional view is being seen as Brute Capitalism, *vis-à-vis* Moral Capitalism. This traditional view has dominated business curricula for decades. Arguably, it still does.

What we are experiencing at the moment is the devastation of societal systems around the world as well as frequent business scandals resulting from a dominant amoral management ideology. Note the use of the word amoral, meaning acting without regard for morality, as opposed to immoral, meaning violating moral principles. The important question is whether corporations do in fact have moral duties. Current influential business, management and leadership theories cover a wide range of academic disciplines including psychology, sociology and economics. Sumantra Ghoshal (2005) reminds us that collectively, these theories have converged on a negative view of human nature and of the role and responsibilities of corporations in our society. Practices in both private and public sector institutions seem to have succumbed to the corrupting influence of money, status and power. Moreover, leadership is still pitched at the person who is at the very head of these responsibilities – the senior manager – 'leader'.

The majority of business schools appear largely to base what they teach on the principles of Brute Capitalism, despite an increasing number of their graduates yearning for a greater sense of purpose and being drawn towards social entrepreneurship (Porter and Kramer, 2011). Witness the Bond Business School mission statement as 'building tomorrow's business leaders: one by one'. The mission statement of Harvard Business School is: 'We educate leaders who make a difference in the world'. The more verbose mission statement of the Wharton School at UPenn is: 'In a world defined by global markets and hyper-speed communications, the challenges of leadership have changed. Wharton is committed to devoting our wide-ranging resources and innovative energy to build and share the knowledge needed by individuals, businesses, and public institutions to excel in this evolving global arena'. Leadership is central to the missions of most (if not all) business schools. There appears to be nothing in these mission statements about ethics and morality, but they all mention leaders and/or leadership and an ominous suggestion of Brute Capitalism. By 'leaders' these business school statements refer to captains of industry. By leadership, they refer to how those people run their businesses.

The results of Brute Capitalism have included missed opportunities and public distrust, and business school curricula will need to broaden in several areas, suggest Porter and Kramer. Many of the worst misconducts of recent business practices arguably stem from a set of ideals which have emerged from business school academicians over the last few decades. Ghoshal (2005) also suggests that business schools do not necessarily need to create new courses; they need to simply stop teaching several of the old ones, leadership for example. Regrettably, by propagating ideologically inspired amoral theories, often under the rubric of 'leadership', business schools have removed any sense of moral responsibility from their students, according to Ghoshal. At best we are misleading students. At worst, we are creating monsters.

By contrast, in a 'stakeholder corporation', leadership fosters contributions to society. Apart from more passive actions such as charity and various forms of corporate giving, stakeholder corporations inspire active engagement for the wellbeing of their communities (Maak and Pless, 2006). We observe a consensus in the literature that the stakeholder framework is useful in the analysis of both the strategic and normative challenges faced by organizations. Furthermore, it appears that good relationships with stakeholders are vital to the success of corporations. Such a relationship is heading towards a new understanding of 'moral' and 'ethical' leadership.

Possession of power places people in office; in political office, social office and in commercial office. Similarly, people in office are attributed with power. With the privilege of holding office comes a range of responsibilities. Some of these responsibilities are ethical. Craig and Gustafson (1998) said that integrity is about *not* doing the bad things, rather than just doing the good things. Moreover, they also recognized the value of supererogatory behaviours, wherein one goes above and beyond normal expectations of altruism or citizenship, even though such behaviour is not specifically called for. We suggest that supererogatory behaviours might be the key to ethical leadership – doing more for the community rather than merely doing enough for the organization. Notions like this do not appear to be in leadership curricula.

We have recently witnessed calls for a change of focus in leadership theory, away from the 'hero' to more of a 'host'. Joanne Ciulla has reminded us that leadership is increasingly becoming a practice of ethics and the careful exercise of responsibility. As Richard Bolden and his colleagues have stated, this responsibility is towards a wide variety of stakeholders, many of whom are currently left out of the discursive practices in corporations.

While the dominant leadership literature has largely emphasized the relationship between leaders and followers in the organization, and defined followers somewhat instrumentally as 'subordinates', Maak and Pless (2006) argue that leadership in fact takes place in interaction with a wide variety of followers as stakeholders both inside and outside the corporation (see Box 7.1).

BOX 7.1   LEADERSHIP AS TRUST

A vital part of creating sustained business success is the leadership responsibility of building public trust, in order to maintain the licence to operate provided by society, and to maintain a reputation as a good corporate citizen. We suggest going past public trust and calling it community trust. Trust is putting oneself at a position of vulnerability, at the discretion of another person. In other words, if you trust someone, truly trust them, you will put your life in their hands. Therefore, people in the community will trust people who help them; and they are less likely to trust people who make money from them. A responsible leader's primary task is to weave an inclusive web where leaders engage themselves among equals. Plato already realized this in his 'Statesman' where he regarded leaders as weavers, whose core task was to weave different people and groups together into the fabric of society (or community) (Ciulla, 2004). People will follow other people whom they trust.

Let's put this idea into the context of intended business school outcomes. If your company exploits your community, then your community will not trust you or your company. Therefore, they will not follow you; they will not patronize your business. Therefore, you are less likely to succeed financially. Who would put their life in the hands of a business that worked only for the benefit of its shareholders; and not for the benefit of its community?

Maak and Pless (2006) propose that a responsible leader must be a steward and a custodian of values and resources; a good citizen and a caring and active member of communities; a servant to various others; and a visionary by offering inspiration and perspective about a desirable future. The concept of the leader as a 'great person' (it used to be 'great man') is arguably no longer particularly valid. Rather, leaders should be regarded as equal humans who earn from their followers a licence to lead. Perhaps leadership should no longer be thought of as actions by individuals within their companies. Rather, it could be thought of as leadership by individuals and their companies within their communities. It is about helping the community (of which the company happens to be just one member). Traditional business curricula state that individuals lead subordinates, within the context of a company. Perhaps, new business curricula could state that companies (led by people) lead their communities. The romance of leadership and our understanding of charismatic attributions will help us to conclude that the person in charge will be attributed with leadership. The example of Richard Branson comes to mind as an exemplar of this narrative.

All things considered, Pless and Maak's (2011) 'responsible leadership' is a multilevel response to the deficiencies in existing leadership frameworks and theories; to high-profile scandals on individual, organizational and systemic levels; and to new and emerging social, ethical and environmental challenges in an increasingly connected world. Responsible leadership is geared towards the concerns of others and asks for what and to whom leaders are responsible. Responsible leaders are trusted. If they are trusted, they are seen as ethical. This comment may seem to be stating the obvious, but it is arguably one of the most under-researched concepts in this field, as well as one of the most relevant. At its core, this discussion seeks to clarify who the 'others' are and what responding to their concerns entails.

In business schools, we suggest that we might be heading towards a new discourse for leadership. Such a discourse might counter the problems of the domination of Brute Capitalism, and might introduce a reality that reflects a more responsible leadership.

WHAT ARE THE CONSEQUENCES OF THIS GAP?

To be fair, all the ills of Brute Capitalism cannot be blamed on business schools. However, the discourse of the teaching of business schools falls too easily into greed, pride, anger and gluttony. By contrast, the discourse of business schools should fall more readily into messages of benevolence, wisdom, prudence and courage, among other virtuous and desirable tactics.

Studies have found that business students are actually less ethical than students in other disciplines. Ferraro and colleagues note that a 'growing body of evidence suggests that self-interested behaviour is learned behaviour, and people learn it by studying economics and business' (Ferraro et al., 2005: 14). Business and economics majors are more likely to 'free-ride'; are more likely to keep more resources for themselves; and are more corruptible than others. Further, Nonis and Swift (2001) found that students who engaged in unethical behaviour in college were more likely to engage in unethical behaviour at work. Wang et al. (2011) found a positive relationship between economics education and students' attitudes towards greed, and McCabe et al. (2006) found that MBA students cheat more than non-business students.

Miller (1999) has proposed that business students do not come into business schools this way, and argues that they learn about the principle of rational self-interest and believe that they are supposed to behave this way. Findings such as these have led some scholars to go so far as to propose that the entire paradigm underlying business education needs to change if we are to overcome the ethical difficulties we are currently facing (see References and Further Reading). There is the possibility at the moment that learning leadership in business schools actually reinforces the semiotic connotation of 'economics' and 'business' as being one that reflects Brute Capitalism. Giacalone and Promislo's (2013) notions of econophonics and potensiphonics, discourses that pervade business school curricula, reflect and reinforce Brute Capitalism. Econophonics is the language of quantification and financial valuation. Potensiphonics is the language of power and domination. These languages eschew virtue and destroy trust (Box 7.2).

BOX 7.2   ARE STUDENTS IN BUSINESS SCHOOLS LEARNING HOW TO BE BUSINESS MONSTERS?

Given the extensive recent media coverage of wide-ranging corporate scandals and misdeeds, public sentiment has increasingly called into question business leaders' willingness to put the public good above the company bottom line. As Michael Porter said in a recent interview: 'High unemployment, rising poverty, and the public's dismay over corporate greed continue to challenge the market system and the legitimacy of business itself' (Porter, 2010: 1). Businesses appear to be facing yet another crisis of public confidence brought on in part by an apparent lack of moral character in some executive suites – the domain of 'leadership'. This crisis of public confidence has recently become more visible as thousands of Americans took to the streets early in the twenty-first century in the 'Occupy Wall Street' protests directed at corporate greed – protests that expanded to other cities nationwide. We suggest that the resultant low public confidence in business leadership leads to reduced trust, which in turns diminishes following. Low following identifies poor quality leadership.

Corporations are commonly perceived to be prospering at the expense of the broader community, and the general legitimacy of business has fallen to worryingly low levels (Porter and Kramer, 2011). This low perceived legitimacy reduces trust considerably. After all, who would put their life in the hands of an illegitimate businessperson? Kochan observed that the main cause of 'recent' corporate scandals in the United States lies in the 'over-emphasis American corporations have been forced to give in recent years to maximizing shareholder value without regard for the effects of their actions on other stakeholders' (2002: 139, in Ghoshal, 2005: 81). Although now several years old, this claim is still relevant, we feel.

We are witnessing a growing discussion about the appropriateness of current leadership theories to address pertinent leadership challenges. This discussion often cites the role and responsibilities of business leaders in society, frequently in light of social and environmental crises. Despite the strong push for reforms, irresponsible leadership was a primary cause of the global economic crisis of 2008.

The summation of our argument is this. Business schools presently treat leadership as influence by individuals over organizations for the benefit of stockholders and other like-minded stakeholders. Instead, it should be treated as ethical influence by organizations over their communities and within their communities for the benefit of those communities. Therefore, business schools can play an assertive role in this by being more reflexive in the way they teach leadership. Also, changing the discourse of leadership, in particular, will aid this.

HOW DO WE PROPOSE TO ADDRESS THIS GAP?

Our propositions reflect a vaccine more than an antidote. An antidote will instantly fix the symptoms; but a vaccine will reduce the possibility of the disease occurring at all. These issues cannot be fixed instantly. After all, business students will still have to study strategy and finance and accounting and 'bottom-line' outcomes. Businesses will still have to make money and be financially resilient. We will need to massage the discourses that students engage in so that they are sympathetic to something other than making money for shareholders.

Leadership is popularly visualized as a social influence process. There is a general consensus for this notion among the leadership scholarly community. We are taking the social influence notion away from just the 'organization' and taking it to the 'community'. We suggest that leadership might be a 'community-enhancing influence process'. To simplify this apparently verbose and possibly even pretentious description, perhaps we could think more simply of 'leadership as community enhancement'. Influence is implied. Social responsibility is implied. The more selfless socialized power motivation is implied (*vis-à-vis* the more selfish personalized power motivation). Trust and therefore following will be generated. Ethical and moral leadership are implied as a result of these outcomes. However, the question still remains of what we can do in business schools about implementing this new mindset.

Changing the curriculum might be just a change in terminology and be seen as a platitude, just as in the past with emasculated terms like 'communication' and 'ethics'. There is more to this problem than just having a new ethics course. This has already been done. We do need more sociology and philosophy to enrich the psychology and finance and accounting and strategy that are still necessary. However, we cannot just add more courses. Also, we will fight a losing political battle to substitute sociology for psychology, for example. Rather than changing through the forced implementation of actual systemic power, which will generate resistance, we should use symbolic power to our advantage. We should change the discourse.

CHANGE THE DISCOURSE ABOUT LEADERSHIP IN BUSINESS SCHOOL PROGRAMMES

For at least the first half of the semester, the context for leadership should be taken out of the domain of the corporate organization. Leadership should be disconnected from business at this point. Followers now are the community, the poor, the underprivileged. Leadership becomes the domain of the student, who now becomes a player in the script that is presented to them. The discourse becomes one of helping the community and the community will follow you (and your organization). Help the community and all people will follow. Students learn leadership by looking at movies and current affairs. Movies dramatize leadership. Examples might be *Whale Rider* or *Milk* or *Hotel Rwanda* or *Moneyball* or *American Gangster* or *The King's Speech*. Current affairs show leadership in action, including how the community reacts to business decisions. Examples might be the UK phone hacking trial in the second decade of the twenty-first century, or world reaction to the typhoon that hit the Philippines in 2013, or the crack-smoking Toronto mayor in the same year or almost anything that is happening in the world. All the core elements of leadership theory and of leadership curriculum are identified in these dramas.

Students need also to reflect upon their own critical experiences and notable people in their life. Perhaps as an assignment or an internship, they must actually help the community with the business they are learning about. This reflexivity becomes important to understanding their own traits, implicit theories, personality, skills, beliefs and habitus. Teachers start to build in examples from history. The example of the BP Gulf oil spill of 2010 might be introduced. The experience of the Philippines tsunami or the Fukushima tsunami-induced meltdown can be investigated. The success of the Mutuals and Co-operatives in the UK in the early twenty-first century might be examined. The following and community support generated by Cadbury in the UK from the mid-1800s, might be explored. In these ways, the core discourse of leadership is not really changed. Rather, the language has virtue built into it and the role of econophonics and potensiphonics (Giacalone and Promislo, 2013) is reduced. Therefore, the leadership discourse is less reflected by greed, symbolic violence, gluttony and domination.

More reflexivity should be introduced into the teaching of management, organizational behaviour and leadership. Students need to experience 'discontent' and 'unease' (Vaara and Faÿ, 2012). The study of leadership will include research about the theory of leadership. At the same time it should focus on students' own experiences. As an MBA student of ours said in support of these notions, 'Don't discredit negative events, adversity, and tragedy. We should embrace them and realize that sometimes important lessons and revelations can come only from these'. Students learn from their own experiences as well as from the Cadbury experience and from the experience of a journalist who is encouraged to engage in phone hacking. Undergraduate students have had at least 19 years of experience of leadership. So, all students have had much experience upon which to anchor a new discourse about leadership. Indeed, by disengaging leadership from the KPIs of senior management, educators are able to unleash a nobler and more reliable understanding of leadership within students, and then to teach it more effectively.

As Vaara and Faÿ said, we should problematize current ideas, values and practices, rather than taking them for granted and reproducing them within teaching. When leadership is taken out of the organization and given back to the community, students will develop their own ethical consciousness. As a skill-building exercise, students will learn how to construct an inspirational leadership speech. They are in the leadership role, and they speak to an audience about a matter that is close to their heart. It need not be a business speech. It is preferable if it is not a business speech. The students could be a representative of the youth community speaking to their parliament about 'boat people' or 'migrants' or 'refugees' who have to pay people smugglers money to make a dangerous voyage across the sea. In this way, the students develop their own discourse of passion, empathy, emotion, sense-making, sense-giving and ethically defensible influence.

It is only when the social processes of leadership are understood, that leadership should then be taken to the context of business. Towards the end of the semester, students can then take their learning about leadership into a business context. They need to look at how their organization might play a leading role in their community. Finally, only then should students look at how they might lead a workforce. To conclude, our discourse about leadership should include a new criterion for the success of any strategy or decision in business. That criterion should be 'how will this decision help the community?' Hitherto, the criterion has been 'how will this decision help the bottom-line of our company?' That flawed criterion must change.

FURTHER READING

Bolden, R., Hawkins, B., Gosling, J. and Taylor, S. (2011) *Exploring Leadership: Individual, Organizational and Societal Perspectives.* Oxford: Oxford University Press.

Cadsby, C.B. and Maynes, E. (1998) 'Choosing between a socially efficient and free-riding equilibrium: nurses versus economics and business students', *Journal of Economic Behavior and Organization*, 37: 183–92.

Ciulla, J. (2004) *Ethics: The Heart of Leadership* (2nd edn). London: Praeger.

DiPiazza Jr, S.A. and Eccles, R.G. (2002) *Building Public Trust: The Future of Corporate Reporting.* New York: John Wiley.

Ghoshal, S. (2005) 'Bad management theories are destroying good management practices', *Academy of Management Learning and Education*, 4 (1): 75–91. Sumantra Ghoshal also speaks freely and cogently about these issues on YouTube.

Sachs, J.D. (2011) *The Price of Civilization: Reawakening American Virtue and Prosperity.* New York: Random House.

Young, S. (2003) *Moral Capitalism: Reconciling Private Interest with the Public Good.* San Francisco, CA: Berret-Koehler Publishers, Inc. Young writes about brute capitalism as a flawed system but also as a challenge for individuals to respond to. It is from the latter perspective that he writes this book.

REFERENCES

Ciulla, J. (2004) 'Ethics and leadership effectiveness', in J. Antonakis, A.T. Cianciolo and R.J. Sternberg (eds), *The Nature of Leadership*. London: Sage, pp. 508–42.

Craig, S.B. and Gustafson, S.B. (1998) 'Perceived leader integrity scale: an instrument for assessing employee perceptions of leader integrity', *The Leadership Quarterly*, 9 (2): 127–45.

Ferraro, F., Pfeffer, J. and Sutton, R.I. (2005) 'Economics language and assumptions: how theories can become self-fulfilling', *Academy of Management Review*, 30: 8–24.

Friedman, M. (1970) 'The social responsibility of business is to increase its profits', *New York Times Magazine*, 13 September: 32.

Ghoshal, S. (2005) 'Bad management theories are destroying good management practices', *Academy of Management Learning and Education*, 4 (1): 75–91.

Giacalone, R.A. and Promislo, M.D. (2013) 'Broken when entering: the stigmatization of goodness and business ethics education', *Academy of Management Learning and Education*, 12 (1): 86–101

Maak, T., and Pless, N.M. (2006) 'Responsible leadership in a stakeholder society: a relational perspective', *Journal of Business Ethics*, 66: 99–115.

McCabe, D.L., Butterfield, K.D. and Treviño, L.K. (2006) 'Academic dishonesty in graduate business programs: prevalence, causes, and proposed action', *Academy of Management Learning and Education*, 5: 294–305.

Miller, D.T. (1999) 'The norm of self-interest', *American Psychologist*, 54: 1053–60.

Nonis, S. and Swift, C.O. (2001) 'An examination of the relationship between academic dishonesty and workplace dishonesty: a multicampus investigation', *Journal of Education for Business*, 77: 69–77.

Pless, N.M. and Maak, T. (2011) 'Responsible leadership: pathways to the future', *Journal of Business Ethics*, 98: 3–13.

Porter, M.E. (2010) 'How big business can regain legitimacy', *Bloomberg Businessweek*. Retrieved from: www.businessweek.com/stories/2010-05-06/how-big-business-can-regain-legitimacybusinessweek-business-news-stock-market-and-financial-advice (accessed 19 December 2014)

Porter, M.E. and Kramer, M.R. (2011) 'Creating shared value', *Harvard Business Review*, 89 (1/2): 62–77.

Vaara, E. and Faÿ, E. (2012) 'Reproduction and change on the global scale: a Bourdieusian perspective on management education', *Journal of Management Studies* 49 (6): 1023–51.

Wang, L., Malhotra, D. and Murnighan, J.K. (2011) 'Economics education and greed', *Academy of Management Learning and Education*, 10: 643–60.

8 DO BUSINESS SCHOOLS CREATE CONFORMISTS RATHER THAN LEADERS?

David Beech

INTRODUCTION[1]

The creative cultural power of competitive market capitalism has catalysed explosive growth in the global population and quality of life over the past 100 years. In 1900 the global population was around 1.6 billion with an average life expectancy of around 25 years. By 2000 the population was almost 7 billion with an average life expectancy of around 65 years. These are astonishing and unprecedented transformations in the demographic profile and quality of life of billions of individuals across the planet. Manifestly people everywhere increasingly benefit from the cultural power of market capitalism. As anticipated in 1960, by 2050 'industrialisation will have swept away most pre-industrial forms of society … The industrial society knows no national boundaries; it is destined to be a world-wide society' (Kerr et al., 1960: 238) establishing an organizational society of pluralistic varieties of market capitalism, with state market (e.g. China), co-ordinated market (e.g. Germany), and liberal market (e.g. USA) capitalism the main early twenty-first-century varieties (Scott, 2009).

Clearly, the cultural power of globalizing market capitalism has generated unprecedented prosperity. In parallel, the destructive forces of capitalism can wreak havoc with people's lives, and there is the real prospect that the human species will not survive the twenty-first century. The threats are multiple and

[1]I am grateful to Chris Mabey and Wolfgang Mayrhofer for their patience, support, and advice, and for the support and advice of colleagues at the Sarum College QBSDA Conference, Salisbury, 23–24 June 2013. I am also grateful to Kirk Chang for comments on an earlier draft.

interdependent, e.g. global climate change due to the humanly created Anthropocene and current consumption by 7 billion people of one and a half times more resources than the earth's ecosystems can renew each year with present technologies and ways of life. Accordingly, working together, the individuals of the ultra-social group-living human species must address profound issues if the astonishing achievements in quality of life catalysed by the cultural power of market capitalism are to be sustained and advanced further.

This chapter addresses the question of who benefits from the cultural power, practices and effects of market capitalism. In particular the chapter asks whether managers are 'conformists rather than leaders in the larger affairs of society' (Kerr, et al., 1960: 245). Business schools aim to educate managerial leaders for business and society (Snyder, 2012). To fulfil this aim there is an obligation on business schools to enable students to understand how the cultural power and effects of market capitalism can be evolved and deployed for the common good. In this chapter I draw upon the work of American sociologist Talcott Parsons and others to address these issues. A scene setting introduction on the challenges facing capitalism and business education in the twenty-first century is followed by three sections: first, on cultural power; second, on value configurations; and, third, on the responsibilities of institutional leadership. I conclude with a call for business schools to deploy, research and evolve the concepts and analytical tools set out here in their curricula for undergraduate, postgraduate and executive education.

CHALLENGES FACING CAPITALISM AND BUSINESS EDUCATION

Edward Snyder, Dean of Yale School of Management, describes three broad sets of issues about market capitalism that business schools need to equip their students to understand and help to resolve over the coming decades (Snyder, 2012). These are, first, energy and environment; second, health and education; and, third, income disparities and political pressures. Colleagues in other chapters in this book write eloquently about these issues and there is a burgeoning literature on them which is not reviewed here. Snyder's key point is that business schools in the twenty-first century must develop a fundamental competence in their education programmes: 'understanding the complexities within and across business and society to enable leadership in a more complex world' (Snyder, 2012: 150). This is a requirement beyond the emphasis in the twentieth century on developing two other competencies, first, to understand 'how markets work and the unrelenting nature of competition', and, second, to understand 'how organizations function and the role of teams, networks, and individual leadership' (Snyder, 2012: 149).[2]

---

[2]Snyder's approach is similar to that of his AACSB colleagues and the AACSB view of the role of business schools.

There is a neglected and fundamental political challenge if business schools are to succeed in educating managers to understand and equip them to help resolve the issues generated by the evolving cultural power of capitalism. A comparative international review of management in 1960 concluded: 'Since they are preoccupied with the internal affairs of enterprise, which become ever more complex, the members of the managerial class are prone to become conformists rather than leaders in the larger affairs of society' (Kerr et al., 1960: 244–5). The tacit reason given for this is that managers work under a contract of employment which obliges them to comply with the reasonable instructions of superordinate managers who in turn comply with the requirements of the owners of the enterprise or a 'board of directors' acting as agents of the owners. Accordingly the primary duty of managers is to ensure the owners of an enterprise benefit from their actions.

Little has changed in half a century in this respect. The asymmetry of power between each individual manager and the owner(s) of an enterprise encourages compliance and conformity. Consequently, yet unintentionally, the structure and control of the economy by privately owned enterprises under the rule of law in competitive markets produces, sustains and accelerates the energy, environment and inequality issues described by Snyder. Private ownership is a key reason, for example, that greenhouse gas emissions continue to increase and for ever widening income inequality across the global commons. Pursuit of legitimate self-interest by the owners of enterprise, or boards of directors acting on their behalf, continues to catalyse a potentially catastrophic and terminal tragedy of the commons. Ecocide through climate change and/or resource depletion is a realistic prospect; as is ecocide due to competing state interests unleashing a nuclear holocaust.

There is a growing, albeit perhaps nascent, appreciation that the cultural power of capitalism is rooted in perpetual co-operation and conflict between the relatively more 'visible' hand of government and the relatively 'invisible' hand of the price mechanism in competitive capitalist markets (Ingham, 2011). According to Weber, the owners of private enterprise 'depend on the state's autonomous power, but they are not subordinated to it' (Ingham, 2011: 33). In particular, since what Weber called the 'memorable alliance' in the seventeenth century between owners of capital and the state, capitalism 'as an economic system [has] operated transnationally in a way that [continues to be] beyond the control of any single state or alliance of states' (Ingham, 2011: 33). Crucially, globalizing market capitalism and its institutional arrangements – e.g. markets under state controlled rule of law, backed by lethal force if required – are an *unintended consequence* of the need in the seventeenth century for states to gain access to finance from the owners of capital, often to finance the conduct of a war.

The institutional arrangements of states and markets enact the cultural power of collective beliefs, values, interests, attitudes and norms. Accordingly, if business schools are to fulfil their mission of educating managerial leaders for business and society then managers across private, public and not-for-profit sectors need to understand how institutional arrangements – institutions and institutional practices – are an expression of the cultural power which enables the enactment and evolution of individual and community ways of life. This requires managers to understand cultural power, value configurations and institutional leadership as they relate to business and society if they are to become leaders rather than conformists in the larger affairs of society. We consider each of these in turn below.

CULTURAL POWER

Cultural power is the capacity to produce collectively based intentional effects, e.g. playing football. It is based in the co-evolving, co-operative and competitive social practices, collective representations and institutions of a community that enable individuals and their communities to survive and flourish (see Box 8.1 below) (Beech, 2013a). Power is often neglected in social science, especially the power created by institutional facts, such as the constitution of the USA and the Universal Declaration of Human Rights, which enable transformations in the conditions of human life (Haugaard and Ryan, 2012). Typically power in social science is construed in terms of the capacity to exercise zero-sum competitive power over others in an interactive decision-making contest.

BOX 8.1   THE STRUCTURE OF CULTURAL POWER AND DECISION-MAKING

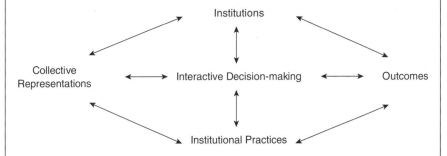

Figure 8.1   The structure of cultural power and decision-making

Cultural power is the capacity that enables individuals and their communities to survive and flourish; it is the capacity to do things together that could not be done alone, like building dams and road transport systems and inventing, deploying

(Continued)

(Continued)

and evolving the institutions and institutional practices of governments, markets, taxes and money.

More precisely, cultural power is based on the co-evolving co-operative and competitive social practices (inclusive interactive decision-making and institutional practices and associated social structures, individual learning and socialization), the collective representations (the collective beliefs, values, interests, attitudes and norms of a group of individuals), and institutions (e.g. language and roles, rules and sanctions) collectively created by individuals that enable individuals and their communities to survive and flourish.

An institution is a system of constitutive rules. Such rules are established as institutions by the interactive social practice of human agreement or acceptance. Institutions include language, marriage, money, leadership, government, property, limited liability companies and markets. Institutions derive from social practices, collective representations and collective intentions. Institutions embody the culture level collective representations and social practices of the individuals in a social group. Collective representations are derived from co-evolving culture level belief and value orientations and individual level beliefs and motivational values and the social practices associated with these.

The institutions and associated collective representations and social practices of a community govern the development, operation and ongoing evolution of social life, including the development, operation and evolution of markets and public, private and not-for-profit enterprises; and the nation state is a large public societal enterprise or polity. In the twenty-first century institutional rules are generally authorized by the state informed by intra- and extra-state interest groups, e.g. non-governmental organizations and international bodies, such as the International Monetary Fund. Institutional rules include arrangements for the institutional practice of agenda setting which establishes the context for the social practice of interactive decision-making and its outcomes, for example terms of citizenship within a polity, terms of national and international trade, and terms of employment. The context for interactive decision-making is individual level beliefs, motives and action as informed by culture level collective representations and institutions and their social practices, including for example institutional practices for deciding what to include in or exclude from an agenda.

Controversially, Parsons defined power as the generalised capacity to mobilize resources and secure the performance of binding obligations in the interest of the attainment of a collective goal rooted in collective value commitments and configurations of culture level value patterns or orientations (Parsons, 1969). For Parsons this collaborative, culture-level concept of power encompassed Weber's concept of power as the capacity of one actor to enforce their will even if another person tries to oppose them. Parsons combined Weber's orientation to individual motivation (social action is the motivated action of two or more individuals) and the exercise of power by an individual *over* other individuals with Durkheim's orientation to collective conscience and collective representations (the need of individuals for a common core of collective values and moral rules) due to the exercise of power *with* others. In the language of contemporary social ontology collective representations are a culture-level outcome of collective intentions. Thus determinate effects can be the outcome of three general categories of indeterminate causation: physical causes, individual motivational causes, and culturally oriented individual causes. This matters for business research, education and practice.

Business scholar Sumantra Ghoshal challenged business schools to engage with the intentional causes of events yet, unlike Parsons, he did not differentiate between individual intentionality due to individual level beliefs and motivational values and collective intentionality due to culture level collective belief and value orientations (Ghoshal, 2005). Yes, there is a decisive difference between physical causes and individual level motivational causes. In addition, there is an equally, and perhaps even more decisive difference between the motivational causes of a bacterium swimming up a sugar gradient (the directionally oriented motivation of an individual organism) and the collective cultural causes of the ultra-social group-living behaviour of human species individuals. Individual behaviour is a function of physical, individual level motivational, and culture level collectively oriented individual causes of events and effects. The operations of market capitalism primarily originate in cultural causes and are due to the effects of the exercise of cultural power as both Weber and Parsons emphasized.

The ontology in this account of evolving cultural power is that cultural causes derive from motivational causes and motivational causes derive from physical causes. There is only one physical, material world and events are indeed due to the actions of separate physical particles in fields of force and to the motivated and culturally oriented actions of separate individuals in networks of relationships (Searle, 2010).[3] If business schools are to develop the capacity of managers to 'understand the complexities across business and society to enable leadership in a more complex world' then they must understand, engage with and contribute to the evolving cultural power that drives the institutions of government, leadership, organizations and markets (Snyder, 2012). Value configurations or patterns of individual level motivational values and culture level value orientations of individuals are decisive for cultural power, and if managers are to become leaders in the wider affairs of society they must understand the nature and implications of value configurations (Parsons, 1969; Schwartz, 2011; Searle, 2010).

---

[3]Schwartz has identified ten pancultural individual level motivational values: conformity, tradition, security, power, achievement, hedonism, stimulation, self-direction, benevolence, universalism. And he identifies culture level value orientations. Recent research identifies an equivalent underlying structure across individual and culture levels. In this chapter culture level value orientations are considered only in terms of culture level ethical value orientations, e.g. individual level conformity, tradition and security are associated with culture level social order.

VALUE CONFIGURATIONS

Adam Smith's political economy of the market capitalist system of perfect liberty among sovereign individuals is based on the world making an assumption (collective representation) that competitive creativity under the control exercised both by the 'visible' rule of law and by the 'invisible' selective force of the price mechanism along with the natural co-operation and mutual sympathy of human beings will ensure the common good (Ingham, 2011).

This assumes that the common good can be generated by the interdependent and evolving dynamics of: a) the *self-interested* and competitive values of power and achievement; b) the *liberty* and creativity (innovation) values of self-direction, stimulation (e.g. risk taking), and hedonism (utilitarian, seek pleasure and avoid pain); with c) self-interest and liberty controlled by *social order* due to natural conformity both to the rule of law and to the relentless selective discipline of the price mechanism along with natural instincts for security and survival; plus natural instincts for d) a sympathetic and co-operative *concern for others* (benevolence and universalism).[4]

Adam Smith's market capitalist system of perfect liberty is a formidable cocktail because it pulls together a compelling configuration of the core culture level ethical values of moral philosophy, which involve balancing *self-interest* with a *concern for others* (e.g. Rabbi Hillel, see Telushkin, 2010), and the core culture level ethical values of political philosophy, which involve balancing *liberty* with *social order* (e.g. Alexis de Tocqueville).

Varieties of market capitalism (e.g. state, co-ordinated and liberal) each involve their own configurations of culture level value orientations and the social practices, collective representations and institutions (Box 8.1) that produce the cultural power of market capitalism. For example, in a very broad way it can be argued that *liberal* market capitalism prioritizes the cultural values of life (competitive and hierarchical power, security and social order), liberty, and happiness (including hedonism) (Schwartz, 2011). In contrast, again in a very broad way, it can be argued *co-ordinated* market capitalism prioritizes the values of liberty, equality (universalism) and fraternity (a benevolent concern for others and conformity to requirements for social order). Further, it can be argued *state* market capitalism prioritizes the values of harmonious social order and conformity to power and achievement hierarchy values along with the value of kindness (a benevolent concern for others, e.g. Chinese 'ren'). These are very broad generalizations and it is, for example, important to note that before the sixteenth century Chinese culture level value orientations resulted in exceptional creativity (the four great inventions of paper-making, the compass, gunpowder and printing). Moreover, looking forward into the twenty-first century and

---

[4]Happiness, in the USA trio 'life, liberty, and happiness', was originally a framing of Aristotelian flourishing. In contemporary Western societal communities it is often associated with the pursuit of narrow utilitarian hedonism.

beyond, state market capitalism could outperform both liberal and co-ordinated varieties of market capitalism. Alternatively, a plurality of value configurations and associated political economy institutional arrangements may persist, including new varieties, e.g. Islamic market capitalism (Kerr et al., 1960).

Leadership contributions to business and society require a reawakening of attention to the political economy of market capitalism (Ingham, 2011; Scott, 2009). Capitalism as a political, as well as an economic, order was neglected in the twentieth century (Scott, 2009). And, yes, both the politics and economics of capitalism evolve through a Darwinian process of biocultural natural selection as Hayek and other neo-liberals argue. Yet, conscious individual intentions and the collective intentionality that generates innovative institutional facts, like Weber's 'memorable alliance', the evolution of the institution of money into credit creation by banks, and the evolution of limited liability companies, all take us into a different realm than the elegant and deceptive simplicity of self-regulated markets under a beneficent 'invisible hand'.

As Weber and Parsons explained, markets and states are socially constructed and evolving institutional economic and political facts (Ingham, 2011; Parsons, 1960, 1969). For example, 'markets' and 'polities' are created by the collaborative cultural power of group-living individuals as their own evolutionary trajectory unfolds into an unknown and unknowable future. If business schools are to do more than develop managerial leaders as conformists to the economic dynamics of market capitalism for the benefit of owners of private property then they must, in addition, engage their students in understanding the political dynamics of capitalism. The requirement is to equip managerial leaders to understand and contribute to the evolving cultural power of capitalism for the common good, including – let me be clear and as Adam Smith insisted – contributing in the process to their own benefit and to the benefit of owners of private property. Self-interest must be respected. In the early twentieth century the USA experimented with institutional arrangements prohibiting the consumption of alcohol with disastrous consequences. The legitimate domination of institutional governance and of *power over others* is only sustainable when it is vested in the authorizing superordinate *power with others* of citizens. Moreover, self-interest is integral to what and who we are: biocultural beasts balancing values-based needs for and commitments to self-interest and a concern for others with needs for and commitments to liberty and social order. Accordingly, an understanding of the cultural power of capitalism requires an understanding of the differences between the institutional governance and executive strategy responsibilities of leadership of an enterprise.

INSTITUTIONAL LEADERSHIP

Leadership and management of economic enterprise are typically construed in terms of: a) executive, top echelon development, change and elimination of the structure of an enterprise; b) operational, senior and middle manager development and the 'piecing out of structure' in an enterprise; and c) front-line, supervisory and technical manager administrative use of structure in implementing executive decisions (Katz and Kahn, 1978). Executive leadership is typically designated as strategic leadership of the enterprise by the top management team (Denis et al., 2011: 71–85). Further, the influential book *In Search of Excellence* catalysed attention to the significance of superordinate goals and shared values for superior enterprise performance and the responsibility of executive leaders for what is often designated as 'institutional leadership' (Peters and Waterman, 1982).[5]

Institutional leadership is typically construed as values-based executive leadership (Selznick, 1957). However, this neglects a distinction between institutional level governing responsibility for the identity and legitimacy of an enterprise and executive level responsibility for strategic purpose (see Box 8.2) (Beech, 2013b).[6]

BOX 8.2   STRATEGIC LEADERSHIP

LEADERSHIP ROLE	Institutional	Executive	Operational	Frontline
RESPONSIBILITIES ↓→	Legitimacy	Strategy	Coordination	Delivery
Identity	###	++	*	*
Diagnosis	++	*	++	++
Purpose	###	###	*	*
Infrastructure	*	###	###	*
Action	++	++	###	###
Benefits	###	###	###	###
Review	###	###	++	++

© Beech, 2014.

primary role responsibility; ++ significant responsibility; * general responsibility

Table 8.1   Leadership roles and responsibilities

Strategy is continuously adaptive goal-directed thinking, resource deployment and learning in action for stakeholder benefits in evolving circumstances. It is 'the direction and use made of means by chosen ways in order to achieve desired ends' (Gray, 2010).

---

[5]Selznick (1957) construed organizations as technical means to ends instruments. According to Selznick organizations become institutions when they are 'infused with value'. According to Parsons all social interactions, relationships and ways of life, including organizations, are rooted in value-commitments; and humanity and human civilization are rooted in institutions such as language and the ethical obligations constitutive of human identity and meaning.

[6]Table and text used with permission.

Leadership is the exercise of reciprocal influence which engages people in action for common aims and mutual benefits in evolving circumstances. It is the exercise of influence in relation to a common goal.

Strategic leadership encompasses responsibility for institutional and executive *leadership of the enterprise* – economic or political – and operational and frontline *leadership in the enterprise*.

Strategic leadership of the enterprise broadens the idea of strategy from the selection, deployment and evolution of means to realize ends to include attention to the choice of ends and their legitimacy. More precisely:

1. Institutional leadership of the enterprise is governing or board level responsibility for enterprise identity, culture and legitimacy. Achieving and sustaining legitimacy requires the board of an economic enterprise or the legislature of a political enterprise (polity) to get ongoing support and authorization from the wider community for the enterprise purpose, actions and outcomes that are in the interests of the common good. This is the governance responsibility of institutional leadership.
2. Executive leadership of the enterprise is the top level management team or cabinet responsibility for crafting, realizing and evolving the strategic purpose – the direction, aims and values of an enterprise and its staff and associates – in relation to competitive position and to external and internal stakeholder configurations of cultures, interests, resources and infrastructures.
3. Operational leadership in the enterprise is the senior and middle manager responsibility for crafting and evolving within and between the enterprise infrastructure – processes, systems and structures – through which people implement, review and evolve the identity, purpose and co-ordinated action and learning for stakeholder benefits.

Frontline leadership in the enterprise is the frontline manager, team leader and supervisor responsibility for realizing the strategic purpose by engaging people in the action and learning processes through which strategy is implemented and evolved for stakeholder benefits.

In the context of the state or polity, power is developed and deployed between the legislature, executive and judiciary; with the executive typically establishing an operational infrastructure for frontline delivery. In his account of formal organizations, including in particular private and public sector organizations, Parsons differentiated between the governance responsibility of institutional leadership for achieving ongoing support for the legitimacy of the enterprise from the wider community, and the responsibility of managerial or executive leadership both for setting the strategic purpose in relation to the external environment and establishing an infrastructure through which to realize the strategic purpose (Parsons, 1960). Parsons' third level of responsibility was the responsibility of technical frontline managers and staff for delivery of the goods and services of the organization. Further, Parsons emphasized that all three levels of responsibility are embedded in cultural power constituted by collective representations and institutional arrangements (see Box 8.1). And he emphasized decisive qualitative differences between the action orientations of institutional, executive and frontline leadership.

Parsons' separation of the values-based community-authorized legitimacy (institutional leadership) from the values-based strategic agenda of community delegated executive leadership is neglected in contemporary accounts of strategic leadership. In these accounts executive leadership is construed as the instrumental implementation of physical cause-effect means to subjective ends; and, institutional leadership is construed as the instrumental implementation of means to realize value-infused subjective ends (Selznick, 1957). Attention to community authorization of the legitimacy of institutional leadership has disappeared. Institutional and executive levels of strategic leadership are brought together and construed as the prerogative of the owners of private property and their agents (boards of directors and other managers) under the rule of law.

Early twenty-first-century citizens have effectively been disenfranchised with values-based, 'authentic' and routinized charismatic change leadership on behalf of private economic enterprise supplanting the political liberty of once sovereign individuals. The transnational creators and owners of financial capital – banks, not governments, create credit and the money supply – now place their bets and take risks in market casinos (e.g. Wall Street) with losses underwritten by nation state (e.g. Main Street) tax payers (Ingham, 2001). And nation states have to-date been unable to co-ordinate with other nation states to establish internationally binding institutional arrangements to enable the creative discovery of competitive market capitalism as far as possible to be subject to co-operative regulation (control) as far as necessary for the common good. Transnational financial speculators on Wall Street and other bourses around the world now seem to benefit more than citizens on Main Street from the cultural power of market capitalism. Have Adam Smith's system of perfect liberty for sovereign individuals and the republican liberal tradition of freedom from dependence sold out to the neo-liberal project?

CONCLUSION

The aim of education is to develop the values-based ethical cultural power 'to frame purposes, to judge wisely, to evaluate desires by the consequences which will result from acting upon them' and the values-based practical cultural power 'to select and order means to carry chosen ends into operation' (Dewey, [1938] 1998: 74). Individual level motivational values and culture level value orientations are defining sources of cultural power (see Box 8.1). And cultural power is deployed and evolved through all aspects of institutional, executive, operational and frontline leadership (see Box 8.2).

Dean Edward Snyder and other business school deans are working vigorously with their colleagues and other stakeholders, including students, to equip their students to understand and help resolve issues emerging from the evolving cultural power of market capitalism. To do this business schools have an obligation to require students to demonstrate they understand: a) how the cultural power of capitalism is constituted by and evolves through the social practices, collective representations and institutions of political economy; b) the nature, configurations and effects of individual level motivational values and culture level value orientations as co-evolving and defining sources of the evolving cultural power of capitalism and its social practices, collective representations and institutions; and, c) the evolving source of the legitimacy and sustainability of institutional leadership in the continuously co-evolving collective intentions, collective representations and related social practices and institutions of interdependent individuals and their interdependent groups and societal communities in the 'struggle for life' on the increasingly global commons in the humanly created Anthropocene.

While the future is unknown and unknowable the evolving cultural power of market capitalism can be subject to the exercise of informed choice about values-based institutions and values-based institutional leadership and their associated representations and practices. Current quality of life benefits and challenges presaging ecocide have evolved from past choices; future quality of life benefits and challenges will evolve from current choices. Business schools and their staff, students and other stakeholders have a duty to be problem finders, problem solvers and solution implementers, enhancing benefits and resolving issues for the common good. I trust they find that the concepts and analytical tools on cultural power, value configurations and institutional leadership presented here prove useful and I also trust business schools and their students will contribute to advancing professional rigour for practical relevance in understanding, deploying, researching and evolving such tools for the common good. Thereby managers could become leaders rather than conformists in the larger affairs of society.

FURTHER READING

For a stimulating and incisive analysis of the political economy of capitalism, see Geoffrey Ingham (2011), and Philippe de Woot (2014).
For important perspectives on cultural power and institutions, see John Searle (2010) and Asa Andersson (2007).
For a classic analysis of power over others, see Steven Lukes (2005).
For an educational agenda for citizen governed policy design and institutional innovations for the good life, see Donald A. Schon and Martin Rein (1994).
For a perspective on the Anthropocene, see Ian Sample (2014).

REFERENCES

Andersson, A. (2007) *Power and Social Ontology*. Malmo, Sweden: Bokbox Publications.
Beech, D. (2013a) 'Cultural power'. *Working paper.* Cambridge Leadership Development.

Beech, D. (2013b) 'Strategic leadership'. *Working paper.* Cambridge Leadership Development.

Denis, J.-L. Kisfalvi, V., Langley, A. and Rouleau, L. (2011) 'Perspectives on strategic leadership', in A. Bryman, D. Collinson, K. Grint, B. Jackson and M. Uhl-Bien (eds), *The Sage Handbook of Leadership.* Los Angeles: Sage, pp. 71–85.

Dewey, J. ([1938] 1998) *Experience and Education* (60th anniversary edn). Indianapolis: Kappa Delta Pi.

De Tocqueville, A. (1848/1994) *Democracy in America* (12th edn). London: Random House (Everyman's Library).

de Woot, Philippe (2014) *Rethinking the Enterprise: Competitiveness, Technology, and Society.* Sheffield: Greenleaf Publishing.

Ghoshal, S. (2005) 'Bad management theories are destroying good management practices', *Academy of Management Learning and Education*, 4 (1): 75–91.

Gray, C.S. (2010) *The Strategy Bridge: Theory for Practice.* Oxford: Oxford University Press, p. 18.

Haugaard, M. and Ryan, K. (eds) (2012) *Political Power: The Development of the Field.* Leverkusen, Germany: Barbara Budrich Publishers.

Ingham, G. (2011) *Capitalism.* Cambridge: Polity.

Katz, D. and Kahn, R.L. (1978) *The Social Psychology of Organizations* (2nd edn). New York: Wiley.

Kerr, C., Dunlop, J.T., Harbison, F.H. and Myers, C.A. (1960) 'Industrialism and industrial man', *International Labour Review*, 82: 236–50.

Lukes, S. (2005) *Power: A Radical View* (2nd edn). New York: Palgrave Macmillan.

Parsons, T. (1960) *Structure and Process in Modern Societies.* New York: The Free Press.

Parsons, T. (1969) *Political and Social Structure.* New York: Polity Press.

Peters, T.J. and Waterman, R.H. (1982) *In Search of Excellence.* New York: Harper and Row.

Sample, I. (2014) 'Anthropocene: is this the new epoch of humans?', *The Guardian* (Science), 16 October.

Schon, D.A. and Rein, M. (1994) *Frame Reflection: Toward the Resolution of Intractable Policy Controversies.* New York: Basic Books.

Schwartz, S.H. (2011) 'Values: cultural and individual', in F.J.R. van de Vijver, A. Chasiotos and S.M. Breugelmans (eds), *Fundamental Questions in Cross-cultural Psychology.* Cambridge: Cambridge University Press, pp. 463–93.

Scott, B.R. (2009) *The Concept of Capitalism.* Berlin: Springer.

Searle, J.R. (2010) *Making the Social World: The Structure of Human Civilization.* Oxford: Oxford University Press.

Selznick, P. (1957) *Leadership in Administration.* New York: Harper and Row.

Snyder, E.A. (2012) 'Five easy questions', in J. Canals (ed.), *Leadership Development in a Global World: The Role of Companies and Business Schools.* Basingstoke: Palgrave Macmillan, pp. 145–61.

Telushkin, J. (2010) *Hillel: If Not Now, When?* New York: Random House.

9 BUSINESS SCHOOLS, ECONOMIC VIRTUES AND CHRISTIAN THEOLOGY

Andrew Henley

INTRODUCTION

The 2008 global financial crisis has brought into sharp relief a sense of unease about what is and isn't taught in the business school curriculum and whether it has in some way contributed to a financial and moral crisis of the global economy (Rubin and Dierdorff, 2013). Indeed for some time business schools have been criticized for teaching too blind a faith in pseudo-scientific economic analysis – an over-emphasis on the 'objective' analysis of market forces and the deterministic interpretation of economic and financial data. It is certainly the case that much of what business schools teach is rooted in the methodology of economics, exemplified in the emphasis on core economic principles, and their application to the teaching of financial economics, international business analysis, marketing, and to the analysis of business strategy. Business schools typically contain faculty drawn from a range of disciplinary backgrounds, notably sociology and psychology, as well as from economics. However, scratch the surface and economics-educated academics are to be found teaching across the curriculum.

Students are traditionally taught that economics is a 'positive' subject. In other words economic analysis is presumed to provide a non-normative technical toolkit for understanding how prices and quantities arise and their relationship to business profits and performance. Economics is in essence a modernist subject, a product of the Enlightenment project to free the individual from higher moral authority or external teleology. It retains very firmly, however, its own meta-narrative, derived from the notion of the rational economic individual.

The absence of an external teleology in economic analysis is highly problematic, and this chapter explores this point from the perspective of Christian theology. This absence confines the subject to the consideration of economic activity which seeks only to further private wellbeing, focusing on individual rationality. It skews the focus onto outcomes rather than the quality of the behaviour or decisions that might lead to those outcomes. This bias is potentially toxic for the education of business professionals. At best these considerations are based on an incomplete understanding of rationality as reasoning. At worst they are based on an understanding of rationality that is circular and devoid of content. Rational behaviour is that which furthers personal satisfaction (although this need not equate to pure egoism), rather than any higher purpose.

However, the unanswered questions here on the tension between rational and virtuous behaviour are hardly new ones. In the contemporary world, as individuals, businesses and governments grapple with present economic and financial uncertainties, the question of how economic decision-makers should behave is never far from the surface. And yet contemporary economics seems ill-equipped to provide answers to what virtuous business behaviour might look like. Instead normative economic reasoning remains stuck in the sphere of 'because we observe Y and X is related to Y, this individual/business/government ought to do this to X' (and by implication doing 'this' would be virtuous). This is perhaps all the more surprising since within the closely related field of academic enquiry in management decision-making, questions of what constitutes a good or bad decision-making process (in an ethical sense) have come to the fore. To extend this normative enquiry into teleological considerations is to ask the question 'for what purpose should my economic behaviour be directed?'.

In this chapter the implicit conception of virtue within neoclassical economics is explored, alongside the limited and contradictory nature of that understanding. The impact of this on the business school curriculum is sketched. The role of virtue in the development of a Christian theological perspective on economic thinking is explored, and a plea given in favour of the reinstatement of a clear emphasis on personal responsibility and virtue in the curriculum as a means to restore a stronger teleological understanding of the purpose of economic and business activity.

'POSITIVE' ECONOMIC ANALYSIS AND THE FICTION OF *HOMO OECONOMICUS*

The academic discipline of economics is an Enlightenment project. It sought to reconstruct a 'rationalist' understanding of human nature on the basis of abandoning any sense of a higher moral order in favour of human nature 'as is'. In his seminal re-evaluation of moral philosophy, Alasdair MacIntyre describes this project as a rejection of classical theological and philosophical perspectives on human *telos*. What remains in economics is a set of principles for behaviour deprived of a teleological context, with the result that the subject *ab initio* existed in a state of tension (MacIntyre, [1981] 2007). Economic analysis might also be regarded as highly ahistorical – economic decision-makers arrive as Lockian *tabulae rasa* and reason for themselves without recourse to past wisdom or narrative (O'Donovan, 1994) (see Box 9.1)

BOX 9.1   UTILITARIANISM AND THE WRONG *TELOS*

Modern economics, having arisen alongside the Enlightenment abandonment of a belief in created moral order and purpose, has readily found an alternative teleology in nineteenth-century utilitarianism. It retained, albeit in diluted form, the Aristotelian notion of *eudaimonia* (human satisfaction or flourishing) but abandoned any higher purpose for achieving it. It also retained the Stoic faith in the harmony of nature, re-interpreted as the idea that markets will tend towards equilibrium fuelled by the invisible hand (Sedlacek, 2011). Utilitarianism is, of itself, thoroughly teleological and becomes the standard *per se* through which economic actions and outcomes are assessed as just or not. However, it is also consequentialist, and can admit no external deontological considerations of the rightness or otherwise of human action. This is regardless of whether those considerations originate from higher ontological considerations of human existence, or from a Kantian moral reasoning that is independent of a reference to a higher moral order. Put simply, from a Christian theological perspective economics is pursuing the wrong *telos*.

In these respects, economics contrasts sharply with other non-economic social sciences usually represented among other business school faculty. In these, greater emphasis is placed on inductive thinking – the formulation of provisional hypotheses subjected to evaluation using a range of quantitative and qualitative research methods. The understanding of human-nature-as-it-is in (neo)classical economics found expression in the 'rational' individual seeking personal satisfaction in the here and now (or looking into the future, suitably discounted). *Homo oeconomicus* is, in essence, the embodiment of these principles.

THE 'VIRTUE' OF SELF-INTEREST IN THE WORLD OF NEOCLASSICAL ECONOMICS

The economist's defence of self-interest appears to be twofold. Firstly, self-seeking behaviour (regardless of questions of virtue) is a reasonable description of human behaviour, *as is*. Employing the characterization of *homo oeconomicus* need not imply moral assent with all observed economic behaviour. Secondly rational economic behaviour need not imply pure egoism. Whether this permits genuinely altruistic behaviour is, however, an open question. So, the most that can be said is that rational choice is revealed by *ex post* preferences, which in turn are deemed to be rational, providing they remain consistent and independent of the choices of others. In a strict sense, for the economist, virtuous behaviour is behaviour that satisfies the axioms of neoclassical consumer preference theory, since that will, by construction, result in the greatest good for the greatest number.

Some recent authors, most notably McCloskey (2006), have argued persuasively that market-based capitalist economies can be regarded as promoting virtuous behaviour, in the Aristotelian sense that this promotes *eudaimonia*. The argument that self-interest (not necessarily the same as selfishness) is virtuous has resonance. The 'private vice' of self-interested behaviour is virtuous because, through the mechanism of the Smithian 'invisible hand', such behaviour promotes the 'public virtue' of the common good. A failure to act in a manner consistent with a focus on outcome could result in the misallocation of economic resources. Productive and financial inefficiencies follow because resources are not allocated by business decision-makers to their best, that is, most profitable use. Prices for some goods are higher than they would otherwise be, and the concomitant reduction in output leads to the under-employment of productive capacity, perhaps particularly labour and skills. The 'virtuous' pursuit of self-interest by economic agents will correct such misallocations and propel the economy back towards optimality.

Self-interest dictates that if a profitable opportunity arises it should be taken. Such opportunities stimulate entrepreneurial 'virtue' to compete for profit. Schumpeter's 'perennial gale of creative destruction' ([1942] 1950: 83) describes the creative and innovative paradox of the entrepreneurial process. This is well understood in business schools, and the recent development of courses on entrepreneurship often takes this important observation as a starting point. On the other hand the persistence of market power, and failure of the entrepreneurial process, are usually attributed to the existence of some barrier to market entry, justifying a rationale for a beneficial regulatory intervention. Where private and social costs and benefits diverge, the power of self-interest to promote the greater good is weakened. 'Virtuous' self-interest pursued in ignorance (wilful or otherwise) of the costs imposed on others can result in externalities such as ecological damage or the over-consumption of non-rival resources (see Scott Cato, this volume). Economists discuss the problem of 'moral hazard', aptly named since it arises from an incentive to behave in a less than virtuous manner, whether this be behaving recklessly after buying insurance, or failing to account adequately for risk in a financial market transaction. I may have no legal or economic incentive to advise you of the inherent riskiness in some cleverly constructed new financial instrument that I am trying to sell; however, I may feel that I have a moral obligation to tell the truth. One might hope that a business school education would not miss this latter point. Without recourse to additional material on the ethics of business practice, an economics-focused business curriculum would, however, falter.

VIRTUE OR *PLEONOXIA*?

The Enlightenment philosophy of classical economics might be regarded as trying, in some sense, to cling to an Aristotelian basis for human action. Indeed Sedlacek (2011) considers economic thought to have begun with Aristotle, since he may be considered to be the first ancient philosopher to have focused attention on issues such as productive and unproductive activity, and the sources of market failure outlined above. For Aristotle the economic problem was that of optimizing good. The issues here are in defining 'good', and in deciding what is optimal. The optimum is not the maximum but a behavioural 'mean' tempered by virtues such as temperance and continence (moderation). But by reinterpreting Aristotelian *eudaimonia* as the utilitarian notion of 'the greatest good (utility) for the greatest number', and by switching the objective from optimization to maximization, neoclassical economic analysis from the later nineteenth century onwards has in effect abandoned questions of the quality of behaviour or actions that might lead to human wellbeing. Thus, in effect, it discarded any useful conception of what is virtuous, in favour of a sole focus on consequence (see Box 9.2).

BOX 9.2 POST-ENLIGHTENMENT RATIONALISM IN SOCIAL SCIENCE

At the heart of MacIntyre's ([1981] 2007) re-evaluation of virtue is a trenchant criticism of the philosophy of contemporary social science, implicit in the business school curriculum. Can post-enlightenment thinking construct rational predictions of the behaviour of economies and organizations in a moral vacuum, and from those infer programmes of efficient management? MacIntyre argues that human action is inherently unpredictable, and therefore not susceptible to rational calculation. However, contemporary economic analysis has developed sophisticated conceptual and analytical tools to deal with uncertainty, allowing theoretical advancement and practical modelling solutions. These tools lie behind many of the sophisticated financial instruments whose flaws were exposed so starkly in the sub-prime crisis that pre-empted the 2008 global crisis. The same tools are taught without significant critique in the finance curricula of many business schools. However, they remain inherently flawed in a moral philosophical sense because they also remain wedded to an underlying deterministic-consequentialist view of the world. The key issue is that a rationalist approach to economic management seems destined to fail because it ignores this unpredictability. The modern social and political world is hostile to considerations of virtue, and creates intractable disagreement about how to act, because the incommensurability of different positions cannot be rationally resolved.

There is an inclination in modern economics towards extending market-orientated consequentialist thinking into an ever-widening range of human activity and experience (Levitt and Dubner, 2005). Recent developments in behavioural economics, integrating insights from psychology and behavioural science, are arguably more enriching for the subject (Kahneman, 2011). Nevertheless such developments can be seen as a marginalization of Aristotelian 'practices' (sport, art, music, academic inquiry, etc.), and therefore the goods that are internal to them, in favour of external goods such as money and status. Those educated for employment in business organizations are implicitly advised that education becomes the means to external goods rather than a practice involving the exercise of virtues in pursuit on internal goods – personal fulfilment, knowledge, skills. Being engaged in business activity for a wider social or creative purpose becomes downplayed in a curriculum which risks undermining virtue in favour of *pleonoxia* (that is, greed or covetousness). Yet surveys of new business founders generally show that motives are as often as not intrinsic rather than financial. The case is therefore made to return to teaching a more prescriptive analysis of economic behaviour, which addresses the important question of how to behave. Once discussion in the classroom advances beyond the 'to what end' question, towards the 'how' question, then the reintegration of virtue in understanding economic behaviour becomes possible. But the next question is what sort of virtue?

A CHRISTIAN REFLECTION ON VIRTUE AND ECONOMICS

Aristotle's conception of happiness is as a state of self-sufficiency that protects against the vicissitudes of the world. In the Aristotelian world virtues are the form of happiness – not the means to happiness (Hauerwas and Pinches, 1997). The happy person is a virtuous one, not merely one who pursues virtuous behaviour, and certainly not one who is satisfied in a utilitarian sense. Contemporary discussion of economics for a Christian theological perspective is often not explicit on virtue. Nevertheless, that discussion has not ignored important questions of how economic agents ought to behave (for example, Hay, 2001; NCCB, 1986; Richardson, 1988). Some argue that 'bourgeois' economic virtues of wealth creation and personal economic responsibility are to be commended (McCloskey, 2006). However, individuals may not earn salvation by virtuous economic behaviour; they fulfil a calling to Christ-likeness by seeking the Kingdom of God in economic and social life. The implications for the understanding of economic activity and behaviour here are twofold. The first is the need to affirm that the economic activity falls within the realm of the Kingdom of God, a Kingdom that is both an eschatological hope and an ontological reality. The second is that the Christian transformation of character applies to economic behaviour as much as to any other form of human behaviour. Economists-as-Christians should seek to understand the underlying moral order, and frame economics in terms of 'how should one live?' rather than 'how do economic agents behave?' (see Box 9.3).

BOX 9.3 A CHRISTIAN *TELOS*

While theologians might not necessarily dismiss psychological happiness as a desirable human state, their understanding of how it might be achieved is profoundly different. Christian fulfilment comes from knowledge of Jesus Christ, the formation of a Christian life in response to His love for humankind through the power of the Holy Spirit, and in the eschatological hope sealed in the Resurrection. Therefore an understanding of virtue from a Christian perspective must stem from that *telos* (Wright, 2010). As O'Donovan (1994) makes plain, there can be no Christian understanding of ethics apart from the created moral order in the universe, from creation to redemption. The early Church held a clear sense of the vision of a future and yet present Kingdom implied by this understanding of Christian *telos*. The Christian truth of the resurrection is integral to this *telos*. Creation has created order and coherence – the resurrection of Christ draws attention to the future redemption of that creation order (O'Donovan, 1994: 31). Order is both description and end, 'generic' and 'teleological'. Thus it might be argued that the end of economic activity is to further the moral purpose of God in bringing forward the Kingdom of God. So a more limited Aristotelian conception in which teleological ordering is a purely natural ordering is insufficient – a point understood by the Scholastic theologians, notably Thomas Aquinas. For Aquinas, the rediscovery of Aristotle's focus on the external world, combined with a distinctive Christian focus, shifted the emphasis from the purely spiritual world to that of creation – a creation that, while still in bondage to sin, was created good and will ultimately be restored to that goodness. Those who enjoy that creation, even in its current imperfection, experience the common grace of the Creator. If a good God created *ex nihilo*, then the material world too must be good – in the words of Tomas Sedlacek in his recent survey: 'worth dealing with, worth improving and worth addressing' (Sedlacek, 2011: 157). Crucially the economic world is part of that created moral order, and it too is part of this *telos*. A Christian re-construction or re-interpretation of economics must begin from this point.

What aspects of Christian virtue have particular salience for economic behaviour and activity? The Scholastics, notably Aquinas, tabulate the virtues as if to present an exhaustive list. The New Testament material seems not to imply this, but rather focuses on the transformation of Christian character. However, there is a parallel with Aristotle's view that the virtues are to be practiced, and that it is only through repeated exercise that they become inherent to individual character.[1] For business schools, this has implications at least as much for pedagogy as for curriculum content – don't try to teach an ethical taxonomy, but rather seek to transform the moral character of present and future business leaders.

Economics specifically in the curriculum requires a focus on the Christian task of the bringing forward being given of the future reality of resurrected creation into the present *kairos*, through specific attention being given to the 'sub-task' of modelling the economic aspects of the future Kingdom. What will characterize that Kingdom? It might promote an economy of care and responsibility, an

---

[1]See 1 *Corinthians* 9.25, *Ephesians* 6.4, *1 Timothy* 4.8 and *2 Timothy* 3.16.

economy of creativity, and an economy where actions as well as outcomes are just (deontology and teleology). Certainly this is likely to entail a full range of virtues, as described in the various taxonomies in the New Testament, particularly Pauline, material.[2] And, as such, the principles underlying this economy are likely to stand in stark contrast to those that underpin modern neoclassical economic analysis, with its 'internal' teleology and absence of deontology.

However, despite this assertion, critics may counter that it is hopelessly utopian to expect virtuous behaviour to arise on a voluntary basis, simply on the basis exhortation from the front of the lecture theatre. The various writers of the New Testament epistles do not appear to think so. On the other hand is the post-Enlightenment economic project unrealistically pessimistic in anticipating that all economic behaviour is motivated by self-interest? Economists are frequently criticized for creating around themselves an aura of intellectual superiority that admits limited engagement with other methodological and philosophical perspectives. The study of economics is also criticized for inculcating within its students a self-interested mindset that undermines altruistic values and co-operative behaviour (Frank et al., 1993). There may be something in this, and therefore a challenge for business school faculty to address.

However, while the development of virtuous character in the conduct of business may indicate the operation of common grace in the world, is it realistic to seek to encourage a framework for virtue based on the eschatological hope of the Kingdom of God in the modern multicultural world? There is often a reluctance to argue an explicitly Christian theological basis for particular courses of action or policies. It is, however, possible here to appeal to an Aristotelian basis for ethics. In the field of business ethics this is often done – concepts of virtue and common good are attractive to those seeking a strong sense of personal responsibility in business affairs, in preference to some blander notion of corporate social responsibility informed by 'enlightened corporate self-interest'. The challenge for business schools is to ensure that such considerations are fully integrated into the core curriculum, and not marginalized as an alternative 'critical perspective'. There is also a tendency to translate the curriculum of corporate social responsibility into too much of an organizational perspective, emphasizing notions of social responsibility as strategy, with insufficient attention given to the thornier question of personal business integrity (see Box 9.4).

BOX 9.4 ALASDAIR MACINTYRE ON 'PRACTICES'

Those higher goods, which MacIntyre calls 'practices', define human relationships with others, including economic endeavour designed to meet the needs of others (MacIntyre, [1981] 2007). Because practices are in essence relational then so is virtue. A simple reflection on the transitive nature of virtuous behaviour illustrates this:

---

[2]See specifically *1 Corinthians* 13, *Colossians* 3, *Galatians* 5 and the avoidance of the 'vices' in *Ephesians* 4 and *Colossians* 3.

'honesty towards whom?', 'justice for whom?' 'care of whom'? etc. Professional communities of practice often situate learning on the basis of historical experience and storytelling. They function on the basis of a shared appreciation of virtues such as trust, honesty, fairness and integrity. While such communities are commonly recognized among professional groups, more recently such communities have been seen to function as learning arena among groups which exist for more straightforward economic purpose – such as small businesses. Economic analyses, which fail to take account of the temporal dynamics of human relationships, and the manner in which virtue may develop through those relationships, will be partial and incomplete. They will fail to recognize that the *telos* of economic activity that may emerge could be very different from that deduced from the ahistorical, utilitarian orthodox model.

It is difficult to be exhaustive and precise on the question of what specific virtues might underpin a Christian perspective on good behaviour in business. Different classifications of virtue may miss the point that Christian virtue is about 'training in righteousness' (*1 Timothy* 3.16). However, virtues such as trust (viz. faithfulness), honesty, creativity, stewardship (viz. temperance), and forbearance to exploit others (viz. self-control) can all be commended to those studying the conduct of economic and commercial affairs. Undoubtedly, however, a key economic virtue is justice. However, justice is a word that seems rather to make an appearance in business school course material, despite having obvious resonance for the manner in which the business leader might engage with employees, competitors, suppliers and other stakeholders.

To choose to be ethical or not in the manner in which business decisions are taken is a free choice. Does such a voluntarist focus in effect let company senior managers, professional and trade bodies and even government 'off the hook' of any attempt to be prescriptive about the conduct of business activity? This question concerns the focus or agenda for any attempt to reconstruct economics around an emphasis on virtue. In business ethics, virtue-based approaches focus on the quality of the behaviour or decision-making of individuals, or perhaps groups of individuals acting in concert, such as a company board. The external legal framework within which those decisions are framed is taken as given. A range of institutions, including professional regulators, codes of standards and government regulations, may heavily circumscribe economic activity. These also include an external framework of contract law, and the institutions required to enforce that. Often the justification for external regulation is to protect individuals against market failure, although sometimes it may be to protect individuals from other forms of harm or exploitation. In broad terms these activities might be framed in terms of society 'doing justice' to those who may be vulnerable in different economic circumstances.

The question here is the extent to which considerations of virtue might guide such activity. To the extent that justice is a key virtue, then virtue has a part to play. However, there will need to be arrangements in place to ensure that public bodies can give expression to that virtue. It is not sufficient to argue that a virtue-based approach to economics pushes all legitimate consideration of the quality of economic behaviour into the realm of the individual, and that economic problems can simply be solved through individual virtuous action. In theological terms governance implies moral order, not voluntarist anarchy. This process starts with education – education about the proper ethical function of professional standards of behaviour.

CONCLUSION

This chapter has argued that a recent revival of interest in virtue ethics has much to contribute to a critique of the modern economics curriculum, and makes a plea for the proper place of virtue at the heart of the way in which future business leaders are educated. That education process begins within a clear and thorough understanding of the proper *telos* of economic and business activity. Economic analysis, grounded in Enlightenment utilitarianism philosophy, flounders on the rocks of internal teleology. Consequently a business curriculum with an over-emphasis on economic modes of analysis self-excludes any ability to comment, in a normative sense, on the quality of business behaviour and actions. This chapter has argued for a Christian theological perspective on virtue ethics – one proceeding from a teleology that is focused on the 'present future' of the Kingdom of God and not on any Aristotelian notion of the common good. So, for example, a theological perspective on the global financial crisis must focus as much on moral and ethical questions relating to personal behaviour and responsibility, as on the technical questions of inadequate government regulation and the consequences of mistaken macro-economic policy. A virtue-based approach would not only focus on underlying issues of global justice, but also on the absence of forbearance, prudence and, as the crisis unravelled, trust. Technical education in the intricacies of financial markets must sit alongside a more moral business school curriculum that seeks to instil a virtuous character on the part of business leaders of the future. Ethical critiques of such technical approaches cannot and must not be 'bolted on' as an afterthought – considerations of decision quality must be taught as integral to the subject matter within the business school curriculum.

As one contemplates that future, the question remains as to whether the 'pull' of such virtuous behaviour is sufficiently strong to effect economic change. The juxtaposition of appealing to 'better virtue' or 'baser self-interest' here illustrates the inherent tension between seeking to develop policy on the basis of how economic agents ought to behave or on the pragmatic basis of accepting economic behaviour as it appears to be. A Christian theological basis ought not to accept the pessimism of the latter, but reflect on the economic and business implications of the optimism of a future Kingdom of justice brought into the present.

REFERENCES

Frank, R.H., Gilovich, T.D. and Regan, D.T. (1993) 'Does studying economics inhibit cooperation?', *Journal of Economic Perspectives*, 7: 159–71.

Hauerwas, S. and Pinches, C. (1997) *Christians Among the Virtues: Theological Conversations with Ancient and Modern Ethics*. Notre Dame, IN: University of Notre Dame Press.

Hay, D. (2001) 'On being a Christian economist', in D. Hay and A. Kreider (eds), *Christianity and the Culture of Economics*. Cardiff: University of Wales Press, pp. 166–90.

Kahneman, D. (2011) *Thinking, Fast and Slow*. London: Allen Lane.

Levitt, S.D. and Dubner, S.J. (2005) *Freakonomics: A Rogue Economist Explains the Hidden Side of Everything*. London: Allen Lane.

MacIntyre, A. ([1981] 2007) *After Virtue* (3rd edn). London: Bloomsbury.

McCloskey, D. (2006) *The Bourgeois Virtues: Ethics for an Age of Commerce*. Chicago: Chicago University Press.

NCCB (National Conference of Catholic Bishops) (1986) *Economic Justice for All: Pastoral Letter on Catholic Social Teaching and the US Economy*, Washington DC: United States Catholic Conference (reprinted in D.J. O'Brien and T.A. Shannon, *Catholic Social Thought: The Documentary Heritage*, Maryknoll, NY: Orbis, 1992).

O'Donovan, O. (1994) *Resurrection and Moral Order: An Outline for Evangelical Ethics* (2nd edn). Grand Rapids, MI: Eerdmans and Leicester: Apollos.

Richardson, J.D. (1988), 'Frontiers in economics and Christian scholarship', *Christian Scholars' Review*, 17: 381–400.

Rubin, R.S. and Dierdorff, E.S. (2013), 'Building a better MBA: from a decade of critique to a decennium of creation', *Academy of Management Learning and Education*, 12 (1): 125–41.

Schumpeter, J.A. ([1942] 1950) *Capitalism, Socialism, and Democracy* (3rd edn). New York: Harper and Brothers.

Sedlacek, T. (2011) *Economics of Good and Evil: The Quest for Meaning from Gilgamesh to Wall Street*. Oxford: Oxford University Press.

Wright, T. (2010) *Virtue Reborn*. London: SPCK.

10 CAN OUR BODIES GUIDE THE TEACHING AND LEARNING OF BUSINESS ETHICS?

Leah Tomkins

INTRODUCTION

I am often struck by the differences between discussions inside the seminar room and outside over coffee or in the bar. The seminar room reflects the language and priorities of corporate life, with its search for models, methodologies and solutions to enhance organizational performance. The bar, on the other hand, is a space occupied by real human beings, grappling with the everyday stuff that is not so easily incorporated into models, methodologies and solutions. One aspect of this disconnect is the treatment of the body. The human beings of the bar have feelings; they experience aches and pains; their performance is compromised by the exhaustions of having too much to do; their advancement is thwarted by their inability to hide the stress they feel; they bond over shared experiences of excess at residential courses; and they experience illness and ageing in themselves, their family and their friends. Few of these corporeal experiences find their way into the seminar room, where the frailties of the body are traditionally seen as inimical to the splendours of the mind.

In this chapter, I explore this disconnect between embodied experience and disembodied curricula, drawing on ideas from two major phenomenological writers, Martin Heidegger and Emmanuel Levinas. Phenomenology is a philosophy which takes subjectivity and selfhood seriously, offering ideas about reconnecting the living human being of the bar with the intellectual, functionalist discourse of the seminar room. My particular focus is ethics, and how ethical thinking can look and feel different when framed in terms of subjective embodiment. Ethics has become a 'hot topic' for business schools, as we reel from massive corporate failures and shocking examples of wrong-doing. With politicians fiddling their expenses, journalists breaching all standards of morality to get a story, and bankers taking breathtaking risks with other people's money, both scholars and practitioners are asking how it is that we have allowed organizational life to develop this way. So, within this context of a crisis of ethics, what can we learn from our bodies?

SENSES OF EMBODIMENT

As the contemporary phenomenological philosopher Mark Johnson suggests:

> Judging from mainstream Anglo-American philosophy, thirty years ago people did not have bodies. But today, it seems like almost everybody has one. They're a dime a dozen. It is as if a great embodiment tsunami swept over the philosophical landscape and deposited incarnate minds as it receded. (Johnson, 2008: 159)

Within this embodiment tsunami, the academic literature on leadership, management and organization is becoming more interested in flesh, blood and guts. There is a growing sense of the limitations of intellect and rationality, and the value of exploring the often messy viscera of our working lives. Bodies now appear in a range of contexts, including gender and power relations, employee and organizational wellbeing, rituals and routines, and feelings and emotions. Bourdieu's work on 'habitus', in particular, has greatly influenced organizational scholars, suggesting that our lives develop unintentionally, as corporeal and habitual engagement, rather than intellectually or as the result of planning (Bourdieu, 1990). Increasingly, it is these habitual, embodied and unspoken qualities of organization that are energizing academic work on the key business school topics of strategy (Chia and Holt, 2009), leadership (Ladkin, 2013), and organizational learning (Strati, 2007).

On the whole, however, bodily concerns have not reached the mainstream work of business schools, despite their growing influence over academic thinking in these key topic areas. Most curricula still revolve around the tools of the mind – logic, theory and models – revealing the extraordinary lingering power of metaphors of humans and organizations as computational machines. The body tends to be thought of as something whose issues should remain firmly on the 'life' side of the 'work/life boundary'; for the perfect employee is the ideal machine component, letting nothing get in the way of delivery and performance. While the discourses of academia and the bar often acknowledge the body, business school curricula have some catching up to do.

Where the body does feature, it is often within the context of 'impression management'. Executives are encouraged to manage the *outsides* of their bodies in order to enhance their professional impact. But embodiment also refers to our *insides*; it is the subjectivity of corporeal, lived experience which provides us with our sense of continuity and coherence of identity. Thus, we have two fundamentally interrelated ways of experiencing and understanding embodiment – our insides and our outsides. And the idea that the very thing that is most intimately and exclusively mine is also an object for other people represents one of the fundamental ambiguities of human existence (Merleau-Ponty, [1945] 1962; Tomkins and Eatough, 2013).

Many of the concepts we use to express psychological welfare – and with it, our discourses of organizational and executive performance – come from the body's logic. For instance, notions of 'containment' and 'balance' have been absorbed into our everyday understandings of successful functioning, but are fundamentally corporeal. This is what is meant when phenomenologists argue that the body shapes the mind (Gallagher and Zahavi, 2008). And if the body shapes the mind, it also influences the way the mind is deployed, including decisions and ideas about morality. Moreover, since the body is more or less the same universally, its constitutive qualities suggest our *common* ways of framing ethical challenges, pointing towards more meaningful ways of interacting with each other.

The particular sense of embodiment that I focus on here is our subjective experience of death and mortality. So, as well as considering the insights and implications of our embodied subjectivity in general, I ask a more specific question – can our *mortal* bodies guide our teaching and learning of business ethics?

DEATH MATTERS!

We all die, and we all know we are going to die. We see reminders of mortality as we ourselves age, and as we care for others, particularly within the context of an ageing population. Death is, therefore, an extraordinary leveller, as relevant to the most successful CEO as it is to the office cleaner. If embodiment shapes us and crafts our engagement with the world, and if mortality is one of the universal aspects of embodiment, then making sense of death must surely be one of the most important things we ever have to do.

In corporate settings, death is most frequently encountered metaphorically, relating, for instance, to the 'termination' of the employee or the 'lifecycle' of the organization. But metaphorical deaths shield us from the sense that death *matters* – being both of-matter and of-concern, that is, we lose sight of its corporeal and its ethical qualities. This encourages us towards a particular discourse of perfection, that of death-denial, where we refuse to see ourselves as finite beings whose efforts at significance are compromised by our impermanence. Within the organizational literature, death-denial has been associated with idealization and the 'buy-in' to corporate objectives: if the organization is perfect and I can identify with it, then I become perfect too (Schwartz, 1990).

Huge self-deception is required to imagine oneself (and one's organization) perfect. Anxiety and shame are inevitable, because there will *always* be a difference between who I am supposed to be (immortal, perfect, heroic) and who I actually am (mortal, imperfect, vulnerable). And such differences between the ideal of the perfect employee and the subjective reality of imperfection are more than just a source of personal difficulty: at the organizational or institutional level, the denial of matter – of the mortal and the ethical – takes us away from what makes us human. As the cultural anthropologist, Ernest Becker, famously argues, 'man's natural and inevitable urge to deny mortality and achieve a heroic self-image are the root causes of human evil' (Becker, 1975: xvii). But if we resist the discourses of perfection and immortality, we are left with real death, and the challenge of what to do with its inevitability. Both Heidegger and Levinas have much to offer us here; both wrote extensively about the significance of death, and give us insights into how we might live our lives both in and out of organization.

HEIDEGGER, MORTALITY AND MEANING

Heidegger is considered one of the most original, influential but also controversial of twentieth-century thinkers. His style is idiosyncratic and notoriously obscure, which makes interpreting his work rewarding but challenging. In his most famous work, *Being and Time*, death has a profound existential significance; in making sense of death, we make sense of life (Heidegger, [1927] 1962). In this sense, Heidegger marks a key shift in a modern philosophy previously more concerned to 'cognize a deathless truth than to face the truth of death' (Cohen, 2006: 22). Humans are always orientated towards death, thus our understanding and acceptance of mortality is something that shapes not just our final years, but our whole lives from the moment we are born.

Although death is certain, its timing is uncertain. Therefore, I must be prepared for it to happen at any moment. But death is not something that I experience directly. Since I will no longer be here when it happens, I can only experience it *in anticipation*. The meaning of death lies in what I *do* with this anticipation – how I make sense of my mortality – how I use it to inspire reflection on what my life and my work are *for*. While I am alive, there is still time to ensure that it is all *for something*, still time to make a difference and realize my potential. When death comes, the meaning of my life will be settled. But if death comes tomorrow, then I should at least have been working towards the life that I want to have led and for which I want to be remembered. Making sense of mortality in this way challenges us to *live each day as if it were our last*, providing our projects of meaning with a temporal urgency: if not now, then when?

Nobody else can die for me. However rich or successful I am, death is something I cannot outsource or delegate to others. Heideggerian mortality therefore signals the importance of agency and personal responsibility. And within the context of business ethics, an emphasis on individual responsibility comes as a much-needed counterbalance to the notion of *systemic* institutional failure.

For the response to the ethical crisis from organizational practitioners has tended to be the creation of protocols and codes of conduct, which require the individual simply to follow the rules laid down by others. The response from policy-makers has usually been the establishment of corrective institutions, such as a Financial Conduct Authority or a Press Standards Commission. (It is ironic, given the focus of this chapter, that these are called regulatory 'bodies', for they seem a peculiarly disembodied response.) The response from critical management scholars, on the other hand, has been to call for macro-ethical solutions, which rise above the mundane goings-on in organizations and position ethics within the realm of politics (Parker, 2003). But focusing on big answers to big questions using the language of crisis management takes our attention away from what individuals can and should do in everyday life (McMurray et al., 2010). A Heideggerian emphasis on personal responsibility re-focuses our attention on the 'mineness' of organizational accountability: if not me, then who?

LEVINAS, MORTALITY AND ETHICS

These themes of temporal urgency and personal responsibility connect Heidegger with Levinas, much of whose work was positioned in response to Heidegger's, particularly in relation to their very different experiences of the Holocaust. Over recent years, Levinas has been exerting a considerable influence over organizational scholars and, as a result, is increasingly visible on business school curricula. He is credited with bringing ethics into the centre-ground of both phenomenological and organizational thinking, and in particular, with the rejection of ethics as codes and rules of conduct (Jones, 2003).

For Levinas, human experience is concerned first and foremost with an ethical orientation to, and responsibility for, the Other (Levinas, 1974). The Other is both the real, concrete presence of another person and a more abstract (non-)entity, a metaphor for all those aspects of personhood and culture that escape thematization and codification. The Other's demands on me are powerful and primordial, but they are also indeterminate, unfathomable and incapable of being represented or known in any certain sense. This is a vision of human beings far removed from the security of procedures and protocols.

For Levinas, mortality and morality are inextricably linked. Like Heidegger, Levinas sees the meaning of death in its *anticipation*. However, Levinas resists the idea that the meaning of my life lies in its totality, in contrast to Heidegger's grander thesis that death will mark and reveal what my whole life will have been about. Instead, Levinas urges us not to wait for the judgement of history to assess the significance of who we are, but rather, to be ready for judgement at each and every moment, to be prepared *now* to be called to account.

Levinas's radical departure from Heidegger comes with the primacy of the Other. The lived experience of mortality concerns not *my* death so much as the death of the *Other*. Thus, what counts is precisely *not* those projects or concerns that might jeopardize or give meaning to *my* life – as per Heidegger – but rather, the projects or concerns of the Other. This takes us beyond a Heideggerian injunction to live each day as if it were our last, and towards a Levinasian alternative that we should live each day *as if it were the Other's last*.

While it is the mortality of the Other that matters, the ethical requirement is *mine*. Levinas's mineness is corporeal; the ethical summons is felt in *my body*. Levinas's subject is a person who bleeds, sweats, sobs and vomits, and who intuits what mortality and morality are all about. The viscera of gut-feel give Levinasian ethics their fire: the belly roar, the bowel tightening and the surges of nausea suggest how we should make sense of our lives and our relations with others. This is ethics not as rules but as a felt sense.

THE FELT SENSE OF ETHICS

For phenomenologists, a felt sense is something that can be explored analytically (Gendlin, 2003; Tomkins and Eatough, 2013). When we feel vaguely troubled or unsettled by something, we can pause to acknowledge this and reflect on what it might mean. A felt sense is not quite the same as an emotion; rather, it is some stirring in the body which feels meaningful before its meaning can be captured, labelled and known. It can inspire interpretation, analysis and potentially action.

A VIGNETTE

Not long ago, I was interviewing an executive – Sue – for a research project into issues relating to 'work–life balance'. Sue started telling me that she was being bullied at work, and her experiences struck me as more than just the normal 'rough and tumble' of corporate life. When I left the interview, I could not get away fast enough! I had an overwhelming sense of relief to get away from her – a 'phew' to be able to distance myself literally and psychologically. When I got home, these feelings of relief morphed into a nagging uneasiness and I felt slightly sick.

The fact that I had felt so relieved to get away began to sensitize me that, for Sue, there was no getting away from her situation, no possibility of distancing. And if I was so keen to distance myself from her, were others in her world responding similarly? Maybe I should not be walking away? Even though her bullying was not my responsibility or my fault, did I have some sort of obligation? Did my unease have something to do with guilt? I was moved by the unfairness of her lot, but unsure whether or how to help, since I had no formal association with her organization. I had a strong sense that someone should *do* something about Sue's situation, and a question started to form: in the absence of anyone else, should that person be me?

I have started noticing how common it is for us to console each other with the words, 'don't blame yourself – it isn't your fault'. However kindly intended, I wonder whether this misses the Levinasian point; whether the ethical summons makes itself felt precisely when it is *not* one's literal responsibility or actual fault. Perhaps we come closest to a Levinasian ethics when we feel moved by a desire for things to be different, even if we lack the words to articulate and explain this feeling or the power and resources to do anything about it. In a Levinasian world, if I knew exactly what I was supposed to do, and had the authority to do it, it would not be ethics. But where I do not have these epistemological and positional certainties, gut-feel may signal that I should at least be *considering doing something*.

My reading of Heidegger and Levinas offers an interpretative frame for why my discomfort at this episode might reveal an ethics of mortality (Table 10.1). From Heidegger, there is the significance and urgency of personal responsibility, as I work towards existential meaning and a positive judgement from history. What if the possibility of supporting Sue were the last thing I were ever to experience? Would I at least *want* to do something to help her, not least, as Heidegger would have it, because I would not want to be remembered as the sort of person who is impervious to pain and injustice? And through a Levinasian lens of Otherness, what if Sue's final experiences of this world were of being bullied, shot through with the knowledge that I knew about it yet raced away from her? My ability to help her, or even grasp what help is needed, may be modest, but the stirrings of unease in my body are a powerful signal that I am engaged and morally implicated in her situation. In the Levinasian ethical summons I am moved by *her* mortality; I need to try – or at least want – to do the right thing while there is still time in *her* life.

Table 10.1 Themes for an ethics of mortality

	Ethos	Primary orientation	Judgement	Temporal urgency
Heidegger	Meaning Mineness	Self	From history, based on one's whole life-work	Now, while there is still time (in my life)
Levinas	Morality Modesty	Other (concrete and abstract)	Uncertain, but felt viscerally	Now, while there is still time (in his/her life)

IMPLICATIONS FOR THE CURRICULUM

In emphasizing the felt sense of ethics, I am not proposing that we sit around talking about our bodies and our feelings all day. I do not seek to replace a fantasy of immortality with an equally reality-denying narcissism, in which we obsess about our selves and ignore the organizational requirement to get on and *do* stuff. What I am suggesting is that members of organizations are more complex and more interesting than business school curricula often imply. The discourses of perfection that underpin so much theory and practice are necessarily simplifications, if not distortions, of organizational life, and they present us with an impoverished model of what being human entails. If we want to explore why organizations seem to be failing us, we need richer pictures of the people who work in them.

One topic that suggests this greater richness is leadership as intuition, using models of executive decision-making as the interplay of expertise and feeling (Sadler-Smith and Shefy, 2004). Seen this way, successful leadership involves drawing on a wealth of available clues, those of the rational mind and those of the intuitive body. Decision-making scenarios can be designed to tease out and probe these various sources of ideas and judgements, moving iteratively and constructively between them (Table 10.2).

Table 10.2 Integrating the rational with the intuitive

From intuition to rational analysis	Do the data back up my hunch?
	Why am I instinctively inclined to take one course of action over another?
	What additional proof will give me confidence in my decision?
From rational analysis to intuition	Does my decision sit comfortably, or are there nagging doubts?
	Do I feel I have grasped the nub of the issue? What does my experience tell me?

These sorts of ideas about leadership often chime with students' own experiences of organizational life, and intersect with academic work that has crossed over into popular literature, such as Daniel Kahneman's work on fast and slow thinking (Kahneman, 2011), and Gerd Gigerenzer's examination of heuristics (Gigerenzer, 2005). Although not explicitly a celebration of the body, let alone the mortal body, such arguments help to sensitize ourselves and our students that the content of our conscious, deliberate minds – the substance of models and methodologies – is only ever part of the executive story.

Mortality and 'imperfection' take us into the uncertainty of leadership, and the radical proposition that leaders – as human beings – might not know all the answers to organizational questions. I think there is a really pressing case for more of this on business school curricula. The discourses of 'best practice' make it hard to admit to not knowing what to do in a particular situation, both as leaders (Grint, 2007) and as teachers (French, 1997). But acknowledging that one does not always know the answer does not have to be seen as a sign of weakness or failure; rather, it can be a spur to exploratory and creative thinking, including tapping into the 'sensible knowledge' of the body (Strati, 2007). It sensitizes us to the need for reflection and consideration of alternatives, rather than the mindless following of protocols and the assumption of 'one best way' (so long as we avoid the pendulum swing of not seeming to know *anything*, that is, I do not think we should answer *every* student question with 'well, what do *you* think?').

The ideas in this chapter concern not only the topics on the curriculum, but the values underpinning it too; that is, the body exerts indirect as well as direct influence (Table 10.3). For instance, the body's commonplaceness signals the value of the personal, the small and the mundane in organizational life, nudging us away from an ethics of big solutions to big problems. The seminar room traditionally encourages big answers, and we probably feel uncomfortable when we address students' questions about 'critical success factors' with answers like 'it is important to talk' (surely there must be more to it than that?). Yet many a successful executive will tell you of the value of 'baby steps' and the importance of small gestures, which suggest a direction or ethos rather than representing a complete solution.

These ideas may not be the stuff of the first semester, especially not when expressed directly, as per my left-hand column in Table 10.3. For students to engage with feelings, let alone death, requires both teaching and teacher to be established as credible, competent and trustworthy, both intellectually and personally. If we engage directly with an ethics of embodiment, we may find students rolling their eyes in dismay (the stuff of an MPhil not an MBA?). But grounding our teaching with the ideas and instincts of the right-hand column uses the logic of the body to resist the nonsense of perfection, and work towards models of organization that are more realistic, more meaningful and more ethical. Thus, we can draw on the *values* of an ethics of mortality and embodiment without necessarily having them as explicit messages or overt topics.

Table 10.3 Direct and indirect ethics of embodiment

Direct: Aspects of embodiment	Indirect: Potential topics, epistemological frames and/or values
Mortality • 'imperfection' • impermanence Felt sense • bodies integral to (constitutive of) identity and lived experience • bodies simultaneously subjective and objective – both intimately mine and available/on show	Meaning: What is it all for? Where does my work fit in with this? Balancing responsibility for self and others; between one's own projects of meaning and organization as the site of collective endeavour Focus on the 'important' rather than the 'urgent' Living (and leading) with uncertainty, while retaining credibility and integrity Limitations of conscious cognition and control; the need to find other ways to lead and relate to others The power and value of intuition and gut-feel The value of the small, personal and mundane Critical reflection as multiplicity, flexibility and acknowledgement of complexity

My call for bodily awareness is not about eschewing the need for solutions. Rather, I think the body helps us to find different kinds of solutions – less perfect but more human – and to find solutions in different ways. Even in the most intellectual of curricula, corporeal logic can be a spur to engage with issues of complexity, flexibility and multiplicity – fundamental qualities for the business of 'critical thinking'. The phenomenological emphasis on the simultaneous objectivity/subjectivity of the body gives us a fundamental blueprint for multiplicity – startling in its simplicity. If we could weave this commitment to multiplicity into our teaching, without this becoming 'flaky' or the relativist's 'anything goes', we really would be learning from our bodies. A curriculum which honours the richness of human being would therefore try to supplement the rational with the intuitive; the grand with the mundane; and the certainties of control with the less certain business of reflection, dialogue and the consideration of alternatives.

Engaging with issues of vulnerability and limitation is difficult personally, and it can be nerve-wracking to do in one's teaching. But these are the things that make us human; they are therefore fundamentally interwoven with, not antithetical to, our organizational achievements. If we can even *suggest* some of these ideas to our students, we begin gently to dissolve the disconnects between rhetoric and experience, between the business person in the seminar room and the human being in the bar. After all, many of those human beings will have been deeply affected by a health scare of their own, or the death of someone important to them, and may well be asking themselves, *what is it all for*? For Heidegger and Levinas, the existential and ethical significance of death lies in our experience of its approach. We can either try to deny this, or we can deal with what really matters and work towards better answers to that question.

In memoriam: For Don Fowler, whose life and death have made a difference.

FURTHER READING

For an erudite yet accessible introduction to the philosophy of phenomenology, see Gallagher and Zahavi (2008).
For the practical application of ideas relating to embodiment and gut feel, see Gendlin (2003) and Sadler-Smith and Shefy (2004).
For a provocative discussion of why death is absent from our organizational conversations, see Schwartz (1990).

REFERENCES

Becker, E. (1975) *Escape from Evil*. New York: The Free Press.
Bourdieu, P. (1990) *The Logic of Practice*. Stanford: Stanford University Press.

Chia, R.C.H. and Holt, R. (2009) *Strategy Without Design: The Silent Efficacy of Indirect Action*. Cambridge: Cambridge University Press.

Cohen, R.A. (2006) 'Levinas: thinking least about death – contra Heidegger'. *International Journal of Philosophy of Religion*, 60: 21–39.

French, R.B. (1997) 'The teacher as container of anxiety: psychoanalysis and the role of teacher', *Journal of Management Education*, 21 (4): 483–95.

Gallagher, S. and Zahavi, D. (2008) *The Phenomenological Mind: An Introduction to Philosophy of Mind and Cognitive Science*. Abingdon: Routledge.

Gendlin, E.T. (2003) *Focusing: How to Gain Direct Access to Your Body's Knowledge*. London: Ebury Press.

Gigerenzer, G. (2005) 'I think, therefore I err', *Social Research*, 72 (1): 195–218.

Grint, K. (2007) 'Learning to lead: can Aristotle help us find the road to wisdom?', *Leadership*, 3 (2): 231–46.

Heidegger, M. ([1927] 1962) *Being and Time*, trans J. Macquarrie and E. Robinson. Oxford: Blackwell.

Johnson, M. (2008) 'What makes a body?', *Journal of Speculative Philosophy*, 22(3): 159–69.

Jones, C. (2003) 'As if business ethics were possible', *Organization*, 10 (2): 223–48.

Kahneman, D. (2011) *Thinking, Fast and Slow*. London: Allen Lane.

Ladkin, D. (2013) 'From perception to flesh: a phenomenological account of the felt experience of leadership', *Leadership*, 9 (3): 320–34.

Levinas, E. (1974) *Otherwise than Being*, trans. A. Lingis. Pittsburgh: Duquesne University Press.

McMurray, R., Pullen, A. and Rhodes, C. (2010) 'Ethical subjectivity and politics in organisations: a case of health care tendering', *Organization*, 18 (4): 541–61.

Merleau-Ponty, M. ([1945] 1962) *Phenomenology of Perception*, trans. C. Smith. London: Routledge.

Parker, M. (2003) 'Ethics, politics and organizing', *Organization*, 10 (2): 187–203.

Sadler-Smith, E. and Shefy, E. (2004) 'The intuitive executive: understanding and applying "gut feel" in decision-making', *The Academy of Management Executive*, 18 (4): 76–91.

Schwartz, H.S. (1990) *Narcissistic Process and Corporate Decay: The Theory of the Organisation Ideal*. New York: New York University Press.

Strati, A. (2007) 'Sensible knowledge and practice-based learning', *Management Learning*, 38 (1): 61–77.

Tomkins, L. and Eatough, V. (2013) 'The feel of experience: phenomenological ideas for organizational research', *Qualitative Research in Organizations and Management*, 8 (3): 258–75.

PART II

RAPPORTEUR

J.-C. Spender

Part II comprises five provocative chapters. Summarizing them with brutal brevity, in Chapter 6 Cato presumes mainstream economics hides an imperative to growth; the pursuit of economies of scale. Against this she proposes an appropriately scaled 'human' economics of self-managed or worker co-operative firms. 'Critical faculty' can help students compare and contrast such economic pluralism; the scale-driven economics of the City and Wall Street versus a human economics for agricultural societies. In Chapter 7 Parry and Fiskerud argue morality and ethics have been left out of leadership studies, leading to Brute Capitalism rather than Moral Capitalism, even as students 'yearn' for a greater sense of purpose. The authors urge extending the business schools' notion of leadership from within firms to embrace leadership within the community. Business education works against such extension whenever it presumes managers should maximize shareholder value. To promote awareness of economics' limits, students should be exposed to media that generate 'unease' at the way Brute Capitalism works. In Chapter 8 Beech argues business schools educate towards ideological conformism, the primacy of shareholder value. Drawing on Parsons, he calls for business education to reawaken disciplinary attention to the cultural power of capitalism. In Chapter 9 Henley follows MacIntyre's arguments that economic thought hinges on a sense of 'the good' that is inattentive to Aristotle's notion of 'human flourishing'. He distinguishes business schools' focus on (a) markets and (b) the hierarchies that trade across them, and goes beyond Aristotle to propose a Christian *telos* that looks towards a more perfect world rather than backwards at the goods economic activity has produced. In Chapter 10 Tomkins notes the absence of 'body' and thus 'human feeling' in business education, leading to an over-emphasis on 'mind'. This erases the human actor's concern with death that *inter alia* underpins the philosophical work of Heidegger and Levinas and the individual's perpetual anxiety about 'What is it all for?' It seems human beings are more complex and interesting than rationality focused business school curricula allow.

These authors help expose some of the foundations of capitalist thought and practice to examination and criticism; and thereby question what business schools are for. For example, Beech cites Dewey's assertion that education is to 'develop the values-based cultural power to frame purposes, to judge wisely, to evaluate desires by the consequences of acting on them, and the values-based practical power to select the means to carry chosen ends into operation'. Generally speaking, these authors are optimistic that business schools can aspire to such lofty goals rather than concluding they are the madrassas of Brute Capitalism, conspiring to overwrite the students' native virtue with the perverted pursuit of personal greed and/or shareholder gain; suspicions supported by the customary appeals to Ghoshal or Ferraro, Pfeffer and Sutton – business school professors all rather than philosophers.

MANAGERS' ECONOMICS

The villain of the piece seems to be economics, taught as a mode of managerial thought along with *homo oeconomicus* as the conceptual model of the human being; to whit, if business schools did not teach this kind of economics most of their deficiencies would disappear. Given business schools educate students to take part in the economy rather than theorize, some kind of economics must be central. But of what kind? We need a thoroughly modern but virtuous economics that recognizes its capacity to contribute to humankind, yet whose complementary capacity for social damage and human degradation is understood and contained. Henley pins this crisply: economics is an Enlightenment project to replace external moral authority or teleology yet 'it retains its own meta-narrative, derived from rational economic thought'. Beech notes Adam Smith's 'formidable cocktail' that 'balances self-interest with a concern for others as it balances liberty with social order'. The implication is that if business education promoted an economics of 'enlightened' self-interest or 'bourgeois virtue' it might get things right – letting market forces rule but not to the extent of denying the other virtues.

However, business schools are not schools of economics. They are schools of private sector enterprise, investment, employment and accounting. Neglectful of their history, business school faculty may be unaware that their thinking differs from that in schools of government, public policy and politics – or even in schools of economics (Van Horn et al., 2011). Business schools take the private sector firm as fundamental to their discourse. Yet, as Coase's 'killer questions' – why firms exist, why their internal and boundary arrangements are as they are, or why their performance is so varied – reminded us in 2012, as in 1937, there is no established or agreed sense of 'the firm' (Coase, 1937; Coase and Wang, 2012). The result is that business school teaching cannot establish any clear connection to 'the firm' or to managing it; what we might call business education's 'dirty little secret'. Instead we find economists of various stripes (e.g. neoclassical, Austrian, Marxist, institutional, behavioural, etc.) framing managing according to their principles. Evolutionary biologists, systems theorists and legions of others have likewise gotten into the act. Yet none offer a viable theory of the firm or to 'managing' as business schools claim to teach it.

Part II's shared anxiety is that managers are failing to apply 'appropriate' economic principles because business schools have failed to codify and teach them. The authors imply a morally sound economics of the firm is possible and teachable even though marginalism and the adoption of rational man methods gutted political economics of its normative dimensions, so no longer able to address the manager's moral contribution (Keynes, 1904). However, this pays insufficient attention to business education's institutional need to establish its own disciplinary territory, and so explain why business schools exist. While Adam Smith's influence is evident in the idea of the firm as a production function, his concern with the legal and institutional foundations of the private sector firm is less so. Economists' assumptions about property, trade and markets are contingent on the laws and politics that shape them. Real economic activity takes place within these constraints, yet neoclassical economics pays them little attention. Business schools likewise ignore corporate law and the history of the private firm (Horwitz, 1992; Hovenkamp, 1991). Does the legal system have a place for the kinds of 'goods' these authors hope for – in contrast to those underpinning neoclassical economics? The new moral economics will not be in a law-free world, rather it will be contingent on appropriate laws and social institutions. What is the intersection, if any, between the private firms' social and legal practices and the economics these authors presume guides them? Put another way, there is no reason to presume management's challenges are essentially economic rather than those of psychology, sociology or the law. Coase, a legal scholar, suggested the 'nature of the firm' arose from the subordination of employees to managers 'within certain limits', these demarcating the firm's legitimate activities from the illegitimate.

BEYOND ECONOMICS

In the background is Knight's intuition that economic growth and profit can only arise from the practice of engaging the uncertainties of the socio-economy. Likewise J.M. Keynes agreed that if the firm is a social and legal apparatus for generating profit it cannot be described or theorized within neoclassical economics, for that discipline is not able to address Knightian uncertainty or its resolution through acts of creative judgement (Spender, 2014). In short, there is no viable theory of the firm as a gain-producing economic actor or entity; it has a different and managerial nature. Put another way, value-creating management and neoclassical economics are axiomatically distinct discourses; while economics theorizes wealth distribution in perfect markets managing is always about wealth creation. In which case bringing moral and ethical dimensions into economics as a move to change its focus from maximizing shareholder wealth will still not tell us much about managing. Bringing in ethics cannot make up for management education's principal lacuna, the lack of a theory of the wealth creating or value adding firm. If the private sector is heading in the wrong direction then criticizing economists misses the real target – the managers whose hands are on their firms' tillers.

The immediate question is 'What should be added to the curriculum or cut from it?' Without doubt business schools tend to be philosophically arid and students would benefit from wider acquaintance with the philosophically inclined writers cited in this section. But without a theory of the firm there is no analytic distinction between the moral and ethical issues that affect us all as citizens and those that characterize us as managers, employees or contractors. If, as Coase suggested, the private firm is a socio-economic mechanism whereby investors profit from the subordination of others, it contains profound moral puzzles at its core. The justification for the private firms' freedom of socio-economic action and impact is far from morally or legally clear. On the one hand, firms exist at law as 'unnatural persons' that have acquired many citizens' rights over the last four centuries. But tensions between investors, managers and the rest of the socio-economy have been both evident and unrelenting since before the Bubble Act of 1720. The political system we have adopted – democratic capitalism – is evidently a Faustian compact; its risks revealed again in 2008 versus the socially beneficial returns Henley lists. Its mechanics are less economic than legal and institutional, tied up with the private firm's 'person-hood' and the nature of managerial power. In recent decisions – *Citizens United* v. *FEC* and *McCutcheon* v. *FEC* – the US Supreme Court has materially extended the person-hood of American firms. What is less clear is how these decisions have altered these firms' duties and, correspondingly, the nature and extent of their boards' and managers' responsibilities. We cannot discover the moral or ethical constraints to managing without a historically and politically situated theory of the firm as a profit-generating socio-legal apparatus. Equally it is clear from the history of corporate law that the inability of the legal profession to define the private firm, along with the inability of the economists, sociologists, or economic historians or others to do the same, has been no impediment to its political health and popularity. Nations have plunged ahead and granted private sector firms freedom of action because some of the wealth they create spills back into the socio-economy at large, not completely captured by share- and bondholders. The resulting social, economic and legal inequalities are the product of our society's political and legal processes. Economists simply provide explanatory rhetorical support and are clearly as baffled by events as the rest of us (Lo, 2012).

Summarizing, economists claim too much when they presume to shape business education, for the firm and its management are phenomena they cannot fully explain. Clearly some familiarity with economics is relevant; but paying attention to business history shows that managers work within constraints that are legal, institutional, psychological and political as much as they are economic. Theorists create a methodological gap as they simplify in their search for generalities. In contrast, managers must engage all these dimensions, using their judgement to arrive at solutions that are not determined by any. Thus business education fails whenever it asserts (a) that the complexities of managerial power and practice can be simplified into a single discipline's discourse, be that economics or any other, or (b) that managers make intendedly rational decisions rather than value-laden judgements.

REFERENCES

Coase, Ronald H. (1937) 'The nature of the firm', *Economica, New Series*, 4 (16): 386–405.

Coase, Ronald H. and Wang, Ning (2012) 'Saving economics from the economists', *Harvard Business Review*, 90 (12): 36–6.

Horwitz, Morton J. (1992) *The Transformation of American Law, 1780–1860*. New York: Oxford University Press.

Hovenkamp, Herbert (1991) *Enterprise and American Law 1836–1937*. Cambridge, MA: Harvard University Press.

Keynes, John Neville (1904) *The Scope and Method of Political Economy* (3rd edn). London: Macmillan.

Lo, Andrew W. (2012) 'Reading about the financial crisis: a twenty-one-book review', *Journal of Economic Literature*, 50 (1): 151–78.

Spender, J.-C. (2014) *Business Strategy: Managing Uncertainty, Opportunity, and Enterprise*. Oxford: Oxford University Press.

Van Horn, Robert, Mirowski, Philip and Stapleford, Thomas A. (eds) (2011) *Building Chicago Economics: New Perspectives on the History of America's Most Powerful Economics Program*. Cambridge: Cambridge University Press.

PART III

ETHICAL LEADERSHIP: PHILOSOPHICAL AND SPIRITUAL APPROACHES

11 INSPIRING RESPONSIBLE LEADERSHIP IN BUSINESS SCHOOLS: CAN A SPIRITUAL APPROACH HELP?

Karen Blakeley

The struggle at the very heart of our business schools and in fact all educational institutions consists of much more than intellectual battles over theoretical concepts or empirical truths. At its very core, this war is about identity, our souls, the very nature of who we are. (Khurana and Snook, 2011: 360)

INTRODUCTION

The past ten years have seen a growing consensus that business schools have lost their way and are facing a crisis of legitimacy. The most influential criticisms can be classified under four headings. Firstly, there has been a slavish adoption of free-market ideology, which is taught to students as 'truth' along with mathematical and 'scientific' models which reduce business activity to the amoral pursuit of profit maximization. This has been at the expense of more complex, human-centred perspectives rooted in moral imagination, emotional wisdom and the existential search for meaning. Secondly, excessive amounts of resources, energy and effort are dedicated to conducting research that is irrelevant to business and fails to impact society for the good. Thirdly, teaching is often disdained by academics who are more concerned with research and career success, than they are with the learning and development of their students. Finally, business schools have failed to define a morally uplifting and noble sense of vision and purpose in relation to their contribution to society as a whole (Giacalone, 2009; Starkey and Tempest, 2009; Wilson and Thomas, 2012). This has led some to accuse business schools of playing a formative role in the 2008 financial crisis and the crisis of capitalism more generally. As Giacalone (2009: 122) maintains, business schools have promoted values whereby 'the only important things in life are power, influence, status, and money – and where people, community, and concern for the next generation ... fall by the wayside in the search for personal and institutional glory'.

It would, however, be fair to assert that many of these criticisms have now been acknowledged as justifiable by increasing numbers of leading business academics. One of the most influential responses to this crisis of legitimacy is the UN Principles for Responsible Management Education (PRME). While laudable, I argue that initiatives such as PRME do not go far enough in addressing the issues highlighted above. This is because many of the social and environmental problems we face in the twenty-first century are, in fact, spiritual in nature, rooted in human characteristics such as greed and selfishness. James Speth, former environmental advisor to President Carter, claimed in a BBC interview that 'the top environmental problems are selfishness, greed and apathy and to deal with these we need a spiritual and cultural transformation. We scientists don't know how to do that – we need the help of religious leaders' (Shared Planet, 2013). Speth's examination of complex environmental issues led him to conclude that the answers lie, partially at least, in an understanding of the role that spirituality plays in mediating human excess. Business schools can play an important role in teaching students how spirituality can help them and their businesses address many of the moral dilemmas and complex problems they will face in the commercial world.

This chapter will therefore address a number of questions: why is spirituality an important addition to responsible management education? What does spirituality in a business school context look like? What might individual academics do to develop their own spirituality in the workplace? While I will focus strictly at the individual level of analysis, it is not intended to underemphasize the significance of organizational and systemic approaches. However, I leave it to other chapters in this volume to explore the meso and macro levels of analysis in promoting spirituality in the workplace. Our focus here will be on the individual, mainly because the starting point for transformational dialogue at group and organizational levels lies in stronger individual leadership in this area.

SPIRITUALITY – THE MISSING DIMENSION OF PRME

In their own words, PRME seeks to 'establish a process of continuous improvement among institutions of management education in order to develop a new generation of business leaders capable of managing the complex challenges faced by business and society in the twenty-first century' (PRME, 2015). In order to become members, institutions are required to incorporate the values of social responsibility into their teaching content, teaching methodology, research activities and stakeholder partnerships while submitting a bi-annual report outlining how they have achieved these goals.

There is, however, already some evidence that PRME is being used purely for the reputational and marketing benefits it confers. While some business schools are highly committed to PRME, others are far less so: they have not introduced any change as a result of joining and have not widely involved their staff in understanding and delivering PRME (Perry and Win, 2013). Further, PRME, through its emphasis on curriculum development, can be accused of placing inordinate stress on individual students to behave in morally uplifting ways while failing to hold business school staff and their leaders to account for living out the values in a systematic and coherent manner themselves. In the UK, for example, the recent row over the excessive pay of Vice Chancellors offered a very real demonstration of how senior academics mimic the values and practices of senior business executives, contributing to the problems of inequality, poor governance and the reduction of trust in society's leaders. In this, business school leaders and senior management teams who are members of PRME can be accused of lacking integrity and of 'blue-washing'.

Pruzan argues that attempting to teach responsibility, ethics and the virtues without embodying them ourselves will lead to 'cynicism and an instrumental approach to ethics in business' (2011: 16). From a more positive perspective, Tabelli suggests that innovative practices should be melded into business schools so that 'students ... feel a sense of belonging to a community. They must be emotionally moved. They should emulate the behaviour of esteemed individuals within the community' (Tabelli, 2011: 137). This implies that if students are going to be inspired to adopt a more socially responsible approach to the role of business in society, they need to be led by staff who themselves demonstrate personal and spiritual wisdom. Muff points out that '[f]aculty and administration are challenged to display the same levels of globally responsible leadership as they would wish to see in their fellow learners and participants' (Muff, 2013: 493). In sum, if academics are to cultivate the responsible business leaders of the future they need to demonstrate responsible leadership themselves.

This does not mean that as academics, we need to be perfect examples of virtue – that would be impossible – but we do need to be seen to be grappling honestly with the challenges of living a life of integrity and wisdom in our own institutions. The main challenge we face here is the problem of 'walking the talk'. Cultivating integrity involves a lifelong struggle to understand our unconscious drivers and to control our selfish urges: spirituality, and its close relation, positive psychology,[1] are important approaches that offer methods for helping individuals to do this. Miller (2006: 14) argues that 'to the degree that an organisation can enable, and support, or encourage a depth of personal morality and dedication to a noble purpose, it possesses spiritual capital'. The question is then, how do we develop spiritual capital in our business schools?

---

[1]Peterson and Seligman's definitive work on positive psychology, *Character Strengths and Virtues: A Handbook and Classification*, drew on the spiritual traditions of Confucianism, Taoism, Buddhism, Hinduism, ancient Greek philosophy, Judeo-Christianity and Islam in order to identify the list of virtues that comprise their volume (Peterson and Seligman, 2006: 34).

SPIRITUAL CAPITAL IN THE BUSINESS SCHOOL – A FRAMEWORK

There has been a growing interest in spirituality both within the general population (Heelas et al., 2005) and more particularly within the business academic community which has a seen a rapid increase in publications in this area over the past 15 years (Karakas, 2010: 90). The 'spirituality at work' literature is still relatively young as a discipline, with the *Journal of Management, Spirituality and Religion* established in 2004. Like many emergent theories, 'spirituality at work' still suffers from definitional ambiguity mainly due to the lack of clarity surrounding the term 'spirituality', which of course, has a much older provenance than the academic discipline of 'spirituality at work'.

In order to arrive at a definition of spirituality for this chapter, 30 key texts and journal articles on the subject were analysed for their definitions and explications of the term. I conducted a simple frequency count of the major themes that occurred in discussions of spirituality; the themes were clustered and ordered into an overarching map (see Figure 11.1). From this process, I define spirituality as the belief in, and valuing of, a transcendent reality which is accessed by means of various practices, in order to support a search for meaning and purpose, wisdom and personal growth, a deep connection with humanity, service to people and the planet and, ultimately, the achievement of a holistic integration of mind, body and soul through one's lived experience of the world. It comprises a number of key elements:

Transcendence – the recognition of a numinous plane of existence that is a source of goodness, elevation, joy, wonder and meaning.

Meaning and purpose – the dedication of one's life to something of personal and social value that is greater than material self-interest.

Spiritual growth – the dedication of one's life to personal and moral development.

Wisdom – the ability to address complex issues by evaluating them from multiple perspectives (rational, spiritual and emotional) while also critically reflecting upon one's own views and opinions.

The sacred – the recognition that some elements of life are not to be treated in an instrumental manner but should be kept pure and protected from material functionalism.

Interconnectedness – the recognition of one's connection and accountability to all forms of present and future life on the planet.

Service – the readiness to spend time in service to others.

Soul – our unique essence which shapes our identity and acts as a source of centredness, inner power and integrity.

Disciplined practice – determined, regular practice of spiritual disciplines such as meditation, reflection, prayer, fasting, volunteering, retreat.

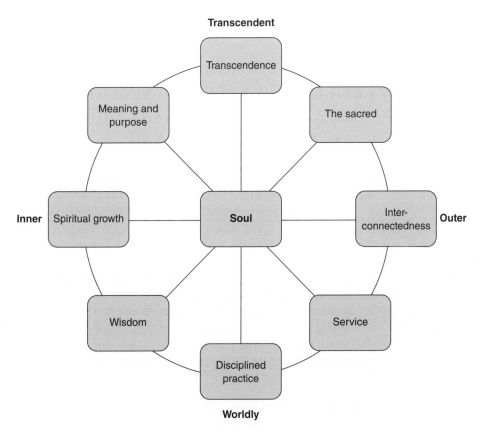

Figure 11.1 Elements of spirituality

Figure 11.1 offers a map of the elements I have included within a spiritual paradigm. At the top there is the mystical, divine or transcendent while the bottom focuses on the more practical implications of spirituality for everyday life. To the left, there is a path tracing the inner life of the spirit while the right-hand side focuses on how spirituality can be seen by others as it is lived out in the world. The middle section (the transcendent, the soul, the practices) provides 'spiritual glue' to the other elements; without a sense of the transcendent, a connection to the human soul and a disciplined spiritual practice, the other elements would lose their spiritual connotations and remain materialist constructs.

Each element poses questions and challenges at a variety of levels. The focus of this chapter is on the individual, but the framework may be used to raise questions at the level of the group, organization or whole system. Ultimately, it offers an alternative focus for our attention, acting as a both a challenge to, and a critical reflection on, the more materialist preoccupations normally associated with business schools. The next section will look in more detail at the individual elements of the framework and make suggestions as to how they might contribute towards helping individual academics demonstrate inspiring responsible leadership to their students and colleagues.

DEVELOPING SPIRITUAL CAPITAL AT WORK – NEW QUESTIONS THAT BUSINESS SCHOOLS MIGHT ASK

For convenience and brevity we will explore the elements under three clusters, each of which raises a number of questions and challenges for business school academics. The first cluster explores 'transcendence', 'meaning and purpose' and the 'sacred', looking at how the mystical elements of life help to shape personal purpose and inner fulfilment. The second cluster comprises 'soul', 'spiritual growth' and 'wisdom' and explores the questions that are raised when human life is reframed in terms of the search for authenticity, integrity and wisdom. The final cluster comprises 'interconnectedness', 'service' and 'spiritual practices' raising questions around 'activity' – what should we be doing and how should we be doing it? Each section will start with questions for personal reflection, followed by a brief exposition of the main themes and one example of how these might be translated into a business school context.

Cluster one: transcendence, meaning and purpose, the sacred

Transcendence – What provokes in you the experience of mystery, wonder or awe? What arouses a sense of deep joy in your life? What do you relate to in your life that is in some way 'bigger than you'? How do you bring your sense of the transcendent into your work practice and relationships?

A sense of the transcendent makes us aware that there is more to life than the material world around us, that the material world itself is a manifestation of the deepest mystery that confronts humanity: the very fact and existence of life itself. For those who believe in divine life, there is a spiritual world beyond our senses that energizes and inspires the human soul. For those who do not believe in the divine, there is an awareness of qualities such as sublimity, beauty, joy and love glimpsed through our earthly inheritance – our planet and culture, the arts and the sciences. Regular reflection upon the transcendent cultivates an awareness that life is not about 'me' but rather about me in some energizing and self-transforming relationship with something bigger – God or the planet or future generations. Our relationship with the transcendent provides us with a sense of joy and love without which it is difficult (some might say impossible) to embody other elements of the spiritual life.

> **Meaning and purpose** – Can you describe what gives your work meaning and purpose? Do you have a vision that inspires you to do 'good work' in the day-to-day? To what extent do you feel that your life has a purpose beyond addressing basic material needs and objectives?

When we have a vision for our lives the energy is infectious and helps us to operate as leaders rather than just academics helping us to inspire others – our students, colleagues and others with whom we come into contact. However, as business academics, if we do not develop personal visions for our work, we may find ourselves hijacked by the default goal of increasing the profitability or efficiency of organizations. While there is nothing intrinsically wrong with this, the obvious question is – who benefits from this increasing profitability? If we are not careful, we may find ourselves reinforcing a system that enriches the few at the expense of the many while contributing to the social and economic problems that flow from this.

We are fortunate since, as business academics, we have a transcendent purpose given to us – the care and cultivation of the next generation of business leaders who will impact the lives of people, organizations and societies across the world (Muff, 2013). This generation will be in charge of much of the technology that has the potential to harm or heal our planet; they will lead organizations that can dehumanize their workers or contribute towards their growth and creativity. At the same time our students will come under great pressure to feed their egoistic drives – for power, wealth, success, fame. How can we help them address these complex challenges?

> **The sacred** – What do you hold to be sacred in life? What do you treat with deep respect, reverence and awe? How consciously and actively do you embody this sense of sacredness in your work?

The sacred is the manifestation of the transcendent in reality – it involves that which is 'holy', related to the divine or 'set apart' from the secular or profane. Borgmann makes a distinction between the graceful sacred (art, nature, beauty) and the rightful sacred (humans beings, invested with inviolable rights) and shows how even the most dedicated atheists have a sense of the sacred. He quotes Daniel Dennett:

Is something sacred? Yes, say I with Nietzsche. I could not pray to it, but I can stand in affirmation of its magnificence. This world is sacred. (Borgmann, 2011: 184)

Business has a tendency to secularize the sacred, including treating human beings as costs or resources to be manipulated at will. As academics we can play a key part in helping our students to reintroduce and retain a sense of what is sacred into the world of business.

Example: developing a personal vision for our work
In order to develop a personal vision for our work we need to spend time in contemplation. Questions we might ask ourselves include: What were my youthful dreams for this world and what do I feel about them now? What, deep down, despite any cynicism that may have built up over the years, do I still feel passionate about? What kind of world/institution do I want to be a part of and how can my work contribute to this?

Cluster two: soul, spiritual growth and wisdom

Soul – To what extent are you able to be deeply authentic in your work and relationships? In what ways are you able to express your full potential and gifts through your work? To what extent do you energize and nourish others around you simply through your presence?

To be overwhelmed by the system is not an unusual experience. Many academics work long hours, managing large cohorts of students, carrying excessive administrative duties, pursuing research, writing papers, seeking funding and trying to keep up with the multiple expectations imposed upon them. Sometimes, they are caught up in the whirl of pursuing career success, driven to publish in prestigious journals and address peers at conferences in exotic locations. Others may be overly comfortable, re-cycling lectures that are years old, content with the adequate rather than the brilliant. It is easy to find oneself out of touch with what one really cares about and difficult to manifest responsible leadership in situations like this. Change has to start at the level of the soul, reigniting passion by connecting again with one's inner gifts, passions, values and commitments.

Spiritual growth – To what extent do you invest time and attention in your own spiritual development? Do you actively seek to examine your motives and cultivate virtues such as courage, forgiveness, love, generosity, joy, humility and self-control? To what extent do your students and work colleagues benefit from your ongoing spiritual growth?

Spirituality is not irrelevant to the running of a successful business. One example is Steve Jobs' Stanford Commencement Address which, at the time of writing, had been viewed by over 19.4 million people on the official Stanford site. In it, Jobs conveyed a number of spiritual 'truths' learned through periods of difficulty, suffering and setback in his life. He claimed, for example:

> Remembering that I'll be dead soon is the most important tool I've ever encountered to help me make the big choices in life. Because almost everything – all external expectations, all pride, all fear of embarrassment or failure – these things just fall away in the face of death, leaving only what is truly important. (Jobs, 2005)

Whatever you think of Jobs (and he was a controversial figure), in his world, soul, purpose, faith, creativity and personal risk were as much at the heart of the business as profits, technology, markets and customers. To what extent do we manifest this in our own lives? To what extent are we living radically authentic lives, demonstrating integrity, doing great work and achieving moments of deep satisfaction and flow?

Wisdom – To what extent do you challenge your own thinking? When was the last time you listened to and learned from someone with a different view or background to your own? How often do your students or colleagues come to you for personal advice?

Wisdom grows through a process of listening to and learning from diverse others so that we continually open our minds to ever more subtle and multi-faceted ideas and experiences. It is from this process that we gain perspective, stimulate curiosity, feed our creativity and infuse our understanding with compassion. Academics may be tempted to isolate themselves, avoiding interaction with business, the community or students, seeking to engage only with other academics. On a more personal level we may avoid questioning our assumptions or challenging ourselves to address issues that we know to be wrong. Engaging with diverse groups, pursuing deeper conversations with our peers and asking penetrating questions that relate to the meaning and purpose of our institutions can release insights and wisdom that transform learning and inspire the necessary social and institutional change.

Example: colleague coaching
Colleague coaching offers a positive environment to explore your personal vision and legacy, your values and relationships and your personal and spiritual growth. Colleagues could engage in mutual coaching, regardless of seniority, so that both partners enjoy and learn from the experience. The coaching pairs could be switched on a regular basis so that colleagues can get to know each

other at a deeper and more meaningful level, thereby contributing to the spiritual capital of the organization.

Cluster three: interconnectedness, service and disciplined practice

> **Interconnectedness** – What is the quality of your relationships at home and at work? Are you deepening your relationships with people over time? Are you modelling responsible leadership principles by connecting your own work across social boundaries and divisions? To what extent do you feel, think and act as someone whose actions can have a profound influence on the world around you?

As responsible leaders we need to acknowledge our connection and accountability to all forms of life on this planet, including to future generations. Indeed, the responsible leadership development literature is specifically focused on the development of empathy, compassion, relatedness and service to others (Maak and Pless, 2009). This means engaging with the notion that our lives really do matter. The Western emphasis on individualism, and in particular on the cult of celebrity, tends to imply that only certain important individuals make a difference in the world. A spiritual perspective suggests the opposite, that every individual matters and that every action we take (or fail to take) impacts the people and the planet around us. Living a spiritual life implies thinking, feeling and acting in conscious awareness of our personal significance and the impact we have on the world around us.

> **Service** – Who do you personally feel called to serve and support? To what extent do you seek to help others without any expectation of reward yourself? Where and how are you generous with your time, skills and other resources?

Part of the challenge for business academics is to connect with others, particularly the less privileged, outside of academic institutions. This might be done through work or outside the work environment; in whatever way we decide to focus our time, energy and talent, demonstrating a practical engagement with a particular social or environmental need is an important element of spirituality. Volunteering or serving others helps us to remain grounded in worlds that we might not otherwise engage with; not only does this result in a deeper understanding of and sense of responsibility for others, it can also provoke profound learning experiences that challenge our sense of identity, meaning and purpose, opening our minds to new insights and opportunities for growth.

> **Spiritual practice** – To what extent do you practise self-control such as resisting food or alcohol? What do you do to consciously practise virtues such as patience, humility and gratitude? To what extent do you spend time in stillness or in silence? What do you do to centre yourself, to develop a sense of peace and control in your life?

Many of the activities described here involve a dutiful element requiring what many of the great spiritual teachers would refer to as spiritual discipline. Like going on a diet, volunteering time as a trustee of a charity or repairing a difficult relationship with a colleague involves a degree of self-control. This is where the final element plays an important role – to become responsible leaders who demonstrate integrity, we need to engage in spiritual practices that strengthen our capacity to exercise discipline and self-control. The core of spiritual practice lies in the subjugation of ego needs and the disciplined application of the will through activities such as meditation, giving, fasting and the conscious practice of virtues such as self-sacrifice, gratitude and courage. It is not difficult to conceive of simple spiritual disciplines that could be applied fruitfully to our academic practice, such as the giving of time in pro bono activities, time on 'retreat' or peer supervision.

Example: cultivating spiritual practice
Spiritual growth is often rooted in a regular spiritual practice. This involves the personal design of a regularly repeated set of activities such as reading, silence/meditation/prayer and committing to a practice that in some way challenges the ego – expressing contrition or asking for forgiveness. One particular practice employed in the Christian tradition is called the examen of conscience. This is a reflexive assessment of one's thoughts, words and deeds from the perspective of a particular moral framework – in this case it might be rooted in the principles of CSR or virtue ethics.

POTENTIAL OBSTACLES TO SPIRITUALITY IN THE BUSINESS SCHOOL

Much has been written critiquing the spirituality at work literature (Case and Gosling, 2010; Karakas, 2010; Lips-Wiersma et al., 2009). There is not the space here to do justice to these works, which are incisive, relevant and important components of the debate. Critical scholars, for example, have long focused their attention on the role played by the management of meaning in creating a sense of wellbeing that can be manipulated by senior management for the purposes of value accumulation and performativity (Case and Gosling, 2010).

Clearly, there is potential here for senior managers and leaders in business schools to manipulate academics for performative ends.

The problems of religious proselytism, peer conformity pressures and a lack of tolerance for diversity (including a lack of tolerance of those who have no interest in or who express a dislike of the notion of spirituality) are also significant (Karakas, 2010). In addition there is potential for the delegitimization of impulses to resist, critique and deconstruct these activities; such resistance can be framed as egotistical or 'negative', causing conceptual and moral confusion and putting pressure on academics to self-censor and self-regulate.

Another problem lies in the fact that hypocrisy and self-righteousness are intrinsic to human nature, hence our attention is naturally drawn to the faults of others while remaining blind to our own moral weaknesses and character flaws (Haidt, 2006: 59).

The practices and suggestions here have been careful to minimize the links between spirituality and the power structures of the business schools (say, for example, linking spirituality to performance appraisals) in the hope that the links to performativity can be avoided. In addition, to combat conformity pressures, it is important that spiritual approaches be deeply rooted in a radical critique of the instrumentalization of our world, with the potential to forge links with critical management scholars as well as with more mainstream CSR and responsible leadership researchers. Critique of spirituality at work should be encouraged and should be seen as an intrinsic part of the debate and ongoing conversation.

CONCLUSION

This short chapter can only offer a basic introduction to how spirituality can help promote responsible management education in business schools. The main argument is that much of what is wrong in our organizations, institutions and societies is spiritual in nature and that both scholars and practitioners have ignored the vital role spirituality plays in sustaining the moral and ethical health of organizations. Business schools can play an important role here. They contain the research capabilities to explore important questions around the relationship between business and spirituality and can provide thought leaders to introduce these ideas to the business community and link them to its needs. Most importantly, they comprise a community within which spiritual values can be lived and taught. Without this community, and without academics willing to explore the spiritual dimensions of life, we are in danger of cultivating a 'do what I say, not do what I do' culture, thereby promoting cynicism or accusations of hypocrisy from our students. Alternatively, academics willing to explore the difficult personal challenges raised by the spiritual perspective can benefit not only from a reinvigorated inner life, but also from the satisfaction that they are helping to cultivate a new generation of responsible business leaders who are able and willing to take on the next set of challenges facing our planet. This is not to suggest that there are not significant problems posed by this approach, some of which have been briefly outlined here. The field is still young, however, and therefore has the potential to offer a rich and meaningful research agenda that addresses these challenges in a way that can make a real impact on the world and on the next generation of responsible business leaders.

FURTHER READING

Calhoun, A.A. (2005) *The Spiritual Disciplines Handbook: Practices That Transform Us*. Downers Grove, IL: InterVarsity Press.

Cox, H. (2009) *The Future of Faith: The Rise and Fall of Beliefs and the Coming Age of the Spirit*. New York: HarperOne.

Howard, S. and Welbourn, D. (2004) *The Spirit at Work Phenomenon*. London: Azure.

King, U. (2008) *The Search for Spirituality: Our Global Quest for a Spiritual Life*. New York: BlueBridge.

Krishnamurti, J. (1995) *On Fear*. New York: HarperCollins.

Sheldrake, P.F. (2012) *Spirituality: An Introduction*. Oxford: Oxford University Press.

Strenger, C. (2011) *The Fear of Insignificance: Searching for Meaning in the Twenty-first Century*. New York: Palgrave Macmillan.

REFERENCES

Borgmann, A. (2011) 'The sacred and the person', *Inquiry*, 54 (2): 183–94.

Case, P. and Gosling, J. (2010) 'The spiritual organization: critical reflections on the instrumentality of workplace spirituality', *Journal of Management, Spirituality and Religion*, 7 (4): 257–82.

Giacalone, R. (2009) 'Academic rankings in research institutions: a case of skewed mind-sets and professional amnesia', *Academy of Management Learning and Education*, 8 (1): 122–6.

Haidt, J. (2006) *The Happiness Hypothesis: Putting Ancient Wisdom and Philosophy to the Test of Modern Science*. London: Arrow Books.

Heelas, P., Woodhead, L., Seel, B., Szerszynski, B. and Tusting, K. (2005) *The Spiritual Revolution: Why Religion Is Giving Way to Spirituality*. Oxford: Blackwell.

Howard, S. and Welbourn, D. (2004) *The Spirit at Work Phenomenon*. London: Azure.

Jobs, S. (2005) Steve Jobs 2005 Stanford Commencement Address, Stanford University. Retrieved from: www.youtube.com/watch?v=UF8uR6Z6KLc (accessed 22 April 2014).

Karakas, F. (2010) 'Spirituality and performance in organizations: a literature review', *Journal of Business Ethics*, 94 (1): 89–106.

Khurana, R. and Snook, S. (2011) 'Commentary on "A Scholar's Quest": identity work in business schools: from Don Quixote, to dons and divas', *Journal of Management Inquiry*, 20 (4): 358–61.

Lips-Wiersma, M., Lund Dean, K. and Fornaciari, C.J. (2009) 'Theorizing the dark side of the workplace spirituality movement', *Journal of Management Inquiry*, 18 (4): 288–300.

Maak, T. and Pless, N.M. (2009) 'Business leaders as citizens of the world: advancing humanism on a global scale', *Journal of Business Ethics*, 88 (3): 537–50

Miller, L.M. (2006) 'Virtuous self interest: in pursuit of a new capitalism', *Leadership Excellence*, 23 (10): 14.

Muff, K. (2013) 'Developing globally responsible leaders in business schools: a vision and transformational practice for the journey ahead', *Journal of Management Development*, 32 (5): 487–507.

Perry, M. and Win, S. (2013) 'An evaluation of PRME's contribution to responsibility in higher education', *Journal of Corporate Citizenship*, 49: 48–70.

Peterson, C. and Seligman, M.E.P. (2006) *Character Strengths and Virtues: A Handbook and Classification*. New York: Oxford University Press.

PRME (2015) 'Principles for responsible management education'. Retrieved from: www.unprme.org/about-prme/index.php (accessed 12 January 2015).

Pruzan, P. (2011) 'Spirituality as the context for leadership', in L. Zsolnai (ed.), *Spirituality and Ethics in Management, Issues in Business Ethics* (2nd edn). Dordrecht: Springer, pp. 3–21.

Shared Planet (2013) 'Religion and nature', BBC Radio 4, 7 October. Retrieved from: www.bbc.co.uk/programmes/b03bqws7 (accessed 8 October 2013).

Starkey, K. and Tempest, S. (2009) 'The winter of our discontent: the design challenge for business schools', *Academy of Management Learning and Education*, 8 (4): 576–86.

Tabelli, G. (2011) 'The role of higher education institutions in the fields of economic and social sciences: has it been changed by the economic downturn?', in A.S. Rovira and M. Morsing (eds), *Business Schools and Their Contribution To Society*. London: Sage, pp. 133–7.

Wilson, D.C. and Thomas, H. (2012) 'The legitimacy of the business of business schools: what's the future?', *Journal of Management Development*, 31 (4): 368–76.

12 IS IT POSSIBLE TO LEARN ETHICAL LEADERSHIP? MACINTYRE, ŽIŽEK AND THE RECOVERY OF VIRTUE

Mervyn Conroy

INTRODUCTION

In recent years we have witnessed an increasing level of corruption exposés in many sectors including finance, media, health and social care and sport. Further dialogue between leadership studies and critical researchers in order to understand more about leadership and the crisis of ethical practice has been urged by scholars. In particular, purpose, ethics, virtue and moral accountability of practices and the relationship to leadership are noted in the literature as needing more attention. In response to this call, in this chapter I suggest that there is an inherent 'ethical distance' between the traditional leading and managing change theories and the virtues of practice excellence. I further argue that an understanding of the ethical dimension of neo-liberal inspired change leadership has, to date, been missing from leadership theorizing. By explicating the leadership–practice gap as ethical in nature, new vistas on leading economic and 'lean' reforms are opened up. For example, the paradoxical nature of the reform process is exposed: the more economic pressure is applied to make practices efficient the more they cost in the long term due to generative practice corruptions. I challenge the practice of the neo-liberal change leadership movement, of which arguably the MBA is on the front line, to take account of the ethical status of practices in institutions. By asking questions business schools tend to avoid I develop an alternative leadership module that takes into account the ethical status of practices. This has been trialled successfully on postgraduate leadership programmes and is outlined in the final section of this chapter.

MacIntyre (2009) suggests that a Christian understanding of the university might restore even to the secular university a sense of purpose for the nature of academic enquiry. He argues that the disintegration of the university curriculum has dangerous implications for global wellbeing and how universities can and ought to renew a shared understanding of their mission. His analysis is that universities once encouraged a unified knowledge of all being, of which philosophy and theology played central roles, bridging findings from the various disciplines. The gradual elimination of theology, the relegation of philosophy to one technical discipline (among many) and the abandonment of the quest for integrated wisdom about the world could mean that all schools, not just business schools, are no longer inclined to ask a whole set of questions relating to mission, purpose and global wellbeing. This chapter specifically challenges the mode of the business school MBA/postgraduate management programme and change/improvement leadership content that promotes a set of ethics removed from a quest for integrated wisdom and argues for an alternative. The main questions that I argue business schools are failing to engage with are related to purpose and moral accountability:

- What are the antecedents of the different standpoints in ethical dilemmas associated with reform?
- What are the originating ideologies informing those standpoints?
- Where does an MBA graduate stand in relation to those ideologies?

Scholars have urged more dialogue between leadership studies and critical researchers in order to understand more about leadership and the crisis of ethical practice, especially in the light of exposés such as those connected with health and social care, financial markets, Formula 1 racing and football. In particular, the ethics, virtue and moral accountability of practices and the relationship to leadership are registered in the academic literature (e.g. Kempster et al., 2011) and enquiry reports (e.g. Francis, 2013) as needing more attention. In responding to this call I propose the notion of 'ethical distance' and argue that an understanding of ethical distance has, to date, been missing from leadership theorizing. Distance in this context means a significant difference in ethics, for example, one virtue of neo-liberal market-based ethics is to be competitive (honing oneself lean to beat another) but this would sit at a significant distance from a public service ethics and a virtue of compassion (honing oneself to be caring for another). By explicating the leadership–practice gap as ethical in nature new vistas on leadership education are opened up. In particular questions associated with the ethics of neo-liberal informed change leadership theories are posed so that the practice of change leadership education is challenged to include a deeper understanding of the ethical status of practices. In bridging this gap through enhancing professional education it is hoped that the average MBA graduate will come across less like Žižek (1991) observes as not really knowing what they are doing; taking on an ideology without questioning the roots of that ideology and the impact of its colonization (Willmott, 1993) on themselves and others when attempting modernizing reforms to whatever type of organization they find themselves leading and managing.

NEO-LIBERAL PERSPECTIVES

Significant investments in time, resources and energy (both physical and emotional) are being made in public and private sector change programmes designed to save money, generate growth and make organizations more effective and efficient. Change leaders, according to the scripts of neo-liberal infused policies and professional education dominated by structural functional paradigms (Burrell and Morgan, 1979); but little is known about the ethics of the practices affected. In this chapter I explore these issues through sociological and psychological theoretical frames from MacIntyre and Žižek respectively. My basic argument is that the intoxicating and addictive (Cook, 2006) cocktail of neo-liberal leadership reform ethics and structural-functional ontology sit at a distance from ethical practice; the consequence is dissonance and corruption to practices. My intention is to broaden existing debates associated with leadership at a distance (Collinson, 2005; Grint, 2010) and the contested purpose of organizations (Hoggett, 2006; Kempster et al., 2011).

Žižek's Lacanian derived theory of ideology presents a radically new descriptive perspective that affords us a unique purchase on many of the paradoxes of the neo-liberal subjectivity. This is politically challenging. Žižek's work prompts us to ask questions about the possibility of socio-political change, including what forms would such changes take and what might justify them or make them possible? Drawing on the work of Žižek (1991), de Cock and Bohm (2007) offer an insight into the Janus-faced nature of neo-liberalism that our society has sanctioned as the saviour of morality, the answer to quality of life for all and the defence against the fear of totalitarianism. One face presents personalization, freedom and innovation and the other a controlling hegemony allied to market brand maintenance: 'You are free to do anything you want as long it involves shopping' (de Cock and Bohm, 2007: 828). MacIntyre (1985) suggests that the harbinger of such misdirected good intentions was the Enlightenment and that we now exist in an era where virtues have been superseded by a disparate, scientifically informed morality. Coping with the loss of a binding narrative of ethical practice in our dealings with others and operating outside social and historical traditions, people have had placed upon them the impossible burden of becoming their own moral authority. Practices in private and now our public and third sector institutions have succumbed to the corrupting influence of money, status and power. Recently reported events in health and social care, financial markets, Formula 1 racing and football would seem to concur with Žižek's and MacIntyre's theses. The perverse (Pidd, 2005) and in some cases fatal outcomes (Francis, 2013) of hospital practices in response to target setting, status chasing and austerity show that the public sector is not immune.

The chapter has four main sections. First, I review recent debates associated with different forms of distance in relation to leader and follower relations; second, I summarize MacIntyre's (1985) virtue ethics in order to define what ethical practice means in this context; third, I consider some of Žižek's arguments which chime with MacIntyre's even though they build on very different schools of thought; and finally, I demonstrate an alternative MBA-style leadership module that was informed by the theoretical frames offered by these two contemporary philosophers and which attempts to bridge the gap in ethical knowledge and understanding for management professionals.

DISTANCE

What do we know about leadership and distance in the modern workplace?

BOX 12.1   KEEPING LEADERS AT A DISTANCE

Grint (2010) explores distance from the perspective of it being a component of the sacred in leadership. He states that leadership has a history of involving some way of providing 'distance' between leader and follower. Grint also suggests that distancing is a device for 'facilitating the execution of distasteful but necessary tasks by leaders and of generating the space to see the patterns that are all but invisible when very close to followers or the action' (2010: 94).

Despite this Grint finds that both in the civilian world of work and in military leadership the belief that nearby leaders perform better than distant leaders is pervasive. One of the issues for leaders in distancing themselves is highlighted by Collinson (2005) who proposes that distance provides significant opportunities for followers to 'construct alternative, more oppositional identities and workplace counter-cultures that express scepticism about leaders and their distance from followers' (2005: 241). Humour is noted as a device used to distance followers from leaders, though like Piccone (1978) originally suggests, space to vent opposition in any form can provide paradoxical support to leaders rather than effective resistance.

In this chapter I explore distance through a virtue ethics lens offered by MacIntyre in a way that builds on the ideas in Box 12.1, but I add another dimension to the distance debate which exposes the dangers of both near and distance leaders when the nature of that distance can be understood in terms of different ethical standpoints and traditions. Evidence offered by Cole et al. (2009) suggests that in close leader–follower relationships followers' behaviour is more likely to emulate that of the leader. They suggest that 'followers' self-concepts, once primed, may be powerful determinants of their subsequent behaviour and connected thought processes' (2009: 1727). Their call is for future research to identify the leadership 'behaviours' that are most relevant to the priming effects of transformational leadership in socially close versus distant situations. In their research there is no consideration of the ethical nature of transformational leadership and whether the adoption of ethical behaviours is good for the institution or the people served by that institution. I argue that there is a paucity of attention given to 'ethical distance' in leadership studies and that neo-liberal leadership ethics, with its emphasis on market, freedom and choice, actually has an inherent distance from ethical practice. Further, when neo-liberal ethics socially constructs practice ethics through follower behaviour it can have a corrupting impact on practice. In the next section the term 'ethical practice' is explicated through the work of MacIntyre (1985).

ETHICAL PRACTICE

MacIntyre's belief is that humans are storytelling animals and one of the purposes of stories is to carry a set of virtues that when enacted in practice with others bring the good life for all those that are part of the polis.[1] For an institution, when viewed through MacIntyre's lens, the importance of individual and collective narratives is emphasized as the carrier of a set of virtues that offer internal goods for all practitioners. What this means in practice is explained in Box 12.2 below.

BOX 12.2   WHAT IS THE RELATIONSHIP BETWEEN PRACTICES, INTERNAL GOODS AND VIRTUES?

MacIntyre (1985) explains that the relationship hinges on practices and their internal goods for the practitioners (fulfilment of a job well done), for others (a product that works well or a service that satisfies) and for the practice (increasing refinement of a process to produce a product or service). Those goods are all internal and for MacIntyre can only be achieved through a continued and communal narrative in the form of a moral debate between practitioners on how best to conduct that practice. The virtues acquired by the practitioners are described as 'an acquired human quality the possession and exercise of which tends to enable

(Continued)

---

[1]Aristotle (*Nicomachean Ethics*) defined a particular type of societal grouping called a 'polis' in which relationships were not just based on friendships but also a shared sense of *telos* (purpose) for the group (city state). Through the polis flows a narrative that carries the virtues that contribute to conducting all practice in a way that brings wellbeing for all (*eudaimonia*) in the polis.

(Continued)

us to achieve those goods which are internal to practices and the lack of which effectively prevents us from achieving any such goods' (MacIntyre, 1985: 187). All practices are reliant on and situated within other practices that contribute to some overall purpose (*telos*). For example, all the different medical and support practices that make up and supply hospital services.

This collective relationship means that practices need to mesh with each other in a moral debate about *telos* to human life that then leads to a refinement of practice virtues for each of the practices, also recognizing that each practice will have its own unique virtues. For instance, a soldier's practice virtue of taking lives is different from a medic's virtue of saving lives but both are needed for the *telos* of winning a war. McCann and Brownsberger (1990: 227–8) extend the notion of *telos*: 'There must be some *telos* to human life, a vision anticipating the moral unity of life, given in the form of a narrative history that has meaning within a particular community's traditions; otherwise the various internal goods generated by the range of social practices will remain disordered and potentially subversive of one another. Without a community's shared sense of *telos*, there will be no way of signifying "the overriding good" by which various internal goods may be ranked and evaluated'.

The ramifications of this perspective are profound in that to form and achieve any particular *telos*, for example global wellbeing, requires the meshing of practice narratives and personal quests in a moral debate about how to conduct our practices across all practices that interconnect to achieve such a *telos*. Moore and Beadle (2006: 332) explain this concept in relation to the communal narrative and bring us back to our own sense of *telos*:

> It is only within the context of this continuing and communal narrative that she can make sense of herself and that she can begin to make some sense of her *telos*. Initially this *telos* is derived from experiences of early childhood, but gradually it becomes hers as she embarks on her own narrative quest.

MacIntyre's view is that we have been deflected from our ability to maintain a unity in moral debate by the liberal individualistic influences from the Enlightenment onwards; further, that we are unable at this point in history to properly reconcile the collision of different ideological horizons and moral traditions that are battled for daily in the workplace. His reasoning is that the premises of competing moral traditions are incompatible and therefore resolution can only be partial and achieved through assertion and counter assertion. The swings in political party fortunes are a good example of this – just as one policy seems to be failing the assertion of a different policy wins through only to be followed later by a swing back to the previous policy.

Leaders practising within the discourse of neo-liberal reform may or may not experience dissonance between the drive for efficiency and effectiveness (that market demands) and building ethical and sustainable excellence in practices. I explore here one contextual example, healthcare in the UK, that has recently attracted much attention due to practice corruptions that have led to scandals (e.g. Francis, 2013). Table 12.1 offers examples of the ethical clashes that regularly arise in healthcare modernization but are also common in other contexts. The first shows the distance between leadership being developed in a person through a learning process about models and theories of leadership and then applying them in practice as opposed to leadership development through an apprenticeship. The second contrasts an evidence-based approach against experienced practitioners working together to find the best solution for patients. The third shows the contrast between individual efficiency and effectiveness in the Tayloristic mode and the practice-based community approach in the Kaizen mode where knowledge about practice excellence is shared across the skill and experience of practitioners. Fourth is personal performance interests in competition with the greater good both for the whole practice and the community they serve.

Table 12.1   Examples of ethical clashes in healthcare

Neo-liberal change leadership	vs.	Ethical practice
Leadership models and theories (predictive knowledge)		Apprenticeship
Evidence-based management		Partnership-based clinical work
Efficiency and effectiveness		Valuing practice-based communities
Personal effectiveness and performance		The greater good

Even when these types of dissonances are brought to the attention of leaders, the virtue ethics perspective of MacIntyre suggests that the nature of the prevailing knowledge system upon which management education is based means they may not have the moral debating resources available to them to resolve these. In short, the current resolution methodology for leaders is limited largely to the power of assertion (or perhaps who can construct the most convincing business case). This challenge to management education will be followed up in the final section of the chapter but for now in order to show that MacIntyre is not a lone voice (albeit a highly respected one) the next section shows how Žižek's theorizing converges with MacIntyre's perspectives in several key areas.

ŽIŽEK

Žižek's theorizing stems from a splicing of Lacanian psychoanalytic theory with that of philosophers such as Hegel, Kant and Marx. This section looks at particular aspects of his analysis which complement and support MacIntyre's viewpoint.

Lacan used the term '*le point de capiton*', literally the 'upholstery button' (Žižek, 1991: 16). Žižek observes the way we succumb to a 'narrative quilting of heterogeneous material into a unified ideological field' (1991: 18). An artificial ideological closure or 'suturing' of raw and incompatible material into a narrative (plot) seduces us with a fantasy. For example, in Žižek's theorizing, as mobilized by de Cock and Bohm (2007), the Janus-faced nature of neo-liberal openness is exposed. De Cock and Bohm (2007) argue that this presents a disturbing and politically dangerous aspect to the ideas put forward by Gray's (2000) two faces of liberalism: the first face of liberalism is based on the principles that universally announce the death of the bureaucracy and replace it with a strong call for leadership on the one hand and communitarian values on the other. Gray's second face of liberalism is one of controlling the excesses of capitalism and managerialism, ensuring the good life through reconciling the claims of conflicting values. By drawing on Žižek's 'other-openness', de Cock and Bohm (2007: 824) argue that there is a major flaw in Gray's suggestion.

Žižek proposes that the main 'social fantasy' that hold us in this era of neo-liberalism is the 'ultimate liberal blackmail' contained in the argument that any alternative to capitalism merely paves the way for totalitarianism. De Cock and Bohm compare Žižek to Mouffe when they suggest 'he [Žižek] posits the public sphere as the battleground where different hegemonic projects confront one another without any possibility of final reconciliation' (de Cock and Bohm, 2007: 827). In our reading Žižek is also very close to MacIntyre's conclusion of irreconcilable moral and social traditions based on different premises. Further convergence appears when we look at their suggested alternatives: 'For Žižek, openness means questioning the ideological workings of the allegedly post-ideological discourse of the open society' (de Cock and Bohm, 2007: 828). MacIntyre (1985) advises a similar path of informing and educating communities of practitioners and policy-makers about the antecedents of their ethical clashes in order to allow them to engage with the moral debate of what kind of business, society and world they wish to build and fight for together. The next section shows how MacIntyre's and Žižek's theorizing was applied to the design of a post-graduate leadership module that has formed part of MBA and post-experience executive education programmes.

AN ALTERNATIVE LEADERSHIP MODULE

It has been argued that a traditional MBA programme based on neo-liberal ideology and functionalist assumptions does not have the ontological flexibility to take account of the ethical dimension of practices. As a result reform applications and proponents will not only sit at a distance from practice ethics but, because of a lack of understanding of how practice ethics are formed and promulgated, could actually contribute to practice corruptions. Furthermore it is argued that neo-liberal approaches combined with structural functional paradigms do not contain the theoretical resources to consider the generative ethical legacy of reform strategies. Even 'ethical leadership' theoretical resources have to date struggled to take account of the ethical dimension and purpose (Kempster et al., 2011). Instead what we have seen in most sectors as a legacy is an explosion from the time bomb of stored practice corruptions. This time bomb is precisely what MacIntyre (1985) predicted as the emphasis shifts to a focus on money (e.g. in the form of either cuts or increased profits), status (e.g. being a brand leader, academy status or foundation trust status) or power (e.g. market dominance) (Cato, 2009). MacIntyre emphasizes that these three are still goods even though they are 'external goods' so they are still important goods for institutions. This position prompts a question: 'How do we engage with this seam of theorizing on an MBA leadership module without alienating students and their employers?' An alternative model was developed and trialled by the author. The headline topics are not radically different from those for a traditional MBA leadership module those for, but the ethical dimension to leadership underpins the programme through the questions posed and the moral debating opportunities provided. The unit topics covered are:

- Vision and strategy.
- Influencing.
- Collaboration.
- Professional relationships.
- Managing change and managing performance.

So what is different about the way these topics were handled? The following is an example from the first topic. Through the theological and philosophical frames offered by proponents such as MacIntyre and Žižek, questions not normally asked by business schools can be asked. The remaining units build on the first and together form a complete package which critically addresses the discourses of neo-liberalism and structural functional paradigms and offers alternatives.

Vision and strategy

For this module we focus on helping delegates gain a deeper understanding of where they stand in relation to their practice dilemmas as a way to develop a personal and collective vision (*telos*) and strategy (virtues) for their practices and organizations and the communities they serve. Typical questions are:

What does it mean to be an ethical leader?

What is the purpose of an ethical leader?

What is the most challenging ethical dilemma you face?

Of what wider battle is your dilemma the scene?

What are the antecedents of the different standpoints?

What are the originating ideologies informing those standpoints?

Where do you stand in relation to these ideologies?

On which side of the fence do you fall?

On whose side do you want to fight?

What does this mean for your personal vision?

How does that relate to a vision for your organization?

How does your corporate vision relate to a vision for your community and society?

What strategies are needed to bring that vision into being?

Naturally these questions encourage an exploration of philosophy and theology, the very topics that MacIntyre (2009) laments as missing from professional education. The students are taken on a journey through a mix of their own studies, peer knowledge of theology and philosophy from many cultures and the lecturer's resources. Very rich debate associated with leadership ensues. For example, the questions help to illustrate for the students the difference between a manager who follows a script written by someone else and an ethical leader who breaks the mould and writes a script of his or her own in a way that resonates with a collective ethical approach and purpose. For others the discussion evokes their anger when they recognize they have been supporting the colonization of practice-corrupting effects and subjectivities (Willmott, 1993). This emotional response comes from them understanding the antecedents of the different standpoints (e.g. liberty vs. equality) and what that means for the people they are serving. They become angry at being pulled unwittingly across the ethical gap and becoming 'emplotted' in a narrative, namely a neo-liberal managerialist ideology, that is in conflict with their own narrative quest as managers or clinicians to enable practices to support health and wellbeing with equality. During learning set time they begin to question rationalizations (Anand et al., 2004) that had led to corrupting influences on the practices they were stewarding. Typical of the feedback received so far, is:

- 'Increased my appetite for reading'.
- 'Made me quite angry'; 'Found it cathartic'.
- 'I came out of Leading Change a changed person'.
- 'Kaboom: it clarified the difference between leadership and management'.
- 'Leadership is about breaking the rules'.

Eventually the debate invariably turns to 'what next?' along the lines of 'It is all very well being clear about my ethical purpose as a leader but how do I build followership?'. The sense from the group at this stage is one of controlled determination fuelled partly by their anger, giving them sufficient momentum to overcome any anxiety they might have felt about putting their heads above the parapet. This leads seamlessly onto the next two units, Influencing and

Collaboration. Having influenced and formed collaborations the next question from the students is usually, 'How do I form these ethically based collaborations into formal and normalized working agreements for my organization and its partners?'. Hence the Professional Relationships unit is a helpful next step for them. Ensuring the organization continues to operate on ethical principles while responding to internal and external changes means the final unit Managing Performance and Managing Change is positioned at the end, and the way it is designed means it also links together all the ethical practice strands from the previous units.

The following is typical of the feedback received at the end of this module:

- 'I am more courageous now in my assertion of doing the right thing in the organization rather than meeting targets'.
- 'I am encouraging more networking – something that I never made time for in the past'.
- 'There is no way we would have taken on this new work without understanding the values at stake'.
- 'Now I feel it is not about who we commission and more about what patients need'.

The general sense from the participants is that the programme seems to (re-) construct their courage, rekindle their 'narrative quest' and develop a clearer purpose for them and their organization.

CONCLUSION

Hoggett (2006) walks some of the same territory of this chapter when he draws on MacIntyre and psychoanalytical theory to argue that liberty, equality and fraternity, three guiding principles of democracy, are incommensurable, inherent and irresolvable. He states that the public official is required to 'enact value conflicts' (2006: 178) every day. His conclusion is that contested purpose should be accepted and worked with as a leader. This is similar to Downing (1997) who observes that, in the midst of change, leaders should try to resolve the storied value conflicts. De Cock and Bohm's (2007) critique of Gray's (2000) second face of liberalism, which claims that only a controlling bureaucracy is able to ensure the 'good life' in organizations, warns against the approach by arguing that it is based on the empty signifier of the open society. What I argue here supports Hoggett's and Downing's initial analysis of contested purpose and conflicting values but then aligns with de Cock and Bohm's warning to argue for an alternative. The alternative emerges by drawing on MacIntyre and change leadership narratives from the frontline of neo-liberal reform. I argue that they expose the inherent ethical distance of neo-liberal informed leadership education from practice ethics, therefore making it difficult, if not impossible, for leaders to engage with the meaningful moral debate associated with those practices. What has emerged at a practice level from this theoretical position, observed through MacIntyre's and Žižek's frames, is an alternative option for leaders facing this dissonance or 'ethical crisis' and not knowing what to do. The option demonstrated here in the form of an alternative postgraduate leadership module begins with questioning the ideological workings and tracing the antecedents of their virtue clashes by asking, 'Of what wider (ethical) conflicts is mine the scene?'. The subsequent journey through perspective broadening concepts from philosophy and theology is precisely what MacIntyre (2009) suggests should be rightfully returned to the academy after being driven out by the neo-liberal movement and all its allies. With this return I argue, based on the evidence presented here, that the MBA graduate will know much more about what they do when given responsibility to lead reform throughout all sectors.

FURTHER READING

Conroy, M. (2010) *An Ethical Approach to Leading Change: An Alternative and Sustainable Application*. Basingstoke: Palgrave Macmillan

Kempster, S., Jackson, B. and Conroy, M. (2011) 'Leadership as purpose: exploring the role of purpose in leadership practice', *Leadership*, 7 (3): 317–34.

MacIntyre, A. (1985) *After Virtue: A Study in Moral Theory* (2nd edn). London: Duckworth.

Spicer, A. and Fleming, P. (2007) 'Intervening in the inevitable: contesting globalisation in a public sector organisation', *Organization*, 14 (4): 517–41.

Žižek, S. (1991) *Enjoyment as a Political Factor: For They Know Not What They Do*. London: Verso.

REFERENCES

Anand, W., Ashforth, B.E. and Joshi, M. (2004) 'Business as usual: the acceptance and perception of corruption in organizations', *Academy of Management Executive*, 18 (2): 39–53.

Burrell, G. and Morgan, G. (1979) *Sociological Paradigms and Organizational Analysis*. London: Heinemann.

Cato, M.S. (2009) *Green Economics: An Introduction to Theory, Policy and Practice*. London: Earthscan.

Cole, M.S., Bruch, H. and Shamir, B. (2009) 'Social distance as a moderator of the effects of transformational leadership: both neutralizer and enhancer', *Human Relations*, 62: 1697–733.

Collinson, D.L. (2005) 'Questions of distance', *Leadership*, 1/2: 235–50.

Cook, C.C.H. (2006) *Alcohol, Addiction and Christian Ethics*. Cambridge: Cambridge University Press.

de Cock, C. and Bohm, S. (2007) 'Žižek and the impossibility of the open society', *Organization*, 14 (6): 815–36.

Downing, S.J. (1997) 'Learning the plot: emotional momentum in search of dramatic logic', *Management Learning*, 28 (1): 27–44.

Francis, R. (2013) *Report of the Mid Staffordshire NHS Foundation Trust. Volume 1: Analysis of Evidence and Lessons Learned.* London: The Stationary Office.

Gray, J. (2000) *Two Faces of Liberalism.* New York: The New Press.

Grint, K. (2010) 'The sacred in leadership: separation, sacrifice and silence', *Organization Studies*, 31 (1): 89–107.

Hoggett, P. (2006) 'Conflict, ambivalence, and the contested purpose of public organizations', *Human Relations*, 59 (2): 175–94.

Kempster, S., Jackson, B. and Conroy, M. (2011) 'Leadership as purpose: exploring the role of purpose in leadership practice', *Leadership*, 7 (3): 317–34.

MacIntyre, A. (1985) *After Virtue: A Study in Moral Theory* (2nd edn). London: Duckworth.

MacIntyre, A. (2009) *God, Philosophy and Universities.* London: Duckworth.

McCann, D.P. and Brownsberger, M.L. (1990) 'Management as a social practice: rethinking business ethics after MacIntyre', in D.M. Yeager (ed.), *The Annual of the Society of Christian Ethics.* Washington, DC: Georgetown University Press, pp. 223–45.

Moore, G. and Beadle, R. (2006) 'In search of organisational virtue in business: agents, goods, practices, institutions and environments', *Organisation Studies*, 27 (3): 369–89.

Piccone, P. (1978) 'The crisis of one-dimensionality', *Telos*, 35: 43–54.

Pidd, M. (2005) 'Perversity in public service performance measurement', *International Journal of Productivity and Performance Measurement*, 54(5/6): 482–93.

Willmott, H. (1993) 'Strength is ignorance; slavery is freedom: managing cultures in modern organizations', *Journal of Management Studies*, 30 (4): 515–52.

Žižek, S. (1991) *Enjoyment as a Political Factor: For They Know Not What They Do.* London: Verso.

13 CLASSICAL GREEK PHILOSOPHY AND THE LEARNING JOURNEY

Hugo Gaggiotti and Peter Simpson

INTRODUCTION

In ancient Greece, philosophy was understood as a way of life, a way of seeing and being in the world, rather than as the abstract intellectual discipline with which the term is typically associated today. For example, Aristotle considered the practice of philosophy as a training to assist in evaluating whether one's actions were good, which was determined in relation to the proper goal or purpose (*telos*) of human existence. That purpose was happiness (*eudaimonia*), which was understood not in the modern sense of pleasurable feeling but in terms of completeness or perfection. This is not entirely unrelated to a more pragmatic understanding of the purpose of business schools, the preparation of students for work, in that it requires attention to be given to right action. However, the questions that might be asked will not be the same because the starting point, the processes of learning and the outcomes will all be of a very different nature.

In this sense it is not enough to be practical, not enough to be intellectual. What is required are leaders and managers who are philosophical in the ancient sense of the term – able to engage with and to ask the deep questions of what it means to be fully human in their practice of commerce and trade as well as in their contribution to society.

Business schools are places of learning, which always involves an inquiry into theory and practice. The description of programmes and modules typically contains learning outcomes that state that by the end of the course students will be able 'to *apply* theories' or 'demonstrate the capacity to *use* theories' in real situations. However, we believe that insufficient attention is given to enabling students to learn how to develop theories of their own; that is, to theorize (Weick, 1995). We have never seen a learning outcome that requires 'the ability to theorize'. This is important because business schools should be expected to prepare students for something more than the 'application of theory'. Some argue that this 'something' is employability, a preparation for work, while others call for the development of more responsible citizens. However, we are more sympathetic to Berry's (1987) discussion of 'The Loss of the University':

> ... what universities, at least the public-supported ones, are mandated to make or to help to make is human beings in the fullest sense of those words — not just trained workers or knowledgeable citizens but responsible heirs and members of human culture ... Underlying the idea of a university — the bringing together, the combining into one, of all the disciplines — is the idea that good work and good citizenship are the inevitable by-products of the making of a good — that is, a fully developed — human being. (1987: 77)

This view of a university education can be traced back to the academies in ancient Greece, the home of the philosophers. The first academy is generally considered to have been Plato's, founded in the *gymnasium* in Athens, where people would also exercise the body – suggesting, perhaps, a particular nuance to Berry's notion of the 'fully developed human being'. Synagogues, mosques, monasteries, libraries, and later universities, took over the role of academies as places to exercise the mind and engage with the deeper questions of being human. The purposes of such institutions were not limited to providing a 'preparation for work', 'the civic standard', or mere 'intellectual competence', but had more rounded and expansive intentions. Moreover, we suggest that central to this intention was the development of the capacity to theorize.

In Greek society prior to the time of Plato there was a particular type of journey or pilgrimage to a religious festival or oracle made on behalf of the community. Relevant to our discussion of *theorizing*, this pilgrim was known as the *theoros*, the spectator of the divine. The whole journey had its focus on *theoria* – the contemplation of the event or object often through participation in a sacred ritual. The *theoros* would return and recount the story of the journey in order to transmit to the community what had been seen. Plato and others took up this image of the *theoros* as a metaphor for the philosopher.

In this chapter we reflect on theorizing using Plato's allegory of the cave as a mythical representation of the journey to see the *eidos*, the Forms or Ideas, which Plato considered the most fundamental reality. The philosopher-as-*theoros* was not taught theories to apply but, by undertaking the philosophical journey, contemplated reality directly and then theorized the experience. We use this image as a metaphor for teaching business school students to theorize – here we imagine the student-as-*theoros*.

The modern notion of theory has lost touch with its linguistic roots in *theoria*, contemplation of the divine spectacle (for an extended treatment of this argument see Case et al., 2012). As a practice of contemplation the philosophical journey gives attention to what is 'seen'. Theorizing involves constructing a way of seeing things. The questions we ask in business schools typically actively exclude aspects of this contemplative vision. We will explore why this is the case in greater depth below. We are interested, however, in what happens to the learning process if we treat the student as a *theoros*, giving attention to what is seen and experienced by the student and how this is then described – both to self and other.

The process of theorizing retains the focus of the learning journey as a pursuit of *truth* or *reality*. However, to name the focus of the journey in such a way is both necessary and potentially unhelpful. Our contention is that the object of theorizing, like Plato's *eidos*, is essentially unknowable in the sense that we, in the modern era, typically think of knowledge. It might seem that this renders our discussion pointless – what value is there in encouraging students, engaged in learning the practical disciplines of leading and managing, to pursue a 'truth' that is unknowable? However, we hope to demonstrate that valuing such truth will influence the manner in which we engage in theorizing.

Firstly, it makes clear the requirement of post-positivist inquiry that we retain a professional humility in the face of the pursuit of knowledge: it is a widely accepted principle of modern science from most epistemological positions that certain knowledge is not achievable.

Secondly – and here we are perhaps more in touch with Platonic thinking – even though we cannot know or properly name truth or reality that does not mean it cannot have an impact upon us. For Plato *transformation* can take place in an encounter with reality.

Thirdly, through paying attention to these transformations, we engage in theorizing – the creation of representations of newly formed knowledge. This will be considered later in our discussion of the Platonic concept of *mimesis*.

A comparison with Czarniawska (2013: 109) is helpful. She uses a different analogy, literary invention, to explore the notion of theorizing the complexities of organizational practice and context. She suggests that such an approach does not create a fiction but rather provides a means to engage with reality by using a narrative plot to explore and make sense of experience. This 'activity of emplotting' produces theoretical knowledge that is then tested against or fitted over the experience of the narrator. It is in this sense that Corvellec (2013: 23) encourages us to consider the learning process as 'something dynamic, that is to say, an invitation to focus on theorizing rather than on theory'.

In Plato's cave we see described the gradual enlightenment that is achieved through the movement from shadowy ignorance through the journey out into the light of the sun. This is a process of 'transformation'.

BOX 13.1 PLATO'S CAVE

In Plato's allegory of the cave, he depicts the typical human being as shackled in the darkness, believing that life consists of the shadows of unseen objects projected onto the cave wall as they pass in front of an unseen fire. The philosophical journey is represented by the story of a person who is freed from these restraining shackles and – with some trepidation – makes a journey not merely towards the fire but also beyond, outside of the cave and into the light of the sun. This is a journey of enlightenment, of discovery, as things previously invisible come to be seen in their true light.

Ironically, but perhaps predictably, when the traveller returns to the cave and tries to explain what has been seen, the account is incomprehensible. To those satisfied with the pale representation of knowledge within the cave, the truth is unrecognisable and, therefore, unknowable.

This allegory provides an idealized view of the philosophical journey – idealized in the sense that such a journey is beyond human capability in anything but a partial sense. The underlying meaning is that we are all in the cave and would struggle to understand the truth even if it were revealed to us. Such philosophical practice is thus framed as fundamentally aspirational; our knowledge of reality is only ever partial and even then difficult to comprehend and accept.

A JOURNEY OF ENLIGHTENMENT

Paradoxically, the initial process of transformation in the journey from Plato's cave is represented by the *theoros* experiencing *blindness* (the first of two episodes). On leaving the shadowy darkness of the cave the philosopher is blinded by the light of the Forms. It takes some time for the philosopher's 'eyes' to adjust. Of course, this is an image of the ideal philosopher and so the analogy does not describe the experience of an all-too-human student *theoros*. The latter will never fully overcome the blindness but may receive a partial vision, as it were, a flash of light, an insight. Prior to this insight, however, the experience of blindness is troubling. Plato suggests that in the experience of being unshackled and coming out of the cave 'all these actions gave him pain, and … he was too dazed to see the objects whose shadow he had been watching before' (Plato, 1971: 208, *Republic* VII 515).

This is one of the reasons that business schools prefer to teach 'theories' rather than encourage their students to theorize: clinging to the illusion of knowing can be a defence against the uncertain, emotional, sometimes painful, experience of encountering the truth. Although being at the edge of discovery, moving to the entrance of the cave, as it were, can be exciting and invigorating, the confusion and unsettling anxiety that also accompany the experience often frighten us off at the very moment when we might catch a glimpse of the truth, when something new might be discovered. Increasingly the context in universities, with requirements for clearly stipulated learning outcomes, contributes to the potential terror that prevents the teacher from putting students in a position where they experience blindness: it is not acceptable to acknowledge ignorance and a lack of answers.

However, if the fear of this blindness, and the possibility that it might be permanent, can be contained then Plato's journey suggests that insight may come – and with it creativity and energy are mobilized. Through the contemplative journey there can be an unexpected broadening of the imagination when one is somehow in touch with or touched by the truth of *this* moment and context, limited and provisional though it inevitably is. This does not have to be a search for some 'grand' truth: it is enough that it is relevant to the demands of the moment. Indeed, the pursuit of some generalized notion of truth can even be a way of denying or avoiding a present situation that is uncomfortable or confusing, whereas addressing the truth of this moment can be exactly what is needed to progress one's learning.

This view of learning involves surviving the debilitating experience of ignorance before coming to see moment by moment what is *actually going on*, in contrast to what was planned for or has been experienced in the past. In order to assess the impact of events, and to adapt as necessary, the theorizing student may have to put their knowledge and familiar ways of thinking to one side, in order to allow their minds to be changed. Such an approach to learning may even require the capacity to downplay what might at first sight appear to be more productive and potentially profitable lines of inquiry. Ironically, it may only be by changing and re-visioning the unfolding reality as it evolves that learning can preserve a focus on what is actually seen and experienced – as opposed to previously conceived answers.

This requires an approach to learning that is based on listening and waiting rather than on the more obvious academic modes of knowing and professing. The poet Keats called this Negative Capability, when a person is 'capable of being in uncertainties, Mysteries, doubts without any irritable reaching after fact and reason' (Keats, 1970: 43). The relevance to students of leadership and management has been recognized in recent years (Simpson et al., 2002).[1] *Theoria*, a journey into not knowing, tends to stimulate high levels of uncertainty and anxiety and is a threat to fresh thinking. As a result, there is often pressure to invoke prior knowledge that may no longer apply or to adopt a new certainty too quickly, before a new vision (or plot, to continue Czarniawska's literary analogy) has had the chance to evolve.

If the philosopher can overcome the anxiety of the first blindness, the journey continues out of the cave and into the light. The philosopher now 'sees' in a new way – the vision of the *theoros* attending the spectacle and not just looking at shadows on a wall – and reality is contemplated directly. However, on returning to Plato's cave, the philosopher is again blinded and disorientated but this time by the darkness rather than the light. Having received the light of insight, the philosopher returns home to a place that no longer looks the same – not because it has changed but because of an inner transformation. It takes time to adjust to this new understanding of reality and new sense must be made of the old. Moreover, on attempting to describe what has been seen, the cave-dwellers either fail, or do not want, to understand the philosopher's description of what has been seen. The philosopher is in danger of being marginalized as mad or politically dangerous. The student *theoros* may suffer the same fate or worse – within many educational establishments a student will run the risk of failing the assignment!

---

[1]The extensive literature on cross-cultural differences and their importance for leadership (e.g. Hofstede, Trompenaars, the GLOBE study) and the psychological construct of ambiguity tolerance might also be considered.

THE RETURN

Plato's allegorical return to the cave suggests two dimensions for the student *theoros* to consider. Firstly, the challenge of managing this second experience of blindness. What had seemed so clear in the contemplative gaze of *theoria* can quickly dim and the sense of enlightenment may dissipate. The 'knowing' of the contemplative gaze on the journey, full of life and vibrancy, is of a different kind to the 'knowing' of the cave, which we might think of as fixed and limited. This requires the emotional re-integration of insight and a re-presentation, the production of an imitation of what has been seen, within the modes of knowledge available in the academic environment. Secondly, the student *theoros* must consider not merely the requirement to find ways to represent these insights in a manner that makes personal sense of what has been 'seen' but also to find ways to communicate this to others.

BOX 13.2 BRIDGING THE GAP – AN ILLUSTRATION

In contemporary education, it is recognized that the virtue of co-inquiring from experience was first addressed at the end of the 1960s with Schwab's (1966) work on the disconnection between teaching science and doing science. Some experiences in inquiry-based learning in business schools have demonstrated the benefits of co-inquiring and theorizing with students. Using the idea of 'bridging' to provoke in business students their own theorizing about change, Page and Gaggiotti (2013) organized tutorials in the middle of the Clifton Suspension Bridge, Bristol:

> We wanted to avoid limiting the invitation to using the bridge as an abstract metaphor to apply to organization change, but rather to invite them to engage with their own embodied experiences of being on the bridge, and to link this to their experiences of change. (2013: 277)

Through this experience, which involved a physical journey from the university campus to the bridge, students were asked to contemplate crossing and being suspended in the middle of a gorge. What was provoked in students and staff was used to theorize the experience of change. This led to the emergence and exploration of concepts and theories of what change was – security, disparity, faith, fatalism, no-turning-back, trust … The students observed that these were ideas that were not addressed in the undergraduate literature. Another dimension of the learning experience identified and explored the experience of anxiety for students and staff. In particular, it was a challenge to hold on to the principles of student-led inquiry as an approach to learning and change. Staff members found themselves under considerable pressure from students to revert to more familiar approaches that were not experienced as emotionally threatening and learning processes that did not involve 'pain'. The severity of not-knowing, like the experience of blindness

(Continued)

(Continued)

in Plato's cave, was immensely challenging. Some students expressed their preference for more didactic approaches and keeping their focus purely on assessment and the successful completion of the modules. The textbook theories on resistance to change were inadequate to capture the emotional and intellectual reality that was found on the bridge over a chasm.

Plato chooses the metaphor of 'blindness' not merely because it can represent the experience of not knowing but also because of the emotional experience of confusion. Seen in this way, theorizing is not merely an intellectual process – it is emotional in all its aspects. Ehn and Löfgren (2013) note that this is rarely addressed in relation to theory:

> Theories are mostly regarded as an extremely intellectual business, a world of abstract and logical thinking. Academic textbooks rarely mention any emotional element in theorizing, talking about the struggles of trying to grasp a new way of thinking or defending it against others. Theories are presented, rather, as finished systems of thought or toolboxes. They are a serious matter, nothing to be taken lightly, to be joked about, or to become too personally involved in. There is not much talk about feelings such as the joy of finally understanding a concept, the security a theory may provide, or the passion that could be invested in it. (2013: 172)

We can see this represented in Plato's allegory of the journey from, and back to, the cave: we see the fear of the unknown, the excitement, delight and wonder of enlightenment, and the confusion and frustration of returning to the shadows and seeking to communicate what has been seen. For Page and Gaggiotti's students (see Box 13.2) the trip to the gorge was emotional. In such circumstances, theorizing is the product of a range of transformations within the individual that arise from an engagement with truth – not merely in the growth of mind and knowledge but also in the use of that knowledge. Plato referred to this process of transformation as *mimesis*.

Mimesis is a term that has gained some popularity in recent times following a long period of neglect (see Gaggiotti, 2012). It is also a term that is used to mean many different things – even by Plato himself, not to mention the array of modern writers. For our purposes we will consider it in its broadest definition, that of representation. For the idealized philosopher, *mimesis* as transformation is the representation of what has been seen through the contemplative gaze of *theoria*, the Form, into a form that is intelligible within the cave, the realm not of reality but of knowledge as we typically understand it.

Plato distinguished between different levels of knowing, valuing most highly the direct engagement of the philosopher with reality through the contemplative gaze (see Gebauer and Wulf, 1995: 6). Other levels of representation are important in the learning process but do not arise directly from *theoria*. In *Protrepticus* Aristotle argues:

In the other arts and crafts men do not take their tools and their most accurate reasonings from first principles ... rather, they take them at second or third hand or at a distant remove, and base their reasonings on experience. Only the philosopher enacts a mimesis of objects that are exact; for he is a spectator of things that are exact, and not of mimemata ... An imitation of what is not divine and stable in its nature cannot be immortal and stable. Clearly, stable laws and good and right actions belong to the philosopher alone among craftsmen. (B48–9). (Quoted in Nightingale, 2004: 196–7)

This relates to the second aspect of the challenge of the blindness on returning to the cave: that the cave-dwellers do not recognize the philosopher's account of the Forms. Their world of knowledge is encapsulated in the shadows on the wall, the representations in flickering images of the objects that pass in front of the fire. Furthermore, the fire is itself a mere representation of the light of the sun, the true source of enlightenment. Thus, the cave-dweller's knowing is not of Form, reality, but of representations of representations. We see the same in relation to the theories often peddled by business schools, which are frequently summaries of adaptations of interpretations of theories – and even then, typically from a different discipline (sociology, psychology, etc.). There is clearly some value in such forms of knowing but it does not have the clarity of vision that is Plato's ideal. The student *theoros* must find a way to make sense of his or her *own* vision of reality in a manner that others might appreciate – not least the tutors if this is to be included in any assessment. Making such a replication of the real is a practice of social justification (Gaggiotti, 2012).

WHY IS *THEORIA* IMPORTANT?

It is for many of the reasons outlined above that theorizing is insufficiently encouraged or facilitated in the learning process in business schools: it can be painful and demanding for the student and a similar challenge for the tutor; it is not controllable, nameable, predictable and amenable to description in a programme specification. It is not easy to audit and requires a high level of trust in the professionalism of the academic as well as moving well beyond the functionalism of a tick-box approach to criteria-based assessment processes. It requires the students to take themselves, their responsibilities and the learning process more seriously than is generally the norm. However, if we are to produce well-rounded human beings who are capable of engaging more effectively in the ethical and relational complexities of the modern organization then finding ways to develop the capacity to theorize is not an optional extra.

Business schools often pride themselves on producing influential leaders of the future. In a recent collection of articles on the future of leadership development, Pfeffer (2011) articulates an 'agenda for change', suggesting that developing leaders has 'at least three components':

- Knowledge – to 'think smart' – 'technical skills required to help them ... make better decisions, organize their enterprises more effectively, and be able to think in a scientific, critical way about strategy and business models'.
- Act smart – 'being able to turn technical knowledge into action – to be able to surmount the knowing–doing gap ... and actually behave in ways consistent with the theories and information that leaders possess'.
- Inculcate values and standards for conduct 'that are socially beneficial and able to engage the workforce'. (Pfeffer, 2011: 219)

These components accord with established wisdom in relation to the requirements of the modern corporate leader. However, they all relate to the questions that business schools typically ask that cluster around questions about *what we (supposedly) know*. In relation to the five ancient virtues of thought (*techne, episteme, phronesis, sophia* and *nous*)[2] we see in Pfeffer's list some attention given to the first three. However, there is a limited – values-based – interpretation of theoretical wisdom (*sophia*) and no consideration of *nous*, the capacity required for *theoria*, contemplative knowing. Consequently we are suggesting that there are several 'components' that ought to be added to Pfeffer's list, which relate to questions about what we love, about what we lack and about what *we do not know*. These questions cannot be answered by reference to others' theories but require the individual students to theorize for themselves.

This presents a challenge to the way that business schools typically operate. As we have seen, the journey of the *theoros* is an emotional one and yet educational institutions legitimate the rational. The student *theoros* is confronted by blindness, which will inevitably evoke confusion. In situations of uncertainty tutors will normally draw upon expert knowledge to tell the student the answer. However, the uncertainty of the *theoros* is of a different order: the tutor needs to be able to provide emotional containment to help the student manage the anxiety of not knowing. The tutor needs a different range of skills and capabilities; and the institution needs systems and procedures that support a different form of learning. For example, learning outcomes cannot be specified tightly in advance – the student needs greater freedom to follow the path of enlightenment that reveals itself. Further, such inner transformation is a spiritual process, requiring the business school, its staff and its procedures to accommodate new levels and dimensions in the learning journey.

A common theme in the literature outlining the differences between leadership and management is that the leadership requires learning to *deal* with the unknowable – new, future, abstract, original – while management requires learning to *deal* with the knowable – old, past, concrete, non-original.

---

[2]These terms do not translate easily but briefly these might be defined as, respectively, skill, teachable knowledge, practical wisdom, theoretical wisdom and intuitive intellect.

Implying a favouritism that we do not share, Bennis states that 'the manager administers, the leader innovates; the manager is a copy, the leader is an original; the manager maintains, the leader develops' (Bennis, 1989: 45). To provide a contrast with this pro-leadership rhetoric, and with an element of sarcasm, Ford et al. (2008: 3) suggest the central task of the leader is an ethereal and futuristic engagement, *promising a bright new tomorrow*. Whether pro- or anti-leadership the literature constantly hints at an unknowable dimension to leadership practice that is rarely given sufficient attention. Business schools typically have interpreted and responded to the demands of the unknowable future by creating a concrete set of 'components', like Pfeffer's list. An emphasis is placed upon what is known in an attempt, like some sleight of hand, to make the experience of the unknowable appear intelligible and predictable.

With a sophisticated nod to the purpose of 'preparing for work' there is a tendency for business schools to adopt a utilitarian approach to determining an appropriate curriculum for leaders. Key terms and phrases in recent decades include 'impact', 'excellence' and 'performance'. The questions associated with such terms are not irrelevant; however, they lack the depth required for a serious engagement with the challenges of the leadership practice of a fully developed human being. Terms and phrases of greater interest in relation to unknowable aspects of leadership practice include the 'relational', 'complexity' and 'ethics' (see, for example, Cunliffe, 2009). The latter offer the potential for the development of leaders with the capability to engage with the challenges of the modern institution.

Unlike Pfeffer's focus, above, which conceives of thinking in a predominantly 'scientific' way, the ancient conception of theorizing integrates spiritual with mental and practical capacities. Importantly, it is in this sense that the philosophy practised by leaders (Case et al., 2011) can be understood as a way of life rather than as an abstract endeavour detached from the everyday demands and realities of work. We are suggesting that greater importance should be ascribed to what the leader sees and receives through the contemplative gaze and how this is then described – to self and other. This has the potential to have a fundamental impact upon the complex processes of thinking not only in the learning process but also in the leader's organization, hopefully increasing the chances of good and right actions.

FURTHER READING

For a developed exploration of key philosophical themes in this chapter, see Hadot (1995).
To appreciate the importance of the journey of the theoros, see Nightingale (2004).
An expansive series of essays on the practice of theorizing and the nature of theory is provided in Corvellec (2013).

REFERENCES

Bennis, W. (1989) *On Becoming a Leader*. Reading, MA: Perseus Books.

Berry, W. (1987) *Home Economics*. New York: North Point Press.

Case, P., French, R. and Simpson, P. (2011) 'Philosophies of leadership', in A. Bryman, D. Collinson, K. Grint, B. Jackson and M. Uhl-Bien (eds), *Sage Handbook of Leadership*, London: Sage, pp. 685–727.

Case, P., French, R. and Simpson, P. (2012) '*Theoria* to theory: leadership without contemplation', *Organization*, 19/3: 15–31.

Corvellec, H. (ed.) (2013) *What Is Theory? Answers from the Social and Cultural Sciences*. Copenhagen: Liber CBS Press.

Cunliffe, A. (2009) 'The philosopher leader: on relationalism, ethics and reflexivity – a critical perspective to teaching leadership', *Management Learning*, 40/1: 87–101.

Czarniawska, B. (2013) 'What social science theory is and what it is not', in Corvellec (ed.), pp. 99–118.

Ehn, B. and Löfgren, O. (2013) 'Theory: a personal matter', in Corvellec (ed.), pp. 159–80.

Ford, J., Harding, N. and Learmonth, M. (2008) *Leadership as Identity*. New York: Palgrave.

Gaggiotti, H. (2012) 'The rhetoric of synergy in a global corporation: visual and oral narratives of mimesis and similarity', *Journal of Organizational Change Management*, 25(2): 265–82.

Gebauer, G. and Wulf, C. (1995) *Mimesis: Culture, Art, Society*, trans. D. Reneau. Berkeley: University of California Press.

Hadot, P. (1995) *Philosophy as a Way of Life: Spiritual Exercises from Socrates to Foucault*. Oxford: Blackwell.

Keats, J. (1970) *The Letters of John Keats: A Selection*, ed. R. Gittings. Oxford: Oxford University Press.

Nightingale, A.W. (2004) *Spectacles of Truth in Classical Greek Philosophy:* Theoria *in its Cultural Context*. Cambridge: Cambridge University Press.

Page, M. and Gaggiotti, H. (2013) 'The bridges that change us: inquiring in the middle of the gorge', in H. Jansen, C. Brons and Faber, F. (eds), *Beeldcoaching: Zet in bewaring [Image Coaching: Set in Motion]*. Baarn: Real Life Publishing, pp. 274–91.

Pfeffer, J. (2011) 'Leadership development in business schools: an agenda for change' in J. Canals (ed.), *The Future of Leadership Development: Corporate Needs and the Role of Business School*. Basingstoke: Palgrave MacMillan, pp. 218–37.

Plato (1971) *The Republic*, trans. A.D. Lindsay. London: Heron Books.

Schwab, J. (1966) *The Teaching of Science*. Cambridge, MA: Harvard University Press.

Simpson, P., French, R. and Harvey, C.E. (2002) 'Leadership and negative capability', *Human Relations*, 55 (10): 1209–26.

Weick, K.E. (1995) 'What theory is not, theorizing is', *Administrative Science Quarterly*, 40 (3): 385–90.

14 FOR WHOSE PURPOSES DO WE EDUCATE? *WAIRUA* IN BUSINESS SCHOOLS

Pare Keiha and Edwina Pio

INTRODUCTION

A community of scholars and teachers, or *'universitas magistrorum et scholarium'* (Newman, 2010), is enhanced through the creation of discursive public spaces where agency, power bases and inconvenient doubt are explored. Spaces where people recognize the interdependency of rights and duties in a shifting world, as knowledge is disseminated and co-created. In the unique transformative, intellectual and emotionally demanding role of business school educators, we believe it is possible to create sparkle and the rich satisfaction of generously crafted miracles (Pio et al., 2013a). For the wellbeing of our students and our communities this involves creating a brightness of spirit, and a steadfastness of purpose embraced within the joy of living. Inconvenient doubt involves opportunities to explore and endorse diverse trajectories in pedagogy and business. We draw attention to the fact that the students who grace our classes are the future CEOs, leaders, police officers, judges, ecologists and the implementers of policies in corporates and the business, educational and social worlds. In other words many are destined for great things beyond the strict confines of the corporate realm.

We use the culturally specific language and tradition of Māori knowledge and practice, encapsulated within the notion of *wairua*. Māori are the indigenous peoples of New Zealand. *Wairua*, albeit poorly translated as the soul, spirit or quintessence of a person, provides the potential for the examination of the role of culturally foreign ideals and their introduction into the orthodox business school curriculum. Less familiar notions such as *wairua* (Māori), *hon* (Korean) or *umoya* (Zulu), force those of us who are educators not only to explore meaning but also to reflect on the meaningfulness of a word. Importantly such concepts provide alternative models for examination and the consequent transformation of our curriculum. Such exploration provides the potential for the negotiation of intellectual spaces to connect individuals and organizations to their communities, including those in the minority (Berryman et al., 2013; see also King, 1992; Spiller et al., 2011; Spiller, 2012). Businesses do not and cannot exist isolated from their communities – and neither should our graduates. Thus the superordinate question that we address to business schools is: for whose purposes do we educate?

We believe that business school education should inform the whole person, including the spirituality of our students, a core aspect of character. Our contention is that foreign notions of spirituality widen the topic for debate in business schools, because they are less constrained by the terminology of religion. Diversity of thought, diversity of language and diversity of culture lead to a more diverse and consequently effective business school graduate. The incorporation of minority or indigenous notions of spirituality, particularly when they are drawn from the local community, has the added advantage of challenging business schools to be more relevant. Consequently, business schools have a duty to educate for community success, not just corporate success. Such an education incorporates ethics and spirituality in the challenge of shaping the character of students. The introduction of metaphor, fable, storytelling, and indeed less familiar terminology such as *wairua,* broadens the mind and challenges students to look within themselves for meaning. This chapter, while focusing on the notion of *wairua* in education, and specifically in business schools, weaves together the importance of collective prosperity for our communities and the utilization of the unfamiliar in making a case for embracing spirituality in how we educate and for whose purposes we educate our students.

COLLECTIVE PROSPERITY

The education in business schools is heavily weighted towards a singular focus, that of success in the corporate world. In our anxiety to educate students for corporate success, we often fail to deal with the social and cultural enhancement of our communities. We are all, however, members of multiple communities – be they described by geography, culture, ethnicity and faith or indeed work. Like businesses, business schools do not and should not exist isolated from the communities they are required to serve. It is a fact of modern life that our communities are becoming more diverse, more complex, more chaotic, less predictable, less certain and less orthodox. In response to this complexity, we use a New Zealand-specific example to illustrate that business schools have a responsibility to educate for both corporate and community success.

A focus on community success in a New Zealand context requires us to examine relationships between a business schools' education and government's social and economic policy. Generally the New Zealand government's university education policy has a particular focus on equity – consequently Māori students are a priority group. In response, many New Zealand business schools have equity programmes and equity targets as a means of improving socio-economic outcomes (Ako Aotearoa, 2014; see also Durie, 2011; Education Counts, 2013). Implicit in such policies is the expectation that through education, members of minority communities will be better off, and so too will their communities. However, fundamental to these policies is the expectation that students from such communities will return as leaders – as agents of change – but there is very little deliberate strategy to ensure that this 'return' is achieved (see Box 14.1).

BOX 14.1   EQUITY SCHOLARSHIPS

Why aren't all students educated for equity? How do we know that in providing equity scholarships to students they will be responsible? The business school at one of the New Zealand universities awards a number of scholarships to Māori students as part of the overall equity strategy. Albeit a silent expectation, equity scholarship recipients have an obligation to their communities – to return to their communities, to mentor others for success. Alternatively, scholarships can also be awarded to the community with the expectation being that the ultimate recipient should maintain and potentially strengthen close bonds with their community. Such recipients are encouraged to maintain their customs, culture and language and thus to strengthen success for their communities based on their terms. That said should it not be the responsibility of business schools to educate for equity generally? And should not business schools ensure that scholarship recipients return or give back to their communities and hold the recipients accountable for this 'return'?

Drew Gilpin Faust (2009), the president of Harvard University, in discussing our 'collective prosperity' wrote about the university's crisis of purpose, noting that universities are much more than a measurable utility for they are meant to have the long view and nurture critical perspectives that look to the future. Universities must be producers of knowledge and (inconvenient) doubt, a source of economic growth, as well as society's critics and conscience. In creating collective prosperity – an intricately woven triad of people-planet-profits – universities are homes to a polyphony of voices that expose patterns of risk and denial, in creating a more ethically conscious, cosmopolitan and interconnected world (Haigh, 2014).

Thus a critical question is this: how do we educate our students for their role as society's critics and conscience? More importantly how do we educate our students for such a purpose in communities other than their own? This is particularly relevant for minority students if not their majority peers. Do we risk impoverishing our communities by unwittingly educating the best and brightest away in order to solely serve the needs of business? For all sorts of reasons we create an education system that is normative but lacking the subtleties and nuances of the wider communities in the society in which we live (Keiha, 2013). In this context the business school is considered a 'place' which is not just geographical, but also a space connecting the learner's narrative with the environment (Sheldrake, 2001). This space can be a source of energy, knowledge and transformation (Pio et al., 2013a; see also Sharley, 2012; Zapf, 2005). This view of place creates tension between the ways spaces are constructed and defined by the multiplicity of learner narratives characteristic of the cosmopolitan nature of our student population. In a New Zealand business school context the introduction of Māori-specific cultural norms to both – curriculum and practice creates both challenges and opportunities for the reinvigoration of learning.

We do not argue for a continuation of the practice of intellectual colonization. Rather we would say that what we need is a business school education characterized by dignity and respect if we are to deliver collective prosperity. Introducing values and beliefs into the classroom can be unearthed from a wide range of cultural sources; and in particular those of an indigenous nature are an important step towards this ideal. Consequently the language of 'others' provides an opportunity to reintroduce universal ideals to the orthodoxy of business school teaching and practice. We place an emphasis on educators as influencers of our students and their communities and in so doing influencers of future generations. Such influences may reinforce, challenge and/or transform Western norms (Trottier, 2010). In a New Zealand context the incorporation of the notion of *wairua* in a business school context would be an important advance. In part we argue that such 'cultural' terms facilitate the discussion, if not the examination, of notions such as spirituality, which regrettably have been eschewed because of their association with matters of religion.

So while we may be arguing for greater diversity in our curriculum we do so not only for the sake of our minority students but also for the sake of all our students, because those students live and work in communities. Thus where minority communities are clearly identifiable, as for example Māori in New Zealand, Aboriginals in Australia, scheduled castes and tribes in India, Sami in the Nordic countries, Africans in Russia, Turks in Germany and Sikhs in Mexico, business schools must be particularly careful to educate students to better serve those communities. In particular such efforts must be cognisant of the underpinning policy environment that advocates for equity through education. Furthermore, where minority communities exist, all students must be encouraged to serve the full diversity of the communities in which they live. This challenge is not a simple one.

WEAVING *WAIRUA*

Wairua, drawn from Māori metaphysics, is a spiralling process of unfolding one's self to truly understand one's spiritual nature (Bishop and Berryman, 2006;

Henry and Pene, 2001; Marsden, 2003; Moorfield, 2010). This unfolding spiral-ling process is different from the linear and progress-oriented process that often typifies the Western mode (Chen and Miller, 2010; Hannah and Peredo, 2011; Pio et al., 2013b). *Wairua* literally means 'two waters' and refers to the interwo-ven flows of energy between spiritual and physical existence (Pere, 2006). Consequently *wairua* provides an opportunity to examine the interconnectedness of collective prosperity through people-planet-profits and is indirect, metaphorical and allusive (Barlow, 1994; see also Coates et al., 2006).

Wairua manifests itself in certain personal characteristics consistent with the notions of spirituality. Like all concepts drawn from Māori knowledge, as with all distinct knowledge systems, it has a particular cache with regard to the men-tal models with which it is associated. People manifest certain behaviours, and collectively we refer to this as character. The question for business schools to consider is whether our programmes and practices should have a role in delib-erately shaping the character of our students. We argue particularly for the shaping of the character of the whole person. Yet the usefulness of a term like *wairua* is akin to the parallel usefulness of metaphor or parable or fable as means of instruction (Pio and Haigh, 2007). That usefulness is as much a prod-uct of the reorientation of the mental models in which current orthodox practice traps us. Why use in an English text a Māori word? We would argue that it is to deliberately challenge ourselves and our students about the way we and they think as, for example, with the parable of the sadhu (McCoy, 1997) – a widely used account for ethics instruction. In the parable of the sadhu, a group of individuals from various countries are in the Himalayas to reach a sacred place. On their journey this cosmopolitan group encounter a sadhu who is ill and they face the dilemma of 'what to do with the sadhu' and 'how much should they do' – should they take the sadhu back to the village or proceed with their plan to reach their destination?

More familiar parables to a Western mind such as the Biblical parable of the sower who scattered seed, some of which fell on rocky ground and did not grow, whereas other seed fell on good soil and produced a luxuriant crop, can also be used. Or parables familiar to Asian minds such as that of the Buddhist parable of the poisoned arrow, whereby when a man has an arrow in his body, should individuals gather around and have long discussions on who wounded the man, who the man is, the kind of bow from which the arrow was shot, or should they not waste time in such speculations, but rather act and remove the arrow. Fables such as those of Aesop, for example that of the ant and the grass-hopper, the shepherd boy crying 'wolf, wolf', or the ass in the lion's skin, may also be used to push and extend the boundaries within which we operate in business schools.

If we accept the notion that business schools have a duty and obligation to shape the character of our students, then we would assume that such shaping and moulding are a deliberative process at the forefront of a business school agenda. However, in most schools theoretical constructs and cognitive reason-ing are characterized by the values and beliefs of the majority culture. We note that while business schools do teach courses such as management and ethics, colossal financial fraud and organizational disharmony have highlighted the fact that managers, created by business schools, often ignore, or express espoused helplessness in dealing with, organizational 'misdeeds'. Perhaps we can attribute this helplessness to the narrow context within which business schools educate, creating a famine in the area of spirituality. Hence a constricted framework of teaching in business schools, where spirituality is not something that is talked about or reflected on, underscores the question – for whose purposes do we educate?

If the strength of one's character is an important comparative advantage in business then how do we identify and shape such a characteristic? How do we build it through education and importantly how do we develop or indeed recruit for character? Or in the case of our particular example, how do we recruit for *wairua*? The challenge can be further illustrated by using concepts from other cultures (see Box 14.2). These concepts are all similar to the notion of *wairua*, yet their nuanced differences (soul, spirit, self, energy, life-force) cannot be expressed in a simple phrase, as this would be like trying to describe the nuances of the colour pink. All these notions we would argue are an important characteristic of the spirit or character of a person. How do we challenge ourselves to think outside the box? How do we embrace the exotic in order to catalyse the transformative power of our curriculum to better shape the character of our students?

BOX 14.2 NOTIONS SIMILAR TO *WAIRUA*

Notion	Nuanced meaning	Source
Atma	The individual enlightened self, soul	Hindi/Sanskrit (India)
Chetana	Consciousness, power of the intellect	Kannada (South India)
Chi	Energy force	Mandarin (China)
Hon	Soul, a state of mind	Korean
Moyo	Heart or soul	Swahili (Africa)
Ruh	Spirit	Urdu/Arabic (Northern Indian subcontinent and Arabic speaking countries)
Umoya	Spirit	Zulu (Africa)
Wairua	Soul, spirit, two waters	Māori (indigenous peoples of New Zealand)

Business schools have usefully borrowed non-Western ideas to advance the critical thinking of our staff and students and thereby advance their mission, for example Sun Tzu's *The Art of War*, and John Heider's *The Tao of Leadership* (1997), adapted from Lao Tzu's *Tao Te Ching*. In an age of cultural relativity and global mobility, a refinement of how we teach students to engage with complexity through giving back to their communities starts with the utilization and knowledge of those communities. Charles Handy (1999) in his book *The Hungry Spirit* argues for educating the whole person and in so doing ensuring the flourishing of humanity. A rounded business school education which borrows from the wisdom of the communities in which we are located is the first step towards developing a better understanding of the layered character of those communities. Consequently we would argue that we would create and develop not only better managers but also better community leaders. Thus, while the concept of *wairua* is culturally specific to Māori, it is universally applicable as a useful tool to deliberate and reflect on one's spirituality and consequently character. Furthermore, *wairua* rescues us from the language of religion and focuses instead on the notion of spirit, albeit in an alternative intellectual framework.

UTILIZATION OF THE UNFAMILIAR

The potential contribution for the use of words, concepts and notions from 'other' cultures is the deliberate creation of uncertainty, ambiguity and complexity from a personal perspective. Can a student's character be shaped? We would argue yes. Can a student's character be strengthened? We would argue yes. That said we would argue that without critical self-reflection, which includes the spiritual nature of our humanity, such opportunities are lost. Box 14.3 presents a short *wairua* exercise as an initiation into what can be done in the classroom and has been used successfully for an MBA class in a New Zealand university. When this exercise has been conducted, students have always enjoyed the quiet time it gives them for reflection and that in thinking of *wairua* they are forced to move out of their usual thoughts and think within a larger perspective. The class seems to get very quiet as individuals delve deeper into themselves. In the sharing, which is voluntary, many students are thoughtful and still within themselves, but others are keen to share their learnings from the exercise. Such learnings include the following: the need to be more inclusive of those on the margins/with fewer opportunities; to understand difficult situations from a number of perspectives; to engage in more meaningful conversations with significant others; to remember to stop and replenish oneself through the use of this exercise. In non-New Zealand settings, the same exercise format could be used with a change in the notion that is being explained. For example, instead of explaining *wairua*, a similar notion can be used from the cultures in which the university is embedded, or from the cultures of visiting/exchange students. Alternatively a short fable or parable could be narrated and the class could be requested to think of the meaning of the parable with reference to collective prosperity (people-planet-profits).

BOX 14.3   A *WAIRUA* EXERCISE IN THE CLASSROOM (25 TO 30 MINUTES)

1. Explain the notion of *wairua* and linkage of one's spirit with what happens inter- nally and externally in our world including our communities (3–5 minutes).
2. Ask the class to individually think of their *wairua* with reference to collective prosperity (people-planet-profits) (5–7 minutes).
3. Encourage the class to share some of their thoughts in this area (10–15 minutes).

Importantly we are not aware that business schools regularly examine the role of spirituality in our curriculum let alone practice. We would argue that the use of notions such as *wairua* is an important first step to strengthening the social entrepreneurship skills of our students. For our minority students it provides them with a locus of familiarity with which they can build their generic man- agement skills. For our majority students it provides them with an opportunity to ground their education in the language of others, while at the same time providing alternative routes for transformation. Like all tools, the use of such notions as *wairua* is only as good as the way they are used. Nonetheless we argue that the incorporation of unfamiliar terms such as *wairua* in business school curricula is a powerful way to catalyse a more thoughtful and deep understanding of how we engage with each other. Therefore the use of *wairua* moves beyond steps in understanding a word to the practice of educating soci- ety and humanity to be better off, and better off not just for parts of society, but for society as a whole.

CONCLUSION

The challenge of cultural relativism (Rachels, 2003), where every standard may be culturally bounded, suggests that tradition may be its own warrant of fitness. Therefore there may be no universal truth, but rather a variety of cultural codes. Despite this variety, there are rules that all societies have in common in order for them to function. We posit that the *wairua* notion is a universal one as it seeks to enhance the wellbeing of communities and therefore the intercon- nectedness of society more generally. In fact the use of the notion of *wairua* in business schools has no negative side effects, as it encourages engagement with oneself and the wider world. Yet the notion of *wairua* in its interpretation is the result of cultural conditioning. This awareness of cultural conditioning enables both students and educators to reflect on their own characters and be more open to discovering their layered selves. Moreover such reflection helps to reduce the arrogance that often develops when we think that our way is the best and only way. Such discovery can be aided by accessing the knowledge and wisdom, rather than resisting suggestions, from minority cultures including indigenous peoples.

In summary, our chapter invites readers to explore the purpose for which business schools exist. In so doing we recommend that the incorporation of the wisdom provided by 'other' cultures provides opportunities for self-examination and transformation. In particular we have reflected on *wairua*, a specifically Māori notion, as an exemplar of such wisdom. In an ever-changing world of multiple realities, as universities struggle to be relevant and thrive through collapsing economies, hegemonic structures and planetary fragility, the introduction of *wairua*, and its expression in business schools in particular, through our curriculum and practice, is a critical dimension of the purpose for which we educate.

FURTHER READING

Berryman, M., Macfarlane, S., and Cavanagh, T. (2009) 'Indigenous contexts for responding to challenging behaviour: contrasting western accountability with Māori restoration of harmony', *International Journal of Restorative Justice*, 5 (1): 1–31.

Grace, P. (1986) *Potiki*. Auckland: Penguin Books.

Hall, A., Poutu-Morice, M. and Wilson, C. (2012) 'Waka Oranga: the development of an indigenous professional organisation within a psychotherapeutic discourse in Aotearoa New Zealand', *Psychotherapy and Politics International*, 10 (1): 7–16.

Mark, G. and Lyons, A. (2010) 'Māori healers views on wellbeing: the importance of mind, body, spirit, family and land', *Social Science and Medicine*, 70: 1756–64.

Pio, E. and Haigh, N. (2007) 'Towards a pedagogy of inspirational parables', *Education and Training*, 49(2): 77–90.

Pio, E., Rasheed, A., Naera, A., Tipuna, K., and Parker, L. (2014) 'A place to hang my hat on: university staff perceptions in multi-ethnic New Zealand', in K. Bhopal and U. Maylor (eds), *Educational Inequalities: Difference in Schools and Higher Education*. New York: Routledge, pp. 212–29.

Scherer, A. and Palazzo, G. (2011) 'The new political role of business in a globalized world: a review of a new perspective on CSR and its implications for the firm, governance and democracy', *Journal of Management Studies*, 48 (4): 899–931.

Sharley, V. (2012) New ways of thinking about the influence of cultural identity, place and spirituality on child development within child placement practice', *Adoption and Fostering*, 36 (12): 112–17.

Shields, C., Bishop, R. and Mazawi, A. (2005) *Pathologizing Practices: The Impact of Deficit Thinking on Education*. New York: Peter Lang.

UNPFII (2007) *United Nations Permanent Forum on Indigenous Issues: Declaration on the Rights of Indigenous Peoples*. Retrieved from: http://social.un.org/index/IndigenousPeoples/DeclarationontheRightsofIndigenousPeoples.aspx (accessed 19 December 2014).

REFERENCES

Ako Aotearoa (2014) New Zealand's National Centre for Tertiary Teaching Excellence. Retrieved from: https://akoaotearoa.ac.nz/mi/ako-aotearoa (accessed 6 January 2015).

Barlow, C. (1994) *Tikanga Whakaaro: Key Concepts in Māori Culture*. Auckland, Aotearoa: Oxford University Press.

Berryman, M., Soohoo, S. and Nevin, A. (2013) 'The confluence', in M. Berryman, S. Soohoo and A. Nevin (eds), *Culturally Responsive Methodologies*. Bingley: Emerald Group Publishing, pp. 389–408.

Bishop, R. and Berryman, M. (2006) *Culture Speaks: Cultural Relationships and Classroom Learning*. Wellington: Huia.

Chen, M.-J. and Miller, D. (2010) 'West meets east: toward an ambicultural approach to management', *Academy of Management Perspectives*, 24 (4): 17–24.

Coates, J., Gray, M. and Hetherington, T. (2006) 'An ecospiritual perspective: finally a place for indigenous approaches', *British Journal of Social Work*, 36: 381–99.

Durie, M. (2011) *Nga Tini Whetu: Navigating Māori Futures*. Wellington: Huia Publishers.

Education Counts (2013) 'Māori Education Targets – Ka Hikitia'. Retrieved from: www.educationcounts.govt.nz/statistics/Māori_education (accessed 21 November 2013).

Faust, D. (2009) 'The university's crisis of purpose', *New York Times*. Retrieved from: www.nytimes.com/2009/09/06/books/review/Faust-t.html (accessed 19 December 1014).

Haigh, M. (2014) 'From internationalization to education for global citizenship: a multi-layered history', *Higher Education Quarterly*, 68 (1): 6–27.

Handy, C. (1996) *Training the Fire Brigade: Preparing for the Unimaginable*. Brussels: EFMD Publications.

Handy, C. (1999) *The Hungry Spirit*. New York: Broadway Books.

Hannah, D. and Peredo, A. (2011) 'Rethinking management education and scholarship', *Journal of Management Inquiry*, 20: 178–9.

Henry, E. and Pene, H. (2001) 'Kaupapa Māori: locating indigenous ontology, epistemology and methodology in the academy', *Organization*, 8: 234–41.

Keiha, P (2013) 'Bad news day', in P. Little and D. Dudek Vinicombe (eds), *Grumpy Old Men*. Auckland: Paul Little Books, pp. 139–43.

King, M. (ed.) (1992) *Te ao hurihuri: Aspects of Māoritanga*. Auckland: Reed.

Marsden, M. (2003) *The Woven Universe: Selected Writings of Rev. Māori Marsden*. Otaki, Aotearoa, New Zealand: Te Wanaga o Raukawa (original work published in 1992).

McCoy, B. (1997) 'The parable of the sadhu', *Harvard Business Review*, 75 (3): 54–64.

Moorfield, J.C. (2010) *Māori Dictionary. Te Aka Māori – English, English Māori Dictionary*. Retrieved from: www.maoridictionary.co.nz/ (accessed 11 November 2013).

Newman, H. (2010 reprint) *The Idea of a University*. San Francisco, CA: Ignatius Press.

Pere, R. (2006) 'A celebration of Māori sacred and spiritual wisdom', in J. Kunnie and N. Goduka (eds), *Indigenous Peoples' Wisdom and Power*. Hampshire, England: Ashgate, pp. 143–57.

Pio, E. and Haigh, N. (2007) 'Towards a pedagogy of inspirational parables', *Education and Training*, 49 (2): 77–90.

Pio, E., Tipuna, K., Rasheed, A. and Parker, L. (2013a) 'Te Wero – the challenge: reimagining universities from an indigenous worldview', *Higher Education: The International Journal of Higher Education Research*. doi 10.1007/s10734-013-9673-1Pio.

Pio, E., Waddock, S., Mangaliso, M., McIntosh, M., Spiller, C., Takeda, H., Gladstone, J., Ho, M. and Syed, J. (2013b) 'Pipeline to the future? Seeking wisdom in indigenous, eastern and western traditions', in J. Neale (ed.), *Handbook of Faith and Spirituality in the Workplace: Emerging Research and Practice*. Arkansas: Tyson Centre for Faith and Spirituality in the Workplace, University of Arkansas, pp. 195–221.

Rachels, J. (2003) *The Elements of Moral Philosophy* (4th edn). Boston, MA: McGraw Hill.

Sharley V. (2012) 'New ways of thinking about the influence of cultural identity, place and spirituality on child development within child placement practice', *Adoption and Fostering*, 36 (12): 112–17.

Sheldrake, P. (2001) 'Human identity and the particularity of place', *Spiritus*, 1 (1): 43–64.

Spiller, C. (2012) 'Way finding in strategy research', in C. Wang, D. Ketchen and D. Bergh (eds), *West Meets East: Building Theoretical Bridges*. Bingley: Emerald Publishing, pp. 61–90.

Spiller, C., Pio, E., Erakovic, L. and Henare, M. (2011) 'Wise up: creating organizational wisdom through an ethic of kaitiakitanga', *Journal of Business Ethics*, 104 (2): 223–35.

Trottier, R. (2010) 'Intellectual property for mystics? Considerations on protecting traditional wisdom systems', *International Journal of Cultural Property*, 17: 519–46.

Zapf, M. (2005) 'The spiritual dimension of person and environment: perspectives from social work and traditional knowledge', *International Social Work*, 48 (5): 633–42.

PART III

RAPPORTEUR

Laurence Freeman

Despite or perhaps because of the intense egocentricity of modern culture and its extravagantly materialistic value system, spirituality and the values associated with it are high on the agenda of many academics concerned with the philosophy of business and finance. In this respect the authors of Part III bravely and strongly reflect what many have thought but not so well expressed.

Business schools appear to be at the interface of theory and practice at this time. But Blakeley even sees a 'crisis of legitimacy' in the very nature and purpose of the business school; and the sense that this kind of academic institution has 'lost its way' is not strange to the other authors in this section. Gaggiotti and Simpson have gone the next step to recover the right direction by the ancient instinct to return to origins. By asking what is the *telos* of business and the true meaning of happiness, they seek a new language in Greek philosophy to substantiate the contemplative thirst that each author in the following chapters in some way reflects. Business schools, to go by these chapters, are in a phase of intense self-doubt, seeking an authentic reason for their existence within academic institutions and a methodology that replaces one that increasingly appears to have failed. Blakeley honestly points out that this soul-searching (in both senses of the phrase) can easily become a mask, an attitude adopted for reputational purposes. Her insistence that business school teachers must themselves embody the values they teach seems to reflect the need for authenticity in a fractured system but it might also seem, for many, to be too idealistic.

The call to make business schools places of *theoria* (contemplation in which one risks oneself and faces the great unknowing) might seem like a blurring of the lines between academia and monastic life. Although universities were culturally products of monasteries they have travelled far apart over the centuries. Universities and their business schools are themselves businesses today. It is hard to be objective about oneself and even harder to disentangle the values relevant to each half of one's soul – a business serving business on the one hand and a place of research and the promotion of universal values on the other.

Is it going too far to expect business school students to 'contemplate reality directly', to try to recover the original meaning of philosophy in the business-oriented environment, to highlight the teacher–student relationship in terms of master and disciple? Is an MBA course similar to the institution of temporary monkhood in Theravada Buddhism?

Keiha and Po propose a kind of academic cloister, a 'discursive public space' in which business schools can become more integrated with the indigenous community around them. Their students will become the 'critics and conscience' of society and the 'famine in the area of spirituality' will thereby be relieved. The authors of this proposal – to recover *wairua* – see business schools responding to an obligation to shape the character of their students; and this requires more than the articulation of ideals but a 'deliberate process'.

Although the need for spiritual values is felt strongly in each chapter there is the predictable sense of the need for something that 'rescues us from the language of religion and focuses on the notion of spirit'. The problem is that language is not so easily filtered without creating non-sense and that 'spirit' is a great deal more than a 'notion'. Perhaps Conroy's approach that focuses more on the ethical and less on the spiritual holds a necessary corrective to this idealism. He asks if it is possible to learn ethical leadership and this question takes us to the heart of the matter. Surely it *must* be learned through experience by those who want to learn it. But can it be taught as merely another form of transferrable knowledge? Or, are teachers there to lead it out of the student by creating the conditions in which as the early Christian monks said *magistra experientia*, experience is the teacher?

Despite the consensus that something seriously different is needed in business schools of the future and that this something has a spiritual dimension, there is only one mention in the chapters of this section of the practice that needs to underpin and authenticate the theory.

The desire of these sincere teachers to serve their students and society better by making them think and feel more astutely and generously is laudable. They want business school students to leave the institution with more than a piece of paper assuring them of a better career. Having a spiritual discipline, however, is critical to an individual's growth. Meditation has a profound impact on the personal, social and spiritual development of its practitioners. As one of the universal treasures of human wisdom, it is a discipline, a *praxis*, rather than just a theory, traceable to aboriginal cultures of forty thousand years ago. It should be taught with awareness of its deep roots in the history of humanity as well as of the results of the recent scientific research by which it has been tested. You can meditate with any or no religious belief system. But one should be intelligently and openly informed about the context of what one is doing.

Meditation yields the insight that the most human aspects in life (peace, truth, wisdom, love) are found within. To discover this truth it is necessary to calm the mind and emotions and descend to a deeper, simpler, clearer level of consciousness where we are free from the images and patterns of conflicting ideas and desires. The authenticity that the authors here are describing is self-knowledge. Meditation, as a way directly into the transformational experience of self-knowledge, is a spiritual framework not just for monastics but for everyone.

As we grow in self-knowledge we understand better the meaning of connectedness and understand that meaning itself is the experience of connection, firstly to ourselves, each other, the earth and ultimately to our unnamable but benevolent source. In meditation we are not contemplating ourselves or ideals. We are transcending our ego, moving free of our desires, thoughts and emotions in the liberating and expanding consciousness of being. However flakey this may sound, it works.

This makes the meditator more empathetic, less severely judgemental and self-righteous and more open to new ideas and people. Inherent in this is the ability to face the unknown, to break rules creatively, establish new parameters and to develop what Gaggiotti and Simpson call the 'contemplative gaze'. It makes us better employers and gives us compassion for those we work with. We become part of the solution instead of the problem. We become better leaders and the theory becomes practice in the act.

Although I have been teaching meditation for many years I learned something new by teaching it at the McDonough School of Business at Georgetown in a course on 'Meditation and Leadership'. It opened with a review of the context of meditation in culture and in all the major religions followed by a survey of the medical and scientific evidence of recent research. While the many approaches to meditation practice were acknowledged and examined, one particular discipline was proposed. Better to dig deep in one well. The students were accepting and grateful for this specificity. The overall emphasis was on developing a personal practice among the students and I was happily surprised at how they responded to the challenge to meditate twice a day (73 per cent). Once the experiential process was under way (within a week) the next step was a shared reflection on its personal and professional implications. As I listened to what the students said or journalled, I was hearing, as if from a textbook, an account of the psychological and physical benefits as well as the spiritual fruits – more awareness, less stress, greater clarity and efficiency of thought, more compassion and gentleness and self-knowledge. The results were felt relationally – with self, others and sometimes a sense of the transcendent. The student who got the lowest grade probably got most out of the course in making the salutary discovery that he or she had discovered a life-inhibiting 'addiction to distraction'.

Throughout these chapters there is a refrain about values and a sense that 'spirituality' can restore or refresh the values in our broken or dysfunctional worlds of business and financial. In fact this same awareness and soul-searching is underway in the other institutions of our society such as education and medicine. 'Value statements' are well and good but they are more easily defined than remembered and applied in practice. They need to be continuously embodied in the heat of the day and, when they are, it becomes clear that there are no real values without an enhanced sense of meaning. Although 'meaning' is less easily defined than 'values', it is readily experienced as connection and it constitutes the heart of any quality of life we are experiencing. Respect for a company's stakeholders or staff members, for example, is more clearly seen in the personal connections and their history than in the abstract.

One would naturally expect academics to be concerned about the language involved in such articulations – whether this involves drawing fresh vocabularies from other academics, from ancient philosophy or from indigenous cultures. We need to think and speak about these issues and these authors have contributed significantly to this quest. But there is also a language or rather an experience of communication called silence, which is the 'work' of meditation, which boosts us out of the self-referential trap of thought and gives words and ideas themselves a new power to communicate meaning. Perhaps my conclusion sounds simplistic. But the simplest, most unifying, refreshing, healing, corrective, integrating – and certainly the cheapest – catalyst to launch this new paradigm and integrate the fields of theory and practice is the personal discipline of meditation. This can be taught in business schools and so far the results have been very positive. Many are concerned about the ethical slide in business and finance with attendant risks associated with various options of statutory regulation; equally, an approach which relies on personal interior transformation attracts its own share of misunderstandings. I would argue that the two are not mutually exclusive and wise business thinking can imagine ways to balance them.

PART IV

RECLAIMING A MORAL VOICE IN BUSINESS SCHOOLS: SOME PEDAGOGIC EXAMPLES

15 WERE BUSINESS SCHOOLS COMPLICIT IN THE FINANCIAL CRISIS AND CAN CLASSICAL FRENCH LITERATURE HELP?

Rickard Grassman

The cynic knows the price of everything and the value of nothing.

The nineteenth century, as we know it, is largely an invention of Balzac.

(Oscar Wilde)

INTRODUCTION

On 15 September 2008, one of the oldest, largest and most respected investment banks went bankrupt and set off a perfect storm across the globe. The collapse of Lehman Brothers sent financial markets into free fall, freezing credit that even manufacturing industries rely on to operate. Global capitalism as we know it was in cardiac arrest and governments across the world committed taxpayer funds for resuscitation. The operation and subsequent purging of financial institutions from their self-inflicted toxicity landed a final bill of several trillion pounds in the US and UK alone. Investment banks, insurance conglomerates and mortgage providers were all implicated in a system-wide trade of subprime mortgages, which turned the failing US housing market into a global financial crisis. While the crisis – the biggest market failure in financial history – dealt a serious blow to the complacency of neo-liberal reason, the ideology of deregulation and private interest as a prime guarantor of growth and stability has nevertheless proved strikingly resilient.

Neo-liberalism is based upon the notion that the market is always a privileged means of resolving problems and achieving human ends (Crouch, 2011), and this chapter ventures to accentuate the complicity of an immensely powerful institution whose ideological impact and reach rarely surface. Yet the argument here is that those who teach in business and finance are as equally, if not more, complicit than those who put theory into practice in financial institutions around the world. Few would dispute that the very *raison d'être* of the business school is to articulate and disseminate knowledge about the nature of the market. Located at the very centre of the most political territory of how to organize our businesses and the economy at large, one would expect business schools to offer a rather nuanced variety and representation of counterbalancing theories, or at the very least, to demonstrate an awareness of the normative position they clearly occupy. Instead, one finds a predominant bias in the most influential theories of business schools towards a totalizing epistemic framework that crudely collapses values into prices, which I contend has been key in ideologically shaping and sustaining the neo-liberal agenda. When value essentially becomes dependent on the market mechanism, activities and skills that do not translate into market prices directly lose their worth. Harney (2009: 318) stresses the particular vulnerability of business students, who 'stand before the university as naked labour, unadorned, unmediated by literature, or art, or even technology, and ask to be made useful to capital'.

The structure of this chapter is as follows. The first section aspires to show how the business school has an ideological bias that goes back to its very foundation. The second aims to show how this ideological bias may result in increasingly unethical and unsustainable business activities, most notably evidenced in the financial industry conducive to the crisis. By examining the eye of the storm, testimonies from employees at Lehman Brothers in association with the collapse of the bank clearly demonstrate the prevalence of extreme individualist discourses and a concomitant lack of concern for the consequences befalling others, society and the economy at large. Finally, in the third and last section, I consider an alternative teaching method that introduces business students to classic literature as a complement and counterweight to mainstream textbooks with this allegedly neo-liberal bias. This, I contend, offers an alternative pedagogical approach that might prove fruitful in denaturalizing the neo-liberal collapse of human values into market prices. The shift in genre, from business textbooks to classical literature, can also provide a compelling, disruptive and creative narrative that may accentuate and contextualize the processes in which values have been undermined historically. In particular, nineteenth-century literature could help reveal the context in which steps towards a capitalist discourse were born and shaped. Here Balzac is used as one of the most prescient novelists of his time – writing in early nineteenth-century France – to illustrate how the fetishism of money (in Marxist terms) leads to a form of instrumentalization of human bonds. As such, Balzac offers a fresh social commentary from another era that both students and teachers may learn from.

THE IDEOLOGICAL BIAS OF BUSINESS SCHOOLS

The birth of the business school some 125 years ago, first Wharton at the University of Pennsylvania, and then Harvard Business School, did not transpire without an onslaught of suspicion and resistance. A parallel development was mirrored in the European universities of Aachen, Leipzig, St Gallen and Vienna at the turn of the twentieth century. Neither side of the Atlantic could smoothly assimilate the emerging discipline of business into the Enlightenment ideals of the university: there was something intrinsically threatening in the very thought of considering business studies as a discipline in its own right (Readings, 1996). In the case of Harvard, university president Charles W. Eliot, between 1869 and 1906, held off for nearly three decades the repeated calls by industry representatives to establish a business school, arguing that 'such a project would be anathema to the university's educational purpose of teaching students how to live worthy lives' (Khurana, 2007: 45). What was so suspect about such a discipline was the lack of any clear object of study along with the apparent incongruence between industry interests and the unbiased ideals of academic knowledge.

One way of resolving this tension due to a lack of clarity in the object of study, or an inability to reconcile Enlightenment ideals with the obvious fads and fashions of something so distorted and inessential as business studies, was actually to foreground the 'truth' of the market as such. Essentially this involved making these incongruent self-interests, not only reconcilable with the disinterested ideals of truth, but also to reconfigure them as truth itself on a more holistic scale. This ideological and epistemological shift is clearly what has come to dominate the theories and disciplines within the business schools, most fundamentally within economics where notions of formulaic purity have undermined any notion of legitimate value existing alongside the market (Friedman, 1982; Hayek, 2009). This ideology sees social interaction, even the organization itself, as essentially a nexus of contracts that should be freely formed by individual agents of infinite self-interest, to guarantee that it is as efficient as it can be (for example, Coase, 1937; Laffont and Martimort, 2002; Williamson, 1981).

The impact of these ideas on the identity and behaviour of students has eventually and decisively influenced the business community and society at large. It is no coincidence that two of the more emblematic figures of our contemporary post-industrial economies in the West are the management consultant and the investment banker. While testifying both to the more individualized fluidity of the workforce and to incentivizing it by a purely performative market logic, these individual incarnations of the supposedly inherent dynamic of market forces are also the most common answer to what our business students want to do upon graduation.

Now this is where the complicity in the financial crisis lies, because in shaping the discourse (not to mention the career choices of our students) the business school has helped to create the conditions through which market-based mechanisms come to eclipse alternative value systems. Investment banking in particular has come to epitomize this logic, most notably through the structure of bonus incentives. This structure was also undoubtedly key in decoupling short-term individual prospects from mounting long-term and systemic collective risks. The former was the most 'natural' striving for a 'rational' agent in the canons of business theory. The latter was essentially precluded by efficient markets theory, which has long been a fixture in university economics and finance departments in the past half-century across the world (Fama, 1965; Schiller, 2005: 177). The curricula of economics and finance departments across the world have not been radically rethought after the crisis, and Eugene Fama, the main mover behind the efficient markets theory, received the Nobel Prize in Economics as late as 2013, so it seems our students are ultimately those who have to shout out against the nude emperor. Rethinking Economics and Post-Crash Economics Society are examples of organized student outcries against the obscenity of being taught by increasingly disconnected ideological curricula within business schools that just cannot keep up with the movement of our time (Inman, 2013)

It is interesting to note that Balzac, to whom we shall refer later, writing in early nineteenth-century Paris, observed the early signs of this modern discourse. Unlike the typical *Bildungsroman*, like any number of Jane Austen's novels which finish with the protagonist eventually finding her place in society (which essentially meant getting married), Balzac shows us a world that changes before our eyes, where nothing is fixed and no one is what they seem. As nobilities fall, fortunes rise from the shady alleyways of Paris, and no one stands unchanged in the wake of the modern world. However, the ascent of capitalism in Balzac's narratives never rises above its discursive and historic contingency. Material objects and financial transactions certainly determine human relationships in his stories, but the cold calculus of capital never fully moves beyond the rich depiction of particular individuals in particular situations. In short, Balzac chronicles the ascent of the capitalist discourse without pretending to articulate anything universal or normative, and it is precisely because of this difference and particularity that the ethical is still possible and discernible according to Levinas (2011). In her contribution to this volume, Leah Tomkins emphasizes the Heideggerian legacy in Western philosophy and how Levinas moves beyond it. Levinas (2011) maintains that any conception of ontology insofar as it is a science, a knowing or a 'logo', reduces the particular other (difference) to the universal (same); a move that always imposes its limits to form a referential totality. Since the particular other always already exceeds the definite limits of such a totality, it is a totality that will always be marked by an absent centre.

This absent centre is ethics, and ethics precedes ontology insofar as responsibility for the other is rooted within our subjective experience and is thereby primordial to the discourses we use to make sense of it in terms of 'knowledge'. This suggests that knowledge ought to be attuned to this ethical relation first and foremost, and this relation is only to be found in the encounter with the particular other according to Levinas. In this sense, Balzac is a much better teacher of what the true impact of the capitalist discourse may entail, because it is only when we become preoccupied with abstract and universal principles that we lose sight of the other, and therewith our abilities to distinguish right from wrong. Whereas most influential business theories have served to *naturalize* universal notions of market interest, Balzac's characters, however much influenced by this same emerging market logic, never rise above their own particularity. This is why a reading of Balzac helps to deter us from disembodied ideological reductionism and universalism. Balzac's characters, viewed through a Levinasian looking glass, raise a powerful warning flag against totalizing ideologies (such as neo-liberalism *vis-à-vis* the veracity of the market), where embodied ethical relationships are suspended, replaced by the ethics of self-interest and market rationale.

NATURALIZING SELF-INTEREST IS A RISKY BUSINESS

It is no wonder then, that before the financial crisis of 2008, when these theories were largely going unchallenged, we find subprime trading on a systemic scale. While 'collateralized debt obligations' and 'credit default swaps' were being repackaged into secondary markets and contaminating the world economy with unprecedented risk and impending crisis, it all made perfect sense according to the business school dogma. In essence, such theories have instilled in us the notion that whatever we can do to favour our own interests in the market is in our nature, and what validates the market itself. Furthermore, the nature of the market will guarantee the overall rationality and morality of all such deeds as long as the valuation, in this case of shares, remains favourable. Regardless of whether 'I' as an individual agent and banker engage in systematically misleading credit agencies and defrauding investors, the market is nevertheless efficient and transparent in a more holistic sense through the rising share prices generated thereby.

In other words this ideology produces a new 'morality'. Ethics are suspended and anyone participating in the capitalist regime is drained of all subjective significance other than being largely subjectified in and through the rational principles of the market. In this sense, identity or subject-hood is constituted by reference to the totality, rather than a body with emotions and idiosyncratic desires. In short, the rational subject is a subject without body, and herein lies the true danger of market fundamentalism – it becomes a self-fulfilling prophecy. The more we rationalize away our visceral emotions of care and concern that particular encounters evoke, by reducing them to instances of universal and totalizing principles, we increasingly lose the ability to feel these emotions.

This ideological shift, whereby the representation of value *qua* price becomes more real than any particular values to be found in visceral reality, is something that emerges from recent research I conducted. In the following passage I show how the accounts from bankers at Lehman Brothers are strikingly symptomatic of this totalizing and existential experience of market prices. The material is based on transcripts from four interviewees.[1] This is obviously not the number of accounts that would be needed in order to make any grander claims of generalization. But the main objective is to provide a brief illustration of broader ideological tendencies that I have foregrounded theoretically throughout the chapter.

In his *Confessions from a Man of Finance* (2009), Knut Ramel, a retired senior executive at Merril Lynch, admits to a feeling a gradual dissipation of existential anxiety paralleling the escalating sense of earning serious money. Ramel's testimony suggests that capital itself offers him existential solace, as opposed to the specific and particular things you can do with it. This is also vividly congruent with the empirical accounts from investment traders Lehman Brothers, wherein every particular relation is reduced to the universal signifier of money and capital:

Banker 1:

Money is the heart and blood of the world, finance is making things happen, and you are at the very top of that food chain. When you became part of Lehman Brothers you became part of something greater, something that is more than the individual and something extremely powerful. You become a cog in that machinery that yearns for the expansion of capital … You felt great, and you were doing well too, making money for the company, for yourself, sometimes even for the customers.

Banker 2:

If I would have wanted to make the world a better place I probably would have chosen something else. Earning lots of money makes me feel good and I don't think there is any shame in that. Lehman Brothers speaks to these kinds of emotions and it makes you feel good.

It is almost as if there is this natural order of oppression, where everyone feeds off of everyone else, and it doesn't matter what you do as much as where you are in the 'food chain' relative to capital.

Banker 2:

Earning money in a great many ways, including most ways in the banking industry, may have a lot of different effects on others, some might be damaging but either way you should not in my opinion worry too much about it. You take care of your business and others theirs. After all, it is a jungle out there, and you don't see lions walking around worrying about whether their eating habits would be damaging to anyone – like the prey for instance.

---

[1] These interviews were part of a more extensive research project associated with my PhD thesis 'The economy of dissociation' in which I conducted a range of interviews with employees at Lehman Brothers in relation to it collapse.

This is clearly in line with the neo-liberal ideology of the market as the only legitimate distributor of wealth, but in the following comment by the same banker, we start to sense the contradictions around the market as a place of justice and truth.

Banker 2:

'Subprime' loans were issued and encouraged as they would yield a high interest and then be passed on to us or to someone else, and we would keep or pass it on. Then the issuer is no longer bound by the loan ... and what is more, and which also was the case on a vast scale, he would be free to bet that the loan he issued would default and earn money in it doing so. This essentially means that you would actually seek out high-risk loan-takers, offer them a loan that they can't afford, sell it on for a handsome sum of money as it yields high interest and then boast the return by betting your money on the loan that you issued defaulting.

Suspending your moral judgement on account of market rationality is one thing but there is apparently another problematic ambiguity which surfaces as a result of identifying so closely with capital which becomes the arbiter of right and wrong. This is how another interviewee describes what can only be seen as a level of contingency in performance:

Banker 3:

You can be extremely diligent and analytical but nevertheless the market proves you wrong, and you have nothing to show for it, and as far as the company is concerned you are failing in what you are supposed to do. On the other hand, you can act on a gut feeling and for all the wrong reasons and if the market proves you right, you are a genius and you will be rewarded for your 'non-efforts'.

Banker 4:

The financial crisis is just a news manifestation of the age-old story about certain men becoming too powerful, it clouding their judgements and they underestimate their vulnerabilities. It is not a new story ... and it certainly does not tarnish the whole of mankind's ambition for profit.

We should recall here what Lacan (2006: 27) says about 'money'. It is 'the signifier that most thoroughly annihilates any other signification'. These extracts from bankers reflecting on their professional domain demonstrate how market value comes to subjugate any other form of value in the neo-liberal ideology. The last quote even indicates that there are no intrinsic values to the work itself other than retrospectively in terms of what kind of work was rewarded in the end. What we are continuously confronted with in this free market ideology, whether in the business school or in the world of banking we encountered at Lehman Brothers, is essentially the totalizing framework around market price as the only credible arbiter of value and concomitantly of right and wrong. Monetary calculations become appropriate guides for relationships between human beings in an absolute sense. We turn now from the neat and abstract theories of economics and human behaviour to literature, and in particular Balzac's narratives which chronicle the way these emergent assumptions of the capitalist order take hold in the private sphere, namely in family, parenthood, marriage and friendship.

BALZAC: A CHILD OF THE NINETEENTH CENTURY

While relatively rare in the Anglo-Saxon tradition, although more common on the European continent, business schools have been known to occasionally use literary classics to assist in teaching certain areas. In England and North America this has been done as a way to illustrate the dilemmas of leadership – one such example being *Lord Jim* by Conrad (1900). Other classics include Dickens and Shakespeare that have been used as part of the curriculum to illustrate the ethical dilemmas faced by pre-modern as well as contemporary capitalist societies. To my knowledge, comparatively little use has been made of Balzac, yet as Oscar Wilde claimed, 'the nineteenth century, as we know it, is largely an invention of Balzac' (Wilde, 2010: 24).

The nineteenth century was of course a time when Western societies moved from feudalism to capitalism, and perhaps nowhere as striking as in post-revolutionary Paris from where Balzac wrote. What's interesting about Balzac is that, unlike Dickens and others who maintain the 'noble' British measure of not quibbling about prices, Balzac was much more precise about the price of everything and how social position became overly determined by material objects and economic transactions in the Paris of his day (Maupassant would later follow suit in this respect). In this sense, he was one of the most powerful commentators on the ascent of capitalism, and therefore I contend the time is ripe to rediscover Balzac, who was also notably praised by Marx and Engels alike.

In essence, Balzac's discourse of capitalism is interesting as it clearly portrays the unfolding dynamic of a market society in the making, subverting values into prices as people are gradually coming to grips with the emerging sensation of the market encroaching into every last aspect of their life. In contemporary society, however, the discourse of capitalism has become so firmly established that it is hardly experienced as anything separate and distinguishable from the life-sphere itself. Indeed, this is why neo-liberalism has proven so successful as well as resilient in the face of obvious catastrophe and crisis. By reaffirming the standard axioms of market rationality taught by respected theories in the business school (see, for example, Coase, 1937; Fama, 1965; Williamson, 1981), neo-liberalism has managed to ingrain its instrumental individualist logic, thus furnishing the market with its own moral dimension. In contrast, Balzac (like Levinas) claims such totalizing constructs actually preclude morality, by reducing every particular relationship to the same transactional basis.

It is difficult to refute that close, intimate relationships have become increasingly defined by economic and political models of bargaining, exchange and equity. This dual process by which emotional and economic relationships come to define and shape each other is called emotional capitalism (Illouz, 2007), and Balzac's writing takes us to the barren end of this ascending logic, which can never be summed up in abstract and generalizing theories (see Box 15.1).

BOX 15.1   BALZAC ON THE COMMODIFICATION OF HUMAN RELATIONSHIPS

No novelist has described this as powerfully as Honoré de Balzac. Himself a staunch monarchist, an incurable snob looking for a rich, noble wife later found in the person of Madame Hanska, Balzac revealed the contradictions and injustices of modern capitalism, dominated by the slogan of Francois Guizot, then Prime Minister, to his fellow citizens: 'Enrichissez-vous'. Make money, get rich. In Balzac's world, everything – including sex, love and intimacy – can be bought, at a price.

And this is especially true of the family. This explains why French novelist Émile Zola claimed that Balzac was one of us (Zola, 1883), and both Marx and Engels (Engels, 2000) praised Balzac for his 'profound grasp of real conditions'. In La Comédie Humaine, as Balzac wrote in the beginning of Le Père Goriot (first published 1835), 'all is true' (a reference to Sheakespeare's King Lear). Goriot is a retired noodle-maker who made a fortune selling vermicelli during the French Revolution. A 'Christ of paternity', he gives up his fortune to his daughters, Anastasie de Restaud and Delphine de Nuncingen. He is deserted by both when he runs out of money, and is left to die 'as an old dog' in Balzac's words. His fatherly love, however, is not as saintly as Balzac would have us believe.

In particular, there are symptoms of incestuous passion and masochism. In one scene, when Goriot helps Delphine and Rastignac, his daughter's lover, to secure a love nest, Delphine profusely thanks her father and kisses him as she has not kissed him for some time. He responds by kissing his daughter's feet, and rubs his head against her dress, which is perhaps not the most appropriate way of demonstrating paternal love (Besser, 1972). The significance of the scene is twofold: first, Goriot buys Delphine a toy boy, just as he would have bought her a piece of candy or a dress when she was a little girl. Second, he gets his reward (kisses from Delphine) exactly like a client who pays for sexual favours (which usually take place after the client presents the 'gift').

Like King Lear, Goriot has an idée fixe, an obsession: his daughters. He monetizes his relationship with them, thus corrupting them to the core. As a result, both daughters repeat their father's mistakes by paying their lovers. This is especially true of the eldest daughter, Anastasie de Restaud, who brings herself to ruin by paying for the gambling debts of her lover, Maxime de Trailles. Delphine's calculated affection for Rastignac is a much wiser investment, but nevertheless she, too, will be abandoned by him, who will end up marrying her daughter, though in another novel. Goriot realises his mistakes on his deathbed:

Ah, if I were rich still, if I had kept my money, if I had not given all to them, they would be with me then, they would cover my cheeks with kisses … Money brings everything to you; even your daughters. (Balzac, 1998: 617)

He compares his love for his daughters to a vice, an addiction: 'I loved them as a gambler goes to the gaming table. This love was my vice you see, my mistress'.

(Continued)

(Continued)

He also understands that he corrupted his daughters by spoiling them, and tells Rastignac that he alone must be blamed for their ruin:

> God would be unjust if He condemned them for anything they may have done to me. I did not behave to them properly [...] The most beautiful nature, the noblest soul, would have been spoiled by such indulgence. I, and I only, am to blame for all their sins; I spoiled them. To-day they are as eager for pleasure as they used to be for sugar-plums. (Balzac, 1998: 625)

How does the study of Balzac (and others like, for instance, Dostoevsky, Tolstoy or Dickens) benefit business school students? It encourages them to think about a much richer depiction of human relations, power, politics, desire, ambition, kindness, cynicism, culture, money and organization and so on, in a more compelling, nuanced and embodied context. It may also help students to think creatively and critically about the abstract theories that have dominated the business school, for example the overarching models from economics, and the way they have influenced theory construction in fields of management and organization studies (such as Friedman, 1982; Hayek, 2009; von Mises, 2010). In this sense, we are looking to the past, so that we can better understand the present. By inhabiting the world of Balzac, we can see the early modernizing tendencies of capitalism as they unfold, and this alerts us to the true costs behind market prices and the neo-liberal attempt to mould naked labour by reductive and essentializing theories. Another advantage of shifting genre (from academic treatise to fictional novel) is that it prompts a richer and more nuanced analysis; it stimulates critical thinking that is more historically informed and more contextually and culturally anchored, as well demonstrating how much of our experiences are still reflected in, and resonant with, the past.

CONCLUSION

It is said that 'the devil is in the detail'. In this chapter we have paid attention to particular details and, in so doing, some of the tensions underneath the abstract and generalizing veneer of neo-liberalism have surfaced. In the literature of Balzac we can clearly see particular human destinies and symptoms of the capitalist discourse as it devours ever more intimate spheres of our lifeworld. Such individual symptoms and particular destinies are otherwise largely overshadowed by an ideology that sustains itself through universalism and reductionism. Moreover, I contend the business school has been key in establishing and sustaining these essentializing principles that have become imperative for the neo-liberal ideology.

We also see the predominance of a similar ideology coming through clearly in the empirical accounts of bankers at Lehman Brothers, shortly before the devastating financial meltdown their business practices helped set off. This demonstrates that when we subjugate our relations to the universal signifier of capital, we forsake our abilities to experience any intrinsic value in our relationship to self and others; all relations are treated as the same insofar as they are merely a means to an end that is always projected anew. We can never catch up with it, as we have confounded means and ends. The end never arrives, as no particular thing can ever satiate our gaze when fixed on the horizon of universality. In the meantime, we are blinded to all the finite ends in front of us, and treat all particular others as a means. By way of contrast, it is in the close encounter with the particular other, in the rich narratives of Balzac as much as in the real lives of investment bankers, that we can start to disentangle human values from the subjugating bondage of the market.

In this chapter I have endeavoured to demonstrate the human costs associated with the discourse of capitalism, and especially the way these costs have been ideologically subsumed under notions of human nature and rationality. Moreover, Balzac has been invoked at some length to illustrate the more intimate reach of an ideology that knows of no distinction between the business world and our private lives. We naively tend to think of domestic life as sanctified and immune to the contractualism that dominates day-to-day economic transactions (see Ng, this volume). Of course, we should know better, as the sociologist Eva Illouz (2007) explains in her book *Cold Intimacies*. Drawing on the theories of Levinas, I hope to have accentuated values hitherto silenced in the study of business, and to do this by turning to the rich landscapes of classic literature in which the humanistic perils associated with such notions are clear to see. Works of art can give us reason for hope. Business studies would greatly benefit from incorporating literature as a way of transcending the simplifying and totalistic tendencies of neo-liberalism: reminding us to stay human and to be prepared for the very constant struggles this demands of us.

REFERENCES

Balzac, H. de (1998) *Father Goriot*. New York: W.W. Norton and Co.
Besser, G. (1972) 'Lear and Goriot: a re-evaluation', *Orbis Litterarum*, 27: 28–36.
Coase, R. (1937) 'The nature of the firm', *Economica*, 4 (16): 386–405.
Conrad, J. (1900) *Lord Jim*. London: Blackwood.
Crouch, C. (2011) *The Strange Non-death of Neoliberalism*. Cambridge: Polity.
Engels, F. (2000) 'Engels to Margaret Harkness in London', from Marx–Engels Correspondence 1888. Trans. Dougal McNeill, Selected Correspondence. Retrieved from: www.marxists.org/archive/marx/works/1888/letters/88_04_15.htm (accessed 8 January 2015).
Fama, E. (1965) 'The behaviour of stock market prices', *Journal of Business*, 38: 34–105.

Friedman, M. (1982) *Capitalism and Freedom*. London: Phoenix Books.

Harney, S. (2009) 'Extreme neoliberalism: an introduction', *Ephemera*, 9 (4): 318–29.

Hayek, F. (2009) *The Road to Serfdom*. New York: Routledge Classics.

Illouz, E. (2007) *Cold Intimacies: The Making of Emotional Capitalism*. Cambridge: Polity Press.

Inman, P. (2013) 'Economics students aim to tear up free-market syllabus', *The Guardian*, 24 October.

Khurana, R. (2007) *From Higher Aims to Hired Hands: The Social Transformation of American Business Schools and the Unfulfilled Promise of Management as a Profession*. Princeton, NJ: Princeton University Press.

Lacan, J. (2006) *Écrits*, trans. B. Fink. New York: W.W. Norton and Co.

Laffont, J. and Martimort, D. (2002) *Theory of Incentives: The Principal Agent Model*. Princeton, NJ, and Oxford: Princeton University Press.

Levinas, E. (2011) *Totality and Infinity*. Pittsburgh: Duquesne University Press.

Ramel, K. (2009) *En finansmans bekännelser* [*Confessions from a Man of Finance*]. Stockholm: Ekerlids förlag.

Readings, B. (1996) *The University in Ruins*. Cambridge: Harvard University Press.

Schiller, R. (2005) *Irrational Exuberance*. Princeton, NJ, and Oxford: Princeton University Press.

Von Mises, L. (2010) *Human Action: A Treatise on Economics*. Auburn: Ludwig Von Mises Institute.

Wilde, O. (2010) *The Decay of Lying*. London: Penguin Classics.

Williamson, O. (1981) 'The economics of organization: the transaction cost approach', *The American Journal of Sociology*, 87 (3): 548–77.

Zola, E. (1883) 'Literary gossip', *The Week: A Canadian Journal of Politics, Literature, Science and Arts*, 1 (4): 61–7.

16 WHY IS IT IMPORTANT FOR LEADERS TO UNDERSTAND THE MEANING OF RESPECT?

Doirean Wilson

INTRODUCTION

Globalization is changing the education and workplace milieux which are now more ethnically and culturally diverse than ever. This creates challenges for business schools which must equip students to effectively engage with these teams to perform well. Moreover, organizations are now required to provide higher quality products and services quickly and cheaply via multicultural teams that are able to work harmoniously (Early and Gibson, 2002). Hence, there is renewed pressure for business faculty to gain insights into culture and to understand how this manifests in teams. If team members are to feel valued in order to work productively with others, this requires greater awareness of what respect means for those from different cultural settings. Most business schools today comprise a multi-ethnic and multicultural mix of students. Rather than seeing this sometimes challenging situation as something to be 'managed', how can this be leveraged as a learning opportunity to explore the subject of respect?

In this chapter I explore the meaning of respect for diverse teams of university business students. I do this via a study, conducted with 27 different nationalities/ethnic groups in two student cohorts, which reveals at least 50 different meanings invested in the term 'respect'. Given that respect is culturally situated, respectful behaviour for one person may be perceived as disrespectful by another. Glossing over or misunderstanding such nuances not only causes conflict in small group work, it also misses the opportunity to prepare students for multicultural working in their future places of employment. My classroom experience suggests that exploring the concept of respect in a business school classroom is risky but highly rewarding; if handled well it can be used to nurture multicultural team harmony, allowing diversity to have a positive impact.

THE BENEFITS AND CHALLENGES OF MULTICULTURAL WORK TEAMS

Operating in learning environments that are more culturally diverse has disrupted traditional identities of time and scholarly communities. Business schools are now expected to work across unfamiliar cultural boundaries. Yet some continue to measure themselves mainly on the rigour of research, preferring to adopt a monocultural theoretical approach to teach business education, instead of ascertaining how well their faculty understand important drivers of business performance such as culturally situated meanings of respect.

The prevalence of multicultural work teams has brought to light the importance of understanding the dynamics of cross-cultural interactions in order to know how to lead such teams. Many organizations acknowledge the benefits that can be gained from multicultural teams that can work harmoniously with those of difference. The same acknowledgement is required of business schools. This places pressure on managers and business faculty to work in a more sensitive and sophisticated cross-cultural manner. This is crucial as multicultural teams are now recognized as appropriate structures for dealing with performance demands and for coping with today's pressures for expedient higher quality performance (Earley and Gibson, 2002).

Although business school faculty have been putting students into teams for numerous years, they have little or no guidance on how teams function (Gabriel, 2000; Hansen, 2006). Business schools are known for their ability to produce impressive research, but are inclined to be limited in actual business practices that reflect a diverse workforce (Bennis and O'Toole, 2005). Perhaps this is due to their inability to understand other people's cultures, making it difficult for them to know how to nurture team respect. My study supports this claim as it demonstrates that promoting respect is difficult without first understanding what it means for those of cultural difference.

THE ROLE OF RESPECT IN TEAM-WORKING RELATIONSHIPS

Respect is recognized as a primary factor that aids relationship success; it is regarded as the primary means to nurture harmonious team working by identifying commonalities from which team norms and values can be developed. Moreover, respect for people is regarded as a paradigmatic example of a universal value that enables people to feel valued, which is intrinsic to one's self-worth (Frei and Shaver, 2002). Conversely, the absence of respect can arguably result in mistrust, low morale, and decreased motivation that can render culturally diverse teams conflicted and ineffective, with a negative business impact (see Box 16.1).

> ## BOX 16.1 FIST-FIGHTS IN CLASS
>
> I recently experienced a conflict that occurred between two executive MBA students in a diverse team working on a business project. They accused each other of being 'disrespectful'. The Greek student said his Indian colleague deliberately took his time to produce work that he felt was substandard. The Indian student retorted by stating that his colleague gave him little time to complete the task. In India business is usually conducted at a much slower pace. The hostility heightened when the Indian student accused his Greek colleague of being aggressive and always shouting. The Greek manner of conversation is usually louder and more emotionally expressive than others. This makes them appear angry when expressing their opinion. These cultural misunderstandings had a negative impact on the team's performance and almost resulted in a physical fight in the classroom.

According to Gibson (2004), those from the same culture tend to share commonly held views and often appraise and interpret management practices and situations in similar ways, while those from different cultures are more inclined to interpret the same situational events and management practices dissimilarly. This can lead to disagreement and disharmony and, *in extremis*, to verbal and physical abuse. The responsibility of respect for people gains its tangible manifestation in their social practices, which akin to respect, is culturally situated. If leaders lack awareness and understanding of what respect means for those of difference whom they manage, then they are likely to misinterpret culturally situated social practices and behaviours. Furthermore, it may be difficult for them to know how to encourage employees of cultural difference to work effectively in teams.

In this chapter I review the meaning of the term 'respect' and follow this with examples of cultural misunderstanding that caused conflict. Based on this experience as a tutor, I argue that business schools need to know how to work across unfamiliar cultural boundaries, to explore what respect means for a heterogeneous student group, and to show how this knowledge can assist business school faculty to nurture multicultural team-harmony both in the classroom and subsequently in their places of work.

WHAT DO WE REALLY KNOW ABOUT RESPECT?

A review of the literature suggests that the term 'respect' is itself a topic for ongoing debate (Quaquebeke et al., 2007). Respect is a commonly used word that still remains abstract so is not easy to define. While the literature acknowledges that respect contributes to relationship success hitherto, limited effort is made to define it or explore how it relates to other relationship constructs such as multicultural teams. This is despite the acknowledgement that respect is culturally situated as a way of life exclusive to a particular group of people (Frei and Shaver, 2002; Quaquebeke et al., 2007).

Gardner (2007) believes that a respectful mindset is one based on an awareness and appreciation of differences among human beings. This suggests that disrespectfulness would limit awareness and make it difficult to appreciate those of difference. Respect is what helps us make sense of global citizenship. Moreover, it is intrinsic to self-respect, itself an essential aspect of self-image regarding the 'I' that represents our identity and one usually happy being at home with the self. The relative disregard of what respect means makes it difficult to measure the impact on how leaders manage diverse teams, team-working relationships and learning outcomes, all of which require interaction and mutual exchange. The literature recognizes that respectful (as against disrespectful intra-group) relations encourage a willingness to engage in group-serving behaviour (Simon and Stürmer, 2003). As a positive self-conscious emotion, being respected instils feelings of happiness, dignity and self-worth. Therefore, it is potentially a driver for forging comradeship in multicultural teams. Yet research in this area is limited.

Despite being difficult to define, it is clear that respect is culturally situated and contributes to relationship success, especially the engaging of group-serving behaviours and the leading of multicultural teams. Business schools are now under pressure to instil norms of ethical behaviour in their programmes, by understanding cultural respect (Bennis and O'Toole, 2005). Sims (2002) asserts that this knowledge would enable business schools to develop students' ethical behaviours and sensitivity to those from different cultural backgrounds, nurturing a respectful mindset (Gardner, 2007). In the rest of this chapter I relate my experiences of developing respect among business school students.

SOURCES OF CONFLICT

My starting point was the experience of intense team conflict among final year business students who were required to identify intervention strategies for addressing real-life business issues as part of a *Consulting* module. Reflecting on this mini-crisis, I decided to build an exploration of respect into the design of the course: a collaborative action research approach which involved the study of diverse teams of four to six multidisciplinary business students. The students (150 females and 95 males) were aged 21–43 and from working- and middle-class backgrounds. The majority (approximately 92 per cent) had no dependents and represented 27 different cultures (see Table 16.1). Some of the students worked part-time for others or for family and some owned their own businesses. The module runs over 24 weeks of an academic year and comprises of lectures, team activities, fieldwork and tutorials. Persistent conflicts were making it difficult for the students to work harmoniously and affected the quality of work produced

Table 16.1 Students' cultural backgrounds and gender

No.	STUDENTS' CULTURES (2007–2008 cohort)	NUMBER OF STUDENTS	No.	STUDENTS' CULTURES (2008–2009)	NUMBER OF STUDENTS
1	White British of English parentage	5 students	1	Srilankan	4 students
2	Spanish of Mauritian Indian parentage	1 student	2	Second generation Pakistani	17 students
3	Somali	18 students	3	Indian	19 students
4	Kenyan	5 students	4	Jamaican	9 students
5	Pakistani	19 students	5	Swedish	1 student
6	Chinese	29 students	6	Black British of Jamaican parentage	11 students
7	Nigerian	19 students	7	Egyptian	1 student
8	Moroccan	1 student	8	Latvian	1 students
9	Sierra Leonean	3 students	9	American	2 student
10	Bangladeshi	8 students	10	Ugandan/Zimbabwean	1 student
11	Malaysian Chinese	12 students	11	Eritrean	4 students
12	Algerian	2 student	12	Bajan	5 students
13	Second generation Nigerian	16 students	13	Second generation Indian	31 students
138 students ÷ into 24 teams			14	Saudi Arabian	1 students
			107 students ÷ into 18 teams		

Total = 245 students, comprising of 42 teams of 141 female and 104 male students over two research phases (2007–2009) and their grades. Furthermore, tutors were expected to resolve the conflict by, for example, agreeing to students' requests to move to other teams, which caused further disruptions. The aims of the study were threefold:

1. to investigate students understanding and meaning of respect, in order ...
2. to determine how this perception of respect manifests in the classroom, prior ...
3. to assessing the implications of these understandings and perceptions for the way students might prepare for working in future cross-cultural environments.

To explore these questions I drew upon four sources of data: audio-visual recordings of stories shared in focus groups, findings from rich picture images, individual learning review essays (ILRs) and participant observation.

Focus group stories

Stories are valuable research communication tools that influence organizational learning (Gabriel, 2000). Prompted by team conflict at the onset of the module, I invited the students to join me to share their stories of respect by forming two research focus groups, at the beginning of the first and second research phase. To my surprise, *all* the teams volunteered, suggesting their interest in discussing the topic. The groups met once-weekly initially for half an hour, but this was increased to an hour due to popular demand. These facilitated sessions were audio-visually recorded, providing rich narratives that were thematically analysed. These recordings provided the opportunity to observe interactions and listen to the participants' discussions, which could be paused and rewound for scrutiny. The intention was to investigate differing opinions and attitudes that the students might have regarding respect (Anderson, 2009). This was achieved by promoting uninhibited team discussions. One such story was shared by a white British female student in the first phase of the study depicted below:

> Having to work in a group throughout this module has resulted in an improvement in my ability to work in a team. My group is very diverse, with people from many different backgrounds, for example Moroccan, Chinese and Iranian. These people's views are not necessarily the same as mine and I have learnt to respect and value these views as this is key to successful team working.

This extract from her story indicates that this student was able to improve her ability to work in multicultural teams due to collaborating in the focus group. Furthermore, she admitted that working with those of difference was something she had previously found difficult and that her interactions with them made her aware that their views were just as worthy and deserving of her respect.

Another story told by a female Chinese student provides insight into what respect means in her culture. That is, not to embarrass so that one can save 'face', a key Chinese concept referred to as *mianzi* and associated with *guanxi*, which refers to a small circle of special relationships, a strong social network. Consequently it is crucial for those visiting or interacting with the Chinese to understand the significance of face to the culture to avoid misunderstandings. Face is a means for protecting self-respect and individual identity, therefore to cause a loss of face can lead to conflict and disharmony. This is part of her story:

> To me the respect is when I do something wrong or make some decisions even though they are stupid, just don't laugh at me! You can try to help me address them, but not to help others is not a respect way and when people have done something and have done some work, respect it like I do and try to treasure it not destroy it.

This student intimates in her story that respect in her culture is also about showing care by helping those in need and to treasure others' work, thus responding sympathetically to those of difference in order to work effectively with them (Gardner, 2007).

A further extract demonstrates how a black male Ugandan/Zimbabwean student benefited from this story-telling process by enabling him to gain a better understanding of other people's respect and its significance in the education arena, in the workplace and in wider society:

> It was great to have a view of how everybody respects each other and what they prefer and expect. And also since it was actually my third year obviously we were finishing the degree and we're going into this big, wide world and it was great to actually see how I can pull all the skills in this focus group into my social life in the outside world [...], it made me aware of how I approach my group members and also people within our classroom and everyone in this university as well. And I'm thinking it's also given me somewhere to start in the life I'm going to start after I finish university ... I'm a lot more aware of people and I tend to ask them about how they are. It's also given me a reason to speak to people to find out how their culture is, what is important rather than just assuming.

It was evident from this part of the study that the stories shared in the focus group sessions enabled the students to gain answers to questions about each other's cultures without causing offence. These stories also provided them with an opportunity to disclose and make sense of what their respect meant and what respectful behaviour looked like through others' eyes. It also helped them identify some commonalities alongside their differences. Armed with these disclosures, members of focus groups noticeably changed their attitude towards each other from one of tolerance, to comradeship and co-operative working.

Rich picture images

Drawing a rich picture is a feature of soft systems methodology and potentially enables an individual to gain new insights to a given, often complex, experience. Their creativity enables them to uncover and clarify the phenomenon via a logical approach (Bell and Morse, 2010; Gardner, 2007). During the early stages of the research, I found myself drawing my own private rich pictures; I recognized that each image was conveying a powerful story of respect and this process enabled me to find my 'empty space', to review and make sense of my role as a tutor. Rich pictures have been utilized in leadership development for many years to enable team members to express their vision of an issue of common concern

(Bell and Morse, 2013) and I realized the students could also benefit by using their creativity to reflect on the meaning of respect and make sense of what was unfolding for them in the learning experience. Figure 16.1 was drawn by a male Somalian student in the first phase of the study; while reviewing it he explained that on his first visit home, he was greeted by villagers who prepared traditional dishes to eat with him. His mother sent him to make tea for their guests, but was horrified when she discovered that instead of making it the traditional way, he opted for boiling the kettle. He could not understand why she was upset, but watched as she placed a pot on the stove, filling it with water before adding tea ingredients. He said this would take longer to brew the tea and his mother responded: 'This is respect … it shows that you care and appreciate your guests', something he did not fully understand beforehand.

Figure 16.1   Findings from rich picture drawn by male student from Somalia

Another image was drawn by a female Caucasian American student showing an image of the globe and herself surrounded by a prism of colours. This, she explained, was how she viewed the world comprising people of various races and cultures in all their diversity; upon questioning from other students, she was able to see the significance of the filter or cultural lens she was using to view others. She commented that she was now able to value people's differences instead of criticizing or seeing them as a threat. These are just two examples of rich picture images used to capture, explore and discuss critical learning incidents, helping the students to uncover their culturally ingrained beliefs about respect. We found that discussing each other's pictures in this way reduced the likelihood of analysing – and possibly judging – another person's image from one's own cultural perspective. Rather, we could see it for what it was.

Findings from individual learning reviews

The ILR essay is an individual piece of work where the students' reflect on their module learning experiences. Because they submit these in confidence, they tend to be very honest. A review of these essays revealed that the overwhelming majority felt others in their class of cultural difference had, at one time or another, been disrespectful towards them. Also, the essays revealed that for the students, respect had either the same, similar or different meanings that reflected their cultural backgrounds (see Table 16.2).

Table 16.2 Students' core meanings of respect from different cultural perspectives

Students' cultural background	Similar meanings of respect
Female overseas Sierra Leonean student	'Listening to and being willing to work with those of cultural difference'
Male overseas Bangladeshi student	'Communicate with others'
Female overseas Chinese student	'Be culturally aware'
Spanish male student of Mauritian Indian parentage	'Recognize personal cultural identity'
White British female student of English parentage	'Valuing people's views and understanding their views of respect'
	Recurring meanings of respect
Male Somali student	
Jamaican female student	
Male Indian student	
Female Malaysian Chinese student	'Respect for elders'
Male Ugandan/Zimbabwean student	
Male UK born Nigerian student	
Male Eritrean student	'Respect can be given and taken away'
	Meanings of respect that were different to all others
Male overseas Nigerian student	'Demanding respect'

As we see from Table 16.2, several students from different cultural backgrounds shared similar core meanings of respect. These include a need to be culturally aware (Chinese student), and a willingness to work with those of cultural difference (Sierra Leonean student), with the latter meaning promoting the former. Respect for elders was a meaning espoused verbatim by a range of students such as the Jamaican and Indian students who were mindful of their approach when among elders. A UK born Nigerian student and those from Eritrea noted respect could be given when earned or taken away if challenged. An overseas Nigerian student was on his own in defining respect as being something one demands. This contrasts with the White British student's meaning of respect, which was to value others' views and understand their respect. The Nigerian student said:

> My team is a culturally diverse team which made me realize that communicating politely and respecting other members' opinions will avoid conflict. The way I related a previously to people where I come from might be seen as offensive by others. My culture demands respect for people.

This student's comments provide insight to the manifestation of his respect, as demonstrated while working with those of difference in a team. Furthermore, respect for elders was another common meaning espoused by the Nigerian students. This helped to explain why conflict would arise when the above student raised his voice and would be more animated than usual while interacting with his other team members. Fellow students found this behaviour intimidating so would accuse him of being aggressive, which was not what he intended. This student was a member of the Yoruba tribe located in south Nigeria where people tend to speak louder, raising their voices particularly when feeling emotionally passionate about something. His fellow group members were all younger than this student, and felt somewhat intimidated by his demanding behaviour. This was more evident when he believed they were not listening to him or when his views regarding team tasks were not sought first. Another male student who was born in the UK but raised by Nigerian parents said:

> In terms of culture I was brought up to be very respectful. From what my parents brought from Nigeria to me is that you respect your elders full stop! If the elders say go outside and clean the bins or whatever, you do it no arguments.

These comments suggest that Nigeria is a hierarchical society where position and age earn respect, therefore when among those who are younger and more junior, little effort is likely to be made to earn their respect.

Participant observations

The audio-visual recordings provided the opportunity to observe, review and reflect on their use of dis/respectful behaviours. This provided insight to some startling revelations. For example, I saw myself in practice on screen saying to the students in the first focus group session (at the start of the study) that I did not want to take the lead, yet immediately did so! This revelation is referred to as a living contradiction, which occurs when one's espoused values are denied by one's practice (McNiff and Whitehead, 2006). Another example of a living contradiction is one that relates to an east African student who participated in the study. He confirmed that observing himself on film conversing with others in the focus group sessions had a profound impact on him. He became aware of what he said and what he did with 'his own eyes'. This made him realize that what others had said about him over the years was correct. He explained that he was often perceived as loud and a poor listener, something he always denied because he believed he was the opposite. I observed this student as he watched himself in one clip for the first time, the way he behaved and the non-verbal responses of others (looks of surprise, folding arms, shaking heads from side-to-side). This realization made him shake his head in disbelief prior to pulling his jumper over his face to hide his embarrassment, as he continued to observe himself on screen. He watched as he interrupted another student whenever he attempted to contribute to discussions. He did this by raising his voice and by leaning forward in front of him each time this student attempted to speak. After watching the clip, he asked the other participants if they had seen the way he was behaving: they nodded to confirm they had, while reminding him of the times they that tried to bring this to his attention.

This student later confirmed that prior to seeing himself in practice he had no idea he behaved as he did nor did he think about how his behaviour affected others. He now realizes that his behaviour is born of his cultural upbringing. He explained that in his culture male children are expected to compete with others by speaking more loudly and getting ahead of them or risk being ignored. This revelation provided insight as to why he behaved the way he did with his team colleagues. This is because in his culture if you are not noticed then you are unlikely to be respected.

This student said he would never forget what he had learnt from observing the audio-visual focus group recordings. Anderson (2009) believes that participant observation is the only way to find out about real life in context with real organizations. As with many other research participants, this process provided the student with insight to the manifestations of his and others' respect behaviours in diverse teams.

CONCLUSION

Despite being a difficult term to define, the literature acknowledges that respect is culturally situated and that culture underpins our behaviour towards others (Frei and Shaver, 2002). This resonates with several key findings from the study. First, for the business students, respect had either the same, similar or different meanings and this was reflected and mediated by their culture. It would be difficult to accurately interpret what constitutes respectful behaviours for those of difference without the self-disclosure and honesty achieved by the four methods described above. Second, it is evident that respect contributes to relationship success: the students' working relationships and performance improved once they began to understand what respect really meant for each of them. A lack of awareness had the opposite effect (disrespect), leading to quite intense conflict that arose among culturally diverse teams. What was evident was the students assumed their understanding of respect was the same as for others, when this was not always the case. Third, the research demonstrated that the business school provides a valuable opportunity to elicit and explore meanings of mutual respect. Cultural diversity is now standard in the majority of business schools, yet there is a tendency for this heterogeneity to remain unexplored; differences are often tolerated rather than respected. By providing a safe, trustful learning environment, my experience is that students are willing to examine their own and others' meanings and boundaries of respect. This mindset (in contrast to disrespectful intra-group relations) has a number of benefits: it builds *self*-respect, one of the most significant goods; it encourages a willingness to engage in group-serving behaviours (Simon and Stürmer, 2003); and it is crucial for nurturing respect for people more generally, and for preparing students to work in cross-cultural contexts so they are able to negotiate global citizenship more effectively.

REFERENCES

Anderson, V. (2009) *Research Methods in Human Resource Management* (2nd edn). London: CIPD.

Bell, S. and Morse, S. (2010) 'Rich pictures: a means to explore the "Sustainable Group Mind"', in the 16th Annual International Sustainable Development Research Conference, Hong Kong, China.

Bell, S. and Morse, S. (2013) 'Rich pictures: a means to explore the "sustainable mind"?', *Sustainable Development*, 21 (1): 30–47.

Bennis, W.G. and O'Toole, J. (2005) 'How business schools lost their way', *Harvard Business Review*, 83 (5): 96–104.

Earley, P.C. and Gibson, C.B. (2002) *Multinational Work Teams: A New Perspective*. London: Routledge.

Frei, J.R. and Shaver, P.R. (2002) 'Respect in close relationships: prototype definition, self-report assessment, and initial correlates', *Personal Relationships*, 9 (2): 121–39.

Gabriel, Y. (2000) *Storytelling in Organisations: Facts, Fictions and Fantasies*. Oxford: Oxford University Press.

Gardner, H. (2007) *5 Minds for the Future*. Boston, MA: Harvard Business School Press.

Gibson, C.B (2004) 'Building multicultural teams: learning to manage homogeneity and heterogeneity', in N.A. Boyacigiller, R.A Goodman and M.E. Phillips (eds), *Crossing Cultures: Insights from Master Teachers*. Oxford: Blackwell Publishing, pp. 221–34.

Hansen, R.S. (2006) 'Benefits and problems with student teams: suggestions for improving team projects', *Journal of Education for Business*, 82 (1): 11–19.

McNiff, J. and Whitehead, J. (2006) *All You Need to Know About Action Research*. London: Sage.

Quaquebeke, Van N., Henrich, D.C. and Eckloff, T. (2007) '"It's not tolerance I'm asking for, it's respect!" A conceptual framework to differentiate between tolerance, acceptance and respect', *Gruppendynamik und Organisationsberatung*, 38 (2): 185–200.

Simon, B. and Stürmer S. (2003) 'Respect for group members: intra-group determinants of collective identification and group-serving behaviour', *Personality and Social Psychology Bulletin*, 29 (2): 183–93.

Sims, R.R. (2002) 'Business ethics teaching for effective learning: teaching business ethics', *Teaching Business Ethics*, 6: 69–86.

17 THE CONTEMPORARY RELEVANCE OF THE HEBREW WISDOM TRADITION

Phil Jackman

INTRODUCTION

Prospectuses and websites for business school MBAs are redolent with USPs about building leadership capability, enhancing business agility and boosting the careers of ambitious middle managers. Less evident is any mention of ethical business practice, boardroom integrity and personal character. This chapter suggests how the ancient Hebrew wisdom tradition can be pressed into service, not by displacing such functionalist discourse, but rather by opening up a new lens through which to view the world, a new language with which to explore leadership development, and a conceptual framework with the inner coherence and resilience necessary to develop more holistic ways of being and doing, thereby challenging the obstacles which persistently block the kind of personal and corporate transformation required to build a better future.

Language is powerful. From a dialogic perspective, it creates and sustains reality. The way we speak about leadership development shapes leaders. It is interesting to note that in the parallel field of training religious/spiritual leaders there is a growing preference for the term 'ministerial formation' rather than 'theological education'. Why is there no such equivalent for MBA programmes? Why is there so little discourse inside and outside of business schools around the 'formation of a business manager' or 'business leader'?[1] Several reasons suggest themselves.

---

[1] A Google search on 'business leader formation' on 9 April 2014 returned just one notable exception on the first page of results, namely the Jesuit inspired Albers School of Business and Economics in Seattle. One other entry, www.leadershipformation.com,

Functionalist dominance. Earlier contributors to this book[2] have already explored the pervasiveness of the belief among both students and faculty that the management techniques enshrined in functionalist discourse are among the most influential in securing career progression, promotion and salary level, further reinforced by business school rankings. Pressured by their own requirement to deliver return on investment, business school deans may well invest more in careers guidance, media coverage, recruiting students from poor countries and placing graduates in rich countries, and publishing in A-listed journals (Adler and Harzing, 2009; Segalla, 2008) than in the kind of intensive mentoring and coaching needed to walk students through the personalized and learner-centred journey required by a methodology of leader formation. Coetzee describes this as part of the 'glass ceiling' that needs to be smashed in order to break through to what he calls the postmodern MBA (Coetzee, 2010: 43).

Fragmented thinking. Tim Harle, in this volume, has noted the silo mentality and lack of integrated thinking that pervade the various faculty members of business schools. Electives are frequently packaged according to the latest fads (Trank and Rynes, 2003) with no organized framework within which the student can contextualize their learning choices in a thoroughgoing reflexive manner. Furthermore the frequent shuffling of teaching faculty makes it difficult for business schools to plan for significant change, since a two-year lead time is generally required from marketing all the way to delivery and there are many stakeholders to engage.

Fear of cloning. Finally, the subjectivist language of 'formation' may well feel more threatening to the student than the objectivist language of 'business education' and 'management development'. Educators operating within a largely instrumental mindset will indeed tend to 'clone' themselves by producing students who subscribe to the values of this framework. The real problem lies in the fact that these performative assumptions are not made explicit or interrogated. An example might be the growing prominence among business scholars of spiritual leadership theory (SLT) which brings together individual spirituality and the creation of an innovative, motivated learning organization with a purported impact on the 'triple bottom line'. The danger, of course, is that SLT renders organizational spirituality as theologically denuded and exclusively concerned with performance – one form of utilitarian rule compliance being replaced with another (Case and Gosling, 2010). The language of 'formation', however, implies a total experience, and a level of trust in the educators themselves who wish to help students explore the deepest recesses

---

used the term in their organization name, but a search of their own website produced not a single incidence of the term being used aside from their name in their online discourse! Two more results produced entries relating to leader formation, but in a theological rather than business context. By contrast, all ten of the entries returned on the first page of a search on 'ministerial formation' made reference to the term in their actual discourse, and no two of these were from the same organization.

[2]Especially Harle, Parry and Fiskerud, Henley and Beech.

of their own hearts. The fear is this: 'They have my intellect and my skills, they've recently taken over my emotions, and now they want my very soul in the service of corporate goals'.[3]

HOW CAN THE HEBREW WISDOM TRADITION HELP?

On the one hand, the dichotomizing Greek influences frequently embraced by Christianity and Western culture have much to gain from their more holistic Hebrew roots. On the other hand, those from the South and East will find much resonance with a wisdom tradition shaped in the crucible of a dialogue with its African and Asian neighbours. A principal Hebrew wisdom text is the book of *Proverbs* known to us through the Hebrew scriptures.[4]

> Like a madman who throws firebrands, arrows and death, so is the man who deceives his neighbour, And says, 'Was I not joking?

My own encounter with this playful and provocative tradition began in the mid-1980s. At that time, in particular, it opened up for me new insights into the relationship between friendship and money. By 2006 I was beginning to draw upon this tradition in my training of business leaders, and in 2010 we designed an MBA leadership elective and a final year undergraduate module around it at Birmingham Business School. Later in this chapter we include unsolicited feedback and extracts from students' reflective essays to give a flavour of the response.

Responding to functionalist dominance

Functionalism is a grand discourse whose power rests in the pervasive intertwining of a multitude of smaller discourses, which in this instance together tell the 'success story' of contemporary business (Alvesson and Kärreman, 2000). For example, Goleman (1995) has justified the use of emotional intelligence (EI) by pointing to the relationship between EI and 'star performers', so although he invokes right-brain intelligence the tendency is for this to be sequestered for instrumentalist purposes. The same might be said for the set of morally, socially and environmentally responsible measures proposed by Segalla (quoted in Adler and Harzing, 2009). Where could I find a competing discourse robust enough to resist the instrumentalist tendencies of functionalism and provide a compelling framework through which to develop well-rounded leaders?

---

[3]See Ricky Ng's chapter in this volume on 'Preparing managers for "exile" at work'.

[4]All references are taken from the *New Revised Standard Version*.

I began to see that the Hebrew wisdom tradition was a strong candidate. Not only is it an intertwining of smaller discourses, it also spans many centuries, emphasizing the intergenerational – versus quarterly – accounting called for by Coetzee (2010) and his research participants. As shown in the Table 17.1, the prologue to the *Proverbs* collection seems to hold in tension two traditions within the same grand discourse – the older pragmatic tradition of detachment

Table 17.1 Pragmatism and intimacy in *Proverbs* 1–7

Avoid the Bad (pragmatism)	Pursue the Good (intimacy)
First cycle (Adoption)	
1:8–18 Avoid bad company	
1:19 Lifetime accounting: Such is the end of all who go after ill-gotten gain	
	1:20–33 Pursue wisdom
Second cycle (Subversion)	
	2:1–8 Get rightly related to God
	2:9–11 Get rightly related to wisdom
2:12–15 Then you will avoid bad company	
2:16–19 Then you will avoid 'Zara'	
2:18–22 Lifetime accounting: Her house leads down to death	
Third cycle (Expansion)	
	3:1–12 Get rightly related to God
	3:13–26 Embrace wisdom
	3:27–35 Treat your neighbours right
	4:1–9 Embrace wisdom as I did
4:10–13 Lifetime accounting: Wisdom breeds longevity	
4:14–19 Avoid bad company	
4:20–27 Build your defences with care and precision. Watch your heart (23), tongue (24), eyes (25), feet (26,27)	
5:1–23 Avoid 'Zara'	
5:21–23 Lifetime accounting: He will die for lack of discipline	
6:1–19 Build your defences with diligence and discernment. Limit your liability (1–5), curb false optimism (6–11), recognize evil behaviour (12–15), shun evil character (16–19)	
6:20–7:23 Avoid 'Zara'	
7:24–27 Lifetime accounting: Her house is a highway to the grave	

which bears the hallmarks of the wisdom of the royal courts of Egypt, and the distinctive Hebrew emphasis on the passionate pursuit of intimacy with God, wisdom and other people growing out of Israel's emerging understanding of covenant faithfulness.

In three successive cycles, the Hebrew tradition develops the older tradition in a relentless assault on the will of the 'simple', the 'fool' and the 'mocker'. While its one thousand year pedigree in the Ancient Near East provides a vast intergenerational perspective, the primary accounting level of the text itself is a single lifetime, stated at the end of each cycle in italics. Taking a straightforward view of 'Zara' as a literal seductive married woman (Forti, 2007), the four Zara passages offer one of the strongest pragmatic/consequentialist lifetime accounting arguments in the entire literature: 'Don't have sex with another man's wife, because her husband might kill you'! It thus accommodates the functionalist concern for success while subverting functionalism's short-termism.

On the one hand, says the Hebrew tradition, pragmatism will get you so far, but not far enough. While the first seven chapters are dominated by the pragmatic and the defensive, the notion of a higher purpose enters epistemologically as early as 1:7, and dramatically as early as 1:20, finally dominating the landscape by the time we reach the end of the prologue in Chapters 8 and 9. Framed as a love affair with wisdom, it evokes all the drama of a passionate pursuit. Parameshwar (2005) has noted how leaders who demonstrate 'ego-transcendence' tend to invoke transcendental epistemologies. Unlike the mainstream Egyptian gods, Yahweh, the God of Israel, is rich with moral characteristics and moral concern: 'He holds victory in store for the upright, he is a shield to those whose walk is blameless, for he guards the course of the just and protects the way of his faithful ones' (2: 7,8).

Nowadays scholars almost universally consider that *Proverbs* 22:17–24: 22 shows dependence on the 30 sayings of Amenemope (Whybray, 1994). Sometimes when borrowing from the Egyptian tradition, a proverb will be lifted more or less intact, complete with its pragmatic reasoning:

Do not make friends with a hot-tempered man, do not associate with one easily angered, or you may learn his ways and get yourself ensnared. (22: 4,25).

At other times the Hebrew version will be distinctively shaped by its transcendental epistemology. Consider the following Egyptian response to a victim of injustice, essentially calling for silence rather than intervention as the wise path:

Call not 'crime' upon a man. Hide the manner of (a fugitive's) flight. (Cited in Simpson, 1926)

The pragmatic Egyptian wisdom, then, was *do what you can, but watch your back*. By contrast, the parallel Hebrew proverb calls for considerable moral courage in the face of injustice:

Rescue those being led away to death; hold back those staggering toward slaughter. If you say, 'But we knew nothing about this', does not he who weighs the heart perceive it? Does not he who guards your life know it? Will he not repay each person according to what he has done? (24:11,12)

The transcendental epistemology is directly invoked in order to press home the higher ethical standard.

This finely tuned blend of detachment and intimacy, enlightened self-interest and higher moral purpose subverts both the short-termism and the reductionism which tend to characterize functionalist thinking. While material prosperity was an important measure of success within ancient Israel, the broader vision of *shalom* embraced a sense of relational harmony, completeness and wellbeing. People and relationships were not regarded as 'resources' in the quest for greater performance. In fact it was the other way around. Wealth was regarded as a resource for building relationships (19: 4,6,7).

Integrated thinking

Fragmentation is a natural result of reductionism. Functionalism has commended itself in public life, but not in private life, for though at other times and places children may have been regarded as economic units which guaranteed parental security, in the twenty-first century West they most certainly are not. Indeed, in the contemporary Western community, *Proverbs* 19: 4,6 generally holds good:

Wealth brings many friends,

but the poor are left friendless ...

Many seek the favour of the generous,

and everyone is a friend to a giver of gifts.

People are not resources in the pursuit of better performance, rather wealth is a resource to be invested in enhancing family relationships. Secularism has driven a whole set of other dichotomies, a sample of which are listed in Table 17.2. With the rules in private and public life so diametrically opposed, integration

Table 17.2 Secularist dichotomies in the modern world

Public world	Private world
Work more important than family	Family more important than work
Relationships serve prosperity	Prosperity serves relationships
Efficiency more valued than beauty	Beauty more valued than efficiency
Science celebrated over art	Art celebrated over science
Numeracy and literacy central	Moral education central
Spirituality marginalized	Spirituality explored
Professional 'distance' with teachers	Intimacy with teachers

comes as a significant threat, for in the long run the needs of one's inner world generally trump the needs of one's outer world. Reductionism is essential to the survival of functionalist exclusivism.

By contrast, the opening section of the book of *Proverbs* sets out the meaning of wisdom as learning, instruction, understanding, insight, wise dealing, right-eousness, justice, equity, shrewdness, knowledge, prudence and skill (1: 2–6), a rainbow of overlapping concepts in which each word can at times stand for the whole. It involves the whole person, not just the mind. It holds together thinking and behaving (1: 2–4); the teacher as a co-learner (1: 5); external behaviour (represented mainly by the eyes, ears, hands, feet and tongue) and inner life (represented mainly by the heart). In the section of short two-line proverbs, all the way from 10: 1 to 22: 14, there are 34 references to the word *lēb* (heart), many of which make connections to various other parts of the body. The randomness of their ordering reflects the wisdom tradition's habit of intertwining the whole of life, and avoiding any possibility of reductionist categorization or spoon-feeding. In its thoroughly dialogic approach, everyone must discover wisdom afresh for themselves, but the student is interrogated from the deepest issues of the heart to the most practical expressions of their behaviour (e.g. 4: 23–27).

Formation without cloning

Fundamental to the ancient Hebrew pedagogy was the role of the 'father'[5] (1: 8; 23: 15,19,26) who instructs (1: 3) and who engages in provocative and cryptic dialogue (1: 6). Setting aside any gender-loaded conceptions of fatherhood which might distract from our main purpose, let us simply note that the father figure was regarded as the chief educator in the ancient world. What then was the 'father's' role?

First and foremost, the father was a mentor, an expert in the relevant field, namely life. The father needed to be a co-traveller on the journey, a model of passionate lifelong learning, a storyteller of past experience and a counselor when appropriate (4: 1–9). Secondly, the father was a master of conversation, using all kinds of cryptic techniques to evoke from the student answers which they themselves had chewed over and could own (1: 6), not unlike the contemporary concept of coaching, but with an additional arsenal of two and four line proverbs designed to provoke penetrating questions, explore tension and para-dox, reveal nuances, foster vision, focus intention and stimulate action.

Thus something akin to what we would today call coaching and mentoring was primal and integral to the wisdom tradition. The acknowledged wisdom of the sage/father figure created a safe relationship in which the student could grow

---

[5]From the exile onwards, the term took on an increasingly metaphorical dimension. The existence of early Israelite schools like the ones in Egypt and Mesopotamia is now seriously questioned, however, and it is clear that the original and primary meaning of 'father' was literal.

and flourish. The fact that the educational curriculum extended way beyond the environment of business and politics was the guarantee that the educational process was not instrumental, but rather training for life, a gift from 'father' to 'son'.

With a cautionary caveat, Grint's analysis of Aristotle may help us here: 'Phronesis, or practical or prudential wisdom or even political wisdom, is a "reasoned and true state of capacity to act with regard to human goods" (Aristotle, 1998: 1140), and it is essentially rooted in action rather than simply reflection. It is something intimately bound up with lived experience rather than abstract reason (episteme) but it is not a set of techniques to be deployed (techné)' (Grint, 2007: 236). So far, so good. But the cautionary caveat is this. The dichotomizing tendency within Greek thought which led to the very classification of these three aspects of leadership development also left the door open for the neo-platonic rationalist preference for episteme to re-emerge, and the subsequent insistence on employee praxis aligning with employer ideals. The Hebrew wisdom tradition avoids this tendency like the plague, preserving and maintaining a more equitable power balance between leader and follower, teacher and learner.

Mabey and Finch-Lees (2008: 124) observe that the relativistic nature of dialogic discourse may not provide a strong ethical foundation for the business student. An example is the ambiguity with which bribery seems to be regarded in the book of *Proverbs* as it once more explores the connection between money and relationships:

He will accept no compensation

And refuses a bribe no matter how great. (6: 35)

Those who are greedy for unjust gain make trouble for their households

But those who hate bribes will live. (15: 27)

A bribe is like a magic stone in the eyes of those who give it.

Wherever they turn they prosper. (17: 8)

The wicked accept a concealed bribe

To pervert the ways of justice. (17: 23)

A gift in secret averts anger

And a concealed bribe in the bosom, strong wrath. (21: 14)

The protection against such relativism is the character and integrity of the sage/father/teacher. For wisdom does not reside in words on paper (contra the trend in modern academia) but in truth is lived and reflected on by human beings in the context of a dialogue.

In my own journey as a business educator, I have been aware of some of the implications that rebound on ourselves, including:

- the need for us as teachers to be passionate learners not just of concepts but of life
- the need for us as teachers to be ready to employ storytelling and transparency

- the need for us to include one-to-one coaching/mentoring such that there is a close heart-to-heart engagement and the possibility of an open dialogue around integrity and ethics.

It is not enough for a teaching/coaching/mentoring team to have the right intellectual grasp of leadership, nor even to have learned good coaching skills. It is vital to employ people with integrity and high ethical standards, who practise what they preach, and are themselves passionate learners.[6]

> I would ... like to thank you for the module this year, I know there were some problems with groups etc. but I have really appreciated having a teaching team who have a genuine interest in the subject that they are lecturing and are so enthusiastic to share this knowledge. (Sarah, undergraduate)

We need to be not just intelligent and well informed, but also wise. When defining 'wise', for the sake of clarity and transparency it is necessary to declare one's wisdom tradition, such as the Hebrew, Arabic or Egyptian. That is to say, borrowing a tree metaphor for a moment, we tutors should identify the roots of our thinking and behaving. But one should also allow students to see and judge the fruit. The foundation of Egyptian pragmatism means that one can easily invite the question, 'Does this person's life work and does it have internal balance and consistency according to its own standards?' This in turn demands a level of transparency on the part of the tutor crossing the public/private divide which contemporary academia tends to eschew.

> Thanks so much for asking me to be involved in the Lifeline assessment. I was really inspired by yours and feel it would be beneficial personally to complete one as I'm currently completing the PG Cert in L&T in HE. (Danielle, postgraduate)

HOW MIGHT THIS LOOK IN AN MBA CURRICULUM?

The conceptual framework in Figure 17.1, used in a course known as 'Habits of the Heart' and integrated within Master's programmes I have led,[7] is deeply influenced by the Hebrew tradition, with the eyes, ears, tongue, hands/feet appearing on the outside: beauty, relationships, discipline and purpose appearing in what Zohar and Marshall (2000) would term the 'associative middle', representing the four phases we take learners through over a four to eight

---

[6]Karen Blakeley makes a similar point on spirituality at work in this volume.

[7]Initially with a group of secondary school teachers in South Birmingham, subsequently in an MBA elective at Birmingham Business School, adapted for use subsequently in an undergraduate programme, and used more recently in development programmes for leaders in health, the arts and business.

month timespan, and spirituality identified with the centre circle with 'my deepest connections' and 'my deepest convictions' – a consistent anchor and reference point for the entire programme. Despite its appearance of neatly a structuring humanity in a typically modern fashion, it too needs to be tempered with the persistent randomness and untidiness characteristic of the book of *Proverbs*. Armed with this conceptual framework, we have attempted to present a compelling vision and a robust context for growth.

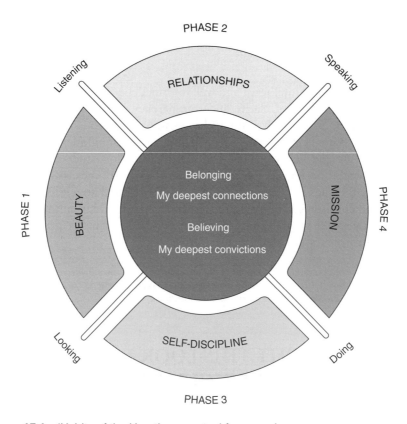

Figure 17.1 'Habits of the Heart' conceptual framework

Although we first used this model in the context of a leadership elective, it makes even more sense to use it to frame the entire MBA programme, designing and marketing the MBA as a unique journey, starting with a vision of beauty, and moving towards a compelling purpose, building relational integrity and new habits of self-discipline along the way.

Adapted from the 34 references to *lēb* in *Proverbs* 10:1–22:14, we developed a life inventory for use at the start, middle and end of the course to track progress across 18 different areas of life. In each phase the students chose one or two development areas revealed by the inventory, while using a learning log or journal to build self-awareness and reinforce learning. The ongoing discussion with the mentor maintained an individual focus with appropriate confidentiality. Throughout the course, we used exercises that keep driving students down to their deepest convictions and their deepest connections.

One of the early exercises we give to our MBA students is to spend ten minutes looking carefully at a tree to consider what lessons it has as a picture of life. We thus encourage our students to connect at an experiential level with what they know to be true. It is at this level that we can often find the most effective global language through more right-brained ways of knowing. This emphasis within the wisdom tradition of dealing with the detail of what is actually happening in front of our eyes (especially in the natural world) can help students from very different backgrounds reflect on and discuss life's meaning without having to travel via the great belief systems of our respective communities, which may too quickly surface conflict and disagreement when approached cognitively.[8] Though students find the process hard at first, they mostly begin to enjoy the fruit with practice. Some of the deepest questions like 'Who am I?' and 'What do I want?' can begin to surface through the 'safe' exploration of what appears to be an external object, but is in reality a metaphor for life itself.

Another key exercise is the writing of one's own obituary, which serves several purposes at once. Firstly, it highlights the issue of lifetime accounting: priorities viewed at the lifetime level look very different from those viewed at the quarterly level. It is a creative way of asking the question *'What is truly important?'*. Secondly, it helps students face the issue of death. In some contexts we have softened this to an eightieth birthday party speech, but in our experience this does not have quite the same bite as the obituary. We have noticed that taboos around the subject of death are particularly strong in regions where atheism is more prevalent, such as the West and China (see Hui, Chiu, Coombes and Pang, this volume). Not until well over halfway through the course are they invited to share some of the content of that obituary with two others. Finally, at the very end of the course, they are encouraged to draw on the insights gained from their obituary to deliver a presentation on one of life's big questions. This careful sequencing, preferably over more than one semester, gives time for trust to develop, first with a mentor, then with one or two fellow students, and finally with the whole group.

Closely related to the obituary is the lifeline exercise already alluded to by a Birmingham postgraduate student above. While the obituary looks to the past and the future, the lifeline looks only backwards to the key events, influences, relationships, etc. in the student's journey so far. Positioned in the middle of the Habits of the Heart course, it provides another stepping stone to deep life

---

[8]In her study earlier in this book of 245 business students from 27 different cultures, Doirean Wilson found that most students felt disrespected by their peers, while storytelling and 'rich pictures' were immensely helpful tools in generating effective communication and mutual respect.

reflection. As each of the mentors will have completed their own lifeline and obituary, this also provides an opportunity for mutual self-disclosure and the richness of storytelling in shaping identity and meaning for both student and mentor. Much more difficult was the use of the exercise on an undergraduate course where there was no one-to-one mentoring component to help build trust. It generated some strong feedback, both positive and negative (see Box 17.1).

BOX 17.1   STUDENT REACTIONS

Negative

The individual coursework was too personal for an UG module. While I can appreciate the extent to which our personal circumstances influence our perception of leadership I felt this was inappropriate … Several of my colleagues were reduced to tears during the presentations with no support being offered by the tutors afterwards. I suffer from ME and was off school for three years. I did not feel comfortable talking about this in front of my colleagues but did not have any other suitable personal issue. (Cally)

Positive

I really have found going through my life story a worthwhile exercise, even if I don't intend to present the whole thing, as it has really helped me identify the events and relationships which have played a part in shaping my insecurities, which is a good start to making a change. (Gabriella)

When we discussed it there seemed to be a general consensus that the course was enlightening, particularly completing the lifeline and seeing where our behaviour and values stemmed from and how aspects of theory gave insight into elements of our experiences – for all of us, it made us think about/notice things that we hadn't before – and has quite genuinely changed how we are likely to lead in the future, which is very useful! (Loretta)

This dialogic analysis of who I am and what my values are has been incredibly insightful in understanding my own identity, recognizing other viewpoints and where my weaknesses lie. (Rebecca)

Before undertaking the LD module, I had very much taken my opinions as they were and didn't question where/how they had come about. However, through exploring my past and the feelings that I experienced throughout certain periods of my life in more depth, it helped me to establish the causality of my current values, and more importantly it has helped me form the basis of what I believe will help me become a successful leader in the future. (Hannah)

Although I have opted for the term 'mentor' to describe the 'helper' who comes alongside the learner, whether in a university leadership elective or a workplace leadership development programme, in reality I am here commending a multi-discourse approach to one-to-one guidance. The mentor is probably most at home in an interpretivist discourse, their own story interweaving with that of the student, reinforcing a plausibility framework in which there is self-awareness, personal transformation, lifeline and obituary. The executive coach may be more at home in a functionalist discourse, in which there are goals, measures of success, numerical inventory scores and strategies for self-discipline. The sage's natural home is in a dialogic[9] discourse, where proverbs in particular are used provocatively and playfully to deconstruct and reconstruct leadership identity without doing violence to the integrity and agency of the student.

CONCLUSION

The dominance of a corporatist, performative mindset, the lack of integrated thinking and the fears associated with opening up parts of the self hitherto regarded as off limits for a leadership development course in a business setting collectively mount a significant challenge to anyone wishing to 'break through the glass ceiling' to the postmodern MBA. Building on a thousand year old grand discourse of international wisdom, the Hebrew tradition offers a way to enhance the richness of learning for business school students willing to engage with it: an integrated pedagogy, a transcendental epistemology and a compelling storyline with which to 'break the glass'.

The fact that this was the normal education system in the Ancient Near East over many centuries should give us courage to think that it could be renovated and shaped for use in a new era, retaining the best gains of modernity, while critiquing the worst from a standpoint of previous intergenerational wisdom.

FURTHER READING

For a scholarly overview of the entire corpus of Ancient Hebrew Wisdom literature, see Murphy (2002).

For a concise, practical and accessible pedagogical aid to using Hebrew proverbs, see Kidner (1964).

For a comparative study into the folk origins of Hebrew proverbs, see Golka (1993).

REFERENCES

Adler, N.J. and Harzing, A.-W. (2009) 'When knowledge wins: transcending the sense and nonsense of academic rankings', *Academy of Management Learning and Education*, 8 (1): 72–95.

---

[9]Corresponding to the radical humanism of Doherty's deconstruction of *Built to Last* in this volume.

Alvesson, M. and Kärreman, D. (2000) 'Varieties of discourse: on the study of organisations through discourse analysis', *Human Relations*, 53 (9): 1125–49.

Aristotle (1998) *Nicomachean Ethics*. London: Dover.

Case, P. and Gosling, J. (2010) 'The spiritual organization: critical reflections on the instrumentality of workplace spirituality', *Journal of Management, Spirituality and Religion*, 7 (4): 257–82.

Coetzee, J. (2010) 'The postmodern MBA: breaking the glass ceiling', *EFMD Global Focus*, 4 (2): 40–3.

Forti, T. (2007) 'The Isha Zara in Proverbs 1–9: allegory and allegorization', *Hebrew Studies*, 48: 89–100.

Goleman, D. (1995) *Emotional Intelligence*. London and New York: Bantam Books.

Golka, F.W. (1993) *The Leopard's Spots: Biblical and African Wisdom in Proverbs*. Edinburgh: T&T Clark.

Grint, K. (2007) 'Learning to lead: can Aristotle help us find the road to wisdom?', *Leadership*, 3 (2): 231–46.

Kidner, D. (1964) *Proverbs*. Leicester: Tyndale.

Mabey, C. and Finch-Lees, T. (2008) *Management and Leadership Development*. London: Sage.

Murphy, R.E. (2002) *The Tree of Life: An Exploration of Biblical Wisdom Literature* (3rd edn). Michigan: Eerdmans.

Parameshwar, S. (2005) 'Spiritual leadership through ego-transcendence: exceptional responses to challenging circumstances', *The Leadership Quarterly*, 16: 699–700.

Segalla, M. (2008) 'Publishing in the right place or publishing the right thing', *European Journal of International Management*, 2: 122–7.

Simpson, D.C. (1926) 'The Hebrew Book of Proverbs and the teaching of Amenophis', *Journal of Egyptian Archaeology*, 12: 232–9.

Trank, C.Q. and Rynes, S.L. (2003) 'Who moved our cheese? Reclaiming professionalism in business education', *Academy of Management Learning and Education*, 2: 189–205.

Whybray, R.N. (1994) *The Composition of the Book of Proverbs*. Sheffield: JSOT Press.

Zohar, D. and Marshall, I. (2000) *Spiritual Intelligence: The Ultimate Intelligence*. London: Bloomsbury.

18 DO BUSINESS SCHOOLS PREPARE STUDENTS FOR COSMOPOLITAN CAREERS? THE CASE OF GREATER CHINA

Pamsy Hui, Warren Chiu, John Coombes and Elvy Pang

INTRODUCTION

More than ever MBA students need advanced business-relevant skills and knowledge to lead in a complex and changing world. Universities worldwide have been working to align their MBA programmes to the goal of training leaders for the future. In North America and Western Europe there is some evidence that MBA holders have better short-term performance than their MBA-less counterparts (Hansen et al., 2010). However, the effectiveness of an MBA for providing for longer-term goals in other cultural settings is more debatable (Pfeffer and Fong, 2002). This is a critical issue as MBA candidates today come from increasingly diverse backgrounds, and live in a world that is becoming more cosmopolitan, with more transnational forms of lifestyle, non-state political entities and global social movements. In China alone, the number of institutions providing MBA programmes has grown from nine (with 91 students) to over 130 (with over 25,000 students) between 1991 and 2010, with possibly an extra million or so graduates in the coming decade (Das, 2013; Warner, 2011). Are MBA programmes, in their current design, equipping students with the necessary skills to lead in such an environment?

Several skills are particularly critical to leading in a cosmopolitan environment. First, one needs strategic skills to understand complexity, make decisions and come up with innovative solutions. Second, one needs to have courage to deal with situations that are bound to arise in complex situations. Third, one needs organizational positioning skills to negotiate the political minefield that comes with a cosmopolitan environment. Fourth, one needs personal and interpersonal skills to relate to diverse others. Finally, one needs a global focus to adapt from context to context. The effectiveness of an MBA programme as a platform that provides these skills depends on careful consideration of students' backgrounds and adaptation to their future contexts. As such, there is a crucial question to be asked: is the programme catering to the specific learning needs of students given their individual social and cultural backgrounds?

In order to provide students with many of the above skills, which are sorely lacking in many MBA programmes (Rubin and Dierdorff, 2013), it is important to understand the social and cultural background of the learner (Schyns et al., 2011). A student from a less cosmopolitan background may be accustomed to an environment that does not expose them to complex decision-making, conflict management, or negotiation with people of different cultures – conditions that an MBA student from a more cosmopolitan city may encounter daily. In contrast, cosmopolitan students need to take into account cultural contexts that are more insular and isolated. Clearly, the learning needs of the two groups are different. In other words, MBA students are increasingly going to require leadership development plans and resources that are tailored to complex and culturally specific learning needs.

A TALE OF THREE CITIES

Greater China provides an interesting setting for studying the effectiveness of MBA programmes, especially in the context of leadership development. There are three main reasons for this. First, China has been developing quickly over the past few decades to become the second largest economy in the world. In recent years, Chinese organizations have begun to expand their reach, but despite this global aspiration there has been a dearth of leadership talent in China. According to an estimate by the McKinsey Global Institute, Chinese organizations will need 75,000 leaders who could operate in a cosmopolitan environment by 2020 – a number that dwarfed the 3,000 to 5,000 leaders they had in 2005. Given the need for leadership talent, good leadership development programmes are in high demand in the region.

Second, the Greater China and Chinese MBA students have shown quite different characteristics from those of typical MBA students in North America and Europe. Yet, they are not the only 'foreign' newcomers to the MBA market. With the rise in the number of MBA programmes offered in Latin America, India, Russia and other fast-developing economies, it is important to understand how the social and cultural contexts matter in MBA education.

Third, Greater China is not a homogeneous region. Some cities are more cosmopolitan than others and provide a spectrum of contexts. For instance, on the more cosmopolitan end of the spectrum is Hong Kong, an international city that has enjoyed a history as a capitalistic trading centre in the Asia-Pacific region. Educational, legal and economic systems have been greatly influenced by the British, though many aspects of daily life have remained traditionally Chinese. Hong Kong is home to many regional headquarters for multinational companies. Xi'an, in contrast, is far less cosmopolitan. Although it was the ancient capital of China, it has grown relatively slowly in cultural, economic, legal and political terms and has lagged behind more coastal metropolitan areas, such as Shanghai and Beijing. Indeed, it has been more provincial than these other cities in terms of its labour-force and funding sources for businesses. Nevertheless, since the late 1990s it has become one of the fastest growing cities in China, with fast-developing telecommunication, transportation, information and financial industries. Falling between these two ends of the spectrum is Shenzhen, a steadily growing city that had spearheaded China's open door policy, and is home to an increasing number of regional corporations and expatriates.

In order to address some of the challenges presented by this diversity, we have designed a series of leadership development workshops embedded in the One China MBA programme run by a Hong Kong university. This affords us an excellent opportunity to investigate the importance of context in MBA leadership training. Details of this programme are given in Box 18.1.

BOX 18.1   THE ONE CHINA MBA

About 230 students in the three above mentioned cities are enrolled in the programme, with backgrounds largely representative of the relative cosmopolitanism of each city. In particular, students from the three cities had different levels of exposure to international perspectives and cultures. The Hong Kong students are mostly middle managers, working in multinational organizations, serving an array of stakeholders with international exposure and fluency in two or more languages. The Xi'an students are mostly senior managers working for government units or state-owned enterprises, dealing with relatively homogeneous stakeholder groups in Western China. Many have limited international exposure, and speak only Chinese. The Shenzhen students tend to be intermediate within these two extremes, exhibiting a moderate albeit steadily growing level of exposure to international cultures as the city develops infrastructural and commercial connections with the rest of the world.

For the purpose of leadership development, students enrolled in the One China MBA programme are assessed on five main competency groups, namely, strategic skills, courage, organizational positioning skills, personal and interpersonal skills, and global focus – captured in 31 competencies via a series of online 360 degree

(Continued)

(Continued)

Strategic Skills	Courage	Organizational Positioning Skills	Personal and Interpersonal Skills	Global Focus
• Business acumen • Learning on the fly • Problem solving • Dealing with ambiguity • Creativity • Innovation management • Perspective • Strategic agility	• Command skills • Conflict management • Standing alone • Sizing up people	• Political savvy • Presentation skills • Comfort around higher management	• Boss relationships • Customer focus • Understanding others • Motivating others • Building effective teams • Managing vision and purpose • Composure • Dealing with paradox • Personal learning	• Global business knowledge • Cross-cultural resourcefulness • Cross-culture agility • Assignment hardiness • Organizational positioning skills • Cross-cultural sensitivity • Humility

Figure 18.1 Major clusters of competencies

feedback surveys embedded in the leadership development workshops (see competency groupings below). Assessment ratings for the 360 degree feedback surveys may include bosses, peers, direct reports and customers, numbering 936 raters in all giving 840 responses, including student self-reports.

Major clusters of competencies

The surveys are built on the concept of competency modelling, in part from Lawler's (1994) idea that competencies form a more parsimonious basis for assessing and developing talent than job-based criteria. Researchers and practitioners have identified common knowledge or skills that are critical to individual and organizational performance (i.e., competencies) across job functions, business units and industries (Shippmann et al., 2000). The surveys used are developed by the Center for Creative Leadership and validated with data collected from managerial participants around the globe. Across the five competency groupings, surveys contained questions about 67 skills (Dai et al., 2010) and the contents, themes and structures, although phrased in layman terms to enhance validity and reliability, are similar to other taxonomies of managerial competencies (e.g. Tett et al., 2000).

All students are required to nominate a set of raters to evaluate them on a five-point Likert scale on each competency, and the importance of each competency, again on a five-point Likert scale, for their jobs.

Our observations

As expected, students from different locations appear to enter their MBA studies with different skill levels, and their jobs *currently* appear to demand different skill sets, according to 360 degree ratings. Interestingly, even within each location, there seem to be skill differentials based on job levels – underlying the proposition that students' backgrounds need to be well understood. As their work environments become more cosmopolitan, students stand to face different challenges. Here we summarize our key findings as to the perceived importance of different skills and how these are currently rated for students from the three cities.

What skills are prized? Different worlds, different dreams

Across all locations, several skills are commonly judged to be of high, moderate or low importance according to the findings of our 360 degree feedback survey. For instance, problem-solving, courage to persist single handedly, boss relationships, building effective teams and composure are considered important skills in all three locations. However strategic agility, conflict management, understanding others and dealing with paradox are all considered moderately important. Finally, creativity, political savvy and many of the global focus skills are uniformly considered as least important.

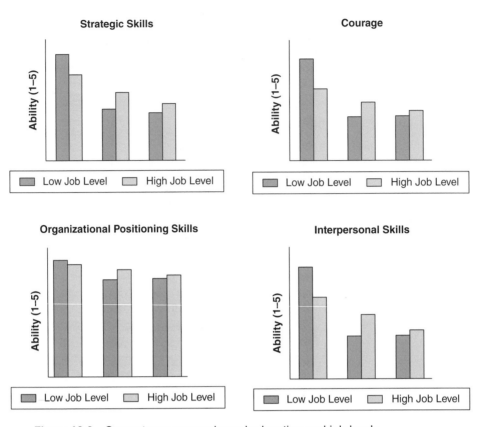

Figure 18.2 Competency comparisons by location and job levels

Despite these similarities, there are also some notable differences across locations (see Figure 18.2). For example, in the fast-developing and growing cities of Xi'an and Shenzhen, it is considered critical to be able to hit the ground running, presumably because the environment is changing quickly. In contrast, other dimensions of strategic skills (i.e. business acumen and dealing with ambiguity) are more important in Hong Kong, where long-term strategic planning plays a more important role than short-term tactical moves for organizations to stay competitive. With little overall experience in an open, capitalist market as a city, Xi'an stakeholders place a lower emphasis on customer focus, quite unlike their more market-facing counterparts. While across all three locations, global focus competencies are placed in relatively low priority, stakeholders in Hong Kong do emphasize two of those competencies (i.e. organizational positioning skills and humility, both related to a willingness to seek advice, learn and share information) more than their counterparts in the other locations, suggesting that Hong Kong is slightly ahead in recognizing the need to develop a more global outlook.

The above observations suggest that for the immediate future, MBA students with different backgrounds and serving different environments will need to pick up different skill sets in their quest for career advancement and to satisfy the demands of their stakeholders. Nevertheless, some skill sets are equally critical in different environments, and can form the foundations for a generic MBA education.

How skills are rated: one world, one dream?

The perceived competency levels of students in the three locations are also important for determining particular levels of skill for leadership development. Xi'an participants are rated significantly higher on most competencies than Hong Kong participants, while Shenzhen participants are sometimes rated similar to the Xi'an participants, and sometimes similar to the Hong Kong participants. If we take these observations at face value, we may then conclude that the Xi'an students are more senior and hence more competent, and would proceed to provide them with more advanced leadership training than the other groups. However, it is also possible that the Xi'an students' raters are more inclined to inflate their assessment ratings than those of the other two locations. If that is the case, then there are not enough substantive differences among locations to warrant training customization. Yet, in a fast-developing and growing environment, individuals who are educated just a few years apart may encounter drastically different political and economic climates, leading to different perceived levels of competence among participants even in the same locale.

This is, in fact, what we observe from the surveys. When looking at the data by both location and job level, a somewhat counter-intuitive picture appears at first glance (see Figure 18.2 for competency comparisons). Typically, we would expect students with higher job levels to be older and educated earlier. However, in Xi'an, students who hold lower job levels are considered more competent in strategic skills, courage, personal and interpersonal skills than their more senior counterparts. This is remarkable considering the possibility that individuals with high job levels may have garnered favourable ratings due to respect from those who rate them. However, on reflection, senior managers in Xi'an in our sample were born around the time of the Cultural Revolution and grew up before China opened its markets to the world. In fact, being in the heartland, they probably received much of their education and training in a more bureaucratic environment where practices differed from those observed in the coastal cities. In fact, some of these relatively senior students might have encountered quite serious disruption to their education. In contrast, the less senior students in this group grew up as China was opening its doors to the world and when the region was becoming more affluent. Most of them received an education with more of a Western influence. Indeed, some of them even have had multinational work experience and training.

The situation in Shenzhen appears to be the opposite of that in Xi'an. Individuals with higher job levels are considered more competent in all skill dimensions than their lower level counterparts. This observation is quite consistent with the development of Shenzhen, a Mainland Chinese city just like Xi'an, but a pioneering special economic zone, with typically entrepreneurial inhabitants, and many university graduates who migrate to Shenzhen in search of better job opportunities. In contrast, those of lower level positions are probably newcomers, still adjusting to life in the city. Thus, through competition and self-selection, it is conceivable that those in relatively high job positions in Shenzhen are more competent in all the aspects measured.

The scenario in Hong Kong is likely the product of its unique historical background. Our findings suggest that there are no significant competence differences among those with higher job levels and those with lower job levels. Among this group of students, regardless of job level, the leadership competence is quite similar. To this assessment of current skill, we need to add a further factor: not everyone is in the programme with the same purpose. While students with relatively high job levels are enrolled in the programme to update their knowledge for immediate leadership challenges, those with relatively low job levels are making a long-term investment in preparing themselves for a job market that is becoming increasingly cut-throat.

What kind of MBA is needed? Toward a cosmopolitan world

Given the above mentioned diversity in terms of leadership competence and the expected goals of an MBA education, by assuming that all students are the same, we risk teaching over the heads of some students while wasting resources on training skills that some who enter the programme already possess. Even students from the same locale may need different levels of leadership development. While they must learn to take what they need and know what they want from the programme – and that is where self-knowledge is critical – we must also make every attempt to tailor the programme to their cultural contexts and the specific demands of those contexts.

If the three cities are all moving toward higher levels of cosmopolitanism in the future, how can an MBA education prepare students better for the challenges ahead? Clearly, this would depend on both the location and the students' job level, among other factors. In Xi'an, more training in strategic skills, courage and personal and interpersonal skills would be necessary for relatively senior students so they can compete with their younger colleagues and survive the immediate future. In the long-term future, however, special attention should be paid to organizational vision and strategic planning, the management of diverse stakeholder relationships, and openness to learn globally, even though these students are not rated as particularly deficient in these skills, possibly because their existing environment does not demand much of these skills, as is evident from our findings.

For the Shenzhen students, those with relatively low job levels would need extra work to pick up strategic thinking, courage, organizational positioning, personal and interpersonal skills for career advancement and to take over from their more senior colleagues in the immediate future. In the long-term future, though, skills related to long-term strategic planning, openness to learn globally and, to a lesser extent, the management of diverse stakeholders need more attention. Indeed, skill deficiencies in some of these areas are detected by the raters in our survey.

For the Hong Kong students in this study, relatively less individual tailoring is required compared to the other two locations. However, skills related to the management of diverse stakeholders would require more work immediately, as clear deficiencies are identified by the raters. In the long-term future, students would also need to develop more openness to learn from cultures that are unfamiliar to them and be sensitive to ideas from these unfamiliar cultures in order to compete in the global marketplace.

TOWARDS A CULTURALLY ATTUNED MBA EDUCATION

As we stated at the start of the chapter, the MBA market is becoming increasingly international. In a class of 50 students, there may be students from 15 to 20 different socio-cultural backgrounds. The country of destination for these students will be equally varied. How can business schools respond to this challenge of ethnic, cultural, linguistic and worldview diversity? Based on our pioneering work at a Hong Kong university with students from Greater China, we offer some early observations.

Culturally sensitive leadership development

Conventional MBA programmes usually include leadership development workshops and related courses. However, workshops and courses are often offered with little co-ordination between them. An increased focus on the socio-cultural context would require more integration and co-ordination in terms of the acquisition of conceptual knowledge and practical skills via different channels. Through carefully crafted workshops using locally derived feedback, students can gain knowledge about their leadership competencies and shortcomings. Benchmarking data can then be provided to enable the process of comparing self and the broader picture to identify strategic improvement. Armed with the data from the workshops, course faculty can then tailor coursework according to the students' general levels of competence. They can even offer extra materials for the less competent students to pick up before class. Similarly, students can walk into the classroom knowing which of their skills needs special attention, and have a chance to prepare themselves to absorb the knowledge conveyed there.

Students as co-producers

Cases, experiential exercises and examples play an important role in MBA education, particularly those that are locally produced. We found that such contextualized materials are sorely missing, and this has been especially problematic for Xi'an and Shenzhen students who are not familiar with many of the contexts and organizations used in materials available in the market. Our experience suggests that under such circumstances, faculty can invite students to reflect on local organizational issues and then use these student-generated cases as a springboard to stimulate further discussion to address competencies that have been highlighted in the workshops. This way, students become co-producers of course materials and exercise greater choice over learning topics. As a result, the coursework becomes tailored to the backgrounds and needs of the students, and this helps students feel more engaged in the lessons.

Contextualization of the workshop materials

The materials used in workshops also require attention to be paid to language and meaning. The language used in learning environments can lose much in translation. Even the phrase 'global leader' can mean different things in different contexts, and as we have found in our study such differences might have created systematic biases between locations. For example, a Hong Kong student who deals with a cosmopolitan work environment may understand 'being global' as being able to deal comfortably with stakeholders from different cultures; a Xi'an student who has had limited exposure to an international market may understand 'being global' as merely buying products and services from different markets, or having an international presence. Such differences call for an adroit balance between competing dynamics. On the one hand the need for locally contextualized vignettes/scenarios as against relying on standard ones developed elsewhere. On the other hand, as the business world becomes more globalized, there is an increasing imperative to avoid learning material which is too localized and parochial.

Integrating 360 degree feedback into the curriculum

In our One China MBA programme, we are finding the use of 360 degree feedback an extremely valuable diagnostic for designing culturally attuned leadership development material. This multi-rater assessment of competencies can be repeated towards the end of the students' MBA education to derive a measure of improvement. However, the challenges associated with this tool should not be underestimated. First, outside the organizational setting it is difficult to include supervisors as raters in the survey. This is possibly due to the existence of a high power distance within the cultures in Greater China. The introduction and use of 360 degree feedback data across the whole programme require careful management as the faculty concerned can fear a loss of autonomy. Involving students in the customization process also means that the workload is higher and class preparation more difficult for faculty. Finally, developing and validating instruments can be time-consuming and costly.

CONCLUSION

This is a challenging time for MBA programmes. In the wake of the 2008 financial crisis, many have questioned whether MBA education is fundamentally flawed. In response to this general doubt, many specialized graduate programmes have mushroomed in the hope of replacing generic MBA programmes. Have MBA programmes lost their value? We are confident that they have not.

An MBA education, because of its generalist emphasis, is especially suitable for leadership development. However, we contend that as MBA students become more diverse and as the world becomes more cosmopolitan, we need to reconsider whether conventional MBA curricula and pedagogy are effective for our students. Our observations of students from Greater China have led us to conclude that in order for MBA programmes to stay relevant and to prepare students for their future careers, we need to put context back into education, and provide students with a forward-looking view of what they need to develop while obtaining their MBA education.

Specifically, our findings reveal a need for MBAs to cater for students whose socio-cultural context may be lacking a cosmopolitan element. This can include more integrated use of interventions such as utilizing particular cases, scenarios and guest speakers that will set the appropriate scene for students to explore and reflect on leadership concepts in context. This will keep learners on the same page in their learning activities, and facilitate learner interaction that is critical to leadership development.

The contextualization effort can also involve a more integrated design of feedback and reflection activities. Feedback instruments such as surveys and 360 feedback should not be seen as a discrete component of leadership development. Instead, they should be designed to be an integral part of the curriculum, with course materials can help students make better sense of the findings. A deliberate transfer of learning is extremely important for the effectiveness of a leadership development programme. In an MBA situation, the transfer can be appropriately facilitated by engaging students in deliberate application of skills and problem-solving within their current set of experiences, but also through the use of thought trials and mental rehearsal in the context of likely future leadership situations. Transfer should also be supported by integrating the leadership development programme with the concepts, cases and materials taught in the various modules of the programme.

These recommendations will likely be neither easy nor simple to implement. But as long as there is an ongoing need for leadership in increasingly diverse situations, contextualizing and integrating MBA related leadership concepts and material will be effort well spent in developing effective leaders. In other words, rather than considering this as a moment of difficulty for MBA education, we see this as a moment of opportunity – an opportunity to reform MBA education and strengthen it with a greater emphasis on adapting knowledge to context.

REFERENCES

Dai, G., De Meuse, K.P. and Peterson, C. (2010) 'Impact of multi-source feedback on leadership competency development: a longitudinal field study', *Journal of Managerial Issues*, 22 (2): 197.

Das, D.K. (2013) 'Management education in Asia: an invigorating growth', *Asia Pacific Business Review*, 19 (3): 421–25.

Hansen, M.T., Ibarra, H. and Peyer, U. (2010) 'The best-performing CEOs in the world', *Harvard Business Review*, 88 (1): 104–13.

Lawler III, E.E. (1994) 'From job-based to competency-based organizations', *Journal of Organizational Behavior*, 15 (1): 3–15.

Pfeffer, J. and Fong, C.T. (2002) 'The end of business schools? Less success than meets the eye', *Academy of Management Learning and Education*, 1 (1): 78–95.

Rubin, R.S. and Dierdorff, E.C. (2013) 'Building a better MBA: from a decade of critique toward a decennium of creation', *Academy of Management Learning and Education*, 12 (1), 125–41.

Schyns, B., Kiefer, T., Kerschreiter, R. and Tymon, A. (2011) 'Teaching implicit leadership theories to develop leaders and leadership: how and why it can make a difference', *Academy of Management Learning and Education*, 10 (3): 397–408.

Shippmann, J.S., Ash, R.A., Battista, M., Carr, L., Eyde, L.D., Hesketh, B., Kehoe, J., Pearlman, K., Prien, E.P. and Sanchez, J.I. (2000) 'The practice of competency modeling', *Personnel Psychology*, 53 (3): 703–40.

Tett, R.P., Guterman, H.A., Bleier, A. and Murphy, P.J. (2000) 'Development and content validation of a "hyperdimensional" taxonomy of managerial competence', *Human Performance*, 13 (3): 205–51.

Warner, M. (2011) 'Management training and development in China revisited', *Asia Pacific Business Review*, 17 (4): 397–402.

19 CAN AN ETHIC OF CARE SUPPORT THE MANAGEMENT OF CHANGE?

Mary Hartog and Leah Tomkins

INTRODUCTION

A common assumption is that business schools exist to serve the needs and interests of private sector corporations, developing curricula which provide the tools and techniques to maximize personal and organizational performance. Recently, however, more and more public and voluntary sector organizations have been engaging with business schools, both commissioning programmes tailored to the public sector context and sponsoring students on general courses in leadership and management. A fascinating consequence of this is how it has started to influence the discourse of organizational strategy and purpose. Thus, it is increasingly possible – perhaps even necessary – to bring issues such as social justice and community responsibility into the classroom, alongside matters of efficiency, shareholder value and return on investment.

A key tenet in this emerging discourse is the ethic of care. The roots of this discourse in the social sciences lie with feminist scholarship, which sees care as a process of moral development based on nurturing and relationship rather than justice and achievement (Gilligan, 1982; Noddings, 2003). In recent years, care has been featuring strongly in organizational conversations too (Kroth and Keeler, 2009; Lawrence and Maitlis, 2012). Often linked to notions of compassion and authenticity, care seems both important and attractive in an increasingly interdependent institutional space, where both problems and opportunities call for ever greater collaboration and relationship with stakeholders. Within this context, the concept of the 'caring organization' is drawing increasing attention in both academic and practice settings:

When an organization embodies compassion, the entire system nurtures a broad range of values, beliefs, virtues, and behaviours that are about both care and caring. (Madden et al., 2012: 704)

In this chapter, we explore a particular instance of care within the context of the experience and management of change in the public sector. We consider the interplay between institutional, interpersonal and personal care, and the ways in which these can cross-fertilize across organizational and pedagogic settings. We cast a critical spotlight on the notion of the 'caring organization' – especially within the public sector – and suggest that business schools have an important role to play and a particular quality of care to contribute.

MAINTAINING CARE WHEN YOUR EMPLOYER DOESN'T

What follows is a case study based on how one manager – Megan – struggled with and adjusted to significant change brought about by public sector cuts (see Box 19.1). The setting is one where we might assume that the qualities of the 'caring organization' would emerge strongly, and where the rhetoric of the organization's care for its external stakeholders would be reflected and replicated in the reality of its care for its employees.

Megan's experience is tracked over the period of time in which she participated in a leadership development programme, which was designed to help managers to lead more effectively in a context of austerity. It was a one-year part-time postgraduate Certificate in Leadership and Management, with several one-day workshops on topics including strategy, change management, team building and performance management. The workshops were interspersed with action learning sets, which involved meeting in small groups of four or five, facilitated by a tutor. These learning sets were intended to provide a space for the sharing of ideas and development of practical solutions geared towards the emerging change context in participants' organizational worlds.

Our intention is to illustrate how Megan's organizational experience of change both mirrored and was mirrored by the pedagogical approach of the programme. As we flexed our approach to working with her, she flexed her approach to working with change within her organization and within herself. Fundamental to an ethic of care is sensitivity to the need to remain flexible in response to the actual and emerging needs of the situation and the people within it, that is, to stay focused on 'the real' (Hartog and Frame, 2013). The space we provided in the programme threw into sharp relief, and perhaps in some way compensated for, the lack of care she felt she was receiving from her employer. In a way, the programme supported her to make sense of the pain of her experience, retain and rebuild a coherent sense of identity, and stay true to her values, while navigating the sort of organizational events that might otherwise have threatened them.

ACKNOWLEDGING COMPLEXITY AND INCONSISTENT EMOTIONS

I (first author) met Megan at the first action learning set which I facilitated on this programme. We only had three such events scheduled, each lasting three hours, so I was very conscious of the need to be task- and output-focused. I was prepared to facilitate the discussions quite tightly in order to achieve the planned outcomes, specifically, the development of concrete action plans for each participant.

As Megan and the other managers introduced themselves and began to share their experiences, my focus on these action plans rapidly began to diminish. It felt like a tsunami of emotion had been released, as feelings of anger towards the organization emerged and their distress became increasingly obvious. Their rage and bewilderment seemed to be exacerbated by an organizational culture that forbade the use of the term 'cuts', and insisted on staff referring only to the notion of 'efficiency savings'.

It became clear that a change of gear would be needed if we were to help these managers to learn in such a complex political and emotional milieu, that is, my task-focus would need to be replaced by paying closer attention to the potency of the participants' emotional experiences. They had come into local government to serve, and they were now experiencing a threat to their personal and professional values which had been based on a 'public service ethos'. There was a strong sense of a rupturing in these participants' life-worlds, and I realized this was something that I would need to both acknowledge and use in my work with them. The most important thing at this stage was to provide a space where emotions could be felt and expressed without fear of being censored or overwhelmed.

One of my instincts during this first session was to nudge this potentially overwhelming sense of rupture into a more manageable consideration of disappointment. When I sensed that Megan was receptive to this, I prompted her to reflect on and try to unpack her own sense of disappointment. She explained that she felt that senior management had demonstrated hypocrisy in espousing the values of care while their actions revealed the very opposite. The shock and hurt were caused by the disconnection between rhetoric and reality, between what should have been and what was. She began to sense that her anger with them had been spilling over into a kind of anger with herself, as if somehow she had let both her colleagues and her young clients down. As she talked, I began to see her increasing ability to acknowledge the emotional complexities of the experience. She began to discuss the possibility of living with two seemingly contradictory emotional responses – disappointment with the event and pride in one's own achievements. Indeed, Megan subsequently described her learning from that first session as follows:

> I was aware that I needed to be in touch with the organisational reality and the emotional reality of my service, staff and young people, as well as my own feelings. In fact, managing all the conflicting emotions and being attuned to the many people affected by the closure of the service seemed at times to be the most important task.

Megan channelled her growing awareness of the need to acknowledge her own emotions into her approach to managing the change. This meant focusing on acknowledging the conflicting emotions of those around her, and encouraging them to acknowledge this, too. She decided that it was crucial to give a voice to all those affected by the closure, just as she had given voice to her experience in the action learning set. She launched a series of informal consultations with staff and service-users, who are increasingly clear that their purpose was not just to share information and facts about what was happening, but more importantly, to encourage people's emotions to be expressed and contained. She subsequently reported that having a space in which people could share their stories and provide mutual support allowed the emotions of anger to be offset by feelings of pride, optimism, belonging and connection.

It is well known that organizational change can trigger deep and unsettling emotions, and that teaching executives to 'manage change' involves moving beyond problem-solving or planning-based approaches, towards working with feelings and defensive reactions (Berggren and Söderlund, 2011; Vince and

Broussine, 1996). What was different here from more conventional teaching of change management was that it truly was 'experience-led'. Megan seemed intuitively to move towards an understanding of communications practice that was emotional more than informational. It was only in later sessions that we introduced models and theories of communications practice to supplement these experiential learnings.

FROM FEELINGS OF SYMPATHY TO ENCOURAGING AGENCY

Closure of the service was scheduled for the end of the financial year. There was a formal period of consultation six months before this time, and initially, Megan's emotional responses included a strong sense of powerlessness and helplessness. Once the decision had been taken to close the service, she felt it would be pointless to engage in further discussions with senior management; she was concerned that the issues and arguments raised by her staff and clients were no longer being heard.

During this period, my pedagogic concern was to continue to work with the conflicting emotions aroused by events, and to support Megan and her colleagues to resist the feelings of helplessness that might accompany them. This involved keeping the notion of action at the heart of our group and individual discussions. This was not to revert to a traditional, exclusively task-orientated model of action learning that would relegate issues of emotional and personal development to the sidelines, but rather to engage in 'critical action learning', which emphasizes the importance of feelings of agency (Hartog and Frame, 2013).

'Critical action learning' is consistent with an ethic of care which goes beyond feelings of kindness and sympathy towards feelings of agency and the possibility of *action* (Gabriel, 2010; Hoggett, 2006). This sees care as solidarity in relationship, not just in terms of empathy or pity, but also as a way of channelling collective acknowledgment of, and dissatisfaction with, injustice. This is care as felt thoughtfulness, an intelligent compassion which can inspire discussion and action, without denying emotion. As Hoggett (2006) suggests, this may be the meeting point between an ethic of care and an ethic of justice; between empathy and challenge. From a teaching standpoint, it was of course crucial that such an acknowledgement of dissatisfaction should not become a general haranguing of any particular organization; instead, the teaching was focused on careful facilitation of discussions around distinguishing between what participants could and could not influence and control.

For Megan, this period marked a shift in attitude and behaviour. She became increasingly energized towards action, embodying and encouraging both optimism and realism, that is, engaging with both the controllable and the uncontrollable:

As I genuinely cared about the staff team as well as the young people, I found it easy to focus them on the common cause – that of not only surviving the closure but benefiting from it. Making this a 'learning for all' journey became the goal. It was important to be both optimistic and realistic in order to build a stronger sense of community, allowing a climate where we could all move forward in the same direction.

Her approach to managing change was now geared towards creating a sense of ownership of potential solutions and alternative ways forward. Table 19.1 summarizes the key change management actions that Megan facilitated during this period, based on the planning and discussions in her action learning set sessions.

Table 19.1 Change management as energized action

- Young clients formed 'support the project' groups
- Staff and clients wrote letters to the director, CEO and local politicians
- Staff and clients engaged in consultation meetings
- Staff and clients invited politicians and managers to visit the project to see the work first-hand
- Staff and clients solicited letters of support for the service from local doctors (general practitioners) and other professionals
- Staff and clients liaised with national agencies working with and for young people to raise awareness of the service and its closure

---

CONNECTED KNOWING: TOWARDS COHERENCE AND THE ENDURANCE OF IDENTITY AND VALUES

Throughout the programme, our facilitation approach sought to support participants at both an individual and a group level. The discussion groups fostered a collective reflection, which seemed to help participants to see that they were not alone in their efforts to make sense of what was happening. While Megan and her peers each had their own individual change project based on the particular issues each was facing in the workplace, it was the power of their shared reflection on the political, institutional and interpersonal dynamics of organizational life that helped them to understand the challenges they faced in coming to terms with both the extent and the limitations of their power and influence.

The power of development as a collective, relational experience goes to the very heart of an ethic of care. In what have become classic studies, care is seen as a process of reciprocity, that is, it concerns receptivity, relatedness and responsiveness, incorporating receiving as well as giving (Gilligan, 1982; Noddings, 2003). Such a process emphasizes the significance of trying to see things from other people's points of view, in what Belenky and her colleagues call 'connected' knowing (Belenky et al., 1986). This is similar to what other scholars have called 'relational' engagement as a kind of knowing-from-within (Bourdieu and Wacquant, 1992;

Cunliffe, 2008). 'Connected' knowing involves a certain immersion in the life-world of the other person, whereas the alternative, 'separate' knowing, is characterized by abstraction, separation and objectivity – a knowing-from-without. In my facilitation work with Megan and her colleagues, I was inspired by Belenky's metaphor of the teacher as midwife – a role which seems fundamentally concerned with intimacy, immersion and relationship – and I held this in mind as I tried to help the participants draw out their learning and give birth to their ideas.

Megan replicated this experience of connected knowing in her change management activities at work. She seemed to reconnect with the importance of her relationships with colleagues and clients – and therewith her care-giving instincts. She re-engaged in discussions and issues with renewed pride in the way in which the service had changed people's lives. Nurturing, compassion and empathy had been her guiding principles while the service was in operation, and she explored ways in which these could continue to guide her actions, attitudes and instincts even now that it was coming to a close.

One particular manifestation of her evolving change management approach at this time was her emphasis on the importance of celebrating the service's achievements. Recognizing that closure was inevitable, Megan's team began to compile a book about the service, involving self-reflection, memories and pictures, seeking to capture and commemorate what the service had achieved and the ways in which it had affected people's lives. Their work on this book was an extremely bonding experience for all concerned. As Megan now recalls:

> For many, it was the first time they were able to express their feelings openly about their fears for the future, as well as their sense of loss. They were also able to balance this with positive reframes of their futures and find some humour among all this. There were many tales and funny stories to share.

Again, this is what change management literature might well have suggested as 'best practice' (Fox and Amichai-Hamburger, 2001; King and Anderson, 2002). But in our view, this was all the more powerful because this was part of Megan's own sense-making, her own experience of the relational engagement of the action learning set, and her reconnection with an identity infused with the giving and receiving of care.

THE 'CARING ORGANIZATION' REVISITED: FROM MIDWIFE TO SURROGATE?

The setting of this story of change management is significant because it is perhaps in the public sector that the differences between an organization's *assumed* values and the *actual* experiences of organizational life – especially during austerity – are felt at their starkest. The rupturing that this can cause in employees' sense of identity and purpose offers us an opportunity to reflect critically on the notion of the 'caring organization', and ask ourselves how we can sustain an ethic of care when the 'caring organization' is found wanting.

Megan had created more than a project; she had created a *home*, most obviously for her young clients, but also for her staff and, indeed, for herself. In blurring the distinctions between work and family life, between weekdays and weekends, Megan's experience is thus a striking case of 'boundaryless-ness' (Arthur and Rousseau, 1996), perhaps suggesting that some public and voluntary sector workers – particularly those whose job is to provide care – have been engaging in such employment psychologies for far longer than their private sector counterparts.

As security of employment diminishes, however, the emerging psychological challenge is how to (re)construct boundaries between *institution* and self, without constructing boundaries between *work* and self. This means disconnecting from the 'caring organization' as a concrete, structural entity, and reconnecting with the less concrete but more enduring values of care, both for other people and for oneself. This suggests something of a departure from much of the current management literature, which sees care as the accumulation of individual empathic responses into an organizational-level caring culture (Madden et al., 2012), supported by the provision of policies, processes and procedures (Kroth and Keeler, 2009).

While this experience involved a certain distancing from institution in the corporate sense, there is of course another sense in which an institution can be caring in this story, namely the institution of the business school. As Megan was receiving less care from her employers, she was receiving more care from her fellow participants and from the teaching staff who were trying to support her as she renegotiated her relationships and attitudes. As I reflected on my role as teacher during this time, I started to move beyond the sense of metaphorical *midwife* (Belenky et al., 1986), and towards feeling that my role was like a *surrogate*. A surrogate is even more intimately invested in a birth than a midwife, and for a longer period of time, both before and after birth. At its best, surrogacy can be a rich experience of connected knowing and of knowing-from-within. A surrogate is concerned with balancing intimacy and involvement with disengagement and separation; it is not a permanent relationship in a structural sense, but it is a relationship whose presence, influence and values can endure.

The idea that the teacher role can feel like, and be perceived as, that of a surrogate parent is not new to the educational literature (e.g. Efron and Joseph, 2001). What seems underdeveloped, however, is the linking of this metaphor with an ethic of care. While surrogacy has emerged as significant in health care (Buchanan, 1989; Tomkins and Eatough, 2013), such treatments have tended to be more literal than metaphorical. The experience with Megan suggests that the surrogacy metaphor can be a powerful guide to a teaching practice informed by an ethic of care. This sort of relationship can provide short-term support during periods when others, such as corporate leaders, are unable or unwilling to invest in the human implications of change.

Care as surrogacy is not easy. It involves dealing with the force of emotions aroused by such intimate involvement in other people's life-worlds, including sometimes powerful feelings of frustration that one cannot do more to help. Even though the teachers on this programme were seasoned facilitators, everyone was profoundly affected by the emotional outpourings of these participants, especially that tsunami of emotion in the first session. I was responsible for our team of facilitators, so after that first session (and each of the subsequent sessions), I created a space for us to reflect on our experience. As part of our own strategy for self-care, we employed a coach to meet with us in between the action learning sets, so that we could attend to our own emotional responses and boost our own resilience to be able to support Megan and her colleagues as they attempted to boost their own.

Throughout this chapter, we have suggested that the manifestations of care in the classroom felt as if they were mirroring, and being mirrored by, Megan's experience in the workplace and, specifically, her emerging practices of change management. Continuing this thread, therefore, perhaps it is not too far-fetched to suggest that Megan's organizational role also took on hues of metaphorical surrogacy. She too had to come to terms with, and make sense of, both intimacy and separation, both pride and disappointment. Like a surrogate, she too had to find a way of making sense of her achievements and investment, while also realizing that there was to be no concrete role for her going forward. In this sense, an ethic of care *is* the management of change; it is support for the personal renegotiation of meaning and, in particular, the question of what to leave behind versus what to take forward into the future.

CONCLUSION

We have grounded these reflections in the context of the changing discourses of organizational strategy, and specifically, the ways in which conversations about both organizational life and business school pedagogy are increasingly orientated around an ethic of care. These experiences with Megan and her colleagues have allowed us to see care as complex and multi-faceted, operating at societal, organizational, intersubjective and subjective levels. This has reinforced our sense that we need to probe and be prepared to criticize the discourses of care, particularly when they emerge in a context of disconnection between institutional rhetoric and experiential reality. That this is something more likely to feature in experiences of the public and voluntary sectors strikes us as important, as we reflect on what we mean by a 'public service ethos' and on where we might expect to find it.

For us, an ethic of care is less about organization in a structural sense, and more about continuity and coherence in a values-based sense. Thus, when one 'caring organization' ceases to nurture its people, another 'organization' can step in to help preserve the values and identities of care while the structural, institutional and consequently psychological furniture is being rearranged. An ethic of care involves working with difficult pairings of experiences – both pride and disappointment, intimacy and separation, importance and redundancy. As business school educators, we are often implicated in relationships of surrogacy during students' processes of disengagement and re-engagement with organization and work; indeed such processes are a core part of their experience of organizational and personal change. Even when we do not have the luxury of intense, one-to-one work with students, we can still attempt to reflect our understanding that these are the processes that our students may be going through. As a community of educators, we have both the challenge and the opportunity to lead the way in embodying the values of care.

Our insights into Megan's life-world also enable us to reflect on the difficulties we ourselves can face in our own experience of organization, and of the occasional disconnections between rhetoric and reality. If an ethic of care can provide a useful framework for understanding change in our students' worlds, it can perhaps also help us to make sense of our own institutional worlds as educators. We also face the need to manage disappointment, to differentiate between what we can and cannot control, and to realize the richness of our potential to influence each other at a micro level even when – and perhaps especially when – this is not mirrored at a macro level. Thus, the appeal from Madden et al. (2012: 704) is as relevant to *our* organizations (business schools) as it is to the organizations whose employees we meet as students:

> We have relied on models of organizations as machines for over a hundred years. It is time to articulate organizations as reflections of our best selves – as communities where compassion, support, and positive energy are expected, natural and normal.

ACKNOWLEDGEMENTS

We would like to thank Megan for giving us permission to use her story in this chapter. Thanks also to Dr Philip Frame for his feedback on an earlier version, and to the Universities Forum for Human Resource Development for providing the research grant used to evaluate this development programme.

FURTHER READING

For classic discussions of an ethic of care, see Belenky et al. (1986).
For more on action learning, see Rigg and Richards (2006).

REFERENCES

Arthur, M.B. and Rousseau, D.M. (eds) (1996) *The Boundaryless Career: A New Employment Principle for a New Organizational Era*. Oxford: Oxford University Press.
Belenky, M.F., Clinchy, B.M, Goldberger, N.R. and Tarule, J.M. (1986) *Women's Ways of Knowing: The Development of Self, Voice and Mind*. New York: Basic Books.

Berggren, C. and Söderlund, J. (2011) 'Management education for practicing managers: combining academic rigor with personal change and organizational action', *Journal of Management Education*, 35 (3): 377–405.

Bourdieu, P. and Wacquant, L. (1992) *An Invitation to Reflexive Sociology*. Cambridge: Polity Press.

Buchanan, A.E. (1989) *Deciding for Others: The Ethics of Surrogate Decision Making*. Cambridge: Cambridge University Press.

Cunliffe, A.L. (2008) 'Orientations to social constructionism: relationally responsive social constructionism and its implications for knowledge and learning', *Management Learning*, 39 (2): 123–39.

Efron, S. and Joseph, P.B. (2001) 'Reflections in a mirror: metaphors of teachers in teaching', in P.B. Joseph and G.E. Burnaford (eds), *Images of Schoolteachers in America*. Mahwah, NJ: Lawrence Erlbaum, pp. 75–92.

Fox, S. and Amichai-Hamburger, Y. (2001) 'The power of emotional appeals in promoting organizational change programs', *The Academy of Management Executive*, 15 (4): 84–94.

Gabriel, Y. (2010) 'Organization studies: a space for ideas, identities and agonies', *Organization Studies*, 31 (6): 757–75.

Gilligan, C. (1982) *In a Different Voice: Psychological Theory and Women's Development*. Cambridge, MA: Harvard University Press.

Hartog, M. and Frame, P. with Rigby, C. and Wilson, D. (2013) 'Learning from the real', in T. Bilham (ed.), *For the Love of Learning: Innovations from Outstanding University Teachers*. London: Palgrave Macmillan, pp. 204–11.

Hoggett, P. (2006) 'Conflict, ambivalence and the contested purpose of public organisations', *Human Relations*, 59 (2): 175–94.

King, N. and Anderson, N. (2002) *Managing Innovation and Change: A Critical Guide for Organizations*. London: Thomson Learning.

Kroth, M. and Keeler, C. (2009) 'Caring as a managerial strategy', *Human Resource Development Review*, 8 (4): 506–31.

Lawrence, T.B. and Maitlis, S. (2012) 'Care and possibility: enacting an ethic of care through narrative practice', *Academy of Management Review*, 37 (4) 641–63.

Madden, L.T., Duchon, D., Madden, T.M. and Plowman, D.A. (2012) 'Emergent organizational capacity for compassion', *Academy of Management Review*, 37 (4): 689–708.

Noddings, N. (2003) *Caring: A Feminine Approach to Ethics and Moral Education*. Berkeley: University of California Press.

Rigg, C. and Richards, S. (eds) (2006) *Action Learning, Leadership and Organizational Development*, Routledge Studies in Human Resource Development. London and New York: Routledge.

Tomkins, L. and Eatough, V. (2013) 'Meanings and manifestations of care: a celebration of hermeneutic multiplicity in Heidegger', *The Humanistic Psychologist*, 41 (1): 4–24.

Vince, R. and Broussine, M. (1996) 'Paradox, defense and attachment: accessing and working with emotions and relations underlying organizational change', *Organization Studies*, 17 (1): 1–21.

20 MANAGEMENT BLOCKBUSTERS: IS THERE SPACE FOR OPEN DISSENT?

Daniel Doherty

INTRODUCTION: A PERSONAL DISCOVERY OF CRITICAL APPROACHES

It came as something of a shock to learn that I knew very little about critical thinking in my mid-fifties when I retreated to business school – exhausted after one overseas assignment too many – to make sense of my career-long consulting experiences. When I signed up for a PhD I had of course expected to be reading obscure texts, in addition to revisiting in-depth concepts that I had encountered in my professional life. What I did not expect to discover was that before I could get down to the business-end of analysing management literature, I would be challenged to learn a whole new language of intellectual critique. One target of my new-found academic colleagues was the populist management guru literature of the type that litters airport lounge bookstalls – and feeds and supports the consulting industry.

Aided by a widely used sociological framework (Burrell and Morgan, 1979) I began to understand different frames of critique through applying them to organizational issues.

When I progressed from research to the teaching of postgraduate business Master's students, it did not surprise me to discover that these students faced challenges very similar to those that confronted me when I left practice, including those challenges relating to applying critical thinking to the debunking of cherished texts that they had once held dear. A turning point in assisting students occurred for me when leading a series of research classes on 'Study skills – doing academic work'. This chapter relates an account of the first two classes where students' comments were collected by flipchart and notes in class; a selection of these comments are represented in italics. (The students gave informed consent for inclusion of their comments in this research.) I realized during this first class that the more enthusiastically I explained the wonders of Burrell and Morgan's paradigmic framework the blanker the students looked. It occurred to me – pausing midsentence – that perhaps I had crossed to the 'dark side', employing the very obfuscatory language that had distanced me not so long ago. I pulled myself up short, confessing to students that I was probably losing them, and asked what would help. Their answer to this query was quite simple and unanimous:

An example of how this works would help! Apply this tool for us please!

My mind turned towards a management book which was perhaps not all that it seemed and which my doctoral supervisor had encouraged me to subject to critical analysis. The text was *Built to Last* by Collins and Porras (1994). This choice was partly because there were lots of copies in the library, but also because it offered some interesting characteristics that distinguished it from other examples of management guru writing. I explained to the class that it was commonly cited as one of the very few business books that satisfied a wide practitioner audience in addition to it representing a management research and theory classic endorsed by many business school academics. Furthermore the authors were explicit as to the research aims and research design underlying their inquiry, and in their opening 'methods' chapter challenged the reader to engage in a critical assessment of their work, which might explain why there were so many copies in the library. Here was our opportunity to take up this invitation (see Box 20.1 for a brief description of the book).

BOX 20.1   A SYNOPSIS OF *BUILT TO LAST*

Since its publication in 1994, *Built to Last* has sold 3.5 million copies worldwide, has been translated into 16 languages, and spent five years on the *Businessweek* bestseller list. It summarizes the results of a six-year study examining the underlying factors contributing to the success of 'visionary' companies. Visionary companies are defined by the authors as widely admired industry leaders with a long-term track record of survival and growth for a period of more than one generation. The research question the authors ask is: 'What has enabled some corporations to last so long, while other competitors in the same markets either struggle, or disappear after a short period of time?' The authors found that the chosen companies operated differently from the comparison companies, and that these differences were as much to do with the companies' cultures as they were to do with how they

(Continued)

(Continued)

responded to their external environment. Central to these characteristics was the need for successful companies to develop 'cult-like cultures' which would bind organization members around a 'core ideology'.

The book is nothing if not wide in its definition of its audience. The preface states that 'we believe that every CEO, manager, and entrepreneur in the world should read this book. So should every board member, consultant, investor, journalist, business student, and anybody else interested in the distinguishing characteristics of the world's most enduring and successful corporations' (1994: 3).

Encouraged by the students' readiness to participate in this exercise, I explained that the next class would involve a 'close reading' of the text. This would require the students to read the book and see what they made of it – first privately and then in conversation with each other – prior to coming to class to walk through the guided reading. I explained that I would lead this reading and seek to promote dialogue. In this invitation I acknowledged the fact this was not a contemporary publication, and that while it stood up in my view as a suitable case for treatment – as it tended to provoke strong reactions – I would be open to challenges that it was no longer relevant. If they wished to read an example of a critique of an equally established management classic then I directed them towards Cullen's (2009) deft deconstruction of Covey's *7 Habits of Highly Effective People* (1989), a text with which most of them were familiar.

THE CLOSE READING OF *BUILT TO LAST*

The first task then was to come to a common agreement on what the book was trying to say. Unsurprisingly there were many and varied responses to the question.

Having established the nature of the book, I then asked if the students had researched the book by reading critics' views on it. A couple said that they had, one indicating that is was interesting to try to locate this book within the broader sweep of management history (see Box 20.2).

BOX 20.2   CONSULTANT GURUS

Built to Last (*BtL*) is recognized as a product of the 'Consultant Guru School' (Huczynski, 2007: 48), its genesis lying within the 'entrepreneurial period' (*BtL*: 153) and sharing a clear lineage from Deal and Kennedy (1982) through to Peters and Waterman's *In Search of Excellence* (1982), the ground breaking business bestseller with which *BtL* shares a number of common characteristics. The first common feature of both texts lies in the breadth of their respective research projects, authored by highly reputable business school academics; the second lies in their encouragement of businesses to emulate the characteristics of their 'winning' corporations if they wish to be similarly successful; a third similarity is that since publication, the performance of both of the books' 'visionary' companies has been monitored closely by business pundits to judge whether the 'success' principles have proved sustainable in business performance terms. And in the case of both publications such sustainability has proved embarrassingly fragile, to the point where vulture-like business commentators have suggested – somewhat gleefully – that inclusion in such a prophetic book becomes some kind of curse.

In our ensuing conversation we found it illuminating to discover that *Built to Last* had not 'come out of nowhere', but that it represented an important moment in the progressive evolution of management books through offering a practical formulae for ensuring sustainable business excellence. We took time to step back from this insight to reflect on the intellectual moves authors such as Huczynski make when contextualizing such literature. We recognized the importance of locating the text in time and place if we were to understand the concepts and mindsets that might be driving the authors at that time. It also occurred to us that if we were critiquing contemporary management fads, then it would serve us to locate these on a historical arc also, rather than embrace them as the contemporary 'answer' never before revealed.

Our conversation turned from exploring the book's context to addressing the question: 'What did we make of it?' We found that this book aroused a wide variety of different responses, thoughts and feelings. These responses varied from a highly enthusiastic embracing of its truths through to sceptical mistrust of the authors' motivations. Several opined that they found the glorifying of the Disney and Wal-Mart corporations as paradigms of business excellence immediately discounted the authors in their minds from serious intellectual consideration. I listened as the class discussed which corporates might be deemed worthy of study, before moving on to share my own reflections on first reading this text, to lend focus to this debate.

On first reading *Built to Last* (in 1995) I was drawn towards the general air of excited confidence it exuded, suggesting that it contained answers to the fundamental management questions lurking at the back of both executives' and business academics' minds. However, as I progressed in my reading I was left increasingly distrustful of its many sweeping claims to discoveries of timeless and universal management truths. As the text gains momentum the advocacy intensifies, while the warrants for its associated claims fade into the background. Part of my disquiet centred on the claims being made by the authors for the quality of their research, especially for the empirical soundness of it, when (disparagingly) compared to the work of other authors in the field.

The class were agreed that there were enough differences of view and lively contentions between us to justify deeper inquiry into this text through closer reading. At that point I walked the class through the Burrell and Morgan (1979) framework, not in detail but more as a reminder of the two axes of *subjective/objective* on the horizontal, and of *change/regulation* on the vertical (see Mabey, this volume p.12). While the class felt comfortable with the distinction between subjective and objective, more dialogue was needed to understand the distinction between change and regulation, and why this dimension would be important in identifying the underlying paradigms.

Which paradigm does *Built to Last* fall into?

After some small group conferring, the general view was that *Built to Last* fell into the *functionalist* paradigm. This was offered tentatively at first, then with a fairly high degree of certainty. I asked the class to locate the reasons for this choice within the text.

Principal in their reasons was to point to the authors' persistent claims to the power of the empirical data that nested within their longitudinal study, gathered over a seven-year period, and supported by a considerable collection of tables and 'evidence' in the extensive appendices. The students also observed that the book was clearly designed to improve practice. This emphasis on practice necessarily drives the authors towards findings that are definitive and translatable into tangible action in the workplace – findings that would prove 'effective to business functioning'. They thought that the practices advocated in the text would be designed to improve control and would be factually or objectively based. They speculated that the changes effected would be measured and monitored – and thus would be functionalist.

They also noted a degree of 'universalism' in the findings, for example where the principles driving visionary companies are said to be 'timeless', i.e. applicable to all places at all times. Thinking back to their research methods classes, they identified that the authors were claiming that their research passed tests of both reliability and of generalizability, which would make it functionalist, or even 'logical positivist'. Further support for their functionalist credentials was discovered in the assertion of continuous 'member checking' with respondents (*BtL*: 20); through emphasizing the sheer weight of unabating popular validity, based on the millions of satisfied book-buying customers; and through persistent claims by their chosen 'visionary' companies that their continued bottom-line financial success was due to their relentlessly following the 'built to last' principles that made them great in the first place.

A quote that seemed to sum up this view was a reference to the research data 'filling three shoulder high filing cabinets, four bookshelves and twenty megabytes of computer storage space for financial analysis' (Collins and Porras, 1994: 21).

If we accept that the work is mainly functionalist, what other paradigms might be in play within the text?

This question was met with a puzzled silence, broken by one student muttering that *'There was nothing to see here but functionalism'*. However, when asked what symbolic devices might be discovered in the text, the responses flowed more freely. Mention was made of the sacred 'principles' of *BtL*, which sounded more like commandments than anything else, as if they were management mantras. They noted that elements of the 'cult-like' cultures' rituals and performances suggested high symbolism, and the use of extended metaphors such as the 'clockwork' nature of the inner workings of perpetual companies. These metaphors suggested that there was something 'sacred' at the heart of these corporations. It proved enlightening to reveal these interpretive devices that were clearly designed to persuade the reader of the truthfulness of the text. Encouraged by these discoveries we were moved towards an exploration of the wider 'interpretive' territory.

As we looked at the criteria for interpretive analysis more closely, we stumbled across the rather obvious truth that many of the book's claims were made not through the power of tables and regression analyses but through the stuff of story and legend which abound throughout the text. We noticed the frequent recounting of heroic 'founders' tales' of almost mythical characters such as Walt Disney and Sam Walton:

> *But don't all books tell stories?* offered one student, frustrated by this intellectual exercise in tripping over the obvious.

> *Well yes, that it is true, we are all captivated by stories and their narrative arcs, it would seem that we cannot resist them ...*

> *Ahh, so all of these empirical figures and tables could be seen to be no more than decorations on the story, rather than the story itself?* interjected another. *Or maybe the story is the paradigm?*

> *Quite possibly so.*

One student took the conversation in another direction, saying:

> *What was playing on my mind was the frequent references to the mysterious 'Darwinian' complexity approach; yet this new age approach is never spelled out in detail anywhere in the book, just alluded to.*

She wondered if this might be evidence of the appropriating of evolutionary theory as metaphor to indicate how these companies sustain and grow. She had clearly been attentive during her study skills, as she pressed on to point out that the analytic process pursued to elaborate the key principles of visionary companies was suspiciously akin to qualitative coding or sorting methods, rather than any working of hard numbers. She remarked that the bulging filing cabinets were as full of narratives that were analysed then mined for meaning, as much as they were stuffed with quantifiable facts. We concluded that while the *BtL* methods' chapter is silent on the explicit use of any type of narrative or ethnographic inquiry, the body of the text draws its narrative arc from executive 'tales from the field'. This 'narrative turn' would suggest that *BtL* strays much further than the authors are comfortable to admit from functionalism into the category of 'interpretive'.

What other paradigms might we see in play?

This question caused a scurrying back towards the definition of the two remaining paradigms. Could *BtL* be seen as falling into the radical humanist paradigm? This question evoked disbelief with students expressing that the worldview *BtL* supported was diametrically opposite to radical humanism. When I asked why that might be, the answer came that the 'cult-like' cultures would imprison people within hierarchical control systems as much as liberate them. They could not see ways in which these cultures would liberate individuals towards radical change, or even allow any dialogue around the same.

I then asked if they could see any traces of the radical structuralist paradigm. Again the answer was that they could not see any evidence of encouragement of a radical change of structures that would subvert the existing power systems. Indeed if anything there was evidence of *BtL* wanting to keep the vestiges of market capitalism in place under the wisdom and guidance of a 'visionary leader', while leaving the invisible hand of the market to do its work. That enabling structures would be built and reinforced by a persuasive culture was a general view, though not expressed in a negative way. Most students could see no place for anarchic or revolutionary principles in the orderly running of a market-facing business.

An ensuing discussion teased out an underlying congruency between the research method that was claimed and the management methods that the authors recommend businesses apply. We had to let this discovery sink in for a little while before we could make sense of it.

> Well it makes total sense doesn't it? said one. It would make no sense at all to use a radical research lens to advocate conservatism!

> And doesn't there need to be means ends congruency or the whole thing falls over?

> But maybe it is more complex than that? For did we not suggest that at least two different paradigms were in play in the construction of BtL; and that they went some way towards complementing each other?

> Well yes but the functionalist and interpretive paradigms were well matched, came the retort. While I could not imagine a radical approach doing anything other than undermining a functionalist argument!

This seemed a good point to introduce into the dialogue the question of whether these paradigms are 'incommensurable'. I pointed out that while it was firmly believed since the introduction of the idea of paradigms by Kuhn (1962) that they could not live together on the same page or in the same social organization, more recent scholars such as Hatch and Cunliffe (2007) are less doctrinaire, believing there is some scope for a merging of paradigms, with cautions. The class was clearly spilt as to the extent to which these paradigms were incommensurable, and which combinations more than others might be exclusive one to another. One student who had been quiet for most of the class suddenly burst into the conversation:

> But I was sure that I came to business school to read scholars who looked at all data in a scientific fashion, going out of their way to consider all points of view. It really concerns me to learn that these academics do in fact exist within separate universes. Surely Collins and Porras should have considered their methods and their advocacy from different perspectives before making the apparent claims they do?

The point was well made, stimulating a debate on how balanced academic thinking and writing should be as opposed to the apparent lack of balance in practice. I indicated that Kuhn was motivated to produce his seminal work on identifying paradigms partly because he recognized the real difficulty in thinking or speaking across these paradigmatic divides. This conversational turn into the territory of balance and contrast left us all very thoughtful, prompting inquiries into research ethics and the question of whether researchers should be asked to consider all paradigms before going firm on their findings. It felt like time for a focussing question to re-join our inquiry into *BtL* critique.

At this point I posed the question 'In how many ways could we critique *BtL*?' The responses to this prompt flowed thick and fast:

> From the perspective of its usefulness to business leaders and change specialists.

> From a researcher's point of view, to assess the rigour of the method.

> From a financial investor's point of view, to assess the extent to which BtL can predict business success.

> From an occupational psychologist's point of view, to look at the impact of strong cultures on people's wellbeing.

> From a trade unionist and organized labour perspective to know what managerialist fad might be coming up next – and to know how to resist it.

> From a consumerist perspective – is this a good read to pass the time on a plane ride?

Class creativity was peaking at this point. It was clear that while there were many lenses for critique, there was no room for some sort of generalized critique that would cover these diverse bases. We speculated that while it might be possible to mix these lenses, the critic would need to be highly attentive to the capacity for reader confusion engendered through this mixing. We reflected that surprisingly few critiques make their critical lens explicit, leaving that detective work for the inquirer to divine.

Someone asked the question 'Is it unfair to judge a text through a lens other than that adopted by the author?', to which a classmate reposted 'It would be unfair on the text *not* to subject it to alternative scrutiny, to road test it for robustness'.

How might different paradigmatic positioning provoke different critiques of *Built to Last*?

As we considered this question, we could easily envisage a radical structuralist perspective usefully majoring on a critique of the 'creation of cult-like cultures'. Such a critique would pick up on quotes such as 'those seeking an empowered or decentralized workforce should first impose a tight ideology, screen and indoctrinate people into that ideology, eject the viruses, and give those that remain the responsibility that comes with membership in an elite organisation' (*BtL*: 138) as evidence that *BtL* advocates power over the workforce which from a humanist perspective must be exposed and resisted.

A radical humanist on the other hand would draw our attention towards *BtL* advocacy of, 'The need to obliterate misalignments ... that promote behaviour inconsistent with the core ideology or that impede progress. Think of misalignments as cancer cells. It's best to get in there and cut them out before they spread too far' (*BtL*: 238). They would ask us to think of the extent to which an approach would inhibit not only individual growth and development but also even eliminate the possibility of discussion of the same for fear that such a debate might destabilize.

We speculated at that point that if these two 'radical' protagonists were in dialogue, they might discover common ground based on a shared wish for change; but we could also imagine these two protagonists engaging in strenuous arguments as to critical priorities in the operationalizing of this change. The structuralist might say it can only come through the overthrow of the imprisoning systems, while the humanist might argue of the need first to encourage all employees to embrace diversity. We could see how those embracing change might find a common cause, just as those seeking conservatism might find the same, even though in each instance there would be a profound argument over the spectrum between subjectivity and objectivity, between feelings and hard facts and concrete structures.

When asked how this exercise might have gone if the students had been directed towards a management blockbuster that was written from a different paradigm, I reminded them of Cullen (2009) who uses 'critical discourse analysis' of Covey's *7 Habits of Highly Effective People* (1989). Cullen does not deploy Burrell and Morgan but instead draws upon a range of sources and approaches drawn from a variety of disciplines. While the Covey work has as its setting personal development rather than business development (he writes of bringing about change in 'personal paradigms'), many of the authorial techniques that Cullen skilfully describes are apparent also in the Collins and Porras (1994) text. Interestingly both of these works were written in the same period and attracted very similar audiences. I also pointed students towards the work of Jackson (2001) who critiques a variety of management fads and fashions from a critical perspective, as does Huczynski (2007). Researchers have long since been occupied with studies of gurus and their paradigms, and much can be learned from the approaches such critics adopt.

Closing out the class and harvesting learning

It was clear at this point that after nearly two hours of dialogue the class was moving towards a natural close. It felt that sufficient insight had been harvested for one afternoon and that it was time to reflect on what we had learned. Feedback suggested that the session had developed more understanding of the constructive role of critique, in addition to placing better the role the Burrell and Morgan (1979) framework might play in sharpening critique. They cautioned that the framework needed to be applied intelligently and not as prescription. They felt that they had learned not only how to be critical of guru texts, but also of how to become more aware of how influential but little stated assumptions underpin all management reading material.

Students suggested that the session had assisted them in reframing their understanding of guru publications. They felt that this critical reading of one such text inspired inquiry and curiosity into the nature of their popularity, rather than previous feelings that had attached to their reading of the same, when they felt a little ashamed that they had been somehow been manipulated into reading (and believing) top-shelf management 'pornography'. One student confessed that the example assisted their understanding of the inner workings of such texts even though they had not read the book beforehand. We then reviewed the success of the close reading as a learning strategy. Someone said that they made sense of it through the Nonaka and Takeuchi (1995) social learning framework. They explained that when I introduced the Burrell and Morgan framework in class it had made no sense at all; but that working through it in open dialogue had materially assisted in the process of 'internalizing' the framework and making it their own. Furthermore they felt they had collectively engaged in some really effective *field building* around the process of critique in general, to the extent that we had *consolidated* a shared understanding of critique among us.

With regard to the commensurability of the paradigms, we had *externalized* our shared understanding of which paradigms might work with each other, and which would collide. Perhaps we had developed our own *combined* theory. Students stated that between us we had developed a shared way of moving into dialogue and critique around any management text without that discussion being conducted exclusively between individuals with polarized opinions. Perhaps we were at last beginning to gain a glimpse of what *double loop* learning might mean in practice.

I conclude from this exercise that while business schools are clear about the need for students to develop critical faculties, they are often less precise as to how these might be developed. This chapter may have provided some insight into how this vital skill could be developed and shared in class, where socialized dialogue through provocative questioning powerfully consolidates the understanding gained from reading critical methods texts.

When I consider where next to direct a future such student group's appetite for further immersion in the field of critical studies, it would seem apposite to point them towards the work of the critical yet highly accessible theorist Cunliffe (2009). In this work she reflects on her experience of teaching the topic of leadership from a philosophical perspective to MBA students, while challenging the dominant functionalist paradigm that drives many MBAs. For a wider review of alternative paradigms at play in management learning I would suggest a reading of Karata-Özkan and Murphy (2009); and for progression into more complex realms of the role of context in shaping our understanding of leadership and culture, then perhaps they could move on to a reading of Fairhurst (2009). In the encouragement of students in this critical direction I take comfort from a quotation from one of Cunliffe's students (2009: 89) who comments on the experience of philosophical immersion in the midst of their busy MBA: 'I was a bit surprised I enjoyed it … I was fairly certain I would not get much out of it. I still dislike writing long academic essays … but I would never probably have read [course readings] on my own … it helped me through some rough times … You were the only professor who encouraged open dissent … it was very refreshing'. I would be delighted if my students, at the conclusion of such critical endeavours, were to express similar sentiments.

REFERENCES

Burrell, G. and Morgan, G. (1979) *Sociological Paradigms and Organizational Analysis*. London: Heinemann,

Collins, J.C. and Porras, J.I. (1994) *Built to Last: Successful Habits of Visionary Companies*. London: Century.

Covey, S. (1989) *The 7 Habits of Highly Effective People*. New York: Free Press.

Cullen, J. (2009) 'How to sell your soul and still get to heaven: Steven Covey's epiphany-inducing technology of effective selfhood', *Human Relations*, 62: 1231–54.

Cunliffe, A. (2009) 'The philosopher leader: on relationalism, ethics and reflexivity – a critical perspective to teaching leadership', *Management Learning*, 40: 87.

Deal, T.E. and Kennedy, A.A. (1982) *Corporate Cultures: The Rites and Rituals of Corporate Life*. Reading, MA: Addison-Wesley.

Fairhurst, G. (2009) 'Considering context in discursive leadership research', *Human Relations*, 20: 1–27.

Hatch, M.J. and Cunliffe, A. (2007) *Organization Theory: Modern, Symbolic, and Postmodern Perspectives*. London: Sage.

Huczynski, A.A. (2007) *Management Gurus: What Makes Them and How to Become One* (3rd edn). London: International Thompson Business Press.

Jackson, B. (2001) *Management Gurus and Management Fashions: A Dramatistic Inquiry*. London: Taylor and Francis.

Karata-Özkan, M. and Murphy, W. (2010) 'Critical theorist, postmodernist and social constructionist paradigms in organizational analysis: a paradigmatic review of organizational learning literature', *International Journal of Management Reviews*, 12: 453–65.

Kuhn, T.S. (1962) *The Structure of Scientific Revolutions*. Chicago: University of Chicago Press.

Nonaka, I. and Takeuchi, M. (1995) *The Knowledge Creating Company: How Japanese Companies Create the Dynamics of Innovation*. New York: Oxford University Press.

Peters, T.J. and Waterman, R.H. (1982) *In Search of Excellence: Lessons from America's Best Run Companies*. New York: Harper and Row.

PART IV

RAPPORTEUR[1]

David W. Miller

THIS MOVIE LOOKS FAMILIAR

It is difficult to overestimate the effects the financial crisis loosed upon the market during the 2007–2008 subprime mortgage disaster and ensuing great recession. The domino effect and eventual toll on governments, global and domestic financial systems, institutions, communities, families, and individuals was historic. How could this happen? Who was at fault? A body of literature surfaced questioning the role of business schools within the collapse.[2] As Kelley Holland wrote in a 2009 article that appeared in the *New York Times*, 'with the economy in disarray and so many financial firms in free fall, analysts, and even educators themselves, are wondering if the way business students are taught may have contributed to the most serious economic crisis in decades' (Holland, 2009).

Professors David Garvin and Srikant Datar, for example, in conjunction with the commemoration of the 100th anniversary of Harvard Business School in

---

[1] I would like to thank and acknowledge Michael J. Thate for his excellent research and editorial assistance in the preparation of this chapter.

[2] See the interesting debate between Jay Lorsch, Rakesh Khurana and Andrew W. Lo in www.businessweek.com/debateroom/archives/2008/11/us_financial_cr.html (accessed 14 July 2014).

2008, convened a number of colloquia and workshops addressing the state of affairs within business schools. The research was eventually published (Datar et al., 2010), and addressed not only the growing concerns and criticisms of standard models (Datar et al., 2010: 75–106), but also offered analyses and provocations for curriculum development (Datar et al., 2010: 43–74, 137–65). Numerous other studies have appeared as well, offering varying historical analyses,[3] and suggestions for reformation (see, for example, Moldoveanu and Martin, 2008), including this chapter, which raises the question of spiritual resources for ethical guidance in business.

And yet, as Michael Grote, professor of corporate finance at the Frankfurt School of Finance and Management, has pointed out, teaching 'ethics in the financial sector is often misunderstood as teaching students to be boy scouts'. What must instead be operative is a teaching of self-reflection, which, in the end, is much more sustainable (Palin, 2013). This chapter seeks to do just that, reflecting next on the six contributions in Part IV, and concluding with offering a modest contribution from my own attempt to reclaim a moral voice in business ethics education at Princeton University.

FROM CRITICISM TO SUGGESTIONS: TOWARD RECLAIMING A MORAL VOICE IN BUSINESS SCHOOLS

The chapters in this section offer a demonstration of the inadequacies of standard business school curricula, a constructive implementation of curricula change to foster student self-reflection, and some pedagogic examples of their enactment of these changes within classroom settings.

Rickard Grassman's chapter argues that business schools were ideologically complicit in the 2008 financial crisis owing to their collapse of all conceptions of value into prices, and the market's creation of its own form of morality. He recommends Balzac as a literary illustration which demonstrates the same point. Grassman's own ideological perspective is provocative and worthy of debate. I embrace his reminder of the role classical art and literature can play in understanding the human condition, motivations, virtues and vices so as to help reclaim a moral voice within business schools. Balzac could be well accompanied by Dostoyevsky, Melville (esp. *Bartleby the Scrivener*) and Trollope, as well as postcolonial voices to name but a few other authors and perspectives.

Doirean Wilson's chapter reminds us of the importance of multiculturalism through the lens of respect and its different interpretations. Worthy of further

---

[3]Note the excellent study of Rakesh Khurana (2007). See, too, Giacalone and Wargo (2010); Hopper and Hopper (2007).

pedagogical exploration is how the cultural location of the classroom and professor, which for example may be Western, impact the concept of respect for students who may be from very diverse cultural backgrounds. While not covered in her chapter, Wilson helpfully gestures toward the question of other forms of culturally influenced behaviours and human interactions that manifest themselves in business, such as different conceptions of loyalty, age, gender roles and/or limitations, and even religion.

Phil Jackman rightly highlights the importance of business schools addressing leadership formation and, intriguingly, suggests wisdom as a pedagogical model as opposed to a merely functional skill set or knowledge transfer. Whereas Grassman turns to classic literature, Jackman draws on the Hebrew wisdom tradition. While this tradition is not as distinct or singular as he seems to suggest, Jackman does helpfully point us towards the practical wisdom found in virtually all religious/philosophical systems, including the various expressions of Judaism, Christianity, Islam, Hinduism, Buddhism and so forth.

Pamsy Hui, Warren Chiu, John Coombes and Elvy Pang, the only authors writing out of the so-called BRIC group of developing economies and countries, recognize different needs from those of other authors in this section. Their notion of 'region of origin' playing a bigger role in determining MBA curriculum needs is a helpful reminder that business schools risk failing their global student body, and perhaps even their domestic students, by presuming a 'one-size-fits-all' curriculum and that all incoming students have the same developmental needs.

Mary Hartog and Leah Tomkins argue that for-profit institutions can learn from non-profit institutions as regards the treatment of other people and broader issues such as social justice. While certainly a helpful contribution, one wonders what bidirectional lessons could be learned from each of these organizational structures.[4] Moreover, their intriguing and important reference to the '(re)construction of boundaries' between the institution and the self, and what this looks like in a digitally interconnected, integrated, 24/7 world, is worthy of further exploration.

Daniel Doherty rounds out Part IV with a marvellous personal and professional perspective on developing critical thinking skills to reassess popular management literature. Doherty enacts an intriguing display of Jackman's call for an accent on leadership formation through a discourse analysis of Collins and Porras's *Built to Last* (1994). Left unexplored but worthy of further consideration is the question: why do so few business scholars successfully transpose their methodological and research skills into accessible vernacular texts that stand up to critical scrutiny?

---

[4]It might have also been intriguing to see some interaction with the critical literature that is arising with respect to the inefficiencies of some NGOs. See, for example, Lupton (2011).

TOWARD AN INTEGRATIONIST APPROACH: RECLAIMING A MORAL VOICE IN BUSINESS ETHICS

In business school education, one is often faced with a disconnected relationship between 'being successful' and 'being ethical'. It is intriguing to consider the different ranking criteria of business schools in this regard. To take the ranking metrics of American business schools as an example, in late 2012, for instance, Bloomberg *Businessweek* ranked MBA schools according to ethical emphases.[5] And in 2014, the *US News and World Report* released its rankings for the 'best [American] business schools'.[6] One would think that these two rankings would have a significant overlap. However, Dartmouth (Tuck) was the only school that was placed within the top ten on both rankings. Does this mean the top American MBA programmes do not value or accent ethics in their curriculum, or are they simply not that effective at teaching it? Is it not possible for top American business schools to design and teach a curriculum that is attentive both to skills development and character formation or do they not have character formation as an objective? Indeed, cynics might trot out the old joke, 'Isn't business ethics an oxymoron?' Yet increasingly, academics and practitioners alike see business and ethics as integrated and related, not oppositional in nature, and central to a successful and sustainable business model. But the question remains, how to teach business ethics effectively. In the remainder of this chapter, I offer my own attempt to tackle this pedagogical challenge, and I do so through a somewhat unusual lens: religion.

A practical and scholarly challenge that often arises when teaching business ethics is: on what basis or criteria is a decision considered ethical or unethical? Typical answers include reference to the law, local customs or a moral philosophical tradition. For the past decade, I have been experimenting with a business ethics class that explores the possible role various religious traditions and their teachings might play in helping to shape and inform ethical decision-making, at both an individual and institutional level.

Not surprisingly, this raises several eyebrows and fair pedagogical questions, including: What about atheists and agnostics? Do students feel they're being proselytized? Isn't religion divisive? Would today's job-seeking and bottom-line oriented students be interested in such an approach to business ethics? And what does religion have to do with business anyway? To my surprise, many of my early concerns proved unfounded. For instance, atheists were often the most interested students, curious to understand how other people and cultures

---

[5] www.businessweek.com/articles/2012-12-17/mba-rankings-top-schools-for-ethics (accessed 17 July 2014).

[6] http://grad-schools.usnews.rankingsandreviews.com/best-graduate-schools/top-business-schools/mba-rankings (accessed 17 July 2014).

draw on religious teachings as part of their ethical foundation. I set clear ground rules that the focus of the class was the 'study of' and not the 'promotion of' any particular religion. Appreciative inquiry techniques were used to explore each tradition's possible contribution to business ethics. Students were intrigued to learn the breadth and depth of religious teachings that applied to modern business, both positive and negative. They also discovered the wide range of commonality among traditions, as well as certain accents or differences. Many concluded that without even a modest understanding of the subject, they would be under-equipped to conduct business internationally and understand different cultural approaches to ethics.

My first version of this course, taught for five years at Yale University, was playfully called 'Business Ethics: Succeeding without Selling Your Soul'. It was an elective course that was dual-listed with the School of Management and Divinity School. Instead of teaching ethics through traditional legal or secular moral philosophical lenses, I experimented by exploring the role of various religious traditions as a possible basis for business ethics and leadership formation. I was unsure if anyone would show up on the first day of class. To my surprise, it attracted an even mix of MBA and MDiv students, and was consistently oversubscribed with students representing a variety of faith traditions, including atheism. The students explored how ancient religious teachings, parables, narratives and wisdom literature could still be relevant to modern business, and how they might help shape and inform a moral voice at the personal and organizational level.

For the past six years I have been teaching an elective course called, 'Business Ethics and Modern Religious Thought' to undergraduate students at Princeton University. It is a refined version of the earlier experiment at Yale. The aforementioned pedagogical challenges remained, as well as some additional ones, including: What department to list the course through in a university that does not have a business department or MBA programme? How to modify the course for undergraduates? How many religious traditions should be covered? And what are the downsides or limitations of religion and ethics? The course was listed through the religious studies department, yet the overwhelming majority of students who take the course are not religious studies majors. Instead, they represent a wide range of degree programmes and academic disciplines, including biology, computer science, economics, finance, languages and physics. Many intend to seek an MBA at some point after graduation. Further, the students represent a diverse range of belief systems and cultural backgrounds. Arguably, one shortcoming of the class is that I limit it to the study to the three Abrahamic traditions (i.e. Judaism, Christianity and Islam) in order to keep the scope manageable. Understandably, this is a disappointment to some students who wish to ask the same questions of other traditions, such as Buddhism, Hinduism or Sikhism. Another ongoing challenge is how to think and talk about religious ideas in a diverse and multicultural business context.

The underlying assumption of the course is that religious teachings are one of the variables that shape and inform individual and sometimes national attitudes towards business ethics. An important pedagogical presupposition is that the course is not about whose tradition or *Weltanschauung* is 'correct' or 'better'. Moreover, students are exposed both to the constructive resources of religious thought, as well as the possible conflicts, limitations and other issues that may arise when applied to contemporary ethical, business and cross-cultural situations.

To combine theory with praxis, I invite several CEOs, each representing different religious traditions, to speak to the students. They share how their tradition helps anchor them, and will shape and inform their leadership and approach to resolving ethical dilemmas in their companies and in the wider marketplace. Students are often spellbound to hear their stories and see examples of how 'successful' business leaders integrate the teachings of their faith with the demands of their work.

The syllabus is organized around what I have come to conclude are five foundational questions of ethics. The '5Qs of Ethics' are: Q1 – what is ethics; Q2 – what is the source of your ethics; Q3 – what is your decision-making framework when facing ethical dilemmas; Q4 – what is your public language for doing ethics; and, Q5 – how do you stay ethically 'fresh'? While each of the 5Qs stand alone as worthy of reflection, they are designed to form an integrated intellectual and practical whole. Exploration of Q2 on the source of one's ethics is typically the place where metaphysical and religious ideas are considered and critically reflected upon.

To be sure, I do not wish to imply or propose that this approach is the ideal or only way to teach business ethics. Indeed there are many pedagogical challenges. Yet I would suggest that, appropriately handled, exploring and understanding the intersection of religious resources and business ethics has a legitimate intellectual and practical place in the business academy, particularly in today's globalized marketplace.

It is my hope that this section offering six pedagogical examples of how to reclaim a moral voice in business schools, and my own modest example here at the end,[7] will constructively raise and engage some important questions that business schools typically don't ask.

REFERENCES

Collins, J.C. and Porras, J.I. (1994) *Built to Last: Successful Habits of Visionary Companies*. London: Century.

Datar, S.M., Garvin, D.A. and Cullen, P.G. (2010) *Rethinking the MBA: Business Education at a Crossroads*. Boston, MA: Harvard Business School Press.

Giacalone, R.A. and Wargo, D.T. (2010) 'The roots of the global finance crisis are in our business schools', *Journal of Business and Education*, 6: 1–24.

---

[7]For more information, visit www.princeton.edu/faithandwork.

Holland, K. (2009) 'Is it time to retrain b-schools?', *New York Times*, 14 March.

Hopper, K. and Hopper, W. (2007) *The Puritan Gift: Reclaiming the American Dream Amidst Global Financial Chaos*. New York: I.B. Tauris and Co Ltd.

Khurana, R. (2007) *From Higher Aims to Hired Hands: The Social Transformation of American Business Schools and the Unfulfilled Promise of Management as a Profession*. Princeton, NJ: Princeton University Press.

Lupton, R.D. (2011) *Toxic Charity: How Churches and Charities Hurt Those They Help (And How to Reverse It)*. San Francisco, CA: HarperOne.

Moldoveanu, M. and Martin, R. (2008) *The Future of the MBA: Designing the Thinker of the Future*. Oxford: Oxford University Press.

Palin, A. (2013) 'Financial crisis forced business schools to change curriculum', *Financial Times*, 23 June. Retrieved from: www.ft.com/intl/cms/s/2/80cba3fc-d9c3-11e2-98fa-00144feab7de.html#axzz39eqWKCt4 (accessed 6 August 2014).

21 CODA: REFLECTIONS ON THE BOOK, ITS GENESIS AND ITS IMPACT

Chris Mabey and
Wolfgang Mayrhofer

Writing a closing chapter is an almost hopeless task. It requires the authors to understand all that has been written in the book, which is difficult at best in a monograph and close to impossible in an edited volume. It also suggests that this is the time for a final wrap-up, a condensed unearthing of the hidden and/or basic themes of all the chapters and a synthesis of them into a single overall message. We are sceptical about being able to do this even if we wanted to, and we hesitate since we wonder whether the contributors would agree with our condensed reading of their work, blurring the boundary between 'theirs' and 'ours' through this type of expropriation. We also wonder whether this is what the reader expects for this book and to what extent it would be helpful. So we are taking another tack in this final chapter. We have chosen to reflect on some issues raised by working together on this book via a conversation between us as editors and we invite you as readers to join us in our conversation through following our viewpoints and adding your own.

CM: The idea of this book has been brewing for some time, hasn't it? I think it was five or six years ago that we first discussed a project of this nature. Then a year ago we organized an informal conference at Sarum College in the grounds of Salisbury Cathedral (UK) with an open invitation for working papers on 'Questions business schools don't ask'. This theme seemed to strike a chord with a lot of people and the response was amazing. There was a real buzz at the conference and a broad range of perspectives discussed ... it seemed that a lot of colleagues were acutely aware of the shortcomings of what business schools were typically doing. But, more than that, there was also a lot of creative thinking about how things could be different ...

WM: ... yes, for a while now, I have felt uneasy about the role of business schools in current times. This relates, first of all, to the spiritual and philosophical realm. I am wondering what business schools do to reflect this dimension of human existence and whether they offer their students an integrated view on human life.

I have another source of unease. Business schools seem to have a tendency to prepare students for their role in the labour market within a capitalist economy in a very one-sided way: as a cog in the wheel which is supposed to function. They have taken over the role of pre-labour-market institutions which train students for the perceived demands of the world of work. In this process, 'we' seem to have lost the broader angle of education. By education I mean giving students a broader picture of the world in the sense of different views, allowing them to experience alternative viewpoints about what economy is or could be, what is the contribution of 'doing business' to the greater good of society, or how business can positively contribute to major problems such as poverty, inequality or malnutrition, which societies all across the globe face these days.

Of course, I am not saying that we do not see a myriad of individual efforts addressing these areas. However, after spending more than 30 years teaching and researching in business schools, I am more convinced than ever that there are systemic 'flaws' with regard to issues such as these.

CM: It is interesting that your little 'diagnosis' picks up on two areas: an unwillingness to engage with philosophical and spiritual matters and systemic shortcomings, because these became the drivers for the book. The sorts of questions surfacing at the Sarum conference were: How can we, in business schools, cultivate wisdom rather than just accumulate knowledge? What worldviews, other than Western-materialist, might guide leadership? What do the arts, philosophy, ecology, theology have to contribute to the development of able leaders? What gets sacrificed if we ignore the spiritual dimension of work? How might a more green and global mindset influence the way we do business? Why do we have so many examples of poor, indeed fraudulent, leadership across all sectors? I remember that in our call for contributions we asked, 'Do you have a burning question which you believe is widely neglected by business schools?' But rather than simply adding to the litany of critique, we asked authors to be imaginative about how their chosen question might be addressed. Finally, and most risky I suppose, we encouraged contributors to be explicit about their personal ontology: to identify the assumptions they are making about knowledge, their worldview, their values, their position of faith or none, and give some justification for the position they are taking. I find this degree of self-disclosure is fairly rare in academic writing.

WM: Looking at the final potpourri of chapters, I am glad that we undertook this endeavour. Four things stand out about the journey leading to this book. First, I was and still am surprised at how differently we can view the world, even the relatively small world of business schools. I consider myself as being a relatively broad-minded academic. Although a business administration scholar by training, I always had a clear interest in interdisciplinary work, which was reflected in my research collaborations both nationally and internationally. However, when listening to my colleagues at the Sarum workshop, getting into a personal conversation with some of them and learning about their background, and then reading their contributions and engaging in 'friendly reviewer' conversations with them, I was stunned: stunned by the breadth of academic background, the diversity of angles resulting from this and the variety of perspectives on a common topic.

Second, I think the contributions in the book demonstrate that faith-related views and secular interpretations share some common ground when it comes to developing alternatives to current realities. Despite different points of departure with regard to the image of who human beings are, what life is all about and, in a teleological sense, where our destiny lies, many of the writers seem to agree on a surprising amount. This includes: business schools clearly fall short of their genuine potential for shaping the development of their students, whether they are in the early stages or well established in life and the world of work; a more audacious approach towards education and research is needed, deviating from the well-trodden paths of the past; and we need a replacement for the narrow, mono-dimensional focus on profit, markets and efficiency by developing (or rediscovering?) more holistic, diverse, paradoxical and ambiguous views of the world – maybe even some kind of re-enchantment which resists or re-casts the accomplishments of enlightenment.

CM: Just to interrupt a moment, I love that word re-enchantment and so many of the chapters do indeed reflect something of the awe, the wonder, the dreams of education. I must say, working on this book has re-inspired me as an educator and a researcher, refuelled me for what universities are all about.

WM: Another reflection on the editing process is the difficulty of avoiding different types of ethnocentric bias when writing for a global audience. Two small examples come to mind. When writing our chapter on the systemic reasons for business schools not being able to ask some questions that they might want to ask, Aidan and I had to make ourselves more familiar with the world of thought and the academic heritage of the other. Being raised in different academic traditions, belonging to different spheres in the world of work made us bump into some issues where we realized that we had a number of implicit assumptions which came from this background. Even more telling were the exchanges with some authors when giving feedback on first drafts. Most of the examples to illustrate their arguments were heavily ethnocentric, using, for instance, sports metaphors that readers from outside the country would have a hard time understanding. When pointed out to them, the reactions were quite mixed. In some cases, it was easy to find a more globally appealing replacement, in other instances it seemed to be much harder. Whether there was no appropriate, universally understandable example or whether there was a deeply rooted feeling that actually everyone should understand this example and if they don't, it is their fault anyway, I cannot tell.

CM: Yes, one of the criticisms of business schools wherever they are located in the world, is that they tend to subscribe to Western management theory and Cartesian rationality (usually in an unquestioning manner) in both the style and substance of their offerings. And I know we also struggled to break free from a dominant Western, Anglo-Saxon mindset when lining up the chapters. I am glad we were able to introduce some cultural and ethnic diversity, but we could have gone so much further. For example, we have no voices from South America or Africa, we have no one offering an Islamic or Buddhist perspective (one author was preparing a chapter on the latter, but sadly had to drop out due to pressure of work), to name just a few omissions.

WM: Being co-editor of the book and being in contact with such a diverse group of authors has also taught me a big lesson about mutual respect when it comes to individual decisions that go beyond the usual reviewer issues. As this book very deliberately digs deeper and invites authors to relate to 'deep convictions', editing the book and giving feedback happen in a tricky minefield precisely because such convictions are involved.

CM: Yes, I must say this book has caused me to wrestle with my own academic and spiritual standpoint. In the opening chapter we discussed theoretical discourses and I placed my own ontological allegiance with critical realism. In plain terms, this means I see most (though not all) organizational activities and events as emergent, socially constructed and open to a variety of interpretations and meanings. So I have resisted – in three business schools where I was employed and in my role as a leadership development consultant – the idea of 'teaching' leadership, because I see this as a contextually based process of social influence and, as such, it is not possible to arrive at universal, replicable leadership theories. It is caught rather than taught. There is a single reality but it is perceived and interpreted differentially. In other words, the social world – and personally, I would go one step further by saying that the *spiritual* world also – is real in the sense that it generates affect and exists independent of its identification.

And why is all this important for a book such as this? If business schools are in some way to fulfil their remit of preparing students to exercise leadership in organizations, networks, communities and the like, this requires some discussion of ethical stance and moral authority: having a sense of one's own personal convictions, appreciating the beliefs of others (not forcing our morality onto others) and collectively determining a sense of direction. Worldview, whether faith-based or not, plays right into these questions and cannot be side-stepped. Yet it is my sense that such side-stepping occurs routinely.

WM: In terms of epistemology, promiscuity is the name of the game for me. Maybe surprising for a 'boring' Catholic Christian, I do not believe in one firm position with regard to access to reality and to scientifically making sense of what goes on in the world. I change my positions according to theme, research project and collaboration partners without the slightest feeling of bad conscience. If pressed further, I would put myself squarely into the constructivist camp, following broadly the tradition of Niklas Luhmann, a late German sociologist and founder of a school of systemic thinking that provides one of the grand views on society, which also, at least in my view, is very helpful for analysing and managing organizations. In short, the world out there exists and is not only a solipsistic phantom engraved in our minds. Yet, ultimately there is no way to have direct access to this world. All we can do, and this is difficult enough, is to construct our views of the world by applying core distinctions (*Leitdifferenzen* in the Luhmannian terminology) which assign meaning and sense to data out there. Imagine people entering a classroom during a seminar on human resource management. What they see as reality has little to do with what is 'really' there. A person trained in ergonomics might describe the situation in terms of the appropriateness of the chairs in relation to the desks; a painter might notice the specific combination of colours and textiles visible in the students' clothing; a feminist activist most likely will see the number of male and female students to get a handle on the situation. I could go on with examples, of course. But the basic message is: you create reality depending on the kind of core distinction you apply to the world out there. Not, of course, completely independent of what 'really' is out there. If you keep applying basic distinctions which are completely incompatible with the hard facts, you learn the hard way that this kind of interpretation does not fit: companies go bankrupt, relationships break up, you hurt yourself, papers get rejected. But in the end reality only appears on your monitor as an individual or social system insofar as you construct it.

CM: Wow, this is heavy stuff with which to finish a book! I didn't know most of that about you ... which just goes to show we can collaborate in academic circles for years (in our case at least ten) and still be in the dark as to each other's personal standpoints and convictions. We can dance around labels, but it sounds like for all our cultural and institutional differences, we have a similar vision of what business schools are and could be. As for the group of authors in this book, we did say at the outset of the project that we wanted to explore options, provoke debate and, if necessary, be controversial. Indeed two things have already happened as a result of starting out on this journey. One is a special issue of the US journal *Academy of Management Learning and Education* on a similar theme: 'Questions business schools don't ask'. Another is an award by the Economic and Social Research Council (ESRC) in the UK to run a seminar series on *Ethical Leadership: Philosophical and Spiritual Approaches*.[1] Hopefully, this Sage edited collection will contribute to an ongoing conversation that will continue to bring rigour and benefit to the way business schools engage with ethical leadership. Maybe, even in some small way, it will help to break the collusive cycle we discussed in the Introduction!

WM: The proof of the pudding is in the eating, as the English saying goes. I dare say that all involved in the genesis of the book had a chance to broaden their horizon, continue their learning journey and reflect on their views about business schools and their personal roles related to them. Of course, I hope this contribution to the discourse within and about business schools will be consequential, i.e. will be heard, picked up and further developed. Using the book in the academic context is one way of doing this. Spreading the content via seminars and presentations is another. But, as another slightly worn-out saying goes: predictions are difficult, especially if they are about the future ...

[1] See www.ethicalleadership.org.uk.

INDEX

Enlightenment, 167
EQUIS, 9
equity scholarships, 191
ethic of care
   business schools and, 257–258, 264–266
   case study on, 258–266, **262**
ethic of justice, 261
ethical distance, 166–167, 168–169
ethics
   business schools and, 211–213, 284–286
   embodiment and, 132–133, 136–141
   felt sense of, 137–141
   leadership and, 98–106, 165–176
   Levinas on, 136–137, 138, **138**, 210–211
ethics of mortality, 138, **138**
European Foundation for Management
   Development (EFMD), 33
'exile', 57–65, 81
Ezzamel, M., 74

Factory Girls (Chang), 61–62
Fairhurst, G., 278
faith-based approaches to leadership, 19, 22
Fama, E., 210
father figure, 237–239
Faust, D.G., 191
Faÿ, E., 105
feminist scholarship, 257
Ferlie, E., 9
Ferraro, F., 102
Financial Times (newspaper), 9, 10
Finch-Lees, T., 238
Fiskerud, A., 143
focus group stories, 224–225
Fong, C., 32
Ford, J., 34, 187
Fotaki, M., 39
Foucault, M., 4–5n4, 20
Freire, P., 39
French literature, 208, 210, 214–217
Friedman, M., 98–99
Froud, J., 74–75
functionalism
   Built to Last (Collins and Porras) and,
      272–274
   Hebrew wisdom tradition and, 231,
      233–237, **234**
   leadership development and, 16, **16**, 232
   overview, 13–14, *13*
Furtado, C., 95

Gabriel, Y., 59
Gaggiotti, H., 183–184, 201, 203
Galbraith, J.K., 75
Garvin, D., 281–282
GDP (gross domestic product), 89
Ghoshal, S., 18, 33, 99–100, 113
Giacalone, R.A., 102, 151–152
Gibson, C.B., 220
Gigerenzer, G., 139
Glengarry Glenn Ross (movie), 76
globalization, 68–69, 90, 92. *See also*
   multicultural teams

Globally Responsible Leadership Initiative
   (GRLI), 33
Goleman, D., 233
Google, 19, 59–60
Gosling, J., 36
Grassman, R., 282
Gray, J., 172, 175
Greek philosophy, 178–187. *See also* Aristotle
Green House (think tank), 88n1
Grint, K., 38, 168, 238
Gross, N., 71
Grote, M., 282
Grugulis, I., 10n7
Gustafson, S.B., 100

habitus, 133
Hamel, G., 37
Handy, C., 36, 195
happiness (*eudaimonia*), 124, 125, 126,
   169n1, 178
Hargie, O., 31
Harle, T., 80–81, 232
Harney, S., 208
Hartog, M., 283
Harvard Business School, 99, 209
Harzing, A.-W., 9–10
Hatch, M.J., 275
health care, 170–171, **171**
Hebrew wisdom tradition
   formation and, 237–239
   functionalism and, 231, 233–237, **234**
   integrated thinking and, 236–237
   MBA curriculum and, 239–243, *240*
Heidegger, M., 132, 135–136, 138, **138**, 141,
   144, 210
Heider, John, 194–195
Henley, A., 143
heroic leadership theories, 20
Hitler, A., 98
Hoggett, P., 175, 261
Holland, K., 281
Holst, J.D., 39
homo oeconomicus, 122–123, 144–145
hon (soul, a state of mind), 189, 194
Hong Kong
   business schools in, 64–65, 246–256
   work culture in, 62–64
Höpfl, H., 58, 60
Huczynski, A.A., 276
Hui, P., 283
human-scale economy, 94–96
The Hungry Spirit (Handy), 195

identity, 57–65, 81
If Women Counted (Waring), 89
Illouz, E., 217
impression management, 133
In Search of Excellence (Peters and Waterman),
   116, 270–271
individual learning reviews, 226–228
inquiry-based learning, 183–184
institutional leadership, 115–118, *116*
integrated thinking, 236–237

National Coal Board (NCB), 94
neo-liberalism
    business schools and, 217
    ethics and, 211–213
    global financial crisis and, 207–208
    See also economic growth
Neubaum, D., 3n2
New Testament, 127–128
New Zealand. See *wairua* (two waters)
Ng, R.Y., 81
Nicomachean Ethics (Aristotle), 169n1
Nigeria, 227–228
Nohria, N., 69
non-profits, 42
Nonaka, I., 277
Nonis, S., 102
nous (intuitive intellect), 186
Nouwen, H., 22–23

'Occupy Wall Street' protests, 103
O'Doherty, D., 32
O'Donovan, O., 127
O'Leary, T., 72–74
O'Neill, D., 90
Onzoño, S.I., 33
organizational change
    alternative interpretations of, 72–77
    case study on, 258–266, **262**
    criticisms of theories of, 69–71
    disenchantment and, 67–69

Page, M., 183–184
Pang, E., 283
Parameshwar, S., 235
Parker, M., 8
Parry, K., 23, 143
Parsons, T., 109, 112–113, 115, 117–118
participant observations, 228–229
Le Père Goriot (Balzac), 215–216
Performance Based Research Funding (New
    Zealand), 9
personal integrity, 36
personal vision, 158
Peters, T.J., 68, 116, 270–271
Peterson, C., 153n1
Pfeffer, J., 32, 185–186
phenomenology. *See* embodiment
philosophy, 178–187
phronesis, 238
Piccone, P., 168
Pink, H.D., 64
Plato, 179–185
pleonoxia (greed, covetousness), 125–126
Pless, N.M., 100–101
pluralist economics, 94–96
Po, E., 202
Porras, J.I.. See *Built to Last* (Collins and
    Porras)
Porter, M., 99, 102–103
positive psychology, 153
power, 111–113. *See also* cultural power
practices, 128–129

Prasad, A., 39
Principles for Responsible Management
    Education (PRME), 33, 152–153
Promislo, M.D., 102
Protrepticus (Aristotle), 184–185
Pruzan, P., 153
purpose, 154, *155*, 156, 157. See also *telos*
    (purpose)

Quakers (Society of Friends), 92

radical humanism, 274, 276
radical structuralism, 274, 276
Ramel, K., 212
rankings, 9–11, 284
rationality, 37–39, 121–126
Rawlinson, R., 51
Reardon, J., 95
reductionism, 236–237
relational engagement, 262–263
research, 6–7
Research Assessment Exercise, 9
Research Evaluation Framework, 9
respect
    definitions of, 221–222
    multicultural teams and, 219, 220
    sources of conflict and, 222–229, **223**,
        226, **227**
responsible leadership, 100–101
rich picture images, 225–226, 226
Rovira, A.S., 34
ruh (spirit), 194

Sachs, J., 103
the sacred, 154, *155*, 156, 157–158
Samuelson, J., 34
Schumacher, E.F., 90, 94
Schumpeter, J.A., 124
Schwab, J., 183
Scruton, R., 7–8
secularism, 236–237, **236**
Sedlacek, T., 125, 127
Segalla, M., 233
self-identity, 58
self-interest, 123–124
self-referential systems, 46, 47–48,
    51–54, 80
Seligman, M.E.P., 153n1
Selznick, P., 116n5
Sennet, R., 69–70, 71
servant leadership, 22
service, 154, *155*, 156, 160
7 Habits of Highly Effective People
    (Covey), 276
Shakespeare, W., 214, 215
Shenzhen, 246–256
Shymko, Y., 80
Sievers, B., 8
Simpson, P., 201, 203
Small is Beautiful (Schumacher), 94
Smith, A., 38, 114, 115, 144–145
Snyder, E., 109–110, 113, 118–119